THEODORE ROOSEVELT.

MASKS
in a Pageant

By

WILLIAM ALLEN WHITE

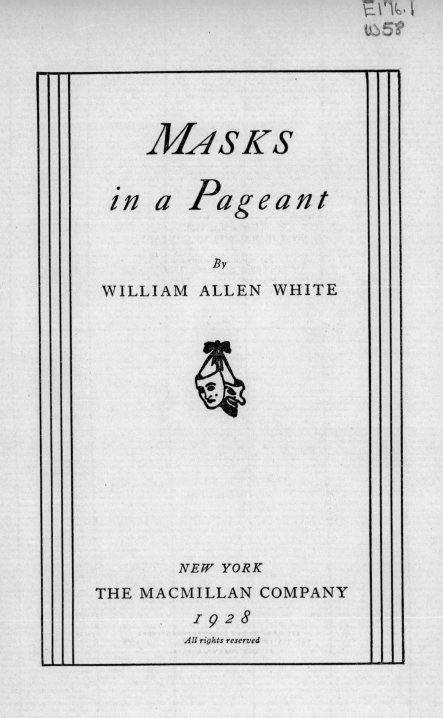

NEW YORK

THE MACMILLAN COMPANY

1928

SET UP BY BROWN BROTHERS LINOTYPERS
PRINTED IN THE UNITED STATES OF AMERICA
BY THE CORNWALL PRESS

INTRODUCTION

PROBABLY life is mostly subjective. It is what you think it is; which means that life is organized memories. And the kind of organization one gives to his memories makes his personal equation—his individual character. Life at its simplest is many-sided, and one's memory must put its beads upon scores of different strings—assorted experiences related in other ways than by chronology; the work-string and the love-strand run through every life. Each may break into smaller chains of remembered things, associated things, as work and love pass through the years. Everyone does many kinds of work, tinkers at odd trades to live or to play.

As I think back and through my forty working years, counting these work-beads of memory, they fall into many kinds of linked successions. One is politics. There, as in all the other forms of passing business and diversion down the long line, faces appear, dim or vivid, dull or significant—which recall the day's work. By a twist of fancy these beads of memory become masks in a pageant—a merry procession of men marching across my consciousness parallel to other pageants that set out from home, from the printing office, from the work desk; pageants of printers and reporters, of story-tellers and poets, musicians and wandering minstrels of festive youth; pageants of the dear and blessed ones who still walk near me, and those whom I "have loved and now have lost a while."

v

This book will set down some account of masks in my pageant of politics. When I was a boy of eight, my father, an old-fashioned hereditary Democrat, took me a hundred miles or so to a Democratic State Convention. I remember the red, sweating, bewhiskered faces of those high-collared, oratorical gentlemen in that convention, clamoring futilely, but with abiding faith in their protest, against the evils of the day—Grant's reconstruction, the padded pension rolls, the debased currency. Ten years later, as a reporter, I was writing about such conventions for a country paper, and on election day I was sitting on the box of the town hack, a pink-faced youth, directing the driver to the homes of recalcitrant voters. I sat as a delegate in a county convention and wrote political editorials before I could vote. I was a Republican then. My mother, who was a "black abolition Republican," had survived my father, and maybe she colored my political thought. But even then I was bedeviled by seeing both sides. All my life the two sides of every political proposal have stood giggling before me so that I never could be as bitter as I should be to convince the suggestible. This cheerful, complacent idiocy in times of stress has often annoyed my deeply passionate friends. Once when we were going over a magazine article that I was to write about President Taft, Theodore Roosevelt took my hand as I left him and cried:

"And now, you old boulevardier,"—such was his sarcastic counter to my swipe at him as Daniel Boone,— "don't hold the knife edge of your balance so perfectly poised in this piece that your readers won't see your bias."

And I paused on the threshold of my going to tell him of old Captain Schilling, state senator from Brown

County, Kansas, into whose safely Republican district I had been shunted by the State Republican Committee to make a speech. The battle-scarred old captain whispered moistly in my ear as he was about to introduce me most fulsomely as some sort of Galahad of reform:

"And now, Bill, for God's sake don't get too damned conscientious in this speech!"

So much for background; now for the figures. They were selected for their news value when the chapters were written. These chapters are for the most part a reporter's notes elaborated. To illustrate: In 1900, William Jennings Bryan was running for President. *McClure's Magazine* asked me to write an article about Bryan. Since then, as a reporter, I have seen Bryan in every National Democratic Convention where he has appeared, or where his name was presented. I came to know him well. I have written many articles about him —always I have written as a reporter. From these articles the chapter about Bryan was prepared. Similarly, the chapters about Mark Hanna, Senator Platt, Richard Croker, have grown from articles written as news—if what is called a timely magazine article is news. Certainly it cannot be called literature. For it is without much perspective, and reflects only the emotion of an hour. And in assembling these reporters' notes I hope to preserve the emotions of some passing moments in the last forty years, so that one who shall really write the story of these times in the calm wisdom of another day may find here a sense of what these figures were in the flesh; of how the particular kinds of men they were affected their peculiar times. For they were strong men, accounted great in their days, and rightly so—probably.

For they did affect political tendency—if not as directors of events, at least as more or less conscious dramatic interpreters. Eight Presidents of the United States are considered in these pages. I knew them all; Grover Cleveland least, Theodore Roosevelt best. With each of them I had a reporter's relation, with six of them—McKinley, Roosevelt, Taft, Wilson, Harding, and Coolidge, political relations—and with Roosevelt I cherish the memory of a friendship that was precious to me.

It is a long time ago since I stood, a young reporter, on the station platform at Lawrence, Kansas,—or it may have been Topeka,—and saw, and even heard across the throng, President Harrison as he was making his "Swing Around the Circle." Since then the liberal movement in world politics has had its rise, its day of power, its hour of tragedy and its passing. The liberal movement sought to make government an agency of human welfare. One of the major mistakes of the liberal leaders was that they sought to make government the *only* agency of human welfare. They forgot that masses who require the stimulation of a just prosperity for their happy well-being must themselves first learn to love justice in their own hearts before they can get much out of prosperity except food and clothes and shelter. Liberal governments brought much prosperity to Christendom, distributed the prosperity with something like equity—only to find that the classes they had improved materially were just as greedy and dull as their oppressors had been in the days before liberalism broke the rusted chains of economic feudalism. Government helped as an agency of human welfare; it failed as the only agency. The men who figure in these chapters that follow were all related to the American liberal movement, one way or another. As pre-Populist agrarianism, liberalism defeated President Cleveland in 1888. As Populism it fused with the Democrats and contributed to President Harrison's defeat in 1892. Advocating an expansion of the currency, wild, new liberalism overwhelmed Cleveland's second administration and offered Bryan to a panic-stricken world. Mark Hanna and William McKinley checked the panic. Roosevelt came, respectabilized and coördinated the liberal policies. They swept Taft out of office. Wilson accepted liberal leadership. War conquered Wilson, but he rallied; and in one supreme intellectual struggle, wherein he was hampered by a heavy armor of moral defects, Wilson—intriguing clumsily, sometimes puerilely, but always for the glory of God—lost his soul to save the peace of the world. That peace, whatever it may be worth, was the first-fruit of the world's liberal movement in the last quarter of the old century and the first quarter of the new.

It is true that prosperity followed the debacle of liberalism after the World War. Also, through modern mass production, in that day prosperity distributed the products of industry with much show of fairness among various kinds of workers. How the steel-throated gods of Mammon must have rattled with ironic laughter at this spectacle of deadly mechanical equity, rising where the prayers of the pious liberals once rose in the fond hope that spiritual progress would follow social and industrial justice! But there are higher gods who always smile —and wait. To-morrow also is a day. So behold, gentle reader, the cat out of the bag. You are now forewarned that these chapters are written by an optimist; alas, by an idealist. Pause, turn back, or expect the worst. It will be a vague, wistful idealism. All idealism is that if it is sane. The materialistic view of life is simple because it is at any time easy to demonstrate the thesis of materialism, even its pragmatic reality, statistically, or actually by any rule of thumb. The materialistic philosophy holds dogmatically that things are bad; so probably will be worse. The premise is unassailable, the conclusion may not be logically gainsaid. And yet—in these two words lies the idealist's creed. For in that nebulous, indefinable hope he is convinced with Job that his redeemer liveth, that life is worth while, that dreams come true, that man's visions are God's reality.

Well, that's that. I have tried to picture these masks faithfully in the pageant of politics. They were men half beast and half god, with the two elements continually battling within them. They were typical of their times, incarnations of various phases of the democratic spirit. Each had his delusions about truth upon which his career was founded, and from which delusions, curiously, came much of his strength. For instance, Harrison and Wilson cherished Calvinistic gods, created in their own image. With these gods they defied the world. In a measure Cleveland and Bryan, also Presbyterians, witched with the same icons. But Cleveland seems to have heard the voice in the clink of a gold reserve, and Bryan was fooled by the ballot box. Although it is the best machine yet devised to get at popular opinion of the hour, Bryan never realized what nonsense and confusion can come out of the ballot box; never knew that it was an invention of the devil just before they put him in chains. So Bryan always was listening at the little hole in the top of the box, sedulously convinced that what he heard there was the voice of God. Roosevelt set up "the average man" as his serpent in the wilderness, and poor Harding, who had no mind of his own, tried to follow what he called the Best Minds. So they go—the long, swiftly-moving line—masks in a pageant; masks that I saw, that I scrutinized eagerly, but—alas!—only with eyes of clay that never could see clearly, much less convey the truth to a mortal heart that never could quite understand.

CONTENTS

name."

Thomas C
bosses who gr
the old century
realms, and typ

CROKER

CHAPTER I

THE RISE OF A CAVE MAN

To the generation who will read these lines the name Richard Croker means almost nothing. Yet for a quarter of a century Richard Croker's name was a power in American politics, a power of the first order—and his kind still rules. It is interesting now only as one looks back to see how he and his kind once lived.

Finite judgments often are biased by immaterial evidence. The thrush, the oriole, the bird of paradise, are esteemed by society, while the unlovely hell-diver is despised. Nature has no favorites. All her creatures are equally beloved; in God's kingdom all the subjects are of royal blood. The earthworm is as useful as the lion; the amœba has full fellowship with man. Contrasts, being human contrivances, are generally unsubstantial—matters of mere whim and viewpoint. When men contrast their fellows the result must make the angels sigh. Each human contrast is the preference for the oriole over the hell-diver repeated. We say this man is not so good as that man, and this other is not so strong as a fourth one, who may be decried for not being as skilled as the fifth. We forget that the hell-diver does Nature's work in the mud, which is as honorable a station

3

as the arbor——even if to our finite eyes the arbor may
seem more beautiful. So when a man rises full of power,
all daubed as to plumage with the muck of the marsh,
we measure him by the oriole. When Richard Croker
appeared in the eighteen-eighties in New York politics,
men gasped and tacitly wondered why Croker could not
be like Charles Eliot. Whereupon his critics began to
throw rocks at the Croker bird, because he was an ugly
bird and had low moral sense. Now rock-throwing is
fine sport, but it does not help scientists to study the
human hell-diver, to find its economic uses, nor to direct
its energies toward the general good.

This Richard Croker, who passed out of the American
picture in the first decade of the new century, is still
important as a type that was, a type that still is, and
always will be in American municipal politics, though the
type will vary a little. The object of this study is to
collect and set down certain data available about the man
Croker; to find his family, genus, and species; to ascer-
tain what he feeds upon; what his place is in the scheme
of things; that is, what part he and his kind play in the
conservation of political and social energy that is slowly
forcing the inevitable triumph of "reason and the will
of God."

Richard Croker was born in Ireland, and popular
belief has labeled him Irish. Yet the blood that governed Croker's character was English, not Irish; for the
Croker family came to Ireland about six generations ago
from England. The English Crokers were people of
quality, and in the family there were a surveyor-general,
a poet and wit, a great editor and literary wrangler of
parts, and there were such courtiers, barristers, soldiers,

and citizens as set the stage for the historical plays of
the period. Until the last generation each Croker lived
a prosperous middle-class gentleman. The fighting devil
seems to have been big in all of them. Richard Croker's
grandfather apparently nursed a particularly active devil,
for the grandfather named Croker's sire Eyre Coot, after
Sir Eyre Coot, a dashing Limerick soldier, who fought
England's battles all over the world. His bones now
rest in Westminster, the wearer of them having grown
black in the face with rage and died of apoplexy in the
heat of battle at the prospect of defeat. Whatever
martial spirit there may have been in Eyre Coot Croker
was spent in finding food and shelter for a large family,
of which Richard Croker was the youngest member.
When the family fell upon evil times, Eyre Coot Croker
emigrated with his flock to America. They passed New
York, and went to a place near Cincinnati. They
remained there but a short time, returning to New York
about 1850. The lad Richard picked up a meager education in the public schools, for the Crokers were Protes-
tants, though Richard became a Catholic after he entered
New York City politics. In the fifties young Croker
entered upon an apprenticeship in the machine shops of
what is now the New York Central Railroad. He was
in his early teens when he began to learn the machinist's
trade, but he was such a strapping youngster that for a
long generation in the shops a Croker myth persisted,
made up of stories of his prowess. As a blacksmith he
could swing a sledge in each hand. They say—and there
are those who have nursed broken heads to remember
Dick Croker—that as a young man his legs, arms, and
chest were covered with swarthy black hair; also that he

not only fought at the drop of the hat, but often jogged
the hand which held the hat, being an impatient lad with
no stomach for dalliance. He learned his trade thoroughly. No mere bench worker was Dick Croker. They
tell how he built a locomotive with his own hands, put it
together, ran it out of the shops, and turned it over to
the company after testing its speed on a trial trip. His
hands were highly educated, if his head lacked knowledge of the stuff of which textbooks are made. He
had a keen sense of things and their relations—which is
all that a man gets from college at best. Young Croker
took his master's degree in the shops and was graduated
as master mechanic, having learned industry, handcraft,
and the simpler uses of physical courage. He left his
alma mater with the welterweight championship of the
institution as a wrestler, a boxer, and a swimmer. He
was admitted to full partnership, and soon thereafter to
leadership, in a political concern engaged in picking up a
more or less honest living, one way and another, known
of men as the Fourth Avenue Tunnel Gang. In the
cloistered shades of this institution Croker took post-
graduate work in sociology, physics, and political ethics.
He availed himself of the rude appliances of the laboratory, which covered an area of ten blocks, from the
Grand Central Station to Madison Square, thence east-
ward to the river. The assistant who was managing the
political laboratory for Boss Tweed in the vicinity of the
Fourth Avenue Tunnel would not supply experimental
chemicals to Croker and his fellow-students, and probably
otherwise this assistant hindered the intellectual development of the gang. So the gang set out to find the holy
Grail in New York politics and to show Mr. Tweed what

a group of young men of high ideals and nimble fists
may do toward attaining the Good, the True, and the
Beautiful. Croker, being a husky boy, was in due time
chosen to run for alderman in the St. Georgian contest
with the dragon Tweed. Croker won. Tweed went to
Albany and legislated Croker out of office. That was
in 1871. Croker ran again. Again he won. Tweed
was overthrown. The young academicians of the Fourth
Avenue Tunnel Gang triumphed. Croker took his Ph.D.
in the study of mankind, and entered upon the active
practice of his profession.

The destiny that shapes our ends probably did her
most effective day's work in Croker's life the day he
joined Tammany Hall. Soon thereafter he became captain of his election precinct. The election precinct is the
base or unit of the Tammany system. The average citizen of the Republic may fancy that the duties of a
Tammany captain of an election precinct, in the days of
rough-and-tumble politics—the days of riot and murder
at the polls, in which Croker took a violent hand—were
solely those of a plug-ugly. Before the days of the Australian ballot the precinct captain had to sit in the saloon
and give out the ballots. Occasionally he had to call
upon the coroner to help the "freeman execute his will."
To encourage misdemeanor and to foster felony were
only incidents of a captain's annual routine. They were
means to an end, and for nearly a century the end and
most of the other means have remained the same.
Indeed, the office is to-day what it was in spirit before
the Civil War, and what in spirit it must be in New York
or any larger American city a generation hence. For the
success of Tammany depends, and always must depend,

upon paternalism strongly fraternal. The Tammany
which trained young Croker, which trained Charles
Murphy, Croker's successor, and which trained Al Smith,
Murphy's successor, is a human institution. Therefore
it rules, not by its vices but by its virtues, and in spite of
its vices. Here is what Tammany taught Croker: To be
kind to those in trouble, to look after the sick in the
tenements in his precinct, to see that the widows had
food and fuel, that the men had jobs and the orphan
children clothes, to mourn with those that mourn and
to rejoice with them that rejoice.

Also Tammany taught discipline. It taught Croker,
by a sort of merit system, that election majorities and
not excuses are desired, and that to get majorities precinct captains may go far, if necessary—may, in an emergency, tiptoe right up to the door of the penitentiary,
and trust to the efficiency of the organization to pull
them back by the coat tails. Croker spent six months in
jail, in his youth, charged with murder. The crime was
committed in an election fracas, and the jury disagreed.
Probably the indictment left no scar upon him, for it was
part of his business.

Tammany holds an amorphous charter. The Society
of Tammany, or the Columbian Order, is a benevolent
organization; and Tammany Hall is a political organization. One set of men belong to both societies so that
Tammany's business is the disbursement of benevolence
and the collection of votes. Being of a practical turn,
the chiefs of Tammany have established a system which
converts the smallest amount of benefits into the largest
number of votes. So district captain Croker, a roystering
young man in his day, learned that it pays to be kind,

that it pays to be generous—perhaps free-handed is a better word—that it pays to keep a promise, that it pays to lend a hand. All this he learned in Tammany, which, in spite of its virtues, is a corrupt, un-American survival of feudal paternalistic government. One wonders if it is not destined to live and wax fat in New York so long as atavism makes the European emigrant and his children stagger a bit under their early burdens of citizenship and grope instinctively for the sustaining arm of a king. Also, one may well pause to ask if Tammany is really as "un-American" to-day as it was when the old century closed. Have not our cities grown in a quarter of a century so far across the land and so fast that the Americanism of the nineteenth century may be modified? Is not an urban civilization, with its problems and its changed relations of men, making to some extent a new morality, a modification of the American ideal, which will make the Croker type much more American than he was when Richard Croker lived? Externally the city boss of 1928, differs from Croker, of 1899. But this modern leader, who seems to be a new type, the product of our new urban life, is probably the old Croker bird in the protective color of a changed atmosphere—not of a different environment.

The courage—largely physical—that became part of Croker in the shops and in the vestibule of politics, combined naturally with the love of kind which he learned in his captaincy. It made him an idol among the lowly. Kings rise from the peasantry with such training; but there was nothing in young Croker's training to teach him moral sense. He saw tributes levied from the saloon, the gambling room, and the brothel, distributed among

the victims of these plagues. His associates regarded
vice as a source of revenue, revenue as a sinew in the
arm of political victory, and political victory as the chief
end of man. In this atmosphere, tainted with the malodorous intrigues of ward politics, Croker's character
was formed. He breathed this air into his spiritual
nostrils, and it became a part of him; but the pollution
which rotted other men merely withered Croker's soul
and left his he-strength—hobbled only by the criminal
statutes. So when he lifted his big, innocent-looking,
unflinching green eyes, and looked squarely at the public
and advised citizens dissatisfied with the election results
to knock down the election judges and drag them into
the street, contemporary gentlemen of sedentary habits,
who delighted in Emerson, gasped and gave Croker horns
and a forked tail in their high imaginings; which was
absurd.

When Croker ran for alderman in opposition to Boss
Tweed's wishes, Croker was elected on the anti-boss
ticket and helped to pull down Tweed. Tweed fell, not
because he was a thief, but because he did not tell the
truth to his fellow-thieves; they found they could not
trust him. And Croker learned in Tweed's downfall the
one trick which gave Croker power—he learned to tell
those who trusted him the exact truth and to make a lie
the cardinal sin in his code. Those who shuddered at
Croker's power in his day shuddered because they fancied
it was generated in iniquity. But the truth is that power
to control men is always the sign of some strong quality.
No man is all good or all bad. Men follow a leader so
long as, in their eyes, his virtues outweigh his vices. And
the Croker who learned industry in the shops and courage

From *McClure's Magazine*.

RICHARD CROKER AT THE AGES OF TWENTY, FORTY-FIVE, AND FIFTY-SEVEN.

in the gang—which was and is the clan in the feudal
system of Tammany—learned a sort of anthropoid honesty in the office of alderman. It is not here contended
that Croker developed a New England conscience. He
was honest according to his lights, and the Croker illumination of that day was a sputtering gas light in the
streets. In a simple way he knew that it was wrong
to steal funds, either public or private, for stealing
requires duplicity, and that was no part of Croker's
nature. But probably he did not understand why successful stealing is iniquitous, further than that it may
not pay in the long run. And anyway he held no radical
economic ideas; he always contended that the proceeds
of theft were sacrosanct if they were large enough.

In those days Alderman Croker's social duties were
about the same as those that confront a New York alderman to-day, and similar to those that have confronted
the gentry for a thousand years. He was patron of
the shire. To him the yeomen looked for succor in dis-
tress. He stood between the young blades of the tenement and their natural enemies, the police. He furnished
amusement and recreation for his vassals. It was his
part to sit in silence on the top deck of a chartered boat,
taking the peasantry to his annual clam-bake, and to
receive his subjects there in stately dignity as his henchmen brought them up. Also, he was expected to lend
the distinction of his presence to the barkeepers' annual
ball and to grace the church fair with his dumb, clumsy
courtesy. It was all medieval, all like the real Round
Table, probably, and all incongruous to the American
point of view as Americanism was defined in Puritan
terms—the quintessence of a rugged individualism—in

the latter part of the nineteenth century. Yet the rise
of Croker in Tammany from peasant to marauder, from
marauder to squire, from squire to liege lord, from lord
to chancellor of the exchequer, from—but that is antici-
pating the narrative; suffice to say that Croker's rise was
not strange; it was typical of the time and the place;
indeed, typical of human nature in any time and place
which develops the need of an overlord. It was like the
rise of Boss Kelly, the rise of Boss Tweed, or the rise
of any of the kings of Tammany whose fall has been
forgotten in the last hundred years.

When in the eighteen-eighties John Kelly rose to the
boss's throne in Tammany, Croker was a district leader;
that is to say, a kind of a county central committeeman
in the political organization, and a Grand Duke in
the Tammany social system. Kelly made Croker a privy
councilor, and gave him the office and the title of city
chamberlain. It may be said to the credit of the system
that produced Croker that he conducted the various
offices he held—coroner, city chamberlain, and fire commissioner—decently and without scandal. No city money
stuck to his fingers. As chancellor of the exchequer,
Croker was thrown daily with the Tammany nobility.
The Irish modification of his English blood in him made
him imitative. He acquired a veneer of manners. He
ceased to be a "gent." His fists whitened. His clothes
grew "mild and lovely," and his voice—strident, harsh,
and full of strange oaths—began to grow "gentle as the
summer breeze" in the days when he was in Kelly's
cabinet. As events crowded power on Croker, a lesson
of silence, which he learned first in the Tunnel Gang,
became more and more a part of his mental habit.

Croker also made his temper bridle-wise. During the season spent in jail charged with murder he learned some philosophy which never deserted him. There is a fine perspective of the world to be had from behind prison bars that gives a man—and Croker got it well—a bird's-eye view of the vanities of this life. Jail makes men silent.

When John Kelly died in the early nineties the Tammany crown came to Croker by natural selection. He was made Chairman of the Finance Committee of Tammany. That was his office for a decade—at the height of his power. The Finance Committee was composed of five district leaders out of the thirty-seven in New York. Under each leader were a score of precinct captains, each of whom was set over four or five hundred people; the people were divided into tribes of nationality and also subdivided into clans. This organization, which has nothing to do with political creeds or platforms, but coheres out of greed for public taxes and public privileges, is the most perfect voting machine on earth. To the royal head of this system, Croker came as a journeyman who had worked up from bound boy. He was made king by grace of his strong right arm, and a steel brain sharpened on a man hunter's whetstone. Passionate— and by that token soft-hearted—simple as a child, acquisitive, shrewd in a narrow groove like a machine, sordid at the core, and ignorant of civilization as a vandal, Croker came to his throne a troglodyte king over a race of cave men.

CHAPTER II

THE TROGLODYTE KING AND HIS KINGDOM

To know what sort of a ruler he made, one must know his domain. It was first of all a material kingdom. There was nothing so ethical about it as a double ledger entry. For his kingdom was not Greater New York; there are spiritual, literary, and commercial estates in New York that never owed allegiance to Croker. He did not dream that they existed. His kingdom was not even the atmosphere of current political thought in Manhattan and the Bronx. For Croker cared little for political economy and the trend of political ideas. The kingdom of Croker was the kingdom of loot, and the old vain heathen in his blindness thought it was one of the principalities and powers. To Croker, or to what Croker stood for, ninety thousand men surrendered their sovereign American rights. This surrender was made, as it was made to Kelly and Tweed before Croker and to Murphy and his successors and assigns after him, without let or hindrance. It carried the right of transfer with it. A tremendous power was generated by this abdication. Croker and four others sat in a secret conference and nominated men to fill every municipal office in New York, from mayor to alderman. Orders came down from this conference to the city convention, to the district conven-

14

tion, to the ward caucus. The only thing that went up
was obedience. Surveying the power of Croker, one
could easily believe that not a policeman walked his beat
in New York City except by Croker's grace; not a brick
was laid on a public or private work that he might not
impudently tear down if the contractor laying it withheld homage to the boss; that not a wheel turned on any
railway in New York, not a car moved up and down an
elevator shaft in Greater New York, which by express-
ing an idle caprice Croker might not have stopped. Popular government in New York City thrived under the
Croker régime as lustily as in Constantinople or Bagdad.

About that time, a New Yorker, seeking to purge the
East Side tenements of vice, sought, not the chief of
police, not the police commissioners, not the mayor, but
the fountain-head of government in New York, Croker
in his council. After introducing the petitioner for
reform to his manor lords, Croker said:

I want you to give close attention to his statement, and I want
that, after you have heard what he has to say, you will use every
effort to correct all those evils as far as it lies in your power.

When the reformer had finished speaking and a committee had been appointed, Croker delivered this ukase:

Right here I want to reiterate again what I said three weeks
ago, and that is, not a dollar comes into my hands from the land-
lords of pool-rooms or houses of ill-fame. If any of you gentlemen have been collecting from these people, you had better get
out of the organization. It hasn't any use for you. You disgrace
it. I am not talking for political effect. I am talking of what
you should do as honest citizens. I hope if this committee should
ask any one of you leaders here for information you will appear
and do the best you know how to make its work entirely
successful.

Some one more venturesome than the other barons attempted to say that the evil complained of was necessary. Let the undisputed report of a half dozen of the best newspapers in New York continue to describe the royal wrath:

Croker bounded from his chair, walked toward the coroner, and pointed his finger at him, shaking it excitedly. "You say you don't know what we can do?" he asked in angry tones. "What you want to do" (raising his voice) "is to act, and to try to do something anyway. You can't stop it, you say. If you do nothing except talk about what you can't do, you can never stop anything. If the people find anything is wrong, you be perfectly satisfied the people can put a stop to it and will. Right will right itself in spite of wrong. It can be righted if this committee here goes to work with a squad of police. And now let's see whether the police can help us."

DR. PARKHURST'S RIVAL, THE REV. DR. CROKER.

Emperor William could have used no stronger language to his Reichstag. The mental attitude of the man who spoke thus was that of dictator. Croker was not giving advice; he was proclaiming an edict. And his proclamation was sincere. The reader must remember that he is not considering a diplomat, nor a chess player, nor even a second-rate politician. Croker was a savage, with a child's mind. Political issues were his toys, and he went from one to another with no thought of design or consequence. Only a year before his retirement did Croker find even a passing interest in his baubles. During the first ten years of his reign the nation was stirred deeply by great events, and moved manifestly by the passing issues of the day. Croker, taciturn, grim, uninterested, furtively concealing his ignorance in stolidity, viewed the panorama of history like an Indian at the show. He had hoarded an untold treasure of golden silence, which in his very latter days he spent like a profligate in wanton speech. Probably some sort of a carnal sense of power had been throbbing in him and awakened a heavy, turgid ambition in this giant and set him to babbling. Bryan's "First Battle" was read to Croker in 1897, when he called the author "Bryant." He was so carried away with the sincerity of the argument that he metaphorically clapped his hands with delight. He never realized to the end of his days that there might be another side to arguments that pleased him. And Croker's enthusiasm for Bryan was unalloyed. They told Croker how the trusts handicapped young men, and Croker retold the story again and again to every listening reporter during the campaign.

It was in the presidential campaign of 1900 that Croker received his highest homage. It came from Bryan, candidate for the second time of the national Democratic party. Bryan was still a young man in those days—barely forty. His emotions were keen, and he was emotionalizing his way through the higher walks of American politics, making moral issues out of economic problems and distributing, as God's Presbyterian viceregent, the white cards of righteousness to such deserving Democrats as followed in his way of light. To others he handed the black curse of his disdain. Millions of Americans of all parties saw in Bryan the Messiah of their pious hopes for a sanctified land. He prayed before battle. He was the prophet of the new day. One night in late September, 1900, Bryan came to New York City—the Sodom that surrounded Wall Street, the plague spot of Bryan's paradise. He appeared in Cooper Union for a speech. He was to attack the very citadel of sin. He stood on the platform of the dingy old hall where Lincoln had proclaimed his faith a long generation before. The gas footlights of the stage shone on a handsome, youthful figure as Bryan stepped out of the group on the platform to hurl his defiance at the forces of iniquity that encompassed him in the Gomorrah of oppression. He put his left hand on his heart, turned his eager young face slightly sideways; shook his black poll regally, waved a beatifying gesture to a dull, square-faced man with sagging jowls, covered lightly by a graying, blotched black beard, who hulked heavily forward in his chair supporting his stocky body with two great paws clasped over a cane between his widespread knees. The old man stared at the young orator, stared catwise, unblinking, expressionless, at the supple, bouncing figure. The flashing, passionate eyes of the young man for a smiling moment flicked the unflinching, unresponsive jade of the tiger eyes before him. Then the soft silvern voice of Bryan quickened the place. Lifting his pontifical hand over Croker's head, Bryan called out:

"Great is Tammany, and Croker is its prophet!"

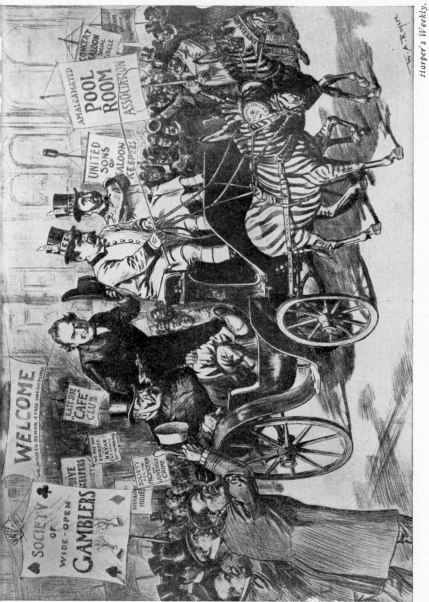

Harper's Weekly.

WIDE-OPEN NEW YORK WELCOMES MR. BRYAN.

It was a terrible instant of silence that followed before the tiger's exultant yowl greeted the orator. In that moment, America gasped and Bryan ceased to be a national leader. His broken scepter was crunched in the tiger's grinning jaws. After that, Bryan was only a partisan; a powerful figure, but a shorn Samson. Croker sat immutable as the crowd yelled. But within his heart the cockles glowed. In November Tammany futilely voted for Bryan. Whereat that debt was paid, the book was balanced, and Bryan was forgotten in Tammany!

Let us look at Croker in another and a lovelier mood. It is in a late year of his reign; Croker is eating dinner in a public place. He sees a city official at a table a few yards away. Calling across the room, he asks:

"Well, how is that Murphy boy doing I sent you?"

The city official replies that the boy is an exceptionally capable young man. Croker is delighted. At the end of his felicitous ejaculations he cries:

"Good boy. How much is he getting?" And then: "You just raise him a thousand to-morrow."

Croker made no attempt at concealment; used no cipher code, nor yet was he brazen about it. He saw no reason why he should not bestow the money of the taxpayers at his discretion. Was he under an oath of office? He was not. And if he wished to do a benevolence, whose business was it? Absolutely no one's! To understand the real Croker one should not confuse him with a sort of mythical Croker that hero-worshipers and a kind of devil-worshipers in his day builded out of the red mud of their own ideals. The real Croker was not crafty. He was not even ordinarily shrewd, either in business or in politics.

When he went into Wall Street he was as ignorant

of the methods there as the Mahdi on the desert. The
men who played his hand for him needed a friend at the
soul of things in New York City, and they knew where
the soul of things was. They did not buy Croker. He
accepted no bribe. He was true to his Wall Street
friends, and his Wall Street friends generally stood by
him. He made real-estate investments, and his advance
knowledge of proposed public improvements made his
investments profitable. He bought stock in city indus-
trials, and his friends in office protected his investments,
and the stock rose and Croker skimmed off the cream.
He frankly acknowledged that what street parlance
called his political pull represented his capital. His
whole life in the years of his power was devoted to
accumulating this influence, and rather proudly than
otherwise he checked on it as an old man would check
on his life's savings. To show Croker his moral responsibility to the city would have required a galvanic vitali-
zation of his moral sense, which was as innocuous
as a vermiform appendix.

Croker knew only the Tammany Hall he made,
an edition *de luxe* of the Fourth Avenue Tunnel
Gang. During the campaign of 1900 he strung some
insolent banners across the line of march of a great
Republican parade. The act was the revival of the
Tunnel Gang instinct—smart, swagger, bullying; not
shrewd, not effective. It reflected merely the mental
processes of a boy.

"I ain't no statesman," said Croker to the Mazet Committee in 1899. "I am looking out for my own pocket
first."

This was literally true. And when Croker said it he

saw no reason for mincing matters. But a year or so
later he grew flabby in his arrogance. A fleshy ambition
for wider influence seemed to have turned Croker's head
along in the early years of the new century. He fain
would have posed as a statesman, and—presto!—he
talked to prove his wisdom. He knew no more of the
sentiment of the country, of its geography, of its mental
and moral attitude, than a Persian satrap. He did not
comprehend the issues of his day even remotely. The
words "seigniorage" and "industrial and sociological ten-
dencies," with Croker, were words to be skipped in reading aloud, and nothing more. He seriously suggested a
compromise with the gold Democrats; he would have
changed the ratio of silver coinage as the silver market
fluctuated. The suggested compromise revealed the
depth of economic thought which he fathomed.

And yet in American politics Croker was for ten years
one of the major powers. He had to be reckoned with.
His death in the day of his ascendancy would have been
a calamity to his city. For no other man in all Tammany
who might succeed him was, just at that time, as honest
as Croker. Negatively his influence, as a sovereign, was
for good, in that the influence of other Tammany leaders
without Croker would have been unspeakably bad. The
ninety thousand Tammany voters who surrendered their
citizenship to Croker might easily have done far worse
with it. They might have used it on their own intelligence
—for instance! This they have never done. If the time
ever comes when they do use their citizenship, unrestrained
by the intervening agency of faith in Croker's heirs or
assigns, heaven protect wealth and social order in New
York City! Take away the steel hoops of Tammany

from the social dynamite, and let it go kicking around
under the feet of any cheap agitator who may come by
with his head in the clouds, and then look out for fireworks.*   A cautious rascal is safer than a vain demagogue. A corrupt king is rather to be chosen than the
anarchy of a million hungry, shifty despots. Croker and
his kind have their place in the scheme of things. The
system that made him a king out of a ruffian grows out
of a need for ruffian kings. It is a case of supply and
demand. Some natural law governs the relation between
the two.

In the quarter of a century since Croker left Tammany
the veneer of civilization has thickened a little. Education has helped some. An improved economic status,
almost revolutionary in its character, has helped more
than education. But education and environment have
not made full-sized men out of the urban masses of our
great cities. They still are children; still need bosses.
Croker will return for generations; modified, of course,
but only as to his skin.

Into the Tammany grist-mill, with benevolence and
civic corruption for its upper and nether stones, the crop
of Ellis Island of the last half of the old century was
dumped. The grist came out a kind of citizen; a poor
kind indeed, but a better kind than no citizen. And with
all the mold of feudalism which the Tammany mill preserved, the Tammany-made citizen was and is more
trustworthy than the citizen that Karl Marx, or Lenin
would make, or than that which any red anarchist or
impatient socialist would make. And right now, in the

*If Tammany would give New York the kind of public schools needed
to elevate the public standard of intelligence, of course this statement
would not be true.

third decade of the new century, with the schools of New
York City what Tammany makes them, it is probably a
choice between Tammany and the dynamiters. For New
York always rejects the middle-class reformer. The good
citizens uptown occasionally, in frenzied hours of peni-
tence, go so far as to send a few political tracts to the
tenements, or to send an officer to kick up a fuss about
the number of people who sleep and work in one room—
a fuss which only irritates the tenements and proves to
them for the hundredth time that the reformers are
enemies of the poor. The good citizens uptown may
even send young men and women to live in the tenements.
But the Tammany precinct captains are brothers of the
people, flesh of their flesh, bone of their bone. The captains understand and are understood. Also, when the
Tammany man rises in the world he comes back to his
kith and kin, not as a scientist examining bugs, not as an
evangelist announcing the last call for social salvation's
dining-car, but as a manor lord returning from a long
and prosperous journey, with an open hand and a warm
heart.

Tammany has preached contentment. It has tolerated
no Jeremiahs. Its philosophy is eat, drink, and be merry,
fight the enemy, and knife the traitor; and Richard
Croker, late of the Fourth Avenue Tunnel Gang, late
precinct captain, later district leader, and finally, in the
days of his glory, haloed with such divinity as "doth
hedge a king," was the same Dick Croker who ran the
caucus and blustered about the polls a quarter of a century before his Tammany coronation. He always did as
much for his friend as he would have done in the old
days, and the friend's morals interested him no more

than his love affair or the color of his hair. And here's
another reason why, in the American scene, Dick Croker
of the Tunnel Gang was safer than the communist to
control the mill that was turning the raw material of the
steerage into American citizens: Croker desired to be a
gentleman. The example is good. For your communist
likes his gentleman broiled on a spit and rather
underdone.

In the closing days of his reign Croker affected foreign
travel—chiefly in Ireland, where he finally went to live
and die a country squire. But when Croker was in
America, he lived at the Democratic Club, which may be
described as the "St. James" of the Tammany nobility
in the days of Tweed, Kelly, Murphy, Croker, and
Hylan. There gathered the beauty and the chivalry of
the institution. In the evening, justices, counselors, captains of police, the chancellor of the exchequer, the lord
mayor, the keeper of the buckhounds, courtiers, nobles,
and gentry, and his sacred majesty the king, all assembled
to pass a quiet hour discussing matters of state. This
Democratic Club was for a generation quartered in a high,
brownstone structure well up toward Central Park, on
Fifth Avenue, where gentlemen passed through the door
all day and as late at night as gentlemen might be out
of bed. Here were four floors upon which lay thick
velvet carpet—bought, they told you, by the "Chief,"
meaning Croker. Complete sets of fat leather furniture
and sets of gilded spider-legged chairs and divans, also
selected by the "Chief," were placed against the wall,
whereon glowing pictures framed in glittering gilt hung
exactly on the line, in the shut-up throne-room of a
parlor. A library, where were government reports and

broken sets of editions *de luxe* of foreign novelists, was
conveniently near the card-room, and under the roof was
a dining-room, splendid with much fine gold, where the
court frescoer had adorned the ceiling with saintly pictures of the Democratic fathers, with allegoric scenes in
pink and pea-green and blue from American history, and
at each corner of the fresco with the smiling, satisfied face
of a tiger on an "animated bust." It is necessary to add
that this room expressed in terms of form and color the
orison that always sang in the king's heart.

In the royal palace Croker was treated with the full
pomp and circumstance that became a king. When he
entered the dining-room robust conversation gasped into
silence until Croker was seated. When he paused before
a table the diners rose. When he left a group of courtiers and went to a quiet corner, with an unlighted cigar
between his teeth, court etiquette required that he must
not be disturbed except on pressing matters of the kingdom. When he appeared in evening clothes he would
not budge a step to meet any human being. Strangers, let
them be who they might—President, senators, allies, or
messengers of kings—had to be brought to Croker for
presentation; for the law of the Tunnel Gang—get your
bluff in first—was as the law of those Medes and the Per-
sians. This I saw with my own eyes one night in the
Bryan campaign of 1900.

And all this homage, all this bootlicking, to a mild-
mannered, soft-voiced, sad-faced, green-eyed chunk of a
man who talked slowly that he might peg in his "seens"
and his "saws," his "dones" and his "dids" where they
belonged, who had a loggy wit, who cared neither for
books, nor music, nor theatrical performances, nor good

wine, nor a dinner, nor the society of his kind! All this
dull obeisance by men of brains and some rudimentary
culture to a slow, emotionless, presimian hulk of bone and
sinew—a sort of human megatherium, who had come
crashing up from the swamps splashed with the slime of
pre-Adamite wickedness! He was throned, and dispensed
a sort of jungle justice, for more than a decade and a half,
while civilization knocked its knees together in stupid,
terrified adulation! And why? What was the secret of
this man's power—this man who scorned the esthetic
joys that delighted his fellows, and was pleased only with
three things: one, the companionship of horses and dogs;
two, the faces of children; and, three, stripped to the
shaggy skin of him, a plunge in the sea far out beyond
the breakers, far out where there is room to romp and
scuffle and wrestle with danger? What set this barbarian
to rule over a free city? What natural selection? What
survival of the fittest? Is society a knock down and drag
out civilization, bloody of tooth and nail? Yet here,
up the natural stepping-stones of a political system of a
great city, came a primitive man with a simple mind, to
which the spectacle of the shifting vitascope of modern
life was as meaningless as the figures in the kaleidoscope;
and men hailed him chief and bowed before him, and lost
their appetite when he frowned, and garlanded him with
roses when he started upon a journey. Why?

Let us put him on the stand and make him answer. In
an interview with W. T. Stead, in 1897, when Stead
asked what is the fundamental law of the universe, Croker
answered:

Sir, the law is that although wrongdoing may endure for a
season, right must in the long run come to the top. Human nature

is so built that roguery cannot last. Honest men come to their own, no matter what odds against them. If you put ten honest men into an assembly with ninety thieves, human nature is such that the ten honest men will boss the ninety thieves. They must do it. They will tell you that Tammany has ruled New York nearly all the time. Do you think we could have done it if we had been the thieves and rogues they say we are? I have been in office nearly all my life. Do you think the citizens would have been such fools as to reëlect me if I had been the bad man they say I am? Things that are rotten do not last. Thieves are not trusted by their fellow-thieves, let alone by their fellow-citizens. It is not by what is bad in them that institutions and parties win, but by what is good.

Over against this virtuous preachment of Croker put the evidence of Captain Meakin's Tammany collector and Croker's cohort, Edward Shalvey, before the Lexow Committee (Vol. I, p. 5, 407):

Q. You collected from these several places—liquor dealers, policy shops, and houses of ill-fame—as you did under the previous captain?
A. Yes, sir.
Q. Did you ever meet with any refusal to pay from the people engaged in this class of business, or did they all pay as a matter of course?
A. They all paid as a matter of course.
Q. So that, officer, even beneath the terrible frown of the Lexow Committee, the collection went on just the same?
A. Yes, sir.
Q. The old, old story continued, is not that so?
A. Yes, sir.
Q. And while, as a matter of fact, exposures were being made as testified to before this Committee since last May or April, the collections continued right along unbroken, did they not?
A. Yes, sir.
Q. And the captains took the money in the same way?
A. Yes, sir.

That, of course, was Croker's idea of honesty—
Tammany's idea, indeed, in that day. How much has
that idea been clarified in a generation? one wonders.
Again, may not one ask, are Croker and his kind the symbol of New York? Here was a city whose clearing-
house reports showed a buccaneer's treasure multiplied
by his fondest dreams, but where, until Croker left the
throne, in the boroughs of Manhattan and the Bronx, no
class had ever graduated from a public high school. Here
was a city with a moral intelligence that permitted hundreds of its policemen to add blackmail to their duties;
a city whose public officers exercised a pirate's honor; a
community that traded its right of free government for
the rule of a boss, not once, but a score of times—and
still needs its boss as an Oriental village needs its caliph;
a community with the sheer brute force of a giant,
whose political history records the giant's low average—
the dead level of it. This was political New York of a
generation ago. It is, more or less, the political New
York of to-day—somewhat improved in housing, in
external beauty, in the statement of its economic equation,
but not greatly changed at heart. What was Croker?
Croker and the metropolis justified themselves. Croker
did not see his own shortcomings. Indeed, it is a question whether or not a difference from others of one's
species is a shortcoming. Each creature has his place in
the economy of nature. When Stead asked Croker:

"Mr. Croker, for nearly thirty years you have been up to the
neck in the rough-and-tumble of New York politics. For nearly
twenty years you have been the supreme boss of Tammany. You
are contemplating a serene old age. Looking back over those
thirty years, is there not a single act or deed which, in the light

of your experience, you regret having done, or that you now feel that you should have left undone?"

Stead says:

"The boss paused. He removed from his lips the cigar of Brobdingnag, and half closed his eyes for a moment. Then with calm, deliberate emphasis he replied: 'No, sir, not one. I do not remember ever having done anything I ought not to have done, for I have done good all my life.'"

Which brings us back to the beginning. Does the hell-diver see mud, and filth, and carrion, and slime-life with the eyes of the bird of paradise?

PLATT

CHAPTER III

THE BLIND EARTHWORM IN POLITICS

THOMAS COLLIER PLATT and Richard Croker were contemporary bosses in New York politics during the last quarter of the nineteenth century. In so far as New York represented a large unit of American population, and in so far as that unit represented the commercial capital of this continent, New York politics and these two New York politicians were important and somewhat identical; although the two men were deeply antithetical. Platt considered himself a scholar and a gentleman. He controlled Republican politics through the manipulation of men of the middle class, often of the upper middle class, in the interests of men of the top crust. His cohorts and henchmen were well-bred, white-collared, kid-gloved, silk-stockinged, plug-hatted. Emotion played almost no part in his hold upon his fellows. Croker controlled the substratum, the cut well under that which Platt manipulated. The immigrant, and the immigrant's children, followed Croker. The under-privileged were grist for Croker's mill. Croker held his liege lordship because he had a loyal heart, an open hand, and a voice in rage which was as shriveling as the wrath of God.

Both were silent men. Croker was grim; Platt was secretive. Croker ruled by force; Platt by intrigue. Yet each was necessary to the political scheme of things as it was ordained by man and permitted by a kind but careless Providence at the opening of this twentieth century. Now we shall consider Platt.

Once upon a time—to be exact, in the first third of the nineteenth century—there lived in the little country town of Owego, New York, a country lawyer of parts and consequence named William Platt—a family man to whom was born, in the course of time—again to be exact, in 1834 —a son. William Platt named his son Thomas Collier Platt, and educated him after his own heart. The townsmen testified to the fact that the younger Platt grew up a rather bloodless, wobbly-legged, flat-chested, squawky-voiced boy. He came to adolescence amid the best culture and refinement that the day and place afforded, and went to Yale College. There he was a fairly good student until his vitality began to ebb, and he left in his junior year. He came back to Owego with notions, and started a literary publication which he called the *St. Nicholas Magazine*. In every man's life there are periods when he thinks he is a born humorist, or perhaps a poet. Platt sowed his literary wild oats in the *St. Nicholas Magazine*. He conducted the joke department. His humor was of the kind that inspires the heathen to tickle the feet of the man in stocks. One sample will do:

THE PREACHER (to the profane boatman) : "Sir, do you know where you are going?"

THE PROFANE BOATMAN: "Up the canal on the 'Johnny Sands.'"

THE PREACHER: "No, no; you are going to hell faster than any canal boat can carry you!"

BOATMAN: "And where are you going?"

PREACHER: "I expect to go to heaven."

BOATMAN: "No, no; you are going right into this canal," and with that he pitched him in.

He was given to puns and quips and jibes, and, worst of all, to bad poetry. This stanza is offered in evidence:

TO STELLA

A little star rode all alone
Along the azure sky,
And sang so mournfully because
No other star was nigh.
But soon another planet swept
Adown the ethereal main,
And twinkled at that pretty star,
Which twinkled back again.
They wove in one their silver crowns
And locked their flashing wings,
And now no rover of the skies
Like happy Stella sings.

Now everything has its use, and this poetry—bad as it is—served its purpose in the world, for it led Tom Platt into politics. Every life has its secret. This was Platt's. He was a musician. In his younger days he could play—by ear—several instruments, and while he lived a myth prevailed in Owego that Tom Platt was handy with the melodeon. Being a rhymer, the inevitable followed. In the campaign of '56—an emotional campaign if there ever was one—the abolitionists had Tom Platt get up the Owego Campaign Glee Club and organize the Republican party in Tioga County. Old men

Harper's Magazine.

FROM POET TO POLITICIAN.

Mr. Platt in 1853, 1871, and 1873. The last picture shows him as a
member of Congress.

and women in Owego for a long generation still held
in their memories the picture of Tom Platt, a gaunt,
loose-skinned youth, rangy and uncertain in the joints,
standing at the head of a drove of wild-eyed human long-
horns, as if to keep them from a stampede, waving his
joist-like arms in rhythm to "down-left-right-up-down-
left-right-up s-i-n-g!" And when they began to sing, the
choirmen would huddle together like cold sheep, and
almost bump heads so that the harmony should be close
and effective. And all the time Tom Platt hovered over
the group, keeping time with a foot or a finger and
chopping out the words of the song with his long, square
flail of a jaw, full of delight at his handiwork. For the
words of the songs were his. Here is one stanza of a
song called "The Greeley Pill," set to the tune of "Captain Kidd—As He Sailed."

> Call us drunkards, liars, knaves,
>   We're so sick, oh so sick;
> Call us cowards, traitors, slaves,
>   We're so sick.
> Call us murderers, as you will,
>   Kick and lash us, we'll lie still;
> Dr. Greeley, just one pill—
>   We're so sick.

These lines are printed partly to show how precisely
the political ballad has preserved its ethical, metrical, and
poetical integrity through the centuries; but chiefly to
show that Tom Platt at the age of twenty-one, a callow
youth, had all the advantages of a high-toned political
education in those good old times which one hears so
much about; when aspirations were lofty, when motives
were pure, when men were exalted by clear patriotism,

and when the recrimination and abuse so deplorable to-day had not crept into our politics. The song of "The Greeley Pill" certainly reflected a political condition existing in Platt's youth. That condition was his early environment. It formed him, gave him his political color and direction. Platt, as the organizer of the Republican party in Tioga County, used music, which hath charms, but not merely to soothe the savage breast; with Platt it was a means to an end. The end of the party organizer in a district is not platforms, nor sentiments, nor aspirations, but votes counted on the tally sheet. Platt sang blithely and in his songs snarled, sneered, and lampooned to get votes. Little of art for art's sake shaped his attitude to the muse. Probably his artistic nature—which really was very big in him despite his practical employment—found expression when he sang in the church choir. Indeed, Platt sang in the church choir until he was nearly fifty years old. His musical taste abode with him to the end; he was a patron of the opera all his life. But music and the fine arts were diversions with Platt, not passions. For Platt lived to work. He was elected county clerk of Tioga County in 1859, but during the early sixties he went into the lumber business, seemingly for his health. He made lumber pay. His health improved. He became president of an Owego bank, and he had money to invest. He put some of it in the Southern Central Railroad, an Ohio enterprise, and went to Ohio to live. He had been dabbling in politics in Tioga County—as the average county banker since Crœsus has dabbled—by the back door of the bank; not enough to hurt, but just to see that the right man is elected sheriff and treasurer, and that the delegations to the State and congressional conventions shall be friendly. In Ohio, Platt was unhappy. Perhaps the thought that the other crowd in Owego was running the Tioga County Convention gnawed at his consciousness. At all events, Platt got his money out of the Ohio venture after the Civil War and came back to Owego. He worked with Cornell and Conkling and Louis F. Payne to give Grant the New York delegation in '68 and '72. As a result he got the Albany habit, and became known about the political hotels at Albany. He used to walk about conventions and whisper things to delegates through the funnel of his hands. In '72 he refused a congressional nomination, but two years later took it, and was elected. At the bankers' convention he was a prominent figure, wearing a Prince Albert coat and fine side-whiskers. Life began to be a serious business with Platt, and it was a great concession to the amenities of friendship when he relaxed himself to make a pun, a mental tipple of which he was exceedingly fond even into his declining years, but which he ever guarded lest it lead to the inebriety of geniality. His business grew. In the course of things he became interested in an express company, and was elected its president. Platt, who dominated whatever he touched, found in Congress neither comfort nor profit. So he left it, and, keeping his clutches on his congressional district and gripping another district, snuggled up closer to Conkling and Cornell and Payne. In 1877, he pushed himself into the king row, and was elected chairman of the Republican State Convention.

At that time he was a pleasant-looking, delicately-built man, a bit slab-sided, restless, nervous, acquisitive. His lean face was covered with a scrawny beard. He had a hard, shifty eye, with a sort of left-over petrified twinkle in it, and his long, broad jaw was the only thing in his face to prophesy his career. He seemed to have had a double ambition: to be a rich man and a successful politician. He had made a good start in his express business, and he was in the last years of his apprenticeship in the manipulation of men. His trade was about learned, and he was getting ready to set up a political business of his own. He began little innocent excursions in state legislation with local bills and private bills, turned out some neat and workmanlike laws, and was becoming so important in state affairs that certain people in his home town hated him. He felt his restless ambition for power—an ambition lariated by the provincialism of Owego. Too many persons walked past his box in the post office peeking at the corners of the envelopes. So in 1879 Platt moved to New York City, where one may be up after ten o'clock at night without causing comment. In a crowd he could play his game unobserved; for Platt had an inborn love of the secretive. It finally went so far that he was noncommittal in the presence of strangers about the state of the weather. He fixed his eyes on an appointive place that pleased him, and pounced upon the office of quarantine commissioner of New York, the only appointive office he ever held. He administered his office well, but played politics in it ten hours a day, which left few hours for the express business. His itch for power was overcoming his love for money. He was familiarizing himself with the political situations all over New York State. He kept his grip on the situation in Owego, and the details of the political life in any community came to have significance to him. About this time he formed a political partnership with Louis F. Payne, a Republican manipulator of some skill and state renown. Platt and Payne were of the same age, reckoned by years, but reckoned by those political experiences which men describe by winks and shrugs, Platt was a bound boy and Payne a journeyman. After the Republicans elected the New York legislature in 1880, Platt and Payne, operating with less than half a score of legislators, went down to Albany to take in the senatorial election. The two herders picketed their legislators to a temporary boom for Platt for senator, and began looking about to see how the game was running. Occasionally they found a maverick legislator, or traded for one, or removed a brand from a stray, and by the time the general round-up occurred it was apparent that Platt and Payne would have enough votes to throw the senatorial election where they chose. They chose to hold it. The people of New York, to whom Platt was merely a carpenter and joiner of politics, considered his senatorial candidacy and his statesmanship a bit Pickwickian. And so one fine morning, when the papers announced that Platt was elected United States senator from New York, the people were amused but bewildered.

Platt as senator in those days was a dwarf on stilts. He entered the Senate as the political camp follower— but not even the creature, and certainly not the ally—of his senatorial colleague, the great Roscoe Conkling, the imperious, who was at the summit of his power.

We must stop a moment and consider Roscoe Conkling, one of the unique figures in American history in the early part of the last quarter of the nineteenth century. He was a stage figure, picturesque to a degree. He seemed to be forever wearing a sort of spiritual make-up which glowed through his body.   Blaine referred to his turkey-gobbler strut.   Yet he had intellectual powers to justify it.   A contemporary, Senator John J. Ingalls, of Kansas, once described Conkling thus:

His presence was noble and commanding; his voice and elocution were superb; his bearing and address somewhat too formal, but marked by dignity and grace.   His vocabulary was rich and ornamental, sometimes almost to the borders of the grotesque, but fertilized with apposite quotations and allusions that showed wide reading, especially in poetry and the drama.   Some hostile critic described one of his speeches as a "purple earthquake of oratory."

Had he learned how to forget where he could not forgive there is no height he might not have reached, even the highest in the people's gift.   But he would not flatter Neptune for his trident, nor Jove for his power to thunder.   In that state of moral typhoid which always follows great wars, an era of profligacy, and of sudden wealth at the price of honor, of Crédit Mobilier and Star Route scandals, he was not contaminated.   He walked through the furnace with no smell of fire upon his garments.*

Platt, in contrast to Conkling, cared little for sentiment, nothing for political issues—he was stalwart—and he abhorred the clash and clatter of rhetorical arms that gave Conkling joy.   Platt could work only under cover. Daylight politics blinded him.   But the very moment he entered the Senate, fate led him to a wide asphalt field under a glaring electric light.   Publicity followed him

* Read these lines on Conkling's career also by Senator Ingalls:
"Patriotic, arrayed always for truth, right and justice, his name is identified with no great measure, and his life seems not so much an actual battle with hostile powers as a splendid scene upon the stage, of which the swords are lath, the armor tinsel, the ramparts and bastions painted screens, the wounds and blood fictitious; on which victories and defeats are feigned with sheet-iron thunder, and tempests of peas and lycopo-dium, and the curtain falling to slow music while the audience applauds and departs."

as a searchlight. A diverting political feud raged in the Republican party in the seventies and eighties between James G. Blaine and Roscoe Conkling. It was deeply personal. No principle was involved; but whoever supported Blaine had Conkling and his friends to fight, while Conkling supporters were proscribed by Blaine and his cohorts. Grant was Conkling's friend. Blaine had helped to defeat Grant for a third term in 1876, when Hayes was nominated by the Republicans and elected— but for one term only; and again, after a bitter fight led by Conkling, the Blaine forces defeated Grant in 1880, and nominated Garfield for President. Garfield, Blaine's friend, gave offense to Conkling; but when Garfield was assassinated, Chester A. Arthur—whom Conkling had nominated for Vice-President—came to the White House; and so Conkling rose to power, while Blaine went into temporary eclipse. So the seesaw teetered. While Garfield was President, Senator Platt tried to avoid a break with him. Because Senator Platt and Senator Roscoe Conkling were from the same state they were thinly allied, but certainly Platt made some advance toward a friendship with Blaine and his followers. The friends of Garfield say that Platt had even given them to understand (they say by explicit promise, which is improbable; he admitted promise by implication) that he would stand by Garfield and Blaine and against Conkling and Arthur. But Conkling, in the end, held Platt's support. As the quarrel neared a crisis, Platt's embarrassment became acute. Suspicion began to leer at him. Perhaps a certain unlovely curve that sloped his shoulders was bent in those days for all time. Anyway, in the historic quarrel with President Garfield in 1881, Platt was forced to take one side or the other. In the bonds of politics, Conkling and Platt had endorsed a candidate for Collector of the Port of New York who did not measure up to President Garfield's standards. The candidate was rejected, and the New York senators—which meant Conkling and, in the slang of the day, "Me Too" Platt —dramatically resigned from the Senate, expecting to rebuke President Garfield by a vindication from their state, and so return to Washington in glory.

When he resigned with Conkling, Platt may have been only hunting cover. The light of publicity had dazed him. Friends declare that Platt expected to go into business, and had decided to make a career in Wall Street. It was in the midst of this row that President Garfield was assassinated.

Platt had acquired such a loathing for politics as a drunkard feels for liquor just after a debauch. He told his friends that he was done with politics. Though for the sake of his temporary reputation he was making a feint at seeking reëlection, they say, Platt had no hope or real desire to go back to the Senate. He went to Albany in a perfunctory way, and began his canvass. Conkling was gratifying a lustful appetite for power and glory; Platt was merely setting up the drinks for the boys, waiting for an opportunity to slip away home. Then a thunderbolt fell. Tom Platt's whole life changed in the twinkling of an eye. A framed-up scandal about a woman came, and smeared Platt's face with shame. Platt laid the blame of the incident on the friends of Blaine. Whether the story they told was true or untrue, no one knows now. Probably the episode was manufactured. They used women in politics in those

days as they used liquor and money and motor cars in
a later day. The truth of the story is really irrelevant.
The effect that the scandal had upon the man's life is
important. The adversity that befell Tom Platt at
Albany when the scandal came seemed to curdle his soul.
He left Albany, withdrew even from the pretense of the
senatorial race, and stole into darkness. All his world
laughed, scoffed, and reviled. When he went back to his
express office, he was supposed to be a dead man with the
lime of shame eating him. But while the grass was
growing over him, down in his grave Tom Platt was
working out. Every wile of his craft, every nerve of
his energy, he summoned to help him. By nature he was
indefatigable, and in that extremity he was implacable
as well. He was ravening for revenge upon those who
had heaped the shame upon him. After two busy years
Platt had acquired less than half a dozen votes in the
legislature, and with these under his arm he tiptoed out
of the graveyard of obscurity back to Albany. About
the lobby he assumed the meek disguise of a modest
peddler doing business in a small way—in a very small
way—in legislative job work. But he handled his votes
dexterously, and he held his growing business in the
express office as a base of supplies. At the next session
of the legislature, Platt came up with a somewhat larger
kit, and with an appetite for vengeance still unsated. At
the end of that session he was a power. He gained
strength not by buying men, but by owning them, by
breeding them and growing them. He worked into the
Republican organization till it became his garment; then
he cut it to fit him, and no man dared dispute his title.

All this he did, working under the surface of things,

burrowing, digging. In those days, very likely, he did not care for power for the sake of power. He seemed to care little for issues, only casually for the measures he furthered. He was interested in winning the game only because, by winning it, he believed that he could destroy his old enemies, and with their destruction he felt he would find some way to wipe the smirch from his name. That came to be Platt's mastering passion, almost a monomania. Untoward fate made him a pessimist. So he scorned to hesitate at means. Ends alone were vital. When, in 1889, Platt became absolute master of the Republican party in New York, when he owned congressmen by the score, he was still unsatisfied. In a measure, he had sloughed off his zest for vengeance. But the habit of work, of incessant political activity, the grinding capacity for the thing before him—these were the things that moved him then. He had worked so far that Harrison's Cabinet was directly in front of him. But he could not make it. When he found Harrison's refusal was final, Platt drew some sort of cartilaginous hood of stoicism over his face, and went on burrowing like an earthworm, making New York history.

When he appeared in national politics again, in 1892, he was leading the campaign of James G. Blaine— Blaine, the man he hated, the man whose friends, Platt claimed, had stained Platt's name at Albany. But Harrison's affront was fresher than Blaine's; so Platt transferred his hatred to Harrison. The only way Platt saw to beat Harrison was with Blaine. The game was the game, the day's work the day's work! Platt supported James G. Blaine in the convention of 1892 faithfully and skillfully. Thus it will be seen that although

Platt traveled with the heavy accouterment of luxurious vengeance, he was always willing to throw it off and make a truce with an enemy when the end required it. Platt kept an alliance with an enemy as honorably as he kept it with a friend. And a friend, unless he was a wise friend who knew his man, was probably as insecure without Platt's express promise, which he never broke, as an enemy. Platt learned well what the politician, ancient or modern, learns in the alphabet of his education: that it does not pay under any circumstances, nor for any reward nor end, to lie. As a class, no men in the world are more absolutely truthful with their intimates than the successful American politicians. Platt's success was won by telling the truth, as well as by hard work. Of course Platt was chary of his word. The man who got a promise from Thomas Collier Platt to do a thing that he disliked to do, accomplished one of the most difficult things in American politics, for Platt was "set" in his way.

CHAPTER IV

THE USE AND ABUSE OF EARTHWORMS

PLATT'S greatness was never in Washington, but in Albany. His work there was permanent for a generation—a long time in politics. And now follows the story of that interesting work.

After the defeat of Blaine at the Minneapolis convention in '92, Platt wormed into his own terrain at Albany. There he had begun a vast system of political tunnels under the institutions of local state government; he went back to finish it. That was Platt's lifework. He was never a national statesman, not even a national politician. He was provincial in his influence; merely a magnified type of hundreds of earthworms—the egoistic forces of life boring beneath the roots of local self-government by cities and states, burrowing silently yet with incalculable power, loosening the soil, sagging vain foundations, putting toplofty visions absurdly awry, changing the aspect of the political landscape.

To appreciate the bulk of the work Platt did, it is necessary to consider the situation that he found when he began to work. Approximately speaking, that was in 1880. At that time the legislature of New York State was much like the legislature of other states. Sometimes the majority was honest, sometimes it was stupid, and sometimes it was venal. Persons interested in legislation took their chances, and acted accordingly. Then, of

44

course, variations of intelligence and honesty appeared in the same session. A legislature that was perfectly honest and reasonably intelligent about the school-book or the canal question might be either corrupt or dull about the railroad question, and a majority adamantine in its honesty about railroads might be open to mercenary conviction about insurance matters. And so it went. Naturally, every interest that might, should, would, or could be affected by state legislation needed a lobby at Albany. The result was a large and expensive third house. Platt entered this third house, and found it a clumsy, inefficient affair. Frequently the legislators voted as they pleased —which, by the way, is not necessarily a wise way—and frequently the demagogues swayed the legislatures, and frequently opposing interests raised the price of legislative votes to figures entirely out of proportion to the actual commercial value of the votes. In short, in the New York legislature an economic disorder prevailed that was painful to a business man of Platt's nice sense of proportion and arrangement. It was his mission in the world to bring order out of confusion.

Of course Platt did not set out consciously to do what he did. Probably no one who plans a new achievement plans far ahead. A man may labor without direction, and with nothing but temperament to guide him, and when his work is done it will be as consistent as it would have been if it had been preconceived. With Platt it was thus. He followed no model—not even an ideal. What he wrought was due to his tireless persistence. At first he had no desire to control more than a few votes, the balance of power. He generally worked in the lower house of the Assembly because it was generally Republican, and because the lower house often takes the initiative in legislation. From controlling the balance of power, Platt grew into the control of the majority of his party caucus in the legislature. Naturally, this growth was slow. Time and again, in a state convention and in a legislature, he was beaten disastrously. Often he was accused of wrecking a state ticket to keep an enemy out of power, and sometimes men and measures that he opposed won in spite of him. But he was as active after defeat as after victory, which is the distinguishing mark of the successful politician. When his man was turned down for the head of the ticket, Platt went into the convention and named the other candidates on the ticket, thereby controlling the executive council; and he nominated the State Central Committee while his opponents were rejoicing over the final overthrow of Platt. From controlling the majority party in the legislature, Platt wormed his way into the administrative branch of the government. During his last decade and a half he tried to own the governor and the state officers as well as the legislature. Occasionally he succeeded, though the proposition was difficult. For the type of man named for governor was often a higher type than Platt; and governors were frequently hard to curry. But governors were mere passing incidents.

It was the control of the Republican Central Committee that chiefly concerned Platt. That was his firm fortress. Through the State Central Committee Platt reached legislators before they were elected. His method was simple. As a rule, a man running for the legislature has no money to spend on his campaign. Platt furnished the candidate with money for election expenses through

the agency of the State Central Committee. How Platt
got that money is another—possibly an important—story.
The candidate for the legislature who believed in the
integrity of his party saw no harm in accepting one hundred, five hundred, or one thousand or more dollars from
the State Central Committee of his party. And be it said
to the credit of the candidates, generally this money was
spent honestly if always wastefully—considering the
standard of the times. But certain things in politics are
changeless. For instance, when the legislature is elected a
legislator is inclined to abide by the decision of the party
caucus on questions that require his vote. If he bolts
the caucus, a new man often appears from his district
the next session. If a corporation, or an interested citizen or business concern has a bill pending before the
legislature, it is evident that the person to see about that
bill is the man who controls the party caucus. That man
is he who sends the campaign expenses to the candidates
for the legislature. This was eternally true in politics
of the last century. It is occasionally true a generation
after. From 1882 until 1902, that particular man to
see about New York legislation was Thomas Collier
Platt. But why should a corporation seeking privilege
or a citizen seeking gain see Platt without a proper introduction? A good way to get an introduction was through
the treasurer of your company, saying that during the
last campaign your company contributed so many dollars
to the Republican State Central Committee and that the
bearer had a "little matter" before the legislature in
which he would be grateful for Senator Platt's assistance.
Upon that basis Platt might be interested. The "little
matter" received attention, the necessity of an expensive

lobby at Albany was avoided, and if the matter was not too palpably culpable, the wishes of the people in the "little matter" carried merely an academic interest. What we call popular government to-day was abrogated in the gallant days of the old plutocracy by a purchase

LATEST ORDERS FROM THE EASY BOSS

From the *New York Herald*, 1896.

of privileges. The process later became a little more surreptitious than it was in the middle nineties. But bootlegging the sale of privilege still is a profitable and, until the bootlegger is caught, a respectable calling. But a generation ago the privilege seeking corporations or those desiring protection from legislative blackmail

learned that it cost less to contribute to the State Central
Committees of both political organizations than it cost to
keep a lobby at a state capital and be forever harassed by
the threat of unfriendly legislation. Also, it was more
certain of desirable results. More than that, the people
approved the system; for stories of individual corruption,
of bribes and scandals, and the salacious gossip that inevitably arose when a numerous lobby was spending
money at a capital, did not arise to "hurt the party."
Then, in addition to all that, this money, which the lobbyists once spent at Albany, was spent under the new dispensation for torchlight processions and picnics, for banners and fireworks, out among the great plain people—
bread and circuses. Hence the contentment!

Now this would have been a wonderfully effective
and valuable machine if its mechanical perfection had
ended right there, but it did not. Platt took it further.
When he got a taste for governors, he found out how
to use them. There was danger that the legislature
might some time be Democratic—which would be embarrassing. So the Republican organization, or Platt—
whichever you will—took as much power out of the
hands of the legislature as it, or he, dared and put the
power into the hands of the executive. The state boss
who controlled the governor, of course appointed commissions controlling the railroads and the insurance companies, the canals and state banks, and as many other
financial and industrial concerns as possible, which were
sources of revenue to the party Central Committee. So
that with a Republican administration in power, and a
Republican legislature, Platt might go away and leave
the legislature for weeks at a time, and have all his

political interests safe in the care of a dozen commissions. If the Republican state ticket should be defeated at the next election, and the upper house of the legislature remain Republican, and the lower house go Democratic, the law—which was the political perfection of the simple legislative thumbscrew—would hold Platt's Republican commissioners in office until their Democratic successors were qualified and confirmed by Platt's Republican State Senate! Thus the reader will see that when the Democrats beat Platt at Albany, they had to make a clean sweep of the legislative and executive branches of the state— an unlikely circumstance. And Platt had one resource left even then. The judiciary was recruited from among the faithful. Too often the judges of the Court of Appeals were Platt's men. A cursory glance at the capital structure of the Platt Legislative Trust and Investment Company would indicate that its stock was a fairly safe investment for New York capitalists looking for anything in that line.

Platt established something more than a personal machine. He established—or grew up with (which it is, heaven knows)—an institution which was as much a part of the government of this country in Platt's day, and certainly as respectable, as the judiciary or the legislature or the ballot box, even though it was not in the constitution of any state. That was the party machine of the last quarter of the old century. This machine was an instrument of government. It stood between what at any time might develop into a mad mob at the ballot box and the ever-present greed of strong men drunk with the power of money. This machine furnished the necessary shock troops in the first line of defense, unconsciously set up by a property-minded nation to defend institutionalized capitalism—the Hamiltonian plutocracy.

Platt's machine, and, indeed, all party machines in all these states and cities and in the nation in Platt's day, had one immovable check—an honest executive. The governor had the state patronage. This power often dominated legislatures. Platt depended on gratitude for favors received as the lever that gave him his power. There is also that gratitude which, as John J. Ingalls once said, is the lively expectation of favors to come. The governor held the lever of that power. If he was independent of the machine, or ambitious to establish a machine of his own, he could carry out whatever honest plans he had and, unfortunately, a few dishonest ones. But, generally speaking, a man who is strong and independent enough to ignore a machine is intelligent enough to be honest. The humanness of the governor was the only weakness in the party machine, whether it was Platt's machine in New York or the machine of any other party manager in the land.

Platt was always a hoodoo in national politics. He was lucky in but one convention in nearly twenty years, that of 1900; he had no eye for currents of opinion. He was elected to the United States Senate in those years of the middle nineties. When Blaine failed in '92, Platt hitched his wagon to Tom Reed's star in '96, and failed. Platt claimed a crumb of comfort in his autobiography in the fact that he brought the Republican convention of '96 to adopt the gold standard, but his claim even to that crumb was disputed by Hanna, who declared that Platt was only one of a hundred who helped.

And right here is a sprightly story. When Governor Theodore Roosevelt went to Albany, it was with the explicit understanding that he would confer with Senator Platt about all important gubernatorial appointments. Platt had no other hold on the new governor. The most important appointment to be made by Roosevelt, according to Platt's mind, was that of insurance commissioner. Platt desired the reappointment of Louis F. Payne, of blessed memory aforementioned. Roosevelt would have none of Payne. Platt blustered and threatened. Roosevelt was firm. The game was this: If the State Senate did not confirm the man whom Governor Roosevelt named as Payne's successor, Payne would hold over for two years. That was Platt's card; for Platt was supposed to control the majority party in the state. On the other hand, if Platt forced a fight with the governor, there might be interesting complications. Roosevelt

"He Wept with Delight When Platt Gave Him a Smile, And Trembled with Fear at His Frown."
—*New York Evening Journal.*
ROOSEVELT'S SUPPOSED DILEMMA.

submitted a list of six other machine Republicans from which Platt might choose. Platt refused to desert Payne. However, Roosevelt dealt Payne a blow squarely between the eyes when, by swooping down on a trust company with a state examination, the governor found that the directors of the trust company were the same men who were directors of an insurance company that Payne was examining as insurance commissioner, and that the trust company had made a loan to Payne of half a million dollars. The security of this loan was interesting. It pointed directly to the work Payne had done in a former legislature for a great street railway corporation. That was Roosevelt's card. But there was not a regular politician on either side of the Senate who was not under obligations to Payne. The insurance companies—under Payne's control—turned out as one man and demanded Payne's reappointment. That was another of Platt's cards. There were twenty-seven Republicans against twenty-three Democrats in the Senate. Under orders from Richard Croker, boss of New York City, the Democrats went solidly for Payne except three, two of whom wanted to vote "furdest away from Tammany," while the third was inspired by civic righteousness. A dozen of the twenty-three Republican senators needed could be trusted to stand by Roosevelt for the gratitude that anticipates its rewards. The others might be influenced by sheer force of public opinion; but if the regular organization of the party stood against public opinion, they would stand by the organization. Conference followed conference. The session was drawing to a close. Roosevelt was good-natured to the point of jocosity; but he was firm. Platt could not budge the young man. Once Platt wired the governor, "Meet me at lunch at the Fifth Avenue," or some such place. The governor replied that he could not do it, and asked Platt to meet him at breakfast at the home of a friend. Platt came to Roosevelt! In a spirit of good-natured teasing, it is said that the governor read the boss's telegram to the company at breakfast and asked them gayly what they thought of that for a message to be sent to the governor of a great state. The company laughed merrily. Platt grinned—bore it. This story illustrates the situation. Good-natured, cold-steel badinage on the part of Roosevelt, smothered wrath on the part of Platt. A crisis came. There was a story that two or three of the machine men had deserted Platt. Platt came for a final conference. The time was getting short. The governor was cheerfully firm; the boss was irascibly arrogant, with a touch here and there of melodramatics. At the close of the interview he had accomplished nothing. He had told the governor that the situation meant a fight and a split in the Republican party. The young governor had smiled toothfully and accepted the situation. The boss got up to go. He got nearly to the door; then he turned back, and surrendered, body and breeches. He accepted Hendricks, the first name on the governor's list of six. The opposition collapsed. This story should go into history; for it is typical of all contests that will come in other years and other times than these between the misdirected machine and the honest executive. The executive who is right and who is brave must always win, no matter what odds seem to be against him. It is written in the very law of the machine that it shall fail when human intelligence in the executive opposes it courageously.

Several times Platt and Governor Roosevelt disagreed, and where a question of honesty was raised Roosevelt won. So Platt conspired to shelve Roosevelt. Platt and Quay made Roosevelt Vice-President to punish him for his integrity. And in disposing of Roosevelt by putting him on the national Republican ticket in 1900, Platt reached his high-water mark in national politics, and also by the same token came to the place of his downfall. Platt's national career was stormy, calamitous, and generally inefficient. When he succeeded, as in the case of naming Roosevelt to be rid of him, fate soured his cup. Roosevelt became President, and patronized Platt.

Then came Governor Ben B. Odell to the governor's chair. Odell in some quarters was believed to be Platt's agent, as chairman of the State Central Committee; but as governor, Odell broke the old relation and defied Platt. Odell had a firm grip on the levers and springs and stop-cocks of the machine, and Odell was a young man and Platt was old. So the contest could have but one end, and that the end of Platt.

But he did not surrender the scepter quickly. Nominally he was the head of the machine and enjoyed his power. But his power under Odell was a shell. This power, which he once craved for what it could give him, he cherished at the close of his life as a miser gloats over his coins. He was more like a dying fox than a miser at the last. Whoever cast even a shadow between Platt and his power heard the click of the old fox's teeth. Platt's whole life was devoted to his treasure; he cared little for and seemed to know nothing of the principles of parties. He was, to the end, always a stalwart. He followed the Republican caucus and the platform faith-

fully. He did not even consider public sentiment in his
reckonings. A long life with the machine blunted his
political sense. A moral issue, where it was opposed by
his party, was a color in the prism which his mental eye
did not discern.

It is only fair, in estimating Platt, to set him in historical perspective. Platt's work was a part of the
tendency of the times. He organized in one state the
alliance between politics and business, a necessary function in the clash between agriculture and industry that
the times were staging. He helped to make it politically
safe for business to amalgamate in great units for
the purpose of multiplying profits by reducing duplica-
tions, cutting down overhead, eliminating competition,
ignoring to a considerable extent the consumer. American capital had been struggling for three decades for just
the privileges which in New York State Platt's leadership
was giving to capital. Hanna was the national champion
of the American plutocracy; a defender of the trust in
politics, who flaunted his banner on the outer wall and
proudly proclaimed the worship of Mammon. Platt in
New York, the city of the temple of Mammon, worked
diligently, quietly, honestly, and most effectively to man
what he regarded as the sacred ramparts, to guard every
point of attack of the holy citadel. And when Roosevelt
came, Platt knew that the battle for which he had prepared was on.

Platt was narrow, both morally and intellectually. At
his home he read an occasional book, and sometimes went
to the opera or to the theater, for his delight in music
remained the soft spot which he turned to humanity.
But in the main the man's existence was wrapped up in

contemplation of the intestinal phenomenon of his party in New York State. It was a matter of absorbing importance to Platt to know that in the tenth ward in Syracuse Bill Jones, who was defeated for a place in the county convention by the John Smith gang, had finally got Tom Brown on his side, and would join in with the Robinson fellows to beat Jim Hughes for ward committeeman, and thereby discredit the Smith gang; or that up in Oswego the fish-eating Irish Democrats had offended the bow-and-arrow French by naming Cahill for recorder, and that there was a chance to "trade in" a Republican over in the eastern wards of the town, and thereby elect an alderman at the next city election. Hundreds of these situations found abiding-place in Platt's mind. He knew the factional fights, and the causes of them, in every county in New York. The knowledge of these fights was power. For he played faction against faction in handling men. He had sat in the Central Committee rooms at the old Fifth Avenue Hotel, now a ghost on Madison Square in New York, hearing these stories of the factions, day after day, year after year. Life meant nothing else at the close. The guile of politics was his meat and drink.

In the United States Senate, where Platt served after 1897, he cut a small figure. He was a negligible man on the floor of the Senate; and generally of small consequence in the Republican caucus. He was for the most part the log-roller, willing to vote for this man's measure if the man would help Platt with some patronage scheme. He took no active interest in the large trend of national events. The social life of the Senate bored him, and he was miserable until the tedious business of

a session was done. Then back at his express office, or
sitting at his desk in the Fifth Avenue, he could gloat
over his power. He clothed his life with few warm personal friendships. His closest allies when death came
were new friends. For he was quarrelsome, petulant,
and suspicious at the last, and those who were nearest
him were always saying they owed him nothing. He
held men by fear rather than by fealty. His tactless
manner repelled strangers, whom he was prone to distrust; and he required at least lip subservience from his
adherents. He was not an "easy boss." Often, as the
years overcame him, his lieutenants defied him, and when
he could not punish them he made the virtue of gener-
osity out of his impotence. But his hate for those who
defied him was obsequious, formal, implacable, almost
salacious! He was always a good judge of human weakness, but he could not comprehend strength. He under-
estimated Roosevelt, Root, and Odell, because he had
no sort of conception of that part of a man which is
called the moral nature. And yet in money matters Platt
was honest—deeply, morally impeccable. Many hundreds of thousands of dollars, possibly millions, passed
through his hands annually for political purposes, and
probably not one penny ever stuck to his fingers. He
made no money out of politics. His tastes were simple.
He never lived extravagantly. He was proud of the
implicit trust the great corporations and their agents put
in his financial integrity, and he would not have parted
with that pride, the foundation of his self-respect, for
all the money in Wall Street. His former friends perhaps may say that he betrayed them, but no man who
contributed a dollar to buy oil for Platt's machine ever

found fault with his investment. Probably his machine was one of the things in the world to which Platt was absolutely true. And as he passed over the hill into the sunset he became a sort of machine himself—hard, impulseless, cunning, acute but witless, immovable, inexorable, grinding; persistent as the power that pulled him, a thing to be taken apart without finding a soul, yet shrewd and with almost human intelligence in his limited work.

Platt could never rule New York City. New York City is essentially feudal, and the king must be of the native blood. Platt was always a foreigner. He never took root in New York. He made an occasional raid into the city and dethroned the nominal king; he even set up once or twice a temporary protectorate or a fleeting dynasty; but he and all his kith and kin were pretenders with the populace. It rose invariably, and drove the usurpers out at the first crisis. Platt knew no more about New York City when he came to town than he knew of Lahore, and he never learned the town. For the spirit of feudal charity and rough kindness to its own people, which is, was, and ever shall be the real spirit of Tammany with all its corruption, is the spirit of New York. A mere cold-blooded, mousy, fidgety little man, who walked cautiously catwise across his own bedroom floor, never could rule New York City. He came to his end a ghost of a statesman shrouded in the wraith of his power. He whom they had been calling "the old man" for so many years passed very gently from his kingdom. He had, in the final years of his reign, the dry, purple-pink parchment skin of senility, and a voice no longer firm. His eyes were often dull. He wore the unkempt

beard of the aged. He slept much in the daytime, and
he worked automatically when he awoke. He attended,
toward the end, a splendid banquet where the leaders
of his national party spoke. While Roosevelt, the greatest of them all in that day, was covertly jabbing Platt
with a merry innuendo, the old man fell asleep. He
drowsed through the evening as gently as a child, and
when it was all over, he came out rather confused on
the arm of a stalwart New Yorker. A group of reporters
in the hallway asked Platt what the national leader
had said at the banquet. The old man paused for a
moment, looking questioningly at the reporters, and
finally replied in a dreary voice: "At the banquet? What
banquet? I know of no banquet." Then gripping his
big friend's arm, and turning from the reporters, the
old man sighed: "Come on; let us go now, Ben." And
so he tottered away—a potsherd flung to the ash heap,
dust to dust!

PART II

THE EARLY STUARTS

"And there were giants in the earth in those days."

Benjamin Harrison, Grover Cleveland, and William McKinley were Presidents of the United States in the eighties and nineties of the old century—a time of gestation rather than birth in their country. These were the last three American Presidents who lived as young men through the Civil War. Their grandfathers brought down traditions of revolutionary times. When the generation of the eighteen-nineties passed, America lost contact with her youth.

HARRISON

CHAPTER V

OUR HAIRY ANCESTORS

AMERICAN men in the eighteen-eighties still were skulking behind the barricade of their whiskers. The whiskers and the moods that maintained them followed the Civil War. Men found beards convenient in battle days; barbering was difficult, and while the war spirit afflicted the land whiskers symbolized war's fierceness and vanity. In the scourge of greed and hate that follows every war, men in the sixties and seventies in America may well have needed beards to hide their shame. General Grant was an honest man, but President Grant's administration, for all Grant's personal integrity, was corrupt and cruel. The South was ridden and ravaged by cheap henchmen of the party in power. The West was going under the plow, but just behind the plow were flocks of evil birds of plunder—railroad promoters, political shysters, real-estate swindlers, fattening on the farmers' seed and on the worms and slugs in the new furrows. It was an era of gorgeous spoilation, a time when bombast concealed larceny. So much wickedness and vanity, so much sham and cupidity were rampant in the land that men did not dare to show their naked faces. So the full beards of the soldiers held

over in popular fashion for more than two decades after
the war.   And because soldiers ran the politics of
America, both North and South, whiskers were the politicians' trade-mark.   One bearded brigadier general
after another had followed Grant into the White House,
and General Benjamin Harrison came the last brigadier,
wearing the last full beard of the Civil War into the
Presidency.   When he left the White House the South
was finally at peace, and the West was done with plun-
derers; the North and East were becoming definitely
industrial, and the country that was to face the new century with its new problems was just beginning to find
itself.   The old day was done; a new dawn was coming.
Men shed their beards and faced a new reality.

Now we are ready to consider this Benjamin Harrison,* twenty-third President of the United States, son
of a congressman, grandson of a President, great-grandson of a Signer of the Declaration of Independence; a
college graduate prepared for college by a private tutor;
a lawyer and a gentleman, an aristocrat of the old line,
a throwback to another century.   He came into the Presidency a man in his mid-fifties.   He was given a pink and
white skin, hair graying from auburn, gentle, often twinkling, and sometimes piercing blue eyes.   He wore
proudly as a badge of masculinity a full gray but always
carefully trimmed square beard.   He had a soft, high,
clear voice which carried well when he spoke out of doors,
but his distinguishing characteristic physically was that

---

* Chronologically, we should come to Grover Cleveland first, who preceded Harrison as President, and who also succeeded Harrison.   But
because Cleveland did succeed Harrison, and because his most important
work was done in his second term following Harrison, we turn first to.
Harrison.

Benjamin Harrison, who signed the Declaration of Independence; William Henry Harrison, ninth President of the United States; and Benjamin Harrison, twenty-third President.

he was a little man, barely five feet six, just a bit stocky; a nimble-footed, quick-moving, but always dignified little man.

The dignity of the little man was an evidence of certain other things unseen in him. Probably his small stature in his youth brought to him a vital need to overcome, with spiritual qualities and mental exercise, the physical handicap which nature put upon him. Little men sometimes grow great because of this early mental training imposed by their physical inferiority. The will to win which an undersized boy puts into life often produces a man who is indomitable. This little Indiana man with the pink and white skin, small hands and dainty feet, who came into American politics in the eighteen-seventies as a national figure and survived there thirty years, moved in a political atmosphere rather different from that which any of his immediate successors knew. McKinley, who came four years after Harrison left came into new issues. And although McKinley was a veteran of the Civil War, he was only a major. And while the Grand Army of the Republic, an organization of Union soldiers, supported McKinley with the enthusiasm of men for the most part in their late fifties and sixties who were making their last fight, Harrison had the support of the Union soldiers of the Civil War at the apex of their power.

He was the apotheosis of their ideal of a patrician, and for all their radical black Republicanism these soldiers did have their visions of grandeur. They were born in the twenties, thirties, and early forties of the nineteenth century. Their fathers had told them of Jefferson, of Madison, of the Adamses, of Alexander Hamilton. So they hailed Harrison, a scholar and a gentleman, with great admiration. Scholars—at least, if a college degree presumes erudition in its recipient—were not strangers in the White House during the forty years before Harrison arrived. Arthur, Garfield, Hayes, Grant—a West Pointer—Buchanan and Pierce carried college degrees. Lincoln, Johnson and Cleveland were not college bred.

Harrison with his college training had a sense of satire, even of sarcasm; but of humor—not much. The basis of his character was an instinct to do the polite, honest, dignified thing in every contingency. He seems always to have felt it more important to be a gentleman than to be an orator with a smart answer in any contest. Now a gentleman may be the joint product of a capable heredity and a sophisticated environment. And it may not be out of place in an account of the career of Benjamin Harrison to glance casually at his ancestry and hastily at his environment.

Harrison's noteworthy ancestral heritage—a great-grandfather who was a Revolutionary soldier, a grandfather who was a President, and a father who was in Congress—was never far from his consciousness. In America grandfathers are uncommon, great-grandfathers are extremely unusual, and the man who has both is as rare as the seventh son of a seventh son. Harrison's great-grandfather, General Benjamin Harrison, one of the signers of the Declaration of Independence and a famous fighter in the Revolutionary War, was a Virginian and of course a politician. His contemporaries describe him as a man of "exceptional candor," which probably means that he was not above practicing the gentle art of making enemies. They say he was a big,

gouty man, and doubtless one who would have his little
nip and his little joke. Legend declares that the sparkle
in the Virginian's eyes was reflected in the kindly light
that beamed in the Indianian's face. William Henry
Harrison, President of the United States, son of the
Revolutionist and grandfather of Benjamin Harrison,
became famous as an Indian fighter, and when he won
the battle of Tippecanoe he garnered his first laurels.
But he accumulated his family quota of enemies. He
was courageous, headstrong, a stickler for his dues, and
an outspoken man little given to salving with oleaginous
tact the wounds his words happened to make. In estimating the character of a grandson it is well to remember
these things of his grandsires, who handicapped him as
well as helped him in the politics of his day. Indeed, if
we may look ahead in the story we shall see Benjamin
Harrison in 1888 battling against a gorgeous cartoon
from *Puck,* a comic weekly, which represented Harrison as a pair of bandy legs and a pussy little body stag-
gering under a big woolly grandfather's hat!

The congressman father of Benjamin Harrison was
a gentleman farmer, and young Benjamin, born at North
Bend, near Cincinnati, Ohio, in 1833, grew up with all
the advantages that accrue to a boy who has to toil in
the open air. Hard work stripped off the bark of family
conceit that might cling naturally to the son of a congressman, the grandson of a President, and the great-
grandson of a Signer. But there was stuff in young Harrison. The enforced industry of life on the farm gave him
an energetic habit.

In the early eighteen-fifties, while yet a boy in his teens,
young Harrison entered Miami University, probably

packing considerable ambition in his trunk. He became
a leader in the school, and was one of the founders of
Phi Delta Theta, a college fraternity which maintained
for a century chapters in the Middle West and South
and in the smaller Eastern colleges. It stands for what
must have been young Harrison's ideals.

Harrison left college, studied law with the great Bel-
lamy Storer, of Cincinnati, married, and went to Indianapolis when he was barely old enough to get his name
on the poll-books. He opened a law office, but clients
hesitated before his door, and his friends say that he
was handicapped by a little man's predilection to pomp.
He looked a boy until his blond whiskers covered his
cherubic face. But he was blessed with industry and
perseverance. Despite his stature, he elbowed himself
into the place of court crier in an inferior Federal court.
But the job enabled him to drive the wolf from the door;
moreover, the pomp and circumstance of the place must
have soothed Harrison's natural grudge against his
diminutive body. In his law practice his first client
escaped conviction for burglary, and the verdict made a
small reputation for Harrison as a lawyer. He worked
hard and kept that reputation polished. No case was too
trivial for his pains. He took up politics, local politics in
his ward, and gave it the same careful attention that he
bestowed upon his law practice. By sheer force of will
young Harrison, behind his fierce beard, became what is
known as a "mixer." He showed himself friendly. He
worked at friendship as a trade. They say he was a
conceited stripling. But by cultivating friendly ways he
certainly sloughed off selfishness, which is the root of con-

ceit. So he widened the horizon of his heart, and in the end this helped him more than his friends—whom he may at first have sought with a fairly low motive.

When the Civil War of the sixties opened, Harrison was reporter in the Indiana Supreme Court, an elective office that carried a liberal salary. He resigned this office to go to the Civil War. He enlisted as second lieutenant, and was made a colonel before the regiment started South. Clearly here was a man. He went at tactics with the brain of a scholar, the heart of a gentleman, and the energy of an ambitious little beaver. Soldiers of the Civil War remember him as a slim-waisted, quick-moving, dapper, affectionate little officer—a colonel; with smiling blue eyes, a brown-red beard sometimes trimmed with a fierce military mustache, fair blond skin, a clear commanding voice, and a ton of dignity. He wore clothes like a manikin, was particular about the amenities of his colonelcy, and a slave to his men.

The official reports say that his strength lay in drill, in preliminary work with his troops, in providing them with food and shelter before action. The caution which he, as a boy smaller than his fellows, must have had ground into his character by the iron of savage youthful experience, rose in him in his battle days, tempered a dashing spirit and gave it craft. Thus the soldier was made, a soldier whom men in the ranks loved and called "Little Ben," and whom President Lincoln made brigadier general at thirty. No hit-or-miss of genius gambled with Harrison's success. It came as the sure consequence of unstinted, well-directed work and vigilant ambition. In two famous Civil War battles, at Peach Tree Creek and Lookout Mountain, Harrison met military glory, but it was a glory that followed his long hours of study, his days of drill and weary maneuver, as surely as harvest follows planting.

Benjamin Harrison came back from the war a general, a man tried and proved. His character was formed. Seventy years after the Civil War it is hard to realize how the form if not the substance of the elements have changed which were mixed in the human character of the middle nineteenth century to make a conventional man. One of the most vital ingredients in the middle of the nineteenth century was denominational religion. Harrison, who joined the Presbyterian church early in life, was a deeply religious man without being pious; a man who believed in the God of his times—a good God who kept books and tolerantly charged off many bad accounts, but still a wise God to whom Benjamin Harrison would have to give account for his talents. He was a praying man, a devout Presbyterian without being sanctimonious; and, recognizing the glory of God, he was modest himself and made no pretense that it was by his own grace that he was chosen, or favored, or shielded by Providence. Citizens of worth and consequence about him were also praying members of some church. The town atheist or the village infidel was a marked man. Before the forces of destiny Harrison presented an humble and a contrite heart. Incidentally, with his piety he was methodical, studious, often punctilious in small matters, always courteous according to his lights, and never slovenly, exacting, or rapacious. Harrison apparently regarded his Presbyterian profession as a part of a gentleman's equipment. To know that he was elected, anointed, and fore-ordained to grace gave the youth a confidence in himself that he needed whenever he considered his five feet six! He was at least sure to be a man-sized angel. Yet a little man's exalted sense of dignity never overcame a big man's innate sense of his own inconsequence.

The lines of his character had deepened; in the Civil War their courses set. He went into the political career of his middle life brave, industrious, gentle, a bit crafty and reserved—but he always was frank where silence might convey a profitable falsehood—and in crises and in routine of duty, however trivial, he was—as much as a mere fleshling may be—a sincere, uncompromising gentleman.

After the war Harrison resumed his place as reporter of the Supreme Court. In that office he broadened his equipment as a lawyer. He had an exceptionally clear theoretical knowledge of law; and during the decade that followed the Civil War, practice gave him skill and acumen. Politics hindered rather than helped the building of his private fortune; honesty was a necessity, not a luxury, with Harrison; and for a poor man in the seventies, honesty in politics was a little expensive for everyday use. So in 1876 Harrison formally withdrew from politics. He declined a gubernatorial nomination and went back to his law office with the sweet serenity of a man who has put Satan behind him. But a few weeks later the gubernatorial nominee withdrew in the heat of the fight, and Harrison came out of his law office,

took the rejected nomination, and set out to carry Indiana
for General Hayes of Ohio, who was the Republican
candidate for President. It was a heavy burden, and
although Harrison led his ticket, the state went Democratic. After that he made no more abstemious vows, but
let nature take its course. President Hayes appointed
Harrison a member of a commission to study the Mississippi as a highway of commerce. After serving on the
Mississippi Commission, he was elected to the United
States Senate from Indiana in 1881. He was elected in
one of those revolts against the low politics of the day,
in one of those passing spasms of yearning for what is
called "good government." The people trusted Harrison. They had never been told things by Harrison
which they discovered after the campaign was over to
be vote-catching tomfoolery. He never deceived them
with promises he did not expect to keep. He did not
try to flatter them by pretending to believe their judgment infallible.

Ambition never left him, and sometimes was unpleas-
antly conspicuous. His ambition was the glory-dream
of a stunted boy coming true. Nothing succeeds like a
well-ordered inferiority complex, pushing a good brain
and a kindly heart to a high goal!

The United States Senate, when Harrison entered it,
was not a sanctuary for sweetness and light. The senators then present there were improving each shining hour.
As senators they were making the desert to blossom as
the rose, and as private citizens they were garnering the
blossoms at handsome prices. Judge David Davis, of
Illinois—an honest man with a sense of humor, a states-

man who had left the United States Supreme Court to enter the Senate—sat with Harrison the day that he came into the chamber to take his seat, and as the senators filed by, Davis called them off as Adam named the animals in the morning of the world: There came the jackal, the vulture, the sheep-killing dog, the gorilla, the crocodile, the buzzard, the old clucking hen, the dove, the turkey-gobbler. Then, as the big hulk of a greedy Westerner—coarse, devious, insolent—came swinging in heavily, Judge Davis pointed his stubby forefinger at the creature and exclaimed:

"A wolf, sir; a damned hungry, skulking, cowardly wolf, sir."

It was accounted a pretty bad lot, the Senate of that day—despite the fact that men point back to the time as the Golden Age! Harrison worked effectively, and in six years came out of the Senate stronger than he went in, with clean hands and a good name. During these six years, before the chatter about high ideals became politically popular, Harrison exemplified, quietly and without advertising it—a principle of civic righteousness. He made the kind of career there that might have been expected from a praying Christian with a college education; from an aristocrat with a burning ambition to sit in the presidential chair from which untimely death had taken his grandfather. It did not occur to him to make an outcry about his ambition or his piety. His Presbyterianism was not ostentatiously self-righteous. His righteousness was a private matter between a patrician and his conscience.

His reserve was never broken. He did not go about

slapping men on the back, calling them by their first
names.   He did not even give quiet assistance to the
other senators with their public larcenies.   He played
the game of practical politics more or less as a lone hand,
but certainly without a marked deck; and he never stole a
trick.   Now let us survey the background from which
Benjamin Harrison came to the White House.

CHAPTER VI

THE "RUDE BARBARIANS AT PLAY"

AFTER the Civil War, the Union soldiers in the Northern States were overwhelmingly Republican in their politics, clannish to a degree, often arrogant in their political organizations, and sometimes selfish beyond the bounds of the highest patriotism; not all of them, but surely many of them. So certain of their leaders gave to politics in the seventies and eighties a low and dangerous tone. Demagogues were not above taking advantage of the passions and prejudices that rose when the Grand Army of the Republic nursed the hates of the Civil War. The Democrats, who had few Union veterans in their ranks, had a phrase for this rebel-baiting— "Waving the bloody shirt." It was in a day when waving the bloody shirt passed for argument, when the bronze button of the G. A. R. was unquestioned in the North as a badge of courage, merit, and distinction; when patriotism was often marked by a swagger, and when it was always popular to "twist the lion's tail," meaning thereby to insult Great Britain; when the cynicism of the day declared that "a public office is a private snap," when the vast agricultural area west of the Mississippi was just coming into economic and political consciousness after a decade and a half of pioneer development. Corrupt politics had marred the Grant administration in

the early seventies.   Corrupt business practices had followed in the Hayes administration in the middle and late
seventies.   In the early eighties, in Arthur's administration, corruption had become less blatant.   It submerged.   An alliance between business and politics in
the late seventies and early eighties was quietly fostered
under the leadership of James G. Blaine.   Into that field
in the late eighties came this rather circumspect, erudite,
self-willed, dainty little aristocrat, Benjamin Harrison.

If he had been more than a gentleman, if he had been
a leader of men, he might have gone far in the world.
If he had been less, he would never have risen above the
Senate.   His Presidential nomination was largely the
result of a compromise.   Blaine was the idol of the
rank and file of the Republican party in the eighties.
Blaine, who had much to explain, a great charm of
manner, that gorgeous surplus of personal grace called
magnetism, a distinction of bearing which he used to
refute the charges of his enemies, Blaine had been nar-
rowly defeated by Grover Cleveland in 1884, but still was
a power in the land.   Senator Edmunds, of Vermont, had
opposed Blaine in the convention of 1884, and had rallied
about him the mugwump support, including a young convention delegate named Theodore Roosevelt, a youth of
twenty-six, from New York, who stood on his chair and
shook his fist in the faces of the triumphant Blaine majority of the Republican convention of that year.   Blaine
waved the bloody shirt and twisted the lion's tail and
was given to oratory and those emotional spasms necessary to the statesmanship of that day.   Blaine was opposed
in the convention of 1888 by John Sherman, who was
backed in that convention by two Ohio managers who

later were to be known to fame—one Mark Hanna; the other, William McKinley. McKinley, a presidential possibility who eliminated himself by a definite refusal to run or to accept a nomination, was a protectionist leader in Congress and Chairman of the Ways and Means Committee of the House of Representatives, and had some following among the tariff beneficiaries of the country. But, alas! Sherman represented the extreme position of the gold-standard advocates, and bore the odium of Wall Street's endorsement. So Sherman's candidacy crumbled. Blaine's strength was not sufficient to renominate Blaine. So both sides, trusting Benjamin Harrison, the meticulous, dignified, quiet little senator from Indiana, a brigadier general of the Civil War with a spotless record, named him in a sort of truce of God; between, on the one hand, the growing power of the mugwumps, who stood for civil service, ballot reform, a scientific tariff, hard money, with only such good times as justice would guarantee; and, on the other hand, the saber-rattling, free-and-easy advocates of manifest destiny and an open treasury led in opposition to Sherman by Blaine, who in a crisis of the convention turned his forces to Harrison. That was the line-up which made Harrison the nominee. And Grover Cleveland, in the White House, by threatening the tariff on wool and—worse than that, by trying to establish an honest government in Washington—let Harrison, the aristocrat, come to the White House.

In the end Harrison owed much to the geography of the situation, which demanded an Indiana man, and to the excellent organization of Mr. Dudley, ill-famed in his day for his "blocks of five." The "blocks of five" was a political invention by which each voter in Indiana was

separated into one of a block of five to be looked after
by a dependable Republican—usually well supplied with
money from the party coffers.*

In the campaign of 1888, which ended with the election of Harrison to the Presidency, no important issues
stirred the people. The Republicans straddled the currency question and the Democrats "sparred for position."
Both parties agreed that from certain imposts, revenues
should be raised, and the debate occurred on the method
of raising the needful amount. To this debate Harrison
brought an editorial writer's gift of lucid, coherent, convincing rhetoric. He wrote in short lengths—from five
hundred to twelve hundred words to a speech—and each
speech was carefully prepared. It was what was called
"polished," in the day's vernacular. It was not an occasion that demanded oratory. The tariff question was one
of expediency. The people decided to try the Republican
expedient—a protective tariff—so they voted for the
Harrison electors.

Harrison on the threshold of the White House was an
anomaly. He represented a decency and dignity above
his party and rather beyond his time. His moral intelligence was backed by moral courage. In harboring
a certain old-fashioned chivalric feeling for the office
Harrison came into trouble. He was probably three-
quarters of a century behind his time. One must remember that he was dealing with the Senate bosses; with
Senator' Quay, with Thomas Platt and with Stephen
B. Elkins, whom he took into his Cabinet, and men of
that type and ilk. Mathew S. Quay may be identified
as the senator whom Pennsylvania returned after he had

* It survives as a political device in Indiana to this day—in 1928!

been rejected by the Senate for an irregularity in his election.

A United States senator in 1889, with few exceptions, represented something more than a state, more even than a region. He represented principalities and powers in business. One senator, for instance, represented the Union Pacific Railway System, another the New York Central, still another the insurance interests of New York and New Jersey. Here, out of the West, came not one but a group representing the Southern Pacific. The Santa Fe divided, with the Gould System, an interest in another. Coal and iron owned a coterie from the Middle and Eastern seaport states. Cotton had half a dozen senators. And so it went. These senators either had campaign contributions directly from the great business interests which they openly championed; or the attorneys for these interests, controlling state conventions and legislatures, named these senators, and so owned them. It was a plutocratic feudalism, not rigidly organized, but eminently respectable. The collar of any great financial interest was worn in pride. No one wore his more proudly than he who represented the New York Central, and Jim Hill's senators from the Northwest flaunted their golden chains. They were faithful. No one charged them with duplicity or dishonor. Their status grew out of the manner, customs, needs, ideals of the times. And after they had served their masters well they served their country incidentally. But these senators, who served their country honorably, felt that their masters' demands and their country's welfare made a common cause. Possibly they were right. America was being developed as a vast capitalistic enterprise, though of course not carefully

coördinated. Whoever served capital well, from whatever motive, probably may not have served his country
badly, in that day. The time had not come to harass
the aggrandizement of organized capital with the Beati-
tudes, nor to compass it about with the Golden Rule.
Even Harrison, high-minded patriot as he was, seems
to have had no great scruples about the rights and
domination of capitalism in American politics and the
alliance between business and politics which was obvious
all over America in that day.

The largest sum of money that had ever been raised to
elect a candidate was raised to elect Harrison President.
National Chairman Quay made a pilgrimage to Indianapolis to congratulate the President-elect and to receive
his gratitude. Men said at the time, and it was undenied,
that Quay, assuming the innocence of Harrison, took with
him a Cabinet slate. Harrison met Quay; and John
Wanamaker, who ought to know, wrote that the Presi-
dent-elect "said in his cold and solemn fashion, grasping
Quay's hand, 'Providence has given us the victory.'"
Quay listened politely to this explanation. But Quay
had taken the Philadelphia cash raised by Wanamaker to
New York, and had overcome an alleged plot which
Elkins and Platt were engineering to turn the election to
Cleveland in return for the New York state patronage.
Naturally, Harrison's pious thanks to Providence pained
Quay. To a friend he sneered at Harrison as the tender-
foot.

"Think of that man! He ought to know that Providence hadn't a damn thing to do with it," quoth Quay.
Quay's hand-picked Cabinet slate was ignored, and Harrison made his own slate. He put James G. Blaine at

the head of the slate as Secretary of State, and did not
give out the names of his Cabinet members until just
before the inauguration. He had method in this, as we
shall see later.

The last Sunday before his presidential inauguration,
Harrison, as deacon in his church, "passed the plate" for
the weekly collection, and the first thing he did in the
White House was to name as Postmaster General John
Wanamaker, the head of the largest Sunday School Class
in the United States at the time. Wanamaker promptly
turned against Quay and became his leading opponent
in Pennsylvania. Wanamaker, in politics, was an outsider. To put him at the head of the Post Office Department was to insult deeply the plunderbund of politics
which fattened on post offices.

Harrison embodied, though he did not politically represent, the ideals of the mugwumps, who were yearning in
a certain vague, inarticulate, bullfrog fashion for reform.
Harrison represented also a revolt in his party and in the
country against a rapidly growing and rather clubby good-
fellowship in politics, typified by Blaine. This good-fellowship tended to form a close corporation of log-rolling,
back-slapping, whispering temple acolytes who assumed
to guard the covenant of the Republican party, but who
were really looking after the main chance for themselves.
These were the Republican "bosses." Blaine was better
than the lot, although he led them. And Harrison, with
his ideals and a clean record, was an outsider. He was
almost but not quite the dramatized leader of the revolt
against certain heavy-jowled scalawags who were making
the Republican organization their exclusive club, whose
arcanum was the United States Senate. In the campaign,

Harrison had met these gentle bandits, but he and they had nothing in common. Neither had he much in common with another type rising to power in those days, the business man in politics; as, for instance, Mark Hanna, who, as head of the financial committee of the Republican organization, had raised the funds for Harrison's election. Hanna was a forthright man who believed that government was organized to promote business, and said so with a certain brutal candor which offended a fastidious person like Harrison, who had an idea that a President was vicegerent of God.

From the day of his inauguration as President of the United States, Harrison began to live the part. He had personal ideas about the presidential office which were exasperating to the Republican politicians familiar with the chummy air of Arthur, with the always inoffensive attitude of Hayes, and with the blunt, frank, cordially nonchalant demeanor of Grant. Harrison decided to be President to his finger-tips, as became the son of a congressman, the grandson of a President, and the great-grandson of a soldier and Signer. In a day of languishing interest in old issues, naturally patronage became the chief end of the man in the White House, and Harrison frigidly declined to sublet certain areas of patronage to senators and congressmen. He recognized all of the time-honored rights of senators and representatives, of national Republican committeemen, to recommend persons for places under the administration, but as President of the United States he held the absolute right to appoint. Recommendations didn't "go," except recommendations of men entirely satisfactory to Benjamin Harrison as a praying Christian! Of course there were exceptions to this rule. Harrison was a man and fallible. But, speaking broadly, if a senator recommended for any place, however trivial, a man against whom there was a sustained charge of incompetency or dishonesty, no matter how earnestly the senator urged, the candidate was liable to be rejected. Now when a senator or a representative had grown up in the notion that a public office is a private snap, that the patronage of his state is his to have and to hold, in fee simple, the Harrison notion of patronage was disconcerting to an alarming degree. When a senator had "promised" a place it was always embarrassing, and often humiliating, to have to break a promise to a bad man and make an alliance with a good man for the sake merely of the crotchet of a runty, soft-voiced, kid-gloved President with hoity-toity Presbyterian notions. Another thing that made the pathway of the place-brokers a hard road to travel was this: President Harrison refused to announce his appointments until they were publicly read to the Senate or to those who as government officials should know them in the routine of duty.

This custom of taking the public business out of the private machinations of the senators was a revolutionary procedure. To illustrate: Kansas in those days was under the political domination of Senator Preston B. Plumb, a Civil War veteran, self-made, a printer, an editor, a lawyer; a banker by turns, a politician by instinct; good-natured, big-hearted, courageous, bluff, greedy for his friends but never implacable with his foes, who ranged the departments, looking for jobs for his army comrades, with all the diligence of a dog on a slop route; Chairman of the Committee on Public Lands in the decade when more public lands were opened, more railroads built across them, more mines located, more wealth created by unearned increment than in any other decade in the history of the world; a downright Westerner, who played his politics like poker and never let a poor hand discourage him; a big man physically, mentally, and a power of the first magnitude politically in the nation. Plumb had a candidate for a vacancy in the Supreme Court. Plumb's candidate was David Brewer, a Yale graduate who had practiced law in Leavenworth, Kansas, gone to the Federal District bench, the Federal Circuit Court, and was in line for promotion—really deserved promotion. Harrison knew it; decided to appoint Brewer. For reasons sufficient to Harrison the appointment was not immediately made. Plumb crashed into the executive office at the White House one day, mad as a bull. He had heard some rumor that Brewer's candidacy had been abandoned. As a matter of fact, the papers for Brewer's nomination were on the President's desk as Plumb came in, signed by the Attorney General and the President. Plumb began a stump speech for Brewer which the little man in the President's chair regarded as bulldozing. He sat fumbling the commission, tempted of all the devils in the pit to tear it up and show it to Plumb spitefully. Plumb raged on, walking up and down the room after his habit, demanding, with many a vigorous damn, the nomination of his candidate; threatening vengeance if the President ignored Plumb. Harrison spoke no word, but looked down his nose at the commission in his hand. He sighed, put away the temptation, dropped the commission in its place on the table when Plumb had finished, mumbled some punctilios into his whiskers, got rid of the senator, went on with his business, and in another week sent Brewer's name to the Senate. Plumb thought he had frightened the President into the appointment and despised him. Harrison knew it, but knew also that to keep an able man out of the service of his country for a personal pique of the President was unworthy of a man whose covenant as a President was with his God. A serious, old-fashioned, deeply religious man was Benjamin Harrison.

Now Harrison seems to have had two reasons for refusing to confide his intention in patronage matters to senators, each characteristic: First, although he probably did not put it first in his self-analysis, was the fear that he might wish to change his mind, and the desire to be uncommitted and free to change. This was the craft in him coming out. Second—and this was his public reason—the instinctive feeling that the functions of the presidential office were, even in small matters, too important, too confidential, to be subjects of gossip. He knew how he was reviled for his course. He knew that he was laying up treasures of hatred and hoarding interest-bearing bonds of vengeance; but he did not compromise.

He did not compromise even with the high priests of the Republican temple. Mark Hanna, of Cleveland, Ohio, who had passed the hat for the funds which made Harrison's Republican victory possible in 1888, had a candidate for a Federal position who did not measure up to Harrison's requirements and the President calmly turned the Ohio candidate down without discussing the matter seriously with Mark Hanna. According to all the rules of the game, Mark Hanna should have been called in, vouchsafed some reason or excuse for the presidential attitude, given a chance to pick another man, and allowed to name the winner. But Mark Hanna received no such courtesy. The dogs that fought with Lazarus for the crumbs that fell from the rich man's table received as much consideration as Mark Hanna, Treasurer of the Republican National Committee, the business man in politics, received from the White House in Harrison's day. It was not that President Harrison scorned money. Money meant much to him in its place, but only in its place. The rich were not denied respectful attention if they came to the White House in a proper attitude. He gathered many rich young men about him, men in politics for careers, men with rich wives or wealthy parents or men with influential, well-placed, respectable relatives. This also angered the keepers of the covenant of politics. They could not endure, for instance, two young gentlemen whom Harrison chose to honor because of their obvious fitness and their high social backing. One of these was young William Howard Taft, from Ohio, a son of the wealthy Taft, a young man with a distinguished father-in-law. The other was young Theodore Roosevelt, of New York, son of the well-known philanthropist. Harrison made young Taft, but a decade out of Yale, Solicitor General of the United States, and young Roosevelt, who had fought Blaine in the New York Republican Convention, and had supported Blaine in 1884, when Blaine was the presidential nominee of his party, by going to a ranch in Dakota—him Harrison made Civil Service Commissioner. It was one of the complaints of the swashbuckling, haw-hawing, hard-drinking centurions as they sat at poker, bragging of their amours, that

the President was surrounding himself with "too many
of these damn college dudes."

In addition to that charge came the allegation of the
undoubted domesticity of Harrison. The President's
grandson, Benjamin Harrison McKee, known as the
McKee baby, was forever crawling over the front page
of the newspapers. Mrs. Harrison's evident dislike for
the wine which the Harrisons were compelled to serve at
state dinners, the fact that the Wanamakers served water
instead of wine at their public dinners, and the further
sad circumstance that the conspicuous piety of Levi
P. Morton, the Vice-President, as straight-laced a
Puritan as either Harrison or Wanamaker did not
prevent him from owning the Shoreham Hotel with its
gorgeous bar—these contributions to "the encircling
gloom," soon gave rise to a deep dislike in the hearts
of the high priests of the Republican temple to the
whole Harrison régime, to his Cabinet, to his household,
and to the President himself.

One stanza of the office seekers' hymn of hate went:

> The baby runs the White House,
> Levi runs the bar,
> Wanny runs the Sunday School,
> And damn it here we are.

These crosses were too much for the flabby flesh and
blood of the spoon-fed Pharisees to bear. So Harrison
was assassinated by an adjective: he was called "cold."
Frigidity was the high crime of American politics in 1890.
A man might be charged with theft, and prove an alibi;
be deemed treacherous, and offer in extenuation the pressure of ambition; be indicted as a demagogue, plead
guilty, and go unscathed; be convicted of every other

crime known to politics, and yet find salvation. But let it be even insinuated that he was "cold," and the portals of political damnation inexorably clicked at his heels.

Harrison's public utterances reflected his gentle breeding. The phrase "a cheap coat makes a cheap man" was one of the epigrams that defeated him. He was a maker of epigrams; yet never what the politicians call a spellbinder. He displayed no emotion whatever in his speeches. He roused no passion in a day when politics was highly emotional. But his words mirrored the man's soul—a well-appointed spiritual area wherein grew wholesome, vigorous ideas, indigenous to the English-speaking races. There was nothing Gallic in his cast of thought, few Latin derivatives in his speeches. His verbs demolished fences of circumlocution, and his adjectives kept him off stilts and close to earth. So he did not pirouette in the elaborate figures used in that day, nor strut with the highfalutin bombast which the tom-tom beaters of politics used, to fire the populace. Here is an example of the way Harrison reached his most effective climaxes. On the occasion of the dedication of the Soldiers' and Sailors' Monument at Indianapolis, August, 1889, after finishing his introductory remarks, President Harrison said:

The suggestion that a monument should be builded to commemorate the valor and heroism of those soldiers of Indiana has attracted my interest from the beginning. Five years ago, when the people assembled to unveil the statue which has been worthily set up to our great war governor, I venture to express the hope that near by it, as a twin expression of one great sentiment, there might be builded a noble shaft, not to any man, not to bear on any of its majestic faces the name of a man, but a monument about

which the sons of veterans, the mothers of our dead, the widows
that are with us yet, might gather and, pointing to the stately shaft,
say, "There is his monument." The hope expressed that day is
realized now.

This is a monument by Indiana to Indiana soldiers. But I beg
you to remember that they were only soldiers of Indiana until the
enlistment oath was taken. From that hour until they came back
to the generous state that sent them forth, they were soldiers
of the Union. So that it seemed to me not inappropriate that I
should bring to you to-day the sympathy and cheer of the loyal
people of all the states. No American citizen need avoid this
monument or pass it with unsympathetic eyes. It does not commemorate a war of subjugation. There is not in the United States
a man to-day who, if he realizes what had occurred since the war
and has opened his soul to the sight of that which is to come, will
not feel that it is good for all our people that victory crowns the
cause which this monument commemorates. . . .

Our spirits have been borne up to-day to meet those of the dead
and glorified; from this place we shall go to our homes more
resolutely set in our purpose as citizens to conserve the peace and
welfare of our neighborhoods, to hold up the dignity and honor
of our free institutions, and to see that no harm shall come to our
country, whether from internal dissensions or from the aggressions
of a foreign foe.

The plain force of the language that revealed his
unpretentious nature was repeated in his public acts. The
craft the man used in lieu of animal strength was called
upon to accomplish legitimate ends. While he was President he confined himself to the legal metes and bounds of
the office. He played politics, but it was on the whole
rather decent politics. He was content to exercise the
simple, constitutional functions of his office. He was a
constitutional President, and, with all his gelidity, this
man whose feet were always under his desk, whose breath
was out of other people's faces, and whose arms were

off their shoulders, was never accused of assuming to be a dictator. The worst they said was that he was running a kid-gloved administration. As President of the United States, he was a plain little man, white as to hair and beard, who kept his elbows to himself at dinner and seemed equally happy in evening dress or in a business suit, who insisted always that public affairs should be conducted in a public manner and not after the informal fashion of the Forty Thieves. Perhaps he was just a shade pompous at times, when he tried to express in one small body the vast weight of dignity that he felt was due to the people from the President of the United States. Yet if he demanded that those who dealt with him in the White House should deal with the President of a great nation, he held just as sacredly inviolable the rights of the people to make their laws. He bought little leadership with patronage. In writing the history of the United States it may be that future historians will go back to the days of the kid-gloved administration of Harrison to find an example of a constitutional President.

CHAPTER VII

FAN-FARE FOR THE "PLUMED KNIGHT"

PROBABLY Harrison's reserve of manner, which came from an exalted sense of official dignity, was contrasted to his apparent discredit by his proximity to the suave, graceful urbanity of Blaine, his Secretary of State. The two men were antithetical. As each was a strong man, and as their ambitions converged, they were bound to clash. Blaine's coming to the Harrison Cabinet was typical of the two men and their inevitable relation toward each other. An early announcement of Harrison's choice of Blaine would have made Blaine the leading man in the Harrison Cabinet, and would have left an easy inference that Blaine had helped to choose the other members of the Cabinet. It was characteristic of Harrison that, while he had decided a few days after his election to call Blaine to the Cabinet, he did not announce his intention publicly until late in the winter, when he gave out the names of the other members of his Cabinet. It was a game of craft against intrigue. Craft won.

We must pause here to catalogue swiftly the "giants in those days," the major statesmen with whom Harrison had to deal. Of course there were the bosses, regional leaders, men like Platt of New York, Plumb of Kansas, Elkins of West Virginia, Logan of Illinois, Quay of Pennsylvania. But above these men were national leaders—John Sherman, for instance, known

as the Gold-bug; Roscoe Conkling; and, greatest of all,
James G. Blaine of Maine. If ever the Republican party
had a god, it was he. He survived longer in politics
than men survive to-day. He was thirty years in the
public eye and most of that time in high public office.
It was a period of feuds. Blaine brought into the Harrison administration the old feuds of a day of personal
politics. Ten years before, in the Hayes administration,
the President had removed Chester A. Arthur, a New
York politician, as Collector of the Port of New York
after an investigation of irregularities there. Conkling,
senator from New York, who was Arthur's friend and
sponsor and Blaine's bitter enemy and rival, led the
assault on President Hayes which resulted in Hayes'
defeat for the presidential renomination in 1880.
Though the contest resulted in a dogfall, Garfield,
Blaine's friend, was. nominated and elected President,
with Arthur, who was Conkling's friend, elevated to the
Vice-Presidency. Conkling turned on Garfield as Blaine's
friend, and the excitement of the hour stirred the poor
addled brain of Guiteau to assassinate the President.
Vice-President Arthur's ascendancy gave Conkling
power at the White House, but not until he and his
Colleague, Senator Thomas C. Platt, had resigned in
pique as senators and had then failed of a vindication by
their state. Blaine was nominated for the Presidency by
the Republicans and defeated by Cleveland in 1884, amid
scandal so appalling that Conkling—a lawyer who had
refused to go to the Supreme Court when President
Arthur appointed him—declared when he was asked to
support Blaine on the stump that he was not in "criminal
practice"! Blaine's friends having joined the majority

that nominated Harrison, Blaine brought to the Harrison administration all the animus of the ancient feud. For the fiendish purposes of Conkling's feudal vassals, and among them were the allies of Grant whose forces Conkling led during the convention deadlock of 1880, the Harrison administration was the Blaine administration; and though Conkling died before Harrison came into the Presidency the evil of Conkling's vindictive nature was not buried with his bones. His friends and factional feudists, seeing Blaine in triumph as Secretary of State, blew on the embers of their hate. The flame of it singed Harrison when he passed them, and seared him when he touched the relics of their idol. Conkling was a bitter punitive reconstructionist and a foe of civil service reform. Harrison had no use for punitive reconstruction and built up the civil service rules with all his might, and—alas!—with all his pious austerity, which was an offense to his enemies and a burden to his friends. And Blaine, the ardent, the gracious, the magnetic, held at arm's length by Harrison, walking with just the hint of a strut down the straight path of rectitude, Blaine finally ceased to be an ally and became a liability of the administration. In a convivial day, Blaine kept open house and a delectable table. The home of the Secretary of State rivaled in political importance the White House itself, and for good-fellowship Blaine's establishment far outshone the Presbyterian ménage on the Avenue.

Through it all Blaine was bitterly attacked, sometimes cruelly exposed; but he never lost the adoration of his idolators. He made friendship a business; but a profitable one. Harrison was friendly for the joy of friendship. Blaine seemed conscious of his talent to charm, and often seemed to be charming those who would be useful to him. He called his fellow congressmen, or his political associates, by their first names on short acquaintance, had a way of putting his arms around them, fumbling with their watch guards. He had a radiant, ingratiating smile and was deeply affectionate in his nature. He was given to intrigue, and, in view of documentary evidence, it is difficult to believe that he was always above profiting by his intrigue. But the times were the times, and standards were in the seventies and eighties lower than now. Blaine was facile and yet not shallow. He saw things with an understanding eye. In Congress and in the Cabinet his vision was often statesmanlike. But the Democrats and a large faction of Republicans distrusted him deeply, searched every utterance for a motive, every action for self-interest.

Blaine did not dominate the Harrison administration, and not being able to rule, unconsciously and without malicious intent or design, he helped to cause Harrison's downfall. For Blaine's very presence at the White House was an object-lesson in rebuke—so thought the offended senators whose treasure-looting prerogatives were abridged—a rebuke to the taciturn, reserved, dignified, self-contained, piously pompous little Harrison. The politicians organized into a sort of unacknowledged, subconscious rebellion. Blaine was the Guy Fawkes. The gunpowder never exploded, but sedition was in the air.

Harrison tried every subtle art known to an honest politician to keep friends with Blaine; but because Harrison merely respected Blaine, his arts failed. Blaine

demanded affection. The President deferred to his secretary in public, and was considerate of him in private.
But Harrison never let go of the reins; there was the rub.
Blaine was respectful and deferential to his superior. As
Secretary of State he often wrote diplomatic notes, but
invariably they were revised by Harrison, and often the
revisions were important. It was always the Harrison
administration. Blaine, who was rather consciously suave,
took a gentleman's part and deferred civilly, probably
with less personal resentment than amusement, to the
changes made by Harrison. But Blaine knew, and Harrison never eased the feeling that Blaine was the second
fiddler; yet the President was scrupulously considerate of
his Secretary of State, after Harrison's cold, impersonal
manner; which, to a warm nature like Blaine's, was in
itself galling. We must not forget that in politics Blaine
came of the hand-holding, tie-fixing, shoulder-rubbing,
fob-fumbling school—a school trained in the county and
township convention system. Blaine was a veteran in
national politics when Harrison entered as a novice.
Blaine had a host of political debtors, the result of thirty
years of office-holding and ten years as candidate for the
Presidency. Harrison would not let Blaine pay his debts
by State Department patronage. Blaine's brilliant mind,
his versatility, his vigorous personality, his firm grasp of
all his faculties, his *esprit* and the indefinite mesmeric
charm of his manner fascinated Harrison. To the very
end of their official relations, Harrison struggled to be
exactly fair—Blaine, to be loved.

But the powder of the Guy Fawkes conspirators
smoldered for three of the four years of Harrison's
term, and finally, in the spring of 1892, a few months

before Harrison was to ask for a renomination for reëlection, the powder flamed up futilely. For three years Harrison had seen disaffection turning to Blaine. Harrison knew that Blaine knew this. Then suddenly Blaine began to overshadow his chief. Blaine had figured prominently in a controversy with Chile. Harrison had forced apology from the Chilean Government for an insult to America. But Blaine, having the newspaper men of Washington all but on his personal staff, was advertised as the hero of the episode. His open house, his generous table, his grace of manner, had captured the reporters whom Harrison had often seemed to snub. As a result of the publicity from the Chilean episode Blaine's stock rose. His friends began to urge him as a candidate for the Presidency. Possibly it was a claque. Possibly the rise of Blaine was the mockery of fate; for his health began to fail. Harrison's friends answered the claque by hinting that Blaine was dying. However, in January, 1892, Blaine was again the "plumed knight" whom Robert G. Ingersoll had touched with the wand of his oratory in the convention of 1880. That "plumed knight," worshiped by millions of Republicans, was the most vital figure in American politics. In the last decade of his life, ending with 1892, it mattered little to the idolatry of his followers that the Democrats had created another figure to represent Blaine—the Tattooed Man, a naked figure covered over with the titles of the scandals through which he had walked. Then, at a Cabinet meeting whither he had gone to discuss the final details of the Chilean settlement, Blaine bolted from the room. The President and his colleagues thought Blaine was offended, and stared aghast at one another in a moment of silence. Elkins, Blaine's

Ardent Advocate: "Now, gentlemen, don't make any mistake i

CAGO Tribunal

Here's Purity and Magnetism for you—can't be beat!"

friend, hurried after him and found Blaine ill and on the point of collapse. Elkins took Blaine home in a carriage, and there, when Blaine thought he was at the point of death, he urged Elkins to assure the President of his confidence and of his wish that Harrison should be nominated for another term. That was Blaine at his best; generous, eager for the approval and affection of his kind. About this time he wrote a formal letter to J. S. Clarkson, Chairman of the Republican National Committee, definitely forswearing his earthly ambition for the Presidency. But with the surge of his old popularity, his old friends and Harrison's new enemies surrounded Blaine and persuaded him to reconsider his abdication of the Presidency. Mrs. Blaine also desired her husband to contest with Harrison for the Republican nomination. There was turmoil in the Republican party and in the land. In the meantime, in 1890, within two weeks of each other, Blaine's son, Walker, and his daughter, Alice, married to Colonel Coppinger of the army, had died. The blow naturally shook Blaine to the core. In that tension which men in sorrow sometimes assume to hide their inner grief, his judgment failed him, as his health broke. Washington reporters declared that after the Chilean episode and just before the Republican National Convention, Blaine, whose face was ashen and whose hair was snowy white, began to assume a vigorous air in public, walked snappily along the street, and paid for his exertion later.

"He is making a great show of being his old self," declared Colonel A. K. McClure, the veteran Philadelphia journalist, in May, 1892. "I never saw a man who had a greater horror of death than he. He dons a jaunty hat and walks briskly along where he may be seen, and then returns home in a state of collapse. He tried to bow to a pretty girl pinning a bouquet in his buttonhole and almost fell prostrate."

All these signs and portents the crafty little gentleman in the White House saw, and the temperature in the White House dropped. Suddenly it rose to boiling point. Mrs. Blaine called at the White House. A story vouched for by the late George M. Pullman declares that she pushed aside the guards and servants, went into one of the private rooms reserved for the family, and sent for the President. When he came she reproached him for the death of her son, Walker. The President had named Walker Blaine Solicitor General of the State Department. The mother claimed he died from overwork. Blaine wished his son to be Assistant Secretary of State. Mrs. Blaine also urged the appointment of her son-in-law, the widower of her daughter who had recently died, to a place as brigadier in the army. Hearing her through patiently, realizing the stress of her grief, the President maintained his impassive dignity and, referring to the ardor of Mrs. Blaine's demands, her reproaches, and possibly what a man of his reserve might regard as her insults, he replied:

"Madam, it is unbecoming my high office and your sex for the conversation to continue longer."

So, punctiliously bidding her good morning, he left her to find her own way out of the house. The legend says that Blaine did not know of this encounter at the time. As a result of Blaine's anomalous position, being a candidate against his chief and yet not a candidate, Blaine fell into a grand sulk, Harrison into a frigid pout. So the spring wore on. If Blaine had his troubles, the little man in the White House was having his. In the early spring of 1892, after the publication of Blaine's letter to Clarkson, Harrison, returning to his home in Indianapolis for a visit, received William McKinley, who had just been elected Governor of Ohio, and one or two prominent mid-Western statesmen who joined with McKinley in assuring Harrison of their support. Later, when Mark Hanna gave a dinner in Minneapolis, just before the Republican National Convention assembled, and tried to organize the sentiment against Harrison, McKinley sat at the dinner, silent, pleasant, smiling, but noncommittal.

It was in late May that Blaine went down to New York to visit a new grandchild, young Mrs. Walter Damrosch's daughter. The New York *World* describes him in the Fifth Avenue throng: "His tall, spare figure dressed in an immaculate close-fitting suit of black, his frock coat cut high, revealing only a bit of the white linen of his shirt and the round collar and black scarf tied in a close bow which he always wears. In one hand he held a high hat with a deep mourning band around it; in the other a pair of black gloves. His somber mourning costume emphasized his white face and the whiteness of his long, thin, nervous hands. His white hair, white beard, repressed air of perfect ease, all gave him a distinguished bearing, yet somehow one got the impression he was not a sound man." To an acquaintance who asked about his health, he said:

"Very well, very well indeed, I assure you," and passed on with a springy step and easy gait.

It was after returning from New York, on Thursday, June 2, that he rode to his last Cabinet meeting with

Secretary Elkins. Reporters declared at the time that
Elkins hinted that Blaine should resign from the Cabinet.
But Blaine gave no sign that it would be his last Cabinet
meeting; perhaps he did not know. The currents of his life
were running swift and furious, far beyond his control.
He was a broken man. Bright's disease had touched him.
His watery eyes peered out of reddened lids above
unhealthy pouches. But even then he towered above the
dumpy figure of Harrison, if Blaine's agile feet sometimes hesitated. Blaine sat in the Cabinet, as he told his
private secretary, "politely"—he was always a gentleman
—"but repressed; speaking when he was spoken to." He
was cheerful, as became a diplomat, but his old smile, that
for more than three decades had glowed its way to the
hearts of his very enemies, under the pressure of sorrow
and pain, was becoming a stiff slit in a mold set on a bias
upward from left to right. When the Cabinet meeting
broke up, Blaine observed the hour's amenities and with
the others shook hands perfunctorily with the President.
Then, Heaven only knows how consciously, he turned and
forever left the Cabinet room, his highest earthly station,
sifting the ashes of disillusion through long, trembling
white fingers.

CHAPTER VIII

A HAPPY ENDING

So there was no parting for Harrison and Blaine. Theirs was simply a cessation of formal official intercourse. A few days later the Republican convention was gathering in Minneapolis. Bellowing through the corridors of the hotel, great marching mobs roared "Blaine, Blaine, James G. Blaine," the old campaign slogan of '84. All across the land the party was in an uproar. The Chilean episode, which redramatized the "plumed knight," had planted strife and rancor in the Republican party. But there was the Clarkson letter; and there in the State Department sat an old thin white man with clabber-colored features, the flames of his life slowly turning to embers. A legend says that on the day before the Republican convention met he learned of Mrs. Blaine's visit to the White House and of the President's frigid reception. Be that as it may, on June 4, after a conference at the State Department with the British Ambassador, Blaine called his secretary, Mr. Dent, to his side and while his old cohorts were clamoring in Minneapolis, dictated a few courteous, formal lines to the President resigning as Secretary of State. The effect in Minneapolis was electric. But the galvanization of the Blaine forces passed with electric swiftness.*

In one quarter was Harrison impregnable. He had the support of the Southern delegates. Perry Heath, in

*Senator John J. Ingalls, a delegate in the Minneapolis convention, gives this account of the farewell to Blaine: "On the fourth day, June 10, Blaine was put in nomination by Senator Wolcott, of Colorado. The scene was indescribably pathetic. All knew he was at the threshold

the Post Office Department, had been effective and loyal.
An Indian politician, who had been Provisional Governor
of South Dakota by Harrison's appointment, and who
had conducted the publicity department of the Harrison
campaign in 1888, Perry Heath, was in charge of
Harrison's nomination at Minneapolis. It was he who
saw that the Southern delegates and the postmasters
were marshaled in a solid phalanx against the foes of the
administration. The defection of Blaine did not seriously affect the result in what was called the "Postmasters' Convention."

But it was a gruesome affair; for the rank and file of
the Republican party were rallying, with pathetic despair,
around Blaine, who was dying. And in the background,
sneering malevolently, were the watery-eyed, flabby-
skinned, hotel-fed politicians, nibbling at the bitter cake
of vengeance they had cooked. The convention to
nominate a Republican candidate for the Presidency went
through the preliminary motion of organizing. It
adopted its platform. It came, under the order of business, to the nomination of a President, and with scarcely
a dissenting vote Benjamin Harrison was renominated.
The applause that followed was almost ribald. Even the
postmasters and the Southern delegates tempered their
enthusiasm at the convention with the lively knowledge
that their joy was short. The Republican party was hope-

of eternity, but at the mention of his name the innumerable hosts broke
into confused and volleyed thunders that for twenty-seven minutes seemed
to shake the foundations of the earth and sky. Like the chorus of an
anthem, with measured solemnity the galleries chanted, 'Blaine! Blaine!
James G. Blaine!' myriads of stamping feet keeping barbaric rhythm,
while plumes and banners waved, and women with flags and scarfs
filled the atmosphere with motion and color and light. It was the passing of Blaine. That gigantic demonstration was at once a salutation
and a requiem. The Republican party there took leave of their dying
leader and bade him an eternal farewell."

lessly split. It was no longer a phalanx of victory, but a cortège. The word "cold" had done its work. Then a bloody riot around the Homestead steel mills—a riot that for a few hours seemed to presage revolution—filled out the funeral train.

One by one, the politicians whose hate Harrison had earned so wisely and so well deserted him. He had ignored Hanna. He had scorned Platt. He had even shown his dislike for Elkins in his Cabinet. Plumb of Kansas despised him, and Plumb, more than any other figure, controlled public sentiment in the Missouri Valley. The Wall Street which had contributed in 1888 the largest sum that had ever been raised to elect a President, began, in 1892, to suspect Harrison of unsound views upon the money question. The high protectionists disliked his academic balance in discussing the tariff and his leaning with Blaine toward reciprocity.

So much for the respectable elements of American politics. But in the South and West another element was making trouble. The new country beyond the Mississippi, which had been opened after the Civil War, had been opened on borrowed capital. Notes were coming due, mortgages were being foreclosed, state, municipal, and county bonds were maturing, and the ancient feud between the creditor and the debtor was appearing in political issues which demanded an expanded currency, asked for control of the trusts, and cried out for regulation of the railroads. These new, strange issues Harrison neither comprehended nor had the vision to study with patience. Populist senators and congressmen were defeating Republicans in the Missouri Valley and overwhelming Confederate brigadiers in the South. They were a queer breed, these Populists, thrown up from the bottom stratum of politics; noisy, often ignorant, sometimes blatant, always disturbing. And as if Populism were not enough, there came into the scene a vast caterwauling against the McKinley Bill. William McKinley, as Chairman of the Ways and Means Committee of the House of Representatives, had introduced into Congress and had pushed into statute a revision of the tariff law by which increased rates were established which made certain articles of common use more expensive than they had been: tin, clothing, chinaware. In 1891, in the midst of Harrison's administration, the President was confronted with a Democratic Congress, and of course his party leaders blamed him for it, which was absurd, considering the fact that he kept so aloof from Congress while it was passing the McKinley Bill that the leaders grumbled that he would not help them. But, under our customs, an administration is blamed for the acts of the party in Congress as well as for the policy of the administration in executive matters.

The industrial unrest of the day was due partly to the dislocation of commerce under the McKinley Bill, due partly to deeper causes coming out of financial conditions in the West and South where debts were maturing, and due partly to booms and collapses that had marked unrestrained finance in America since the Civil War. The country had suddenly caught up with its industrial visions. Enough railroad, wires, pipes, and girders had been laid to complete the needs of that generation. The closing steel mills culminated in a strike of the steel workers of western Pennsylvania. Riots brought bloodshed and assassination. The country for a few weeks shivered under the fear of anarchy in the industrial centers of the Middle States. With that fear beclouding the land, Harrison went into the autumn campaign for his reëlection.

In the midst of the struggle, after a lingering illness, the wife of his youth died. He was unable to go to the people. He made a few speeches in Philadelphia, in New York, in Baltimore. He had a pleasant campaign presence, possibly convincing at times. But the stars in their courses were against him. The people chose Grover Cleveland for the second time and Benjamin Harrison was numbered among the one-term Presidents of his country.

The three months between Harrison's defeat and the inauguration of the new President were months of virtual boycott upon the White House by the Republican politicians. The President went about his work alone. Even the office grabbers and self-seekers, realizing that he could not help them, kept away from him. It had been, and still is, an ancient custom for the friends of the outgoing President and his political associates to call upon him the morning before the inauguration. On that morning Harrison sat in his office waiting for his friends to come. No congressional leader appeared. Only Perry Heath, his political manager at the "Postmasters' Convention," and a newspaper correspondent for some Western papers, came to break the solitude which gathered about Harrison before the President-elect appeared.

Leaving the White House, Benjamin Harrison went back to Indianapolis, where he "used to be so happy and so poor." He "passed the plate" in the Presbyterian Church the Sunday following his home-coming. He took up his life as a prosperous Hoosier, resumed the practice of law, and became part of the spirit of his town. He lived the last nine years of his life decently and in order. Enough law business came to him to occupy him by day, and during his hours of leisure he devoted much time to books;

for Harrison was always a student. The degree he received from the little Ohio college did not satisfy him, and he did not cease growing while he lived. He read widely—general literature, fiction, poetry, essays, science, psychology, law, economics, sociology. In all these departments of learning he kept abreast of his times. This is uncommon. The average American politician, indeed the average American statesman, knows shop and can talk shop; beyond that——

Harrison, on the other hand, after he left the White House, came to know his country better than he knew it in the White House. He knew every side of it; knew its literary side as well as its political side; knew what aspirations were moving the people; came even to comprehend the roots of Populism, which puzzled him when it arose. He knew what movements were current in American art, what scientists were striving for. When he left office he merely relinquished one routine of duty for another. Life was not bound up in the gratification of his own ambition. Harrison's spirit was anchored deeper than politics. Political defeat left him serene. It did not change his viewpoint, much less his character. Before 1888 he spoke his mind freely—alas!—not caring who was offended. After 1892 he did not see any reason for cringing before popular opinion. He realized that the people and the wind are fickle and that election results have little to do with the justice of any cause, nor with its ultimate success or failure. He used the best means at hand in a civilized world to find out what was right, and if he happened to believe the politicians and the people wrong, that was their affair.

In 1896 he threw himself vigorously into the fight for the gold standard. He overlooked his dislike of Hanna and his distrust of McKinley in their cause. He believed it was right. In 1900 he stood by the gold standard, but he refused to go into the campaign for McKinley; for Harrison did not believe in colonial expansion. He felt that we should not take over Porto Rico and the Philippines. The world of politics stood aghast that a Republican ex-President should not declare for a Republican national ticket. It was urged that Harrison owed it to the Republican party to support it in every emergency, to which he replied in effect that his conscience and his self-respect had helped him when the Republican party was powerless to do so, and he would stand by his conscience and keep his self-respect. It was a simple matter; political gratitude put in the balance against his sane judgment of the right of the question. His judgment outweighed his gratitude, and the fact that he knew he would be execrated, called a traitor and even a sorehead—which is a much more biting epithet—did not weigh a hair's-breath. He was a gentleman unafraid.

And so Benjamin Harrison lived his life to the end in peace and—for such was the serenity of his temperament—in contentment. He died before old age had shriveled his mind or shaken his body or left him lonely. He gave much service to his country. It honored him, and will always honor him, though mildly, for what he gave. He fought gallantly and well upon his country's battlefields. He sat in the United States Senate and helped there to overcome the partisan bias and bigotry of the day. He stood in the place of honor, and was a just ruler and a brave one. But most of all, he gave to his generation—and rather palely to the generation that shall follow—the example of a courtly, wise, ambitious American who was never afraid in any crisis to be a dignified Christian gentleman, a pious, praying Christian gentleman of an old, old fashion.

GROVER CLEVELAND

CHAPTER IX

"HIS ACCIDENCY"

GROVER CLEVELAND came to the White House—the twenty-second President of the United States—in March, 1885, on a day that closed twenty-four years of unbroken Republican rule. In those years the Republican party, which was born of an ideal, had degenerated sadly. It could not withstand the fleshpots of reconstruction during the sixties and seventies. The administration of Lincoln was purely a war administration. Andrew Johnson, Lincoln's successor, by reason of his liberal reconstruction policy, lacked but one vote of impeachment. Grant's eight years in the White House came as nearly bringing corruption there as it ever came. And while President Hayes battled four years ineffectually with the spoilsmen he was unable to subdue them, and they made him a one-term President. A nation-wide feud between Blaine and Conkling broke out in the Garfield administration. Garfield was assassinated. Arthur came to the White House, an amiable pacifier of the factions. He did little to check the hunger for spoils which dominated his party. Then came Grover Cleveland, a Democrat, and broke the Republican succession, and the Republican politicians referred to him as "his accidency." There was much justification in the phrase. His experience in national politics was negligible. He had been Governor of New York but two years when he was elected President of the United States, and his nomination as a Democratic candidate for governor was an accident. Another man was slated for the job; but the night before the convention opened the other man was weighed and found wanting by the powers that ruled the convention. Less than four years before Cleveland became President his chief political distinction was the fact that he had been elected Mayor of Buffalo at the head of a reform movement. The Republican faction—fighting in New York in 1882 between the Conkling "half breeds" and the Blaine "stalwarts," made Cleveland's election as governor possible. In the campaign of 1884, when he was nominated for President, Cleveland's political enemies referred to him as the "hangman of Buffalo," recalling the fact that as Sheriff of Erie County, in 1871, he had hanged a condemned criminal with his own hands instead of turning over this unpleasant duty to a deputy. Republican demagogues, waving the bloody shirt, called attention to the fact that although Cleveland refused to hire a deputy to hang a criminal, he hired a substitute during the Civil War to serve for him when he was drafted into the Union Army. His record as mayor and as governor before he was nominated for President was a record of ruthless honesty. He offended Democrats and Republicans alike, scorned Tammany Hall in New York City, flouted the labor element in his party, vetoed a legislative bill to compel elevated railways to maintain their passenger rates at five cents, and disported himself generally in those guber-

natorial years like a bull in a china shop. As governor
he would have no private secretary. He wrote most of
his own letters by hand. He organized no kitchen cabinet,
had few friends, played a lone hand. The refreshing picture of this solitary figure stalking through the corruption
of his day even into minor offices, the mayor's office and
the governor's office of his state, so captivated the national mind that he was elected President. But here again
the element of accident contributed to his success. Cleveland's opponent in the election was Blaine; Blaine, the
idol of the Republican party; Blaine, who was a powerful
orator, a man of pleasing personality who had that mys-
terious quality of super-charm called magnetism in those
days—Blaine the unbeatable. But a few nights before
the election a preacher named Burchard, at a Republican
banquet, had denounced the enemies of the Republican
party as the cohorts of "Rum, Romanism, and Rebellion."
And so by a narrow majority, most of which was garnered
from those whom the term "Rum and Romanism" offended, Cleveland carried New York, and with New York
won the Presidency. He made his second visit to Washington when he came to be inaugurated President of the
United States. He was not merely innocent of national
affairs, but ignorant of them for the most part, and
equipped chiefly by his indomitable honesty. He was
forty-eight years old; stood about five feet eleven. His
two hundred and forty pounds were loosely incased in a
hulking, clumsy figure. His two or three fat chins receded
from a strong jaw. A large and rather hard mouth was
masked by a heavy brown mustache, and an immobile face
—rarely but brilliantly lighted with a smile—screened
the hidden purposes of a resolute spirit, which sometimes

GROVER CLEVELAND.

gleamed out from his pale gray-blue eyes; eyes that in anger took a greenish cast. His party had been out of power since Buchanan's day, and the crowd that assembled to hear his inaugural, a curious, critical, and turbulent mob, was divided into two elements: angry deposed Republicans and restless, eager, joyously hungry Democrats. Before the thousands who gathered to hear his inaugural address, Cleveland stood unperturbed, stolid. He looked indeed "the hangman of Buffalo." Those who saw him did not realize what a sentimental, overgrown boy was behind that heavy face. They did not know that the Bible which he kissed in the hands of Justice Waite was the Book his mother gave him when he left home to make his fame and fortune. There was no trouble in his voice, nor did nervousness in the slightest affect the perfect coördination of all his muscles and his splendid physique. He was anything but a handsome man as he stood there. Charles A. Dana, of the New York *Sun,* seeing him, a towering mass of beef, dubbed him "the stuffed prophet." The long skirts of his double-breasted Prince Albert coat fell like a pall from a beefy torso to his knees as he rose to take the oath and kiss the Bible. He lifted up clear eyes from the Book. Then, placing his hands behind him, disclosing the fact that he had neither notes nor manuscript, he delivered to the gaping, critical, strange congregation before him his inaugural address without hesitancy or faltering! John J. Ingalls, the polished, erudite orator, a lean and hungry Cassius out of New England stock, senator from Kansas, seeing the spectacle of this sheriff-mayor-governor facing a hostile crowd, and discarding his notes and taking the terrible chance of blundering in that high moment, turned to his senatorial colleagues and, unleashing his dramatic voice, exclaimed at the astounding spectacle:

"My God, what a man! What a gambler! Not since Ajax defied the gods has the world witnessed such sheer audacity!"

From that moment the Republican leaders knew that they were confronting a fighting man. Thus Grover Cleveland sloughed off his garments as the hangman of Buffalo and became a gladiator of reform, a major figure in his times, the incarnation of an ideal, the personification of honesty in a day when honesty in politics was languishing.

Grover Cleveland's father was graduated from Yale in the early part of the last century, and became a Presbyterian minister. In 1837 he was stationed at Caldwell, Essex County, New Jersey, and there a son was born to him, christened Stephen Grover, for the minister who had preceded the Rev. Richard Cleveland in the Caldwell pastorate. The baby's grandfather was William Cleveland, a Connecticut watchmaker and silversmith, and the Clevelands were sturdy, honest, hard-working people. The baby's mother was Anne Nealy, the daughter of an Irish bookseller and a German Quakeress. With Yankee, German, and Irish blood in him, young Stephen Grover may be said to have had all the advantages of a liberal ancestry in forming his character and career. In 1853, after the boy Grover had fought his way into the respect of the schoolboys at Fayetteville and Clinton in New York State, the family moved to Hollandpatent, where the father died, leaving the mother, Anne Nealy Cleveland, with nine children to support. Grover was the fifth

child. His school-teacher has described him as at that
time a large, apple-cheeked boy, who paid enough attention to his books to keep up with the boys of his age; an
out-of-doors boy who fished and swam, trapped, hunted,
and skated; living in, on, and around Limestone Creek as
many hours a day as he could. Yet he came from a home
where there were books, and he was always familiar with
the things that attract cultivated people. These things he
acquired by unconscious absorption. He was essentially
masculine—lusty, ruddy, full-blooded, close-knit, big-
boned, and as virile as a young ram. He did not differ
from other boys of his town save in one thing—he always
had a job. He clerked in a store for a time, and when his
father died he went with his elder brother to New York
City and found work as a teacher in an institution for the
blind. When he was eighteen he borrowed twenty-five
dollars from a family friend and set out for Cleveland,
Ohio. He was attracted by the name of the town, and
hoped to get a place there in some attorney's office. On
his way to Cleveland he stopped to visit an uncle in
Buffalo. The uncle was rich—for those days. He owned
a fancy stock farm on an island in the Niagara River,
and as he was compiling a Shorthorn herd book, he hired
young Grover to help with the book. The trip to Cleveland was abandoned. The uncle was a man of parts and
consequence in Buffalo, and he put his nephew into one
of the best law offices in the town. The youth was
admitted to the bar in 1859, and four years later, when he
was twenty-six years old, he was made assistant district attorney of Erie County. The six formative years
of his young manhood were spent in a city of one hundred
thousand people, where he met men and women of force,

character, and attainment at his uncle's home and in the daily routine of his work in court. The best homes in Buffalo were open to him, but he could not be called a social butterfly. Indeed, if he owned a dress suit before he went to Albany as governor, no one ever saw him wear it. He chose to live a man's life. He devoted his leisure hours to hunting and fishing. He was a familiar figure on the Niagara River in his fishing-boat. As soon as he could afford it, Cleveland left his uncle's home, and moved his traps to a bedroom over his law office. In those days he was a tall, burly, leather-faced, soft-voiced, but quick-spoken fellow, hard-headed, hard-living, hard-working, close-fisted, honest, sturdy, manly. He had the young animal's desire to drink and to eat well. When he loafed, he loafed with men, in clubs, and in the resorts—the saloons, to be explicit—and other haunts of the young bachelors of the city. A man is said to be no stronger than his stomach, and Cleveland's stomach was as hard as his head or his face or his hand. Whatever he put into his stomach by night did not trouble him by day. Certainly he never lost an opportunity to make the most of himself.

In the law he was a plodder. He won his cases by digging, not by inspiration. As assistant district attorney he became a good trial lawyer, but he was never an orator. He was a good talker, because he knew his case. He impressed a jury with his passionate sincerity. The Irish in him led him into politics, possibly made him a party Democrat. He was nominated and defeated for district attorney, but he was prominent enough in the party organization to be one of the men consulted when any action was taken by his party in Erie County. In

1866, at twenty-nine, he became the head of the County Democratic Central Committee. Politics came to him as a duty of citizenship; the law was his occupation. He recognized the wisdom of saving, and started a bank account. Because it would help his bank account and keep him around the courts and in the atmosphere of the law, also because he was in politics deeply enough so that it came his way without much effort, Cleveland took a nomination for sheriff on the Democratic ticket and was elected. That was in 1870. When he came out of office, in 1874, he entered, as a partner, one of the most important law firms in northern New York. He was then a man formed, thirty-seven years old; unconsciously, unimaginatively brave; with an ox-like honesty, and with a huge body which furnished unlimited power for a tireless brain lusting for work. This was the Cleveland who was a notable lawyer in his town, in his county, in his state during the seventies. He made money, and he saved some of it, though he was cultivating an able-bodied man's love of good living. He was convivial on occasion, and at times he softened enough to be called sociable—but always man-wise, never in parlors. Many men about town thought they knew him because he loafed with them when he wanted to loaf, and because in living his own life as he pleased to live it he met them and was merry with them on his way. These men deceived themselves. Cleveland was, in reality, always apart from them. They were creatures of the play which amused him. He lived without romance, with few friends, but close ones; and, save these few, all his relations with men and women in the world about him were businesslike and commonplace transactions. He was straightforward, trustworthy, true.

Probably he never willfully deceived a human being in his life. But he deserves no special credit, for, with his heavy mental and moral equipment, deception was a jugglery he would hardly have tried. Cleveland might throw the hammer or put the shot, but he could never work a shell-game on man or woman.

So Cleveland, in his thirties, lived and waxed strong. He knew no master save an indomitable will. His only guide was a conscience balanced on common sense and that sum of ancestral wisdom in action called integrity. His mind was not brilliant, nor his conscience poised on a nice balance; his life moved in a powerful current because it went simply and directly. He was full of the work in hand—stuffed full—mind and body and soul. His capacity for work was expanding, and his appetite for work grew with his increasing capacity. Finally came a joy in working, and Cleveland was branded for a life of toil. After he reached that point it mattered little what the work was; he did what his hand found, and had small choice.

While Cleveland was growing in power, the people of the country were passing into an epoch of mental and political unrest. The desire of men for a change is savage and unreasoning, but it is as strong as the force of a tide. The Republican party had been in power for sixteen years when the national impatience broke forth in the popular presidential majority for Tilden, the Democratic nominee. The country clearly desired a change. Hancock, the next Democratic nominee, four years after the people voted for Tilden, could not call the spirits from the vasty deep, but they were there nevertheless. After the defeat of Hancock came unmistakable evidence of

Republican misgovernment. Added to Republican corruption came factional wrangles in New York and Pennsylvania, which revealed more corruption. The exposures of political villainy in the Star Route scandal and in other flagrant abuses of the public trust were startling the taxpayers all over the land. The political air was charged with the electricity of protest. It needed only to gather into cyclonic form to become resistless. In 1881, while this storm was brewing, Cleveland was elected Mayor of Buffalo by an unprecedented Democratic majority. The man was not magnetic in himself, yet curiously, the myth that gathered about his name or political trade-mark became a magnet which drew men to him.

CHAPTER X

HIS EXCELLENCY

As Mayor of Buffalo Cleveland was a working machine, automatically following an intelligent conscience. He tackled the work in the mayor's office like a new railroad manager; cleaned out the dead timber and gave the stockholders the worth of their money. He had no paper ideals, no municipal program, no sort of policy to try on the city. He took the work as it came through his office every day, and measured it by one rule—to give a dollar's worth of value to the people for every dollar's worth of taxes spent. Every scrap of municipal business which wouldn't fit that rule he cast aside. His vetoes made him famous all over New York State. He was plain-spoken. If he thought a proposition was a steal he said so, and he used the short word. A robber, a thief, a sneak, a liar, and a cheat wore no perfunctory titles in the bright lexicon of Cleveland's veto messages. Naturally the people were pleased. Nothing wearies the flesh of the taxpayers so quickly as to find their servants putting in valuable time arranging rhetorical feather-beds with which to break the fall of scoundrels. Also, the people were tired of statesmen eternally saving the country with their vote-getting plans of salvation. What the people desired just then with a furious passion was a vigorous, uncompromising man without any plans, who would save the State from its statesmen. The times crying out for an obstructionist to stem corruption found young Grover Cleveland. And six months after he became Mayor of Buffalo the Democratic party of his state whirled around him in a cyclone of enthusiasm and made him Governor of New York. This enthusiasm the real man Cleveland could no more inspire than he could flit from flower to flower. Yet the people of his state, who had never seen him, who knew nothing of his personality, made Governor of New York an ideal creature of their own conjuring, who bore Grover Cleveland's name.

The real Cleveland went to Albany with almost no acquaintance with public men, unfamiliar with the affairs of the state, with no constructive plan for running his administration, and with no known capacity for the work before him. The only attribute common to the ideal Cleveland whom the people chose, and to the real Cleveland who took the office in 1883, was a dumb honesty. He was swept onward by the tidal power that was moving the protesting heart of the country. He became a man of destiny because he embodied the spirit of the times. He did not make the wave, he rose with it. The revolt against Republican rule was brutal, unplanned—a barbaric yawp of disgust. Cleveland was that revolt in flesh and blood. He sat at his desk in Albany twelve or fourteen hours a day; a big man, rather loggy in person, with a heavy German jaw, a nose with fight in it, a broad forehead, under which peered two pale blue, guileless, inquiring eyes, like embers in a banked fire. He did not look the part of a statesman, hardly that of governor. And when he took up the day's business, he did not try to direct or manage it. He took it as it came, and when a piece of work appeared unfit, he threw it out without any manifestation of emotion, whether it was a party caucus measure or a private bill. Day after day and month after month Grover Cleveland sat at his desk at Albany, measuring the work, selecting the good, rejecting the bad. At the end of the legislative session his veto pile was astonishingly large, and platoons of gentlemen engaged in the gentle art of public larceny were amazingly mad. But the blue eyes of the big man at the desk did not bat under their sluggish lids; the heavy, muscular hand went scratching away at its work; and the people did not know when it was time to cheer, for he gave them no sign. He worked this way for two years, with no sense of scenic effect, stage business, or curtain time. Occasionally he did a great thing, but he did it without any relation to anything else, and merely because it was part of the day's work. It was without climax, and sometimes passed without applause.

But it was all honest, all true, and mutely brave in an impersonal way, as a rock in a fortress is brave because it cannot realize danger nor avoid it. This spectacle was most remarkable in American political life. Living men had seen nothing like it. For two years, as Governor of New York, Grover Cleveland stood the one strong, looming figure in the nation. The Democratic party was chiefly a flock of chattering daws, under the fumbling leadership of Samuel J. Tilden, who had all but won the Presidency in 1876. The Republicans were under the dangerous leadership of the brilliant Blaine, whom they idolized. But the soul of the people was sick of politics, and was nauseated at all politicians. Cyclonic conditions prevailed everywhere. The electric spirit of protest against things as they were was so thick that sparks of profanity snapped from the conversation of mild-mannered men at the slightest irritation, and Cleveland had gathered to his name the electricity of discontent from a wide area. When the tornado broke, in the campaign and election of 1884, it took up Grover Cleveland, the Democratic candidate for President, and hurled him into the White House.

When he landed in Washington he was literally an unknown knight. He might have passed undisguised through the inauguration throng, and not a citizen in a hundred would have known him. The man was so utterly without vanity that he had never been "the subject of this sketch" in the local biographical annals of Buffalo. Not a speech, hardly a scrap of all the writing he had done until he entered the gubernatorial office, was available for the newspaper writers of the time. There were no anecdotes about him to illuminate his character. He had lived a life as prosaic as an index to an auditor's report. In the campaign against Mr. Blaine, preceding the presidential election, the only story told on Cleveland was an unlikely and unimportant scandal, which he did not take the pains to deny; instead he assumed a somewhat disinterested judicial attitude, and advised the scandalmongers to "tell the truth." After that the story lost its point, and was, perhaps, the only slander in American public life which ever died of neglect in the house of its friends.

On that raw March day in 1885 when Cleveland took his oath of office as President of the United States, he faced the largest crowd he had seen in his life, but not five hundred people in the multitude had ever seen him before. He was so new a quantity that not fifty men in the world could have guessed what position he would take on any pending political problem, nor whether or not he would straddle all the fences of equivocation running through the domain of current political and social economy. At the end of his eight-thousand-word speech, to which he came without a tremor in his voice or a perceptible evidence in his manner that he was doing anything more important than addressing a jury in a court at Buffalo, the country knew exactly what he thought about every issue he cared to discuss. Also, men who knew human nature saw that there was a man in the President's chair who was color blind to fear. He was not producing an effect by delivering his inaugural without manuscript or notes. He did not know he was doing anything unusual.

Cleveland entered the White House twenty years after the close of the Civil War. During those twenty years the country had been governed by the voters in the Northern states. The largest group of votes in the Northern states was the ex-Union soldier vote. Both parties were bidding for it in the North. The Republican party held practically all this vote. But in holding it the Republicans had made the word "soldier" a sacred word; and many demagogues and rascals were using the word "soldier" as a passport to public treasuries, which the shysters were looting brazenly. By their action the deserving soldiers were discredited, and much of the money which should have been spent honestly for soldiers' pensions was turned to fraudulent uses. President Cleveland's first important official position was taken as an obstructionist. He registered the protest of the whirlwind by checking the pension frauds. He vetoed private pension bills by the hundreds. His record of vetoes during his first term was greater than the number of vetoes of all the preceding Presidents of the United States combined. Men whose schemes were frustrated hid behind the magic word "soldier" and began attacking Cleveland viciously. It was charged that he was an enemy to "the old soldier"—a terrible indictment; also that Cleveland himself, not being a veteran of the war, was venting his envy and spite on those who had sacrificed their youth to their country. There is no doubt that the country sympathized with the animus of this attack during its progress. But Cleveland kept sitting up nights until two or three o'clock, poring over the pension papers, finding flaws, looking for frauds, and vetoing the bills he deemed unworthy. He trusted no clerk, commissioned no assistants. Indeed, he had no stenographer during the early part of his term, and after hours answered at first hand the calls which came to the White House over the one telephone. There was Jeffersonian simplicity. There also was Jacksonian courage. The storm of popular abuse raged, but with a grave, dull stare in his eyes he gazed for a moment at the political turmoil, and then went on signing his vetoes as placidly as though he were writing virtuous mottoes in a copybook. Even when the storm reached Congress, and Congress began passing his vetoes over his head, Cleveland still toiled through the mass of papers, reading the evidence and setting forth his reasons for his veto, absolutely sure that each veto would be unavailing and that even the moral lesson he was teaching would be lost. As a climax to his course he vetoed a general

pension bill—the dependent pension bill. It was the first
solar-plexus blow the bloody shirt wavers had taken for
twenty years.

During his first year in the White House, President
Cleveland seems to have discovered that he would be
more efficient as a President with a wife than as a
bachelor. He married Miss Frances C. Folsom, a young
girl just out of college, the daughter of a former law
partner. The marriage strengthened him with the people. Probably Cleveland had no thought of this, but
certainly he had a thought of his duty to give the office
its greatest efficiency. He was that way.

When Cleveland was not vetoing pension bills, during
the first years of his first term, it was pretty safe to guess
that his midnight oil was burning over the records of
Republican officeholders. He turned out thousands of
them. Probably most of them were better out than in,
for twenty-four years of an uninterrupted official incumbency will corrupt the best party in the world. But it
is certain that Cleveland worked conscientiously to "turn
the rascals out." He worked over the charges against
these men with the same almost fanatical industry that
he had used in his law business. And years of legal
experience had given him a judicial mind. He was as
fair as a man could be in those offensive partisanship
cases where he was judge, jury, attorney for the defense,
and public prosecutor all in one. Being a stamp-licking
executive, he spared himself no pains. While he was
creaking drearily through his heavy grist, the United
States Senate, which was Republican, and sore, jauntily
asked Cleveland to let it see the papers in some of the
cases in which he had made removals. With one absent-

minded smack of his heavy hand, the presidential mastodon knocked the senatorial impertinence aside with the remark that the constitutional duty of the Senate in the matter was limited to confirmation. Then he resumed his inexorable grind, and the years wore away.

When he came to the White House, Cleveland knew little of national affairs. Once Carl Schurz, who had been in American politics for twenty years and was a leader of the American mugwumps in his time, called on the President, who asked Schurz what he thought was the most important question of the day. Schurz told him that he thought he ought to take up the tariff.

"I shall never forget what happened," said Schurz. "The man bent forward and buried his face in his hands on the table before him. Finally he straightened up with the same directness and spoke:

" 'I'm ashamed to say it, but the truth is I know nothing about the tariff. Will you tell me how to go about to learn?' "

Cleveland had a clear, well-trained brain. He tackled the tariff question and mastered it, as he also mastered the currency question after he came to the White House. So in 1893 he vetoed the Seigniorage Bill, which would have provided for the purchase of silver bullion at a price less than the value stamped on the metal when it was coined. It represented the difference between a silver dollar and a dollar's worth of silver. By that time Cleveland knew the currency problems as he knew the tariff. Cleveland's first brush with William Jennings Bryan occurred over the vetoing of the Seigniorage Bill. Bryan, a congressman on the Committee of Ways and Means, chairman of a sub-committee which had to do with the public debt, felt that his power on the committee gave him the right to name the postmaster of Lincoln, Nebraska, his home town. The President seems to have turned the patronage over to J. Sterling Morton, a fine old Democratic war horse who was in Cleveland's Cabinet. Bryan fumed and fretted. Cleveland was immovable. When the Seigniorage Bill came up, in spite of the warning of his political advisers Cleveland vetoed it. Bryan rose on the crest of the wave of protest, traveled up and down the land for a bi-metallic League, and became a national figure. Which is running ahead of the story a little.

While the business of the nation was passing across his desk in his first term, Cleveland gradually became conscious of the fact that the country was taking in more money than it was paying out, and that a surplus was accumulating rapidly in the Treasury. When this fact found secure lodgment in his mind, he did a simple thing—for Cleveland. He devoted an entire message to Congress, in 1887, to a constructive plan to reduce the national revenues and divorce them from the business of the country, making a tariff not to encourage new industries nor to protect existing ones, but to produce revenue, and revenue only. To Cleveland's mind it seemed a logical proposition that tariff was for revenue and for nothing else. But just then the country was not of that opinion. That was easily demonstrable. Some of Cleveland's friends, to whom he read the message before delivering it, told him how the matter stood with the people. Their showing affected him about as deeply as the buzzing of flies. He did not change a syllable of the message. He knew it might defeat him. But he

"A LOCAL QUESTION"

"WHO IS TARIFF, AND WHY IS HE FOR REVENUE ONLY?"

A cartoon by Thomas Nast in *Harper's Weekly*, suggesting the confusion into which politicians were thrown by Cleveland's advocacy of a tariff "for revenue only."

did not regard himself as a martyr. His friends seemed to imagine that Cleveland made a noble sacrifice for his country's good when he sent in his tariff message in 1887. Probably nothing was further from his view of the matter. He believed that what he said was true, and that as a mere incident of the day's work it should be said. He did not dramatize the situation by putting his personality into it; to him the matter was impersonal.

CHAPTER XI

HIS OBSTINACY

PRESIDENT CLEVELAND went into the campaign for his
reëlection in 1888 in a cheerful but not a hopeful frame
of mind. He was happy, not in the sense of duty well
done, but with the felicity of a man who has nothing
undone to worry him. He fished and hunted and worked;
and being a bridegroom of two years, life, as he puts it
himself, was "one grand, sweet song." As for the people,
he liked to meet them, to shake hands with them, to hear
them talk and cheer, pushing and crowding about his carriage. For he was human enough, and all the world was
brother to him; but the color of his brother's hair or the
complexion of his votes was a matter of indifference to
Grover Cleveland the President. He was easily renominated by the National Democratic Convention in 1888,
and was heartily praised by the mugwumps in the
Republican party. James Russell Lowell led off. Young
Theodore Roosevelt spoke well of Cleveland, though he
voted the Republican ticket.

Cleveland was running for reëlection on his record.
His record for his first term was this: He recommended
the repeal of the Silver Purchase Clause of the Bland-
Allison Act. He suppressed an insurrection in the
Isthmus of Panama, occupying the Isthmus with three
thousand marines and soldiers; he put down a threatened outbreak among the Mormons in Utah by the con-

129

centration of infantry and artillery in Salt Lake and
threatened during a Canadian fisheries dispute to stop
Canadian traffic from entering the United States except
by American railroads. Congress had created an
Interstate Commerce Commission, had passed an anti-
polygamy bill aimed at Utah, the Chinese Exclusion Act,
the Presidential Succession Bill, and another limiting the
powers of Congress to count the electoral votes. These
were minor measures. The President's demand for a
revision of the tariff passed the House but was shattered
in the Senate. He went into the campaign of 1888 tremendously popular with the independent element in the
East, and strong in his own party save in New York,
where Tammany disliked him instinctively. Out West
the independent element of the party was suspicious of
Cleveland. The farmers disliked his tariff views. They
were educated to believe in the free coinage of silver, and
out West new, strange issues affecting the currency were
being discussed which did not concern the East. Then,
as a result of the loosely organized financial system of the
day, a period of business depression appeared about election time in certain parts of the industrial East. Times
were hard. The administration was blamed, and the
country returned to the Republicans. Cleveland lost the
election to General Benjamin Harrison, who had two
hundred and thirty-three electoral votes against one hundred and sixty-eight for Cleveland. Tammany elected
David Bennett Hill, Democratic Governor of New York,
but significantly gave the electoral votes of the state to
General Harrison.

Cleveland went to New York City and practiced law
for four years. While his defeat in the electoral college

was fairly decisive, the fact that he had a majority of one hundred thousand ballots in the popular vote made him available as the national Democratic candidate in 1892, although Henry Watterson, the leader of the Kentucky democracy and a national figure in his party, declared that the renomination of Cleveland would take the Democratic party "through a slaughterhouse to an open grave." Bourke Cochran, Tammany's silver-tongued orator in the convention, could not stop the rush to Cleveland, who was renominated and carried the country; at least, the solid South, plus four doubtful states—Indiana, Connecticut, New Jersey and New York, and three Republican states—California, Illinois, and Wisconsin. He defeated President Benjamin Harrison.

In the West new issues had sprung up. The Populist party presented these new issues. In several states fusion between the Democrats and the Populists was effected, and the Populists carried twenty-two electoral votes for General James B. Weaver of Iowa. These votes were from normally Republican states. This was the beginning of a movement that in another decade was to change the politics of the nation; indeed, it was a symptom of a world-wide drift to liberalism, which reached its peak in Christendom twenty-five years later.

During the four years between '89 and '93 in which Cleveland had been a private citizen, he did not gratify his enemies by uttering a sign of regret at the course of human events. He even concealed his ambition to regain his power. He cloaked himself in no ex-presidential dignity, but remained an unassuming, reticent, hard-working lawyer in a great city. The Democratic masses had forced his renomination in 1892. He owed nothing to Democratic leaders. He came back to the White House in 1893 on a cold, raw March day. With no attempt at concealment he fortified himself with a tumbler of whisky, stood up before the multitude, delivered his second inaugural, and began the most vigorous administration that the United States had seen for two generations. His platform was his only war cry. He made it himself with one issue—tariff for revenue only. He was notoriously a hard money man, a supporter of the gold standard. He had signed the only prepared letter he ever authorized, addressed to Samuel J. Tilden, denouncing free silver in 1883. But because Tilden had insisted upon the letter Cleveland cut loose from Tilden's guidance and patronage rather bluntly; for Cleveland wished to declare himself for the gold standard in his own way and in his own time. Yet for all his obvious belief in sound money, the Populists out West and in the South who were rising to power put some of Cleveland's phrases on their campaign banners. As, for instance, this: "The communism of combined wealth and capital, the outgrowth of government cupidity and selfishness." In the West and South the Democrats in 1888 had campaigned under the banner "Cleveland and Free Silver," which probably angered Cleveland, for he turned upon the Populists and Free Silverites when he came back to the White House with a vigor that was deadly because it was without emotion. Excepting for the tariff issue, his second term to all intents and purposes might have been Republican in name rather than Democratic, so completely did he turn to the protection and conservation of property and the privileges of capital during his second administration, while his party was taking the other road.

From 1885 to 1889 Cleveland was an obstructionist; from 1893 to 1897 he was a militant obstructionist, protesting against the new protest. Always his best talents functioned when he was an obstructionist. No other period of American history since the days of the Civil War and reconstruction was so filled with riot and tumult, nor was any other period so hazardous to our national life as were those four years of Cleveland's second administration. The rise of Populism was quick and menacing in its early stages. The debtor and creditor faced each other angrily in a dozen Western states, and somewhat in the South. Idle workmen glared at the lockout sign on factory doors all over the industrial area of the nation. Strikes were called as a protest against reduced wages. Unrest was everywhere. It stifled business, dominated politics, flared out in crisis after crisis. It was then that Cleveland rose as a towering national figure. He was the Man on Horseback. He performed a service to this country as important as any President ever performed in time of peace. Populism, new and in ferment, but for Cleveland might have exploded in anarchy. Looking back over those days, one is forced to believe that Cleveland—like all men who do great necessary things in this world—must have been a man sent. His character was so exactly molded to the task before him, and the work he did was so entirely the reflection of that character, that one wonders if the fatalists are right and that the things to be must be, and are planned before they are. That, however, is idle speculation. This is what happened:

The twenty years before 1893—an era of good times —had been marked with financial fluctuations; now and then came panics, which passed like thundershowers in summer. The depression of the early-seventies had been followed by recuperation, and that by stability; prosperity had been followed by growth, growth by speculation; and then came the grand boom of the eighties. The Missouri Valley and the Pacific coast states had been settled and developed on borrowed money. The West was mortgaged. Real-estate speculation became rather crass gambling. In the Missouri Valley the boom broke in 1889, but elsewhere it lasted two or three years longer. In 1892 the wheels of trade began to slow up; in 1893 they stopped stonestill. Production had caught up with development. No more railroads were needed; no more towns required on the Western prairies. Lumber, stone, steel and oil were without markets. Then came collapse. When Cleveland entered the White House the second time he was facing the financial ruin of his country. The treasury surplus which worried President Harrison in 1889 had disappeared. There was no longer talk of a gold surplus anywhere. Gold coin was in hoarding. The demand for gold, which is always worth its weight, had put the gold reserve in the national treasury down to a dangerously small sum. The drain increased rather than abated. Bond plates which were made in the government printing office just before Harrison left were used by the Democrats who issued bonds to protect the treasury gold reserve. There was clamor against the issue of bonds in time of peace; but rather than buy silver and debase the currency, Cleveland went ahead with the bond issue. The moment the government should cease paying gold and begin to pay silver for greenbacks, that moment the country would be on a silver basis, and

stand on a financial footing with the half-civilized countries of the world. Cleveland felt that the national
degradation would have been unspeakable, and the financial ruin immeasurable. And the hopeless side of his
case was that the Democratic party, which had come up
strong in the West—tainted with Populism—was a
rampant silver party. But Cleveland was for gold, and
for a year he tried to maintain the gold reserve in the
treasury. In the meantime the Democratic congressional
leadership was in the hands of politicians—Cal Brice, of
Ohio, and Gorman, of Maryland, and Hill and Murphy,
of New York, the voices of Tammany. Out West the
congressional leadership of the Democratic party was
more than half frankly fused with Populism. Thus while
calamity was clouding the country, the Democratic leaders
were scurrying about like rats, with their mouths full of
straw intrigues no more important than petty larceny.
The President stood alone. All he could be certain of
was impending disaster and the treachery of his partisans.
He moved slowly—perhaps not so much from caution as
from a ponderous habit of mind. He was not afraid, but
he desired to be thorough in his preparation of the case
before he went to trial. Cleveland was an indefatigable
workman before he was a statesman—or anything else.
He ruminated four long months on the subject in hand
before he acted. Then he knew his case. He had no
fear of the outcome; for Cleveland's mental make-up provided no place for fear. He called Congress together in
special session to repeal the Sherman law, which drained
the gold reserve by compelling the purchase of silver
bullion; and although Cleveland knew that his party was
ulcerated with the silver evil, and although he felt that

the party leaders who had intelligence were cowards, and that those who had courage were mad with raw Populism, Cleveland's imagination could not dramatize the situation. He saw only what he deemed the wise thing to do, and he did it in a superb serenity. Congress assembled, ready—almost eager—to push the country over the edge of the precipice on to a silver basis. Then Cleveland did a characteristic thing. He trusted to the sheer righteousness of his cause, left Washington for a vacation when Congress assembled, and came back to find that his cause had won. Blandly in the first meeting of the Cabinet he said to Carlisle:

"Well, you boys have done a splendid thing."

Very likely he did not realize how they had done the splendid thing. They had bought the way through Congress for their measure with patronage. Cleveland did not know it. He denied it vigorously later. But Western Democratic senators testified to the fact that when their votes were doubtful on the repeal of the silver purchase clause, their patronage was held up until they aligned themselves for the administration measure. If incompetent men got into the public service while Cleveland was away, recommended by purchasable congressman who traded their votes for patronage, Cleveland—coming back innocently—did not know it. What he knew was that the Sherman law was repealed. One crisis was past.

When Congress assembled in regular session in December, 1895, it began an affair—perhaps liaison is a better word—with the tariff. As the session grew, men began to sniff the odor of unsavory gossip. Cleveland could not control his party. He had no tact, no diplomacy, no faculty of persuading men. In the mass, men may be governed by pure reason. Individuals may be governed by self-interest. Cleveland could never dramatize his convictions so that a man would find himself a hero in following Cleveland. That was Roosevelt's trick. The Democratic Congress under Cleveland, in 1894, became publicly indecent; and when the Wilson Tariff Bill finally became a law it literally stank with scandal. Cleveland would not touch it with his signature, and he reviled the party that framed it.

Again the gold reserve ran low. Again Cleveland sold bonds, and again the Populist faction of his party in Congress and in the nation spat upon him. Cleveland turned his back upon his party, and set out alone to find some way to break the "endless chain." Bonds were being sold for gold, and greenbacks were being presented at the treasury for the gold purchased by the bonds; and when the greenbacks had drained out the gold, more gold was bought by the issuance of more bonds. Industry was paralyzed. Banks were failing. Gold was going into hiding. Populism was rampant, and Democracy was a bedlam. There was neither a market for bonds nor time for a bond issue. When Cleveland saw the blight coming, he turned from the madhouse of Congress to Wall Street. There a syndicate was organized, which, for a consideration that Cleveland considered fair, agreed to help in maintaining the gold reserve for a specified time. The syndicate offered better terms if Congress would make the bonds payable in gold instead of in "coin." This offer was deluged with a torrent of congressional wrath. Cleveland's name was execrated by the Populists in the Democratic party as no other man's ever was before in his generation. Naturally, the hard-money Republicans were too partisan to rally to the President's support. Hatred is a mild term to apply to the attitude of the Western and Southern Democracy toward its former idol. But opprobrium did not disturb him. His isolation only gave him free swing for his shoulders. He walked forward, trampling on the party organization, kicking its wreckage right and left as it fell across his path. Probably there was no passion—no resentment in his heart. By night he toiled till cockcrow, working to find his duty; by day he did that duty with a stoicism that would have been splendidly urbane had not the assertive grit of the man been all over it.

There came a time when discontent broke out in riot. A great railroad strike centering at Chicago clutched business by the throat in the Mississippi Valley. In Illinois Governor Altgeld, a Populist Democrat, was clearly in sympathy with the strikers. He claimed that they were about to win the strike. Altgeld's opponents feared that the strikers' victory would be a surrender to anarchy. Altgeld held that the strikers had a just cause. His foes declared that the mob should be quelled before the merits of the strike could be discussed. Then Grover Cleveland rose again as a despot of law and order, and with the arms of the Government of the United States quelled the mob, and of course broke the strike. To do this he had to violate the Democratic bugaboo of States' Rights; he had to snap traditions and make his own precedent. But because he believed that in the day's work that was the thing to do, he did not hesitate longer than it took to reach for a blotter with which to dry the ink of the order. It is hard to-day, in another time and generation, with the solid success of material things bought and paid for and set into their appointed places, to realize how the nation

trembled in the balance between order and anarchy in
that summer day of 1894. Freight cars were burning
in the Chicago yards. Soldiers were meeting rioters at
division points. Rifles flashed and cavalry charged into
mobs all over the Mississippi Valley. It is true that
only a few people, compared with the millions, were
involved, but it takes but a few in times of flux to make
a revolution. And again other things besides industry
were disturbed and questioned—finance, farming, commerce generally all were in a state of shock, quite apart
from the menace of revolution. It was in that hour that
Cleveland acted on his own wisdom, to put down what he
felt was an industrial rebellion. After it was put down,
slowly the courses of life began to re-function; business
began to breathe regularly, the menace of anarchy van-
ished. Cleveland dismounted as a dictator and went back
to the constitutional Presidential chair.

He reached the climax of his unpopularity and usefulness toward the end of his term. He had been in public
life at that time, counting his term as governor, a dozen
years. They were fighting years. Outwardly, Cleveland's face expressed little emotion. Without batting an
eye he once told Henry Watterson, a national leader
of the Democratic party, to "go to hell." Whatever
spiritual struggle shook him as he faced the angry
mob of his countrymen during his second term, it
did not make him wince. But some inner and cor-
roding care began chiseling the fat away from his jowls
in the middle nineties, and cut down the roll of adipose around his abdomen, which sagged a little. His hair
was thinning, his mustache turning a brownish gray.
There came into the poise of his head a certain forward

slant like that of an old bull lowering his head for combat.
The pinkish brown of his skin in his forties blotched a
little and paled in his late fifties, and he walked with more
of a roll than a stride. But when he stood up in a group
of his fellows he towered over them, dominated them, led
them. Henry Watterson, who knew him well, always
maintained that Cleveland was two men—one before his
marriage and the end of his first term; the other afterwards. Watterson seemed to feel that Cleveland
sloughed off his old friends and advisors in the course of
his first term. Certainly during his second term Cleveland
stood like a Brobdingnagian in American politics; a giant
in those days; an oldish giant; obviously disillusioned, yet
not disheartened. He may have shed the friends of his
early Presidential days, but he did not lose his Buffalo
ways. He referred to Watterson as a "dirty little scoun-
drel" with no reason except his dislike of Watterson.

   The President loved to spit out a good God damn, and
was not ashamed of a big drink if he wanted it, or two or
three, which he carried steadily. He loved to fish, to
shoot, to roam the fields, and was always masculine to
the core. Apparently he cared little for social amenities.
He was an out-of-door dog that never was thoroughly
"housebroke." Always he was the "hunter home from
the hill," who loved his wife, adored his children, and
prized a good dog beyond rubies. If he wanted to go
fishing on Decoration Day he did so, and let the Grand
Army of the Republic sputter and be damned. If he had
but fifty dollars to send to the relief fund for the
Charleston earthquake sufferers he sent it unabashed,
even when the South lifted its astonished eyebrows. He
surrounded himself with strong men in the Cabinet, fol-

lowed their advice often, but always in his own way. He turned his back on Tilden, as Taft afterwards disentangled himself from Roosevelt. His was the Cleveland administration.

In December, 1895, he performed the most far-reaching act of his administration. The President found that Great Britain was encroaching on the Venezuelan boundary. Our diplomatic protests had been ignored with bad manners by the Salisbury government in London. Under the Monroe Doctrine, President Cleveland claimed the right of the United States to protect its interest in Venezuela. Without mincing matters and without wasting time in diplomacy, Cleveland sent a message to Congress asking for an appropriation to pay a commission, and for authority to appoint it, which should settle the Venezuelan boundary dispute. The American right to act in the matter was assumed with a bald audacity that made the world gasp. Wall Street threw a momentary panic. Cleveland's mugwump supporters threw a fit. But Congress backed the President. The Monroe Doctrine was translated into a policy. Our first forward step toward South American imperialism was taken. England winced, Europe grew black in the face, America cheered herself hoarse, and Grover Cleveland, as much astonished as any one at the turn affairs had taken, grunted and went on with his work. In a month he was closing the details of the arbitration treaty, in six months the incident had faded from public interest. But it remains one of the really significant episodes in Cleveland's public life.

And so the four years of his second term wore away. With Democracy fusing into Populism in the West and South, Cleveland plodded ahead, guided by "the brave old wisdom of sincerity," tranquilly, almost cheerfully, crashing through the wreckage and débris of his party organization, blundering with men, and mending with measures. When the Democratic convention met in Chicago in 1896, his enemies mocked him with the phrase— "his obstinacy!" But enemies were the only ones brave enough to mention his name. And no man ever went to the stake with more enthusiastic and cordial approval of his former supporters than Cleveland went in the National Democratic Convention of 1896, when the Democratic orators roasted his effigy.

It was this convention that gave Bryan the presidential nomination and so paved the way for his leadership in the party—a leadership which lasted for more than a quarter of a century. If ever two men were absolutely antithetical they were Grover Cleveland and William J. Bryan. The things Cleveland despised Bryan honored. Cleveland would serve the people according to his own judgments of their needs. Bryan would first know what the people desired. Cleveland was a benevolent despot— reasonably wise; Bryan a conscientious Democrat—pretty dumb! When Cleveland departed as a leader of his party, with him went a host of gentlemen of the old school; rich, respectable gentlemen, high-minded and courteous; men of family and social distinction; the silk-stockinged men who placed principle far above preferment, knew good food and good liquor, loved fair women and sought brave men; men who in a changing era made the Democratic party in the United States the last stronghold of a political aristocracy. When Bryan came in he brought with him the mob—rabble-rousing leaders, the sans culottes, the rag-tag and bob-tail, the discontented, the visionaries, the prophets of a new order. They dropped away from Bryan in a decade or became respectable, well-shod, clad, and stall-fed, but still remained servants rather than masters of the people. The current which brought this change had been swift and devastating. Bryan rode the wave triumphant, while Cleveland, ashore, must have looked with consternation at the tide.

Grover Cleveland wrecked the machinery of the Democratic party. The cataclysm was complete. But he did not wreck it willfully, and certainly not with careless malice. The Democratic party was wrecked as a mere detail in the daily routine of the work of an honest man who felt he was engaged in the patriotic task of saving his country's honor. When he looked around and saw what he had done, perhaps Cleveland was surprised; but it is safe to say that he harbored no regrets; that he would surely have done the same thing if he had it to do again.

In his great day he stood at the crossroads in a crisis of American history. Out of the West and South were coming strange new turbulent currents; a new idea was bringing new issues into men's hearts. The old agricultural era which had lasted upon this continent for nearly three hundred years was passing—the time when every man on his farm or in his store or in his little factory was self-sufficient, could be independent and need not fear nor favor any man. The political ideals of those three centuries concerned, naturally, the production of wealth; but in a new era that was rising after the Civil War, industry was piling up tremendous masses of wealth in a few hands all unrestrained. Deep in the consciousness of the people was the idea that this great wealth accumulating around the factory door should be equitably

distributed among those who work and those who buy
the products of industry. So issues concerning the distribution of wealth rather than its accumulation were
coming into the hearts of the people. Conservatives
called this Socialism—this creed of the mob which saw
things askew; these clamoring ne'er-do-wells who had the
first urge for rebellion, these idle workmen, these foreclosed farmers, these bankrupt merchants, who were
beginning to form in politics disturbing minorities, even
majorities, in certain sections of the land. Obviously a
rabble was forming which sought to redress its wrongs
rather than to establish its rights. For a few years the
rabble rousers and the mad mob behind them threatened
to overrun and ruin the orderly processes of civilization.
Grover Cleveland stood like Horatius at the bridge and
held back the invaders, although they were to come
later in serried ranks and well led by wise men, and the
movement was to occupy the land.

Cleveland, as a statesman, will be remembered as the
man who checked abuses, prevented conniving men from
accomplishing their ends, warded off impending calamity,
reduced revenues a little and saved some taxes. He
stayed the ebbing tide of public credit. He stopped
foreign aggrandizement on the American continent. He
brought no new doctrine to the people—not even imperialism. For he did not foresee the far-reaching implications of his act in the Venezuelan controversy. He had
no peculiar theory of government—merely an ideal of
duty for the hour. He founded no institution; in the
political life of his time he constructed nothing, but
every hour of the working day he did what he thought
was exactly right. While he never attempted to guide

the current of the public business, he did try to see that
the business was wisely and honestly done. He was a
modest, industrious public servant, who lived as well as
preached the motto, "A public office is a public trust."
He lived it so well that people came to believe that he
invented it—which he did not. No law on the statute
books of his country is known as Cleveland's law. He
tried to efface his personality, but it was so strong, so
distinctive, and smelled of masculinity so pungently that
his personality dominated everything he did in spite of
his aversion to personal politics. Yet he will never be a
hero, because he did not live a dramatic life. Nothing
may be found in his biography to amuse or interest a
Plutarch or a Boswell. He must remain to posterity a
disembodied spirit, an ideal of honesty bearing a man's
name—the symbol of a national aspiration toward public
virtue.

CHAPTER XII

"HIS COMPLACENCY"

On March 4, 1897, when he shook hands with William McKinley, his successor in the White House, Cleveland finally left public life. He established a law connection in New York, downtown in the financial district, but he made his home at Princeton, New Jersey, and went from Princeton to New York three or four times a week to earn an honest living. Time mellowed Cleveland, and experience taught him a kindly philosophy. A tinge of humor brightened his outer face in his late sixties, and a strong, placid light of happiness glowed from his heart. At Princeton he lived in a big white house with a hall through the middle of it. On the wide shaded blue-grass lawn his children played, while inside he and his wife and his books and his pleasant memories were happy together. The college boys from Princeton congregated in his yard on occasion, and frequently he returned their calls and went down to the chapel and talked to them in a good-natured, felicitous way. He filled in those quiet golden days with writing, reading, and recreation. Youth, always big in his heart to the last, tempted him out fishing and hunting. He loved the fields and woods and waters as he loved them when he was a boy. Nature checked in his face the lines that followed the days and nights of hard living and hard working in the years of his maturity. But behind those lines was another face—

146

a serene, exalted face which shone out of a strong, uncon-
querable soul—a righteous, rock-anchored Presbyterian
soul—honest to his own hurt.

He lost twenty-five hundred dollars by selling all his
coal-carrying railroad stock, in 1902, when President
Roosevelt would have named him on a committee to
settle a coal strike, and the loss was serious. He had
salaries from various corporations; at one time managed
an insurance company which was in difficulties, but a few
hundred thousand dollars constituted his fortune. Two
terms as President satisfied him. He had no political
ambition, but kept a lively interest in the Democratic
party and once expressed an old man's desire to live long
enough to see a Democratic President in the White
House. But he had no stomach for Bryan, who had
abused him by referring to him as an "office boy in a Wall
Street law firm." He became a trustee of Princeton University and was embroiled in a bitter cat-and-dog rumpus
on the board opposing Woodrow Wilson, president of the
university, whom local legend declared Cleveland loathed
heartily. Probably the legend was founded on fact. It is
inconceivable that two men like Cleveland and Wilson
could entirely respect one another in a college board fight.
Cleveland was as different from Wilson as he was from
Bryan; and as different as Bryan was from Wilson. Wilson surrounded himself with men of soft approach;
Cleveland liked the he-man type. Wilson was given to
rationalizing his expedient conduct jesuitically to win a
contest. Cleveland metaphorically grabbed a caveman's
maul and walked in "and damned be him who first cries,
hold! enough!" Wilson in the Princeton brawl was
standing for democratic ideals which Cleveland might

well have espoused. But he couldn't follow Wilson's
ways, and so rejected Wilson's cause and made Wilson's
enemies Cleveland's friends. Princeton tradition says
that a letter exists, which some day may be published, in
which Cleveland pours out the wrath of his heart about
Wilson, little dreaming that Woodrow Wilson would succeed Cleveland as the next Democratic President at the
White House. The tradition may have no foundation
other than the wish of Wilson's enemies.

In those later days of his life, in 1907 and 1908,
Grover Cleveland, entering his seventies, stood like an
old tree—stark and lonely. He had lived a hard life.
Never was he dissipated, but he had cared little for his
body; ate what he would, drank what he pleased, went
out in all weathers, suppressed to a great extent the outward expression of his passions, though he was never
above a good mouthful of imprecations if it helped him.
At seventy he was gaunt. His paunch had slumped, great
veins stood out in his scrawny neck. His skin foreshadowed a coming senility. His blue eyes looked out of
reddening lids with the astonished stare that comes into
the eyes of old men, his jowls were pouched, and his
mouth line sagged sadly. He turned more and more to
the faith of his fathers, to the Bible of his youth. Always
he cherished the little Bible in which were two inscrip-
tions: "My son, Stephen Grover Cleveland, from his
loving Mother"; and the other in the handwriting of
Justice Waite: "It was used to administer the oath of
office to Grover Cleveland, President of the United States,
on March 4, 1885." A few weeks before he died he
sent to his old home for one of the worn hymn books that
were used at family prayers in his boyhood, and at the

end, on a little oak box beside his bed, they found Whittier's beautiful hymn, "At last" opened in the book:

> When on my day of life the night is falling,
> And, in the winds from unsunned spaces blown,
> I hear far voices out of darkness calling
> My feet to paths unknown.

His seventy-first birthday was his last. He was greatly weakened, his stomach had failed him and an organic disease of his heart and kidneys had developed. He could scarcely move about his home, and soon was confined to his room. But his mind was clear and he often sat thinking, probably of the days of his strength, his power, his glory; the strong man measuring the conduct of a busy, useful life by the measuring rod of a rather primitive religion; for surely he was a primitive soul. There were in his staring blue eyes visions of Buffalo during the Civil War as he roamed over the place, a young lawyer in politics. There was the hard decade of his thirties—a work time when, as a young bachelor, he moved up toward the head of the Erie County bar by dogged plodding by day, and relieved himself by night, as young bachelors will, with such diversions as the town and countryside afforded—a good horse, a good meal, a good friend, and a good drink,—for he had no time for the soft amenities of female society,—and then a good sleep before another good day's work. Politics came in his forties, and probably his attitude never changed in his relation to politics. The night when he was elected governor, in 1882, he wrote to his brother:

I have just voted and sit here in the office alone. If Mother were alive I should be writing to her, as I feel as if it were time to write to someone who will believe what I write. . . . I have tried hard to properly appreciate the responsibilities that will rest upon me, and they are much, too much, and under-estimated. . . . In point of fact I will tell you, first of all others, the policy I intend to adopt—and that is to make the matter a business engagement between the people and myself . . . with an eye single to the interests of my employers. . . . Do you know that if Mother were alive I should feel so much safer? I have always thought her prayers had so much to do with my success. I shall expect you to help me in this way.

And in that mood he went into the tasks of his life. Possibly, looking back from his seventy-first birthday, he did not understand the deep significance of his service at the end. But in those days of the middle nineties, Grover Cleveland, the obstructionist, held back the clamoring, unthinking hosts until they could find their reason and march in order. Did he see this in those last days as he lay in his room at Princeton? Did he realize the import of his service? Probably not. But surely he saw— trooping across the land he cherished, under the leadership of Roosevelt and a thousand of his kind in both the parties—only the devastation of an old order that he respected. Yet the new order, that phase of liberalism which passed for progress, by which new ordinances of political justice were being established and old ordinances abandoned, was coming into the world. Cleveland wrote to a friend in those days, "I feel like a farmer who started at the bottom of the hill with a wagon load of corn and discovered at the hill top that his load had slid out under the tail board." To a passing neighbor who asked why he did not swear, he replied, "Because, by God, I can't do the subject justice." He felt that he was right. Always he hoped against hope for sanity to come back to a mad world. Again to a friend he wrote, "I can not help feeling that the light is still brighter" ahead for the Democracy. But Bryan continued to hold the Democratic party under his leadership. And to Cleveland, the light was a will-o'-the-wisp. The next great Democratic leader was to be anointed by the hand of Bryan and to be not of the Cleveland succession.

It was in June, 1908, after his mother's hymn book had come to him from his sister from their old home, that he sat a broken, tired, old man, with thin, graying hair and gaunt features, but with the fire of ancient combat unquenched in his eyes. He had been dozing, dreaming the dreams that are an old man's solace. He opened his eyes and spoke wistfully to her whom he loved, who was near him: "I have tried so hard to do right." Was it the old warrior's benediction on his life of combat? or was a doubt winging its black shadow across his mind? "I have tried so hard" carries some of the pathos that follows futility. As his brave old eyes glared at the changed world it was natural that Pilate's bleak, unanswered question should flutter in his heart.

McKINLEY

CHAPTER XIII

A CITIZEN BECOMES A POLITICIAN

WILLIAM McKINLEY, twenty-fifth President of the
United States, was a career man in American politics in
the strictest sense; a typical politician who had studied
the science of government as he climbed. He held office
practically all his life, and the only appointive offices he
ever held were those of school-teacher and major in the
Union Army. He was elected Prosecuting Attorney of
Stark County, Ohio, in 1869. He made speeches for
General Rutherford B. Hayes in the Ohio gubernatorial
campaign in 1875, and the year following McKinley
was elected to Congress from an Ohio district, serving
for seven consecutive terms and surviving various
Democratic gerrymanders, designed to keep him at home.
He became Chairman of the Ways and Means Committee of the House of Representatives, succeeding James
A. Garfield when the latter went to the Senate. McKinley
was Republican National Committeeman, Chairman of
the State Convention, and delegate to various Republican
National Conventions, being Chairman of the Committee on Resolutions in '88, when he and Mark Hanna
together managed the campaign of John Sherman, who
sought the presidential nomination before that conven-

tion. The convention might have turned to McKinley. He knew that the rules of the game against treachery would be violated if he allowed the drift to proceed, so he protested publicly against votes in his own behalf. He went back to Congress, prepared the McKinley Tariff Bill, which lost the House of Representatives for the Republicans in the election of 1890; and in 1891, the year that he quit Congress, he was elected Governor of Ohio by a handsome plurality, and reëlected two years later. A few weeks after the end of his gubernatorial term he was inaugurated President of the United States, and served until he was assassinated in September, 1901. So closed a career and an epoch.

McKinley was the last of the soldiers of the Civil War to occupy the White House. Excepting Cleveland, every President, for thirty years, had been a veteran of the Civil War. The issues of the Civil War dominated politics. The pension plank in a Republican platform, whether state or national, in the generation that followed the Civil War, was as important as the tariff plank, generally vastly more important than the currency plank. All other issues were minor issues—except Pensions, Currency, and the Tariff! Pensions and Currency were issues which rose out of the war. The tariff was an issue which came out of the changing conditions in America that overthrew slavery.

The black man, even sixty years after slavery, does not tend a machine as well as the white man. And as agriculture itself began to pass from a cottage industry into a highly complex industry requiring capital, machinery, seasonal labor, slavery had to go; indeed, would have gone without the war under the pressure of economic evolution. And the Protective Tariff had to come to replace slavery in protecting American white labor against competition from countries which maintained lower standards of living than America. Incidentally, the tariff was heavily loaded in favor of capital. But even though our gates swung open to millions from Europe, our standards of living remained high, and wages inevitably followed our standards. So much for the tariff. The currency problem rose because we had gone to a paper basis in the war, established a metallic basis after the war to pay the bondholders, and later virtually went to a gold basis as a necessity in obtaining credit to do the vast work of opening the American continent beyond the Mississippi. Pensions became an industrial necessity because hundreds of thousands of men had devoted the four years of their youth to the Union Army and were either broken, disorganized, or impoverished by the martial experience. In the nineties, the Federal Pension Bill was virtually an old age pension north of the Mason and Dixon Line. In the South the states pensioned the Confederate soldiers.

Those were the issues upon which McKinley fought his way up in politics from prosecuting attorney to President of the United States. His father was an ironmaster in Ohio. Young McKinley went to the common schools, went to Alleghany College, quit college to enter business, quit business to enter the army, virtually quit the army to enter politics, and made politics the major business of his life. He was deeply, essentially, a politician; honest enough, brave enough, intelligent enough for politics— and no more so. He knew the rules of the game, and played the game like a gentleman when gentlemen in politics were scarce. McKinley had no ideals of service to justify, no principles to glorify except the bundle of jargon and prejudice known as Republican principles in that day, and he had no ideals outside of politics to hamper him. He was as good as the best in politics, but no better. In politics the first maxim is to take care of yourself; the second maxim is to take care of your crowd. Politicians of the better grade often put the second maxim first. McKinley did. He was never too selfish for his own ultimate good. But, living thirty years in politics, having no other visible means of support, or recreation, or ambition, McKinley became galvanized with a certain coating of publicity. He lost his private life and his private view. His wife for many years was an invalid afflicted with a nervous disorder, gentle, sweet, with an effaced personality; so that at no point of his existence did he touch deeply any private relation. He had no friends but politicians, no conversation that did not affect issues, the "situation," or the ballot box. He became as one "affected by public use." He walked among men a bronze statue, for thirty years determinedly looking for his pedestal. Not that he was greedily ambitious. He was concerned entirely with the political game. Incidentally he was a patriot, but he rarely confused his patriotism with the game. He was a friend, but even his friendship—that with Mark Hanna—was a sort of public relation which might easily have been controlled by a commission or bureau. Joseph Cannon, the incarnation of reaction in the Republican party, Speaker of the House of Representatives and for a dozen years colleague and contemporary of McKinley, being angry with McKinley once declared:

"McKinley keeps his ear to the ground so close that he gets it full of grasshoppers much of the time."

Which, though only approximately true, was well said. Physically, McKinley was a handsome man. They say he was a dashing soldier, most gallant, with the fine self-conscious gallantry of a sort of gilded chivalry that rose out of the Civil War when cavalry charged and infantry fought in the open and artillery was a-wheel. As a young man he was given to eloquence, political eloquence always. He made few speeches outside of politics. He talked on the resumption of specie payment when it was a Republican doctrine, talked on the tariff when it was a Republican doctrine, and always spoke beautifully of pensions. In Congress he rose rapidly because of his facility of speech, but also because he had a logical mind, a sound, healthy body and could work in committee, talk on the floor, and hurry through the departments getting jobs for his friends. He played no poker and drank little whisky. Not that he was a moral young man; he was wise in the day and generation when whisky, poker, and women were the diversion of statesmen. He was abstemious, frugal, and continent; and yet, strangely enough, not so toplofty about his habits that his virtues became vices. He was just a busy, genial, kindly, serious young man in Congress who took leadership, worked hard, went to bed at decent hours, remained aloof from the gang, and kept his leadership somewhat because no one ever could approach him with the soft, insinuating familiarity which breeds contempt. Possibly he knew, possibly not, that his aloofness, his dignity, his frock-coated immaculacy gave him a prestige which a hand-shaking, shirt-sleeved, perspiring, back-slapping cordiality could never have brought to him. Perhaps the political technique of Blaine made McKinley wince. He took his defeat in Congress in 1890, when the McKinley Bill went down with the Republican majority, like a gentleman, when many of his Republican colleagues went out and drowned their sorrows in the flowing bowl and publicly damned the Democrats. But McKinley, being unctuous, left Congress for the governor's chair with only a few months' hiatus.

In the meantime, he had begun his friendship with Mark Hanna. Hanna had everything which McKinley lacked. Hanna was impulsive and intuitive where McKinley was calm and reasonable. Hanna had money where McKinley was comparatively poor. Hanna had imagination where McKinley had industry. Hanna would rip out a good red double-distilled God damn where McKinley would stifle a scowl with a smile. So far as Hanna was concerned, the affection was deep to the point of abasement. McKinley put his affection on a meter, kept books with his emotion, was just, even generous, but never infatuated; pleased, perhaps flattered at times, deeply, if gently, moved, but never passionate as Hanna was in their relation. McKinley met financial reverses. Hanna, his friend, restored McKinley's fortune.* The two men had met some time in the seventies, probably before the classic episode in which McKinley, as the miners' attorney, faced Hanna, the employer, in a strike. Their meeting must have been casual. And for nearly ten years it remained an acquaintance. The association with John Sherman, in

*McKinley had endorsed a bad note. Hanna, Myron Herrick, H. H. Kohlsaat, and Judge Day gathered together sixty thousand dollars and paid the note, saving McKinley's name and fortune.

which Hanna was the financial agent, McKinley the convention floor leader, brought the two into intimate relation.* And in the early nineties Hanna's attachment to McKinley was much more than platonic, as associations go in politics. McKinley was the apple of Hanna's eye in those early days of their friendship. McKinley could stand up and make a speech. Hanna was a splutterer. McKinley wore his clothes well, Hanna only indifferently. McKinley could control his emotions. McKinley knew the intricacies of the political maze, which Hanna would crash through rather than follow circumspectly. Hanna had a higher ambition for McKinley than McKinley had for himself. It was Hanna who first saw the White House at the end of McKinley's road. Hanna caught a glimpse of it in 1892, when Benjamin Harrison was nominated for the second time. The politicians had come to hate Harrison because he was a gentleman always before he was a politician. Possibly Hanna was late in revealing his ambition for McKinley. At any rate, in the spring of '92, the year of the presidential nomination, Governor McKinley of Ohio was one of the first of the Middle States governors to make the holy pilgrimage to Indianapolis to assure President Harrison of the support of the Ohio delegation. Yet four months later, when Hanna had drawn the curtain showing McKinley the White House at the end of McKinley's road, McKinley sat at a dinner given by Hanna to a group of Harrison's bitter opponents at the Republican National Convention in

*In 1888, when Hanna and McKinley were supporting Sherman, a Connecticut delegate voted for McKinley in the convention. McKinley quickly protested. He stopped the balloting to say: "I do not request—I demand that no delegate shall cast a ballot for me." He created a dramatic moment and made himself a hero. Politicians remembered that hour and trusted McKinley ever after.

Minneapolis. Without protest McKinley heard Hanna discuss the possibility of defeating Harrison in the convention a few days later by switching to McKinley the Harrison opposition which was gathering around Blaine. Harrison had rather publicly humiliated Hanna in some matters of Cleveland patronage. Hanna was troubled by no inflamed and ingrown conscience. Out of his heart his mouth spoke. But McKinley sat by and said nothing; for he knew politics. He knew, probably, that it was a vain hope which Hanna cherished, that the nomination of Harrison was on the cards, and that to defeat Harrison in the convention would defeat the winner in November.

So they made McKinley chairman of the convention which nominated Harrison and he spoke glowing words about Harrison and smiled at his friend Hanna—the kind of smile that politicians give business men who intrude.* Then the governor went on his way; for if McKinley was a calm man he was not always sure of himself. He changed his mind several times on the currency. He was uncomfortable in the presence of men of academic training, and knew virtually nothing of economics outside of tariff schedules. Even there he was uncertain, and his friends on the Ways and Means Committee of the House of Representatives testify that he was the least certain man on the committee about many important tariff rates though he was its chairman. Time and again he agreed to set up a tariff schedule in the committee and

*When, on the first ballot, McKinley's Ohio alternate in the convention voted for McKinley with forty-three others, McKinley stopped the balloting, demanded a poll of the delegation, voted himself for Harrison, and settled that defection. Later he called Elliott F. Shepard to the chair, and moved to make Harrison's nomination unanimous. It was the second time he refused to be a Presidential candidate.

then kicked it over. But his uncertainty was the result
of study—not of caprice or cajoling. He was earnestly
trying to be fair. He was a protectionist only because
he lived north of the Mason and Dixon Line. In politics
generally, certainly until he came to the White House,
McKinley was never distinguished as a man who had
championed what the people should have, but rather he
was known as one who sensed what the people desired.
Hanna was protection incarnate. McKinley, in politics,
was more or less Hanna's attorney—not actually, but in
their political relations. .

To McKinley, Hanna was the human personification
of McKinley's political creed; never more than that. But
Hanna gave McKinley his heart. Hanna was intensely
personal in his relations with men, thousands of men.
McKinley had relations with the people. Hanna was the
stronger man. Perhaps his fame, which may be slight
as the centuries roll by, will exist only as his name is
linked with McKinley's; as Achates comes to us with
Æneas, Mæcenas with Horace, Boswell with Johnson.
For McKinley, by reason of the political position to
which Hanna led him, became the stronger influence in
human affairs. Such are the ironies of life. In passing,
let us note this: that McKinley was diverted from his
real ambition by Hanna. McKinley desired to go on the
Federal bench and to round out his career as a judge in
one of the higher courts. He was put on the Ways and
Means Committee of Congress when he went to Congress,
as a second choice. Judiciary would have been his preference. Thomas B. Reed's election as Speaker forced
the checkers on the board to move so that McKinley
became Chairman of the Ways and Means Committee;

and when he was defeated for Congress in '90, Hanna's hero worship made McKinley go to the people for endorsement for governor in '91. So does destiny shape our ends.

McKinley and Hanna, in their day together, were great men, which means they were also average men in the main, and nothing that happened to them in the higher walks of politics was peculiar. The thing that happened in Minneapolis, in 1892, when Harrison was renominated, happened in miniature at a hundred thousand county conventions and state conventions all over the land in those convention days. Indeed, probably little happens in the White House that has not been enacted before in every county court house in America. The difference between the average run in statesmanship and the average run in peanut politics is merely in the size of the counters, and not in the rules and the run of the game.

CHAPTER XIV

A POLITICIAN TURNS STATESMAN

IN '94, having secured the reëlection of McKinley as governor, Hanna went out in the highways and byways of Wall Street, New England, Cleveland, Chicago, and raised a fund to finance the presidential candidacy of McKinley. He knew that game. He had raised money in the national campaign of '84. He had been the head of the Republican commissary department in the battle of 1888. He was known as the business man in politics, seeking no particular acclaim, but motived by a healthy appetite for power.

Hanna was an unconscious agent of a deep tendency in American politics which had been growing since the Civil War; a tendency toward industrialization as against the agricultural dominance of the continent. Mills and mines were opening from Boston to the Mississippi River. Smokestacks of industry were jutting into a thousand horizons. Workmen were coming from Europe to toil in factories, and boys were leaving American farms to work with machines. Mill towns were no longer limited to New England. Yet it was not so easy, this industrial conquest of the continent. If industry was to grow, it required special legal privileges—in short, protection. This need for protection, chiefly a high protective tariff, required an alliance between business and politics. If America was to industrialize, her politicians must help;

hence Hanna went forth from Ohio seeking funds which should amalgamate the protected industrial interests against the attacks of the agrarians. It was not his first venture; but under Hanna the efforts of the manufacturers to control government had become an orderly branch of politics.

Therefore Hanna went out seeking money. He knew where to go, how to get it. But the other end was vastly more important; he knew where to spend the money he got. Most politicians have easy consciences about the money entrusted to them by other politicians for political purposes. Forty per cent of all political money in all campaigns since the ballot box was invented has stuck to the fingers of each recipient. Hanna probably reduced the ratio to fifteen or twenty per cent, keeping nothing for himself. He reduced the percentage of loss by avoiding the more greedy crowd in every state. He had his choice of crowds. No one else was roaming America with money in his pockets in 1894, establishing political headquarters for a Republican presidential candidate. Hanna

MR. HANNA CALLS ON MR. WANAMAKER.
—*Chicago Journal.*

picked the most effective crowd and the least prodigal, and used the most effective means and least expensive to promote his plans.

The most expensive device he used was a private car, and occasionally a special train in which McKinley from time to time darted out of Columbus, Ohio, where he was governing a sovereign people, and visited remote states in the West and the North and New England. McKinley's technique on those visits was perfect. It will be interesting to observe it. Consider first the private car: A kitchen in the front, dining room amidships, berths and staterooms aft, and back of that section a small glass-windowed reception room ending in a broad rear platform. Visiting statesmen came up the steps of the car onto the broad rear platform and were shown into the reception room. On each side of the room were chairs, at the farther end toward the engine a small table. Back of the door leading to the rear platform was a large chair filling the corner. It filled the corner so amply that no other chair could sit beside it on the left on account of the door, nor on the right because its position was veered around so that the man on the right would have only McKinley's shoulder. No one could drop into that chair nor into any other chair and monopolize McKinley, thus getting next to the throne. McKinley sat or stood before this chair. The visiting statesmen stood before McKinley, or sat remotely from him in some other parts of the reception room. Thus he met all comers, kept everyone aloof, greeted everyone kindly, treated all alike, played no favorites, gave everyone a chance, and so strung the politicians through the gills like fish on his string as he sped on his way. Only the wisdom of a deeply crafty man who knew humanity well but himself better, who was too self-satisfied to be cynical and too cunning to be fooled, could have arranged that pleasant device of the large armchair in the corner behind the door. The arrangement perfectly represented McKinley. Roosevelt, going across the country in his private car, was fluttering all over the place, out on the steps, dragging favorites into his stateroom, buttonholing men over the rear brass railing of the observation platform, slapping his hat in delight as the train pulled out. Taft moved with a sort of megatherium leisure through his car, restlessly, sitting down here, putting a hand on this man's knee, on that man's shoulder, smiling into this dumb face or that reptilian eye, with all his own dignity and charm. Wilson, yearning for affection, clumsily tried to coax it out of men by fatuous gestures that often, more often than not, offended rather than won them. But McKinley, in his little throne room, ruled; a wise and gentle potentate, who knew the game and loved it for its own fine sake. Sometimes at a station he stepped—rather nimbly for a man in his early fifties—to the rear of the platform and stood while he spoke with a sort of sweet solemnity to the crowd at the train's rear end. In that day and time, and from then on to the close of his career, he wore the politician's garb: a circumspect, well-tailored, carefully pressed suit; a coat with tails, dark gray pinstriped trousers, an immaculate white vest, unwrinkled over a decently rotund paunch that never was fat, a white starched shirt with a flat, narrow black or white bow tie, and a high choker collar which enclosed a rather large neck, a strong jaw, and supported a fine, massive head.

He had a splendidly molded head, well proportioned,

fit for the "animated bust"; a broad, noble brow not too high, heavy but not shaggy eyebrows, a clear, firm, steady eye that could be piercing at will but rarely was roused; a large, assertive but not pugnacious nose, a decently long Irish upper lip, a broad but never sensitive and hardly generous though conspicuously strong mouth, and a good chin just slightly cleft. It was the statesman's face, unwrinkled, unperturbed; a face without vision but without guile. Of all the masks in the long pageant of the generation that has led up through politics into the White House, this face of McKinley's, this placid, kindly, unchipped mask of a kindly, dull gentleman, is a cast most typical to represent American politics; on the whole decent, on the whole dumb, and rarely reaching above the least common multiple of the popular intelligence. In McKinley our politics reached its finest flower. He was of it—the perfect product, a public man; the public man who hid his cigar from the camera lest the picture should corrupt youth!

As Governor of Ohio, McKinley was just a good average governor. He went along signing requisition papers, appointing state boards, making occasional speeches, wearing his gubernatorial silk hat at perfunctory ceremonies, keeping away from all local issues and entanglements that might embarrass a presidential candidate. Ohio never had a more cautious governor. Unconsciously, McKinley covered himself with conservatism; not economic conservatism, but political caution. Upon the surface, no word of McKinley's indicated that he was thinking of the White House. Yet Mark Hanna was devoting his life to the McKinley presidential campaign. Hanna built a steel-ribbed, fire-proof machine for

McKinley in Ohio, the like of which was never known before, for it was held together not by the politicians but by business interests. Out of the principles and practices of that machine—but through another faction—in which business interests contributed for tariff favors to come, the Ohio gang grew. In Hanna's day it was little more than a close corporation for McKinley, with the voting stock in the hands of Hanna as general manager. It had one object, a tariff for protection. With the fighting enthusiasm of a champion, Hanna organized a political syndicate in business circles to name McKinley for President. It was the first mobilization of class-conscious industrialists. Great manufacturers and their allies in transporation, with their supporters in high finance, had been taking root widely but without premeditated purpose in the administrations of Cleveland and Harrison. But growth came suddenly, and their vague visions came to flower and fruitage in the Hanna organization of business and politics behind McKinley. No wonder the farmers of the West met this organization in revolt. The Populists had carried four states in 1892—Kansas, Idaho, Colorado, and Nevada; also, they had secured one electoral vote in North Dakota and one in Oregon. Four years later when McKinley ran against Bryan the agricultural West was against McKinley and his platform. This rise of the Western farmers came from a disquieting belief that the old order was threatened in which agriculture had dominated American politics since the beginning. On the other hand, the strikes, riots, the menaced anarchy which came in Cleveland's administration, were the protests of labor against the inequitable distribution of the privileged profits which industry was reaping under the

protective tariff. Hanna with his money bags represented
the heart of the thing that menaced the farmers. He was
a sort of super-salesman, selling stock in what seemed to
him to be an immortal corporation, ageless and impregnable, for the domination of business in government
through the control of politics.

He floated his presidential stock with a daring and
frankness that astounded McKinley's enemies and gave
McKinley's friends that flare of success which is two-
thirds of the political battle. Hanna went South, opened
a home in Georgia, called the Southern politicians to him,
and created there also his own effective machine. He
minced no words, used no hoity-toity phraseology in dealing with the politicians of the South. Business was business, and that ended it. But up in Columbus, Ohio,
Governor McKinley, being a shrewd politician, realized what Hanna was doing. Yet probably the only place
on earth where Hanna covered the blunt artillery of his
language was in the presence of McKinley. There,
Hanna spoke of his bargains as arrangements, and
referred to his deals as combinations. Whether McKinley knew, or did not know, about the manipulations of
delegates in the South which nominated him for President,
must be a matter of mere conjecture. But after his election he turned the patronage of the South over to Hanna.

All through the campaign for his first nomination
for President, McKinley was complacent under his plaster
cast of gubernatorial dignity. Days and nights and Sun-
days he had worn the josslike countenance that politicians
put on for public functions, until his features finally
became set to it. But Hanna, who hurried through real
events of world-wide importance during those days of

'94, '95, and '96, never could assume what has been
called the poker face. His mobile lips twitched when his
mouth was full of angry words, and he spat them out. He
glared with his big, frank, hearty eyes, or he smiled with
them, and those about him made no mistake in his meaning. Only in this they misread Hanna, and it was cruel
and unjust to him: men thought that his ambition for
McKinley was ambition for personal power, ambition to
control a President of the United States. The power that
moved Hanna was fine and strong and clean as a father's
love. Hanna's worship of McKinley was the passion of
his life. It was utterly unselfish, save as Hanna had
invested his own reputation as a fighter in it, and had in
the outcome of the game a consuming desire to win—for
the stake is the largest in all the world.

Senators Platt and Quay, Thomas B. Reed, Speaker
of the House of Representatives, and the New England
contingent of the Republican party, representing banking
interests rather than industrial organizations, changed
the issue of the campaign of '96 from the tariff to the
currency, and demanded the flat endorsement of the gold
standard. Hanna, whose first thought was for McKinley's safety, mouthed a momentary protest but accepted
the inevitable. McKinley, being a politician and used to
suddenly changing figures on the chessboard, calmly
ignored his silver speeches and took up the demand for
"an honest dollar and a chance to earn it" with the sea-
soned zeal of an old convert. After he was nominated in
1896, he refused to go racing up and down the land making speeches from the rear end of a railroad car. Bryan
did that. As a vice-presidential candidate Roosevelt did
that. But McKinley, as the presidential candidate of

the Republican party, received guests upon his front lawn
at Canton. Train-load after train-load came to him;
and came not so spontaneously as they seemed to come.
Their spokesman was rehearsed. His speech of greeting was edited. No ruler, or king or potentate, was ever
more careful that no untoward event should occur and
that no ill-advised words should be spoken in his presence than was McKinley as a candidate for the presidency;
for McKinley was never rash. He handled himself with
automatic poise. And in the campaign for sound money
no one was so unruffled as he, who in his day had trod
the path of dalliance—though quite circumspectly, to be
sure—that led toward fiat money. McKinley was trustworthy, as the phrase goes in politics. He was not given
to illusions of leadership. The advocates of sound money
had confidence in McKinley after he became their candidate, and his former record did not worry them any more
than it worried him. They apparently construed his
silver utterances as the Pickwickian deliverances of a
gentleman indulging in the harmless pastime of soft-
soaping the electorate. McKinley grew into their respect
and confidence later, but when the gold standard champions in the Republican party took him they did not think
particularly well of their bargain, though it was the best
they could make.

Hanna was McKinley's bondsman. And what might
be called the Gold Trust, which became the holding company of the stock of the original tariff operating company,
regarded the McKinley candidacy, in the early days of the
campaign of '96, as merely the plant in the vote-making
business, of which Hanna was general manager. When
the two went to Washington, McKinley as President and

Hanna as senator, if the popular opinion of their relations had unconsciously affected Hanna's sense of the real facts, McKinley set Hanna to rights quickly. McKinley and Hanna lifted John Sherman out of the Senate and into the Cabinet to make room in the Senate for Hanna. But when that job was finished, McKinley seems to have felt his political obligation to Hanna was ended. After that McKinley was President in fact as well as in name.

CHAPTER XV

AND THE STATESMAN TURNS TO MARBLE

THERE was never a moment after the election of 1896, which made McKinley President, when Hanna was even fourth assistant President or chief clerk to a deputy. As President, McKinley generally kept Hanna—as most of the time he kept every other human being—in merely an official relation to him. McKinley was President, and Hanna was senator from Ohio, and as chairman of the National Republican Committee he was ex-officio proconsul from the South. McKinley was a consummate politician; at the last perhaps a statesman of sorts, but clear down to the core of his soul he was in politics. He played politics with Congress—perfectly honest politics, and as clean as the times would permit. He played politics with the people—always deferring to them when he could not persuade them, using them with craft rather than with force. He played politics with his Cabinet—picking its members with an adroitness that displayed his highest genius, so that no member of his Cabinet was indebted to the ruling state boss or dominated by a United States senator, and so that every Cabinet member might, therefore, choose his subordinates freely and honestly. And, finally, McKinley played politics with Hanna, his friend. When the Cabinet was formed Hanna found that he had no more influence with Cabinet members than any other chairman of the National Committee might have had.

McKinley at the age of fifteen and on the eve of his assassination.
The later pictures are used by courtesy of Judge Publishing Co., Inc.

Flesh and blood would have given Hanna a partnership in the Presidency, which would have been wrong and unjust to the country. But McKinley knew the rules of his game and played the rules fairly. He was not ungrateful for what Hanna had done. But what Hanna had done was for a friend, for a man, not for a President; and the friend's affairs were not matters of prime importance to the President, whose duties were purely official.

There are these degrees of intimacy at the White House: to shake hands with the President at a reception—that is the citizen's prerogative; to eat dinner there—which is a politician's royal arch degree; to go there for breakfast—which is the mark of presidential preference; to bring your valise and to sleep there—which is a distinction accorded to the Truly Great; and to bring a trunk and get your laundry done there—that is to be a member of the household and to be accepted into full fellowship with the nation's ruler. Hanna brought his valise to the White House, but he always left his trunk at the hotel.

Hanna and McKinley were close enough friends to spat, to quarrel in a friendly way, and to wrangle a little. But if there was pouting to be done, Hanna always had to do it, and to get over his pout, too, for that matter. Once, in a campaign, Hanna—as Chairman of the National Republican Committee—wrote to the President protesting against laying off certain men in the Brooklyn Navy Yard, and against a certain Sergeant Dugan, who was charged, in this letter from Hanna to McKinley, with having "contemptuously thrown aside a letter of recommendation from a member (of Congress) of that district." McKinley's reply went into the matter rather fully. His position was unassailable. He made it plain that the action of the Treasury Department in laying off the men at the Brooklyn Navy Yard was necessary, and that Sergeant Dugan, at Iona Island, was acting clearly in the line of public policy. Then McKinley, at the end of the letter, put in this bit of pleasant moralizing apropos of Hanna's protest in these matters:

This is a time when every effort will be made to have the administration do questionable things. It is a period of great temptation, just the sort that will require the highest courage to meet the cause. If elected, I have to live with the administration for four years. I don't want to feel that any improper or question-able methods have been employed to reach the place, and you must continue as you have already done to stand against unreasonable exactions which are so common at the present time.

Hanna read the letter and threw it on the floor angrily. It was obvious that the President had written the letter with studied care. More than that, the President's letter bore evidence of having been particularly copied for the White House files. The man behind the mask, that was McKinley, had not written to his fides Achates, but to posterity! Hanna was put in the attitude of being a messenger boy to some future historian. McKinley could not even for a moment step out from behind the memorial bronze which had galvanized him to reply to a friend as a friend. A dozen words, a mere "no, it cannot be done, you're wrong," would have satisfied Hanna. But when he saw the data for the McKinley biography in a letter addressed to him, Hanna raged for a moment, flared up, subsided, sighed, spent his passion, had his pout, and forgot it.

In the same campaign, Hanna functioned after his kind. He started to South Dakota to make a speech against Senator Richard F. Pettigrew, a Populist, who had tried to get the United States Senate to investigate the legality and morality of Hanna's election to the Senate. Hanna was hungry for vengeance when he turned his head toward South Dakota. He was going on his own errand, though he was Chairman of the Republican National Committee. At Chicago, he met Mr. Charles Emory Smith, Postmaster General, who began beating about the bush to persuade Hanna that the Northwestern adventure was ill-advised. Smith even indicated that Hanna might meet personal violence if he protested too viciously against Pettigrew in South Dakota. Finally Hanna looked up, opening the searchlight in his big brown eyes, and cried to Smith:

"The President sent you, didn't he?"

Smith hesitatingly admitted that he was an emissary of McKinley. Hanna rose, and twitching his mobile mouth in rage, cried:

"Go back and tell the President that God hates a coward!"

Thus Hanna comes to posterity, not as his friend in the White House came—behind a mask—but full of blood and passion, an unconquered soul. This much must be said, however, for McKinley: The Democratic newspapers of the day were lampooning the President as the creature of Mark Hanna. Comic papers cartooned Hanna holding McKinley in leash like a monkey. As a matter of fact, the President was a better politician than his chairman, knew more about men, had a better knowledge of public affairs, was more intelligent outside of business than Hanna. Yet in the public eye, particularly in the eye of the President's enemies, Hanna seemed to be the dominant figure. McKinley held his relations with Hanna pleasant to the end. And in spite of his pouts, Hanna clove to the President as to a brother.

Sometimes Hanna addressed McKinley reverently as "William"—but probably he did not see McKinley as often as he wished to see him, and too many times merely had audiences with the President, whom Hanna did not always like. For the official cast was coating McKinley deeper and deeper as he grew older. He never stepped from his pedestal, not even when he was using his greatest strength and coming into his highest responsibility. The period of his highest responsibility and greatest strength came just before the war with Spain. That war revealed the blood hunger of a democracy. McKinley tried earnestly to prevent war. It is hard to realize, a generation after, how the waves of public wrath at the delay of the war with Spain beat in breakers about the White House. The tyranny of Spain in Cuba had excited the mob spirit in America. One wonders also if the deep lust for conquest was not in our heart in those days. McKinley, with vision and courage, quietly prepared for war while urging peace. The mob cursed him for a poltroon. He turned to them an unwincing, bronze face. It was the face of a ruler; but whatever agony was in the man's heart was hidden. With Lincoln, at such times, it was always the man that men saw; it was ever the grief mounting in his own soul, not his public sorrow, that the nation caught. Each, in times of popular fury, was doing in secret what the people desired, hoping the need for action would pass. Lincoln's face furrowed. Heartache was written all around his closed lips. When

McKinley passed through this ordeal in the spring of '98 the President's face was impassive, whatever the man's soul may have suffered.

McKinley was a good president; Lincoln a great man!

And Hanna in that hour was a panic-stricken bondsman, who feared he would have to pay the forfeit. He was for peace. The conservative part of Wall Street was largely for peace, being timid about its new prosperity. Stable business everywhere was for peace. But the speculators were for war. Hanna went on record publicly for peace. All that expostulation and unrestrained insistence could do for peace Hanna did. The vigor and simplicity of his nature were never more plainly seen of men than they were in the days before war was declared. But when he saw the inevitable approach he rallied to McKinley, and was the President's faithful servant. And if he passed out to the good fellows at the gate an occasional loaf of bread in the form of an army commission or a contract, or a place as director of the Cuban posts, put it down to gratitude to his friends, to the kindness that was in his frank, honest brown eyes, rather than to cupidity or greed for spoils. For Hanna was a man who liked to keep out of debt politically, and he regarded public office as a public trust, the stock of which would stand considerable watering! He secured the appointment of Charles G. Rathbone as director of the posts in Cuba. Rathbone had been named, in an affidavit filed with the United States Senate, as a go-between who might have furnished funds in an alleged attempt at bribery in the legislature when Hanna was elected United States senator. Rathbone, in Cuba, failed to meet the standard of honesty which McKinley held, and was incontinently removed at the end of a scandal. Hanna could not hold him.

McKinley, who grew intellectually every day of his presidential life, did what he did in those hurrying days of the war in the main with clear eyes upon his duty. He was deceived sometimes, and mistaken sometimes, but he knew what the people had a right to expect, and he was faithful to them so far as an erring human being may be faithful to a wayward people who tied his hands with many strings. The country was keen for war, but the politicians knew that many patriots were as keen for jobs as for war. Every office under the government in that war was regarded as a job. Whether the applicant desired to be commander-in-chief of the army or com-missary-sergeant, his friends in pushing him regarded the place as a job. The army was stiff-kneed and the navy was rusty; but for all that, McKinley and the American people conducted the war—a little war to be sure—with precision and vigor to the end. McKinley handled the soldiers with tact and civilians with tact, and in closing up the affair the President handled the civilized world with tact. Hanna would have blurted out his real desire, and did, so far as that goes; but the President chose to let his opinions come from the country, and then to appear not as a leader but as a follower of public thought. This studied indirection must have irritated Hanna, but he was too loyal a friend to show it. He was ever the faith-ful heart. He was McKinley's guardian rather than his adviser. Hanna was the more energetic man, yet he did not overcome the President's quiet force. Indeed, there were times when, in McKinley's presence, the bubbling humor of the senator, his bald recognition of apparent facts, his incisive, unmincing metaphors, which revealed his strong convictions and his frank prejudices, were turned by the furtive, bland, impartial McKinley into a kind of obsequious, abashed repression, and Hanna, almost squelched and ill at ease, simmered down from respectful inanition to enthusiastic silence as he watched the President play the game.

McKinley's life in the White House was not distinguished by any important personal achievement. He had no program save to establish the gold standard as per agreement, and to maintain the protective tariff as the keystone of the national economic arch. The tariff was revised under his administration probably as justly as any tariff was ever revised. That revision stood for a decade with few changes. The gold standard had been adopted by administrative custom, to all intents and purposes, during the Harrison and Cleveland administrations. It was merely legally established by McKinley. But the opening of gold mines in the Klondike and in South Africa expanded the currency to a per capita circulation as large as the advocates of bi-metalism could have desired.

The annexation of the Hawaiian territory gave America her first colony. McKinley had no experience in colonial affairs and no theory about colonial government; but he set over the colonies men of the highest integrity, and for rules in administering colonies turned to such academic experts as our country afforded. Certainly McKinley showed no weakness, no lack of ideals, no dumb partisan blindness in guiding America's first steps along the highway of imperialism. He was not an im-

perialist. His utterances indicated that he feared imperial expansion and desired to remain at home in peace.
He even held ideals about our tariff relations with the
new colonies—as, for instance, Porto Rico—higher than
the protectionists in his party would endorse. He had to
retire from his position. It was this episode which drew
from Roosevelt the classic remark: "McKinley has a
backbone like a chocolate éclair!"

McKinley in the White House was a conscientious protectionist, but there is evidence in his presidential speeches
that he felt that the greed of the protected industries
needed curbing. He favored reciprocity with Cuba and
aroused the ire of the sugar-beet growers. His chief
strength and the glory of his administration came from
his knowledge of politics and men in politics. For his
major places in the Cabinet, in diplomacy, in administrative jobs, he picked men better, on the whole, than any
President of his generation has picked. The state bosses
were stepchildren, scrupulously washed and fed and
attended, but not dearly loved. Thirty years later Harding loved these political stepchildren so fondly that he
let them steal the family silver.

CHAPTER XVI

AND SO MOUNTS HIS PEDESTAL

McKinley's reëlection in 1900 was a triumph. Bryan, his opponent, carried little outside the solid South. McKinley had established himself in the public confidence. The people believed in him preëminently as a good man. There can be no doubt that his governing desire was to be a faithful servant. Certainly his chief and most useful instrument was not erudition, for he was comparatively unlearned; not oratory, for he was a dull speaker; not courage, nor character, nor foresight, for he was on the wrong side of many propositions and went back as easily from the right side to the wrong side as he went from the wrong side to the right side—and never suffered by his meandering. His most useful weapon was his knowledge of politics, which gave him an insight into the hearts of men. No President since Lincoln knew men better than McKinley. His courage was generally tact. His wisdom was often the experience of others. But his knowledge of men came out of a long, successful life in politics as a candidate, as a servant, as a sort of consecrated follower.

In the eyes of its contemporaries the McKinley administration seemed to stabilize a paternal benevolent plutocracy as the permanent form of American government. Prosperity was McKinley's ideal. Under his rule our plutocracy hoped to grow richer and richer, allowing the overflow from the larger fortunes and the greater corporations to trickle down to those of next smaller size, and so overflowing, flood the lower level and keep labor in its place, business growing substantially, wheels whirling busily interest coming in regularly, and, in the salubrious capital structure, the melon-vine of speculative promoters' profits growing larger and larger melons unto the perfect day. This order carried in its roots the seeds of its own destruction, the germs of protest which were bound to destroy it. But destruction was to appear in another time.

As McKinley rounded his first term and turned into his second the relations between him and Hanna remained stationary. They did not grow closer, nor did they weaken. Hanna was always welcome at the White House, sometimes as United States senator, sometimes as national committee chairman, and occasionally as friend. But he never headed for the White House to see McKinley in any other capacity than as friend, however he may have been received. His affection for McKinley never waned. Probably he always thought of him as "William," though he was as chary of that name in public as a schoolgirl is of her first lover's endearments. The President found many advisers, and came to trust their wisdom—for it was of a high order. Mr. Hay, Mr. Root, Mr. Knox, General Wood, Mr. Charles Emory Smith, and a score of others came into the President's councils. Some of these men liked Hanna; others disliked him.

But Hanna had but one friendship, one master passion: that was for McKinley's fame and welfare. He arranged, together with his friends in the Senate, a *modus vivendi* with "high finance," by the tacit terms of which the trusts were not to be disturbed. Hanna ironed out the wrinkled front of the Senate when it would have frowned at McKinley; Hanna was even ready to pare the horns of Protection that McKinley's reciprocity ideas might have full play. Always he was the friend in need; always his life was centered on McKinley's; always he was the soul of devotion.

He did what he did expecting no rewards and indeed asking few favors. And the President, whose outlook was always official and large, paid back the kindness Hanna gave him with such gentleness and manly gratitude as a man may bestow upon another, but little more. McKinley was just. He was so just, indeed, so colorlessly fair, that his personality is elusive. We know men best by their faults, by their little human weaknesses; in the shadow of these their virtues stand out more clearly. But McKinley had no little vices. He was truthful without being exactly frank, and brave without being sufficiently candid about it for the people to realize it. He was so careful that his style in writing is heavy. His utterances read like a sheriff's sale notice, full of restrictions and exceptions and painful exactitudes—not academic, not so much qualifying as timidly reiterating, unnecessarily explaining. His whole life seems to have been spent before an audience. He was an elective public servant continuously for a generation, and became so cautious lest he should tread on a public corn that any private character he may have had was hidden. He was the incarnation of the ballot box in its noblest mood.

McKinley's last public performance was in Buffalo, New York. He came to Buffalo with a retinue of statesmen to visit the Buffalo Exposition, a sort of exalted country fair, not so large as the World's Fair at Chicago, but better perhaps than the average of the expositions that were fashionable in those days. His appearance in Buffalo was a triumph. He rode many miles through multitudes who saw him sitting easily in an open barouche with his silk hat in his hand, bowing to the cheering thousands. His hair was thin on the top of his head, but his face was virile. His virility was not conspicuous as was Roosevelt's, yet McKinley's physical vigor glowed in his countenance as he beamed upon the crowds. He stood to speak before the multitude and revealed a fine upstanding figure of a man in his middle sixties, soldierly, dignified, commanding, yet without vain pride. He wore the conventional statesman's garb; a skirted coat, gray trousers, an immaculate white vest, a black bow tie, and a high choker collar—a decent lineal descendant of the old chokers that the statesmen wore before the Civil War. He stood easily and spoke from notes. Even in a fairground crowd he received excellent attention, and his speech launched out into a new policy, the policy of reciprocity with other nations in tariff duties. It was an attempt at popular leadership, and McKinley's conviction must have come from a sense of the injustices that arise necessarily from a purely political tariff written by its beneficiaries through control of politics. It was the high day of McKinley's life.

The next day the President again journeyed through throngs that gathered about the street, and at the end went to a reception in the Temple of Music. As the handshaking throng filed past the President, a Pole, named Czolgoz, carrying a revolver wrapped in a handkerchief, approached McKinley, who, thinking the man's hand was wounded, reached for his left hand. As he did so, Czolgoz fired twice. For a second there was dumb amazement. The first man to recover his senses was a negro named J. B. Parker, standing directly behind Czolgoz. He hit the assassin an awful blow on his nose, and the two fell to the ground. A special officer grabbed the pistol and a marine officer jumped on the special officer. The crowd began pummeling the wrong man. The negro and Czolgoz lay wrestling on the floor. The President sank back, wounded twice in the abdomen.

He lingered in the Milburn home, where he was a guest, for several days. From all over the land Cabinet members, statesmen, senators came hurrying to Buffalo. The President seemed to rally, seemed out of danger, then came the collapse. It was all curiously unreal, like a stage picture. The official record of his death is a newspaper story. It reads:

> After the Cabinet officers left the sickroom the physicians rallied him, and the President asked that his afflicted wife be brought to him. The doctors fell back into the shadows of the room as Mrs. McKinley came through the doorway. The strong face of the dying man lighted up with a faint smile as their hands clasped. Probably Mrs. McKinley did not realize the significance of his tender farewell. She moved from the spotlight, and the watchers gathered again about the bed. They heard him chant, in a murmur, the words of the old hymn, "Nearer, My God, to Thee."

He was an historic figure, making a perfect exit.

The most vital figure in it all did not seem to be the dying President, but the stocky little man who came in clicking his cane; who walked over to the bed, and, looking long and lovingly at the stricken form, finally broke out with a horrible sob:

"William—William—don't you know me?"

That was real; that was anguish. A strong man has strong emotions. Hanna cried like a child at McKinley's deathbed. For he probably knew, even if from afar, the heart that no one else knew, the real soul that hid itself from men under the cover of official garments— the soul that shone in kindness and gentleness through all the life of William McKinley, whose last audible conscious words were publicly recorded by the doctor:

"Good-by, all—good-by. It's God's way; His will be done!"

Then he turned officially to marble, leaving no imperfections to ignore when animation left the clay.

And so passed the twenty-fifth President of the United States into history. McKinley was the last of an old order. He exemplified that order in two distinct ways: First, because he dramatized the issues of the day. They were issues which he knew, upon which he had come into power. These issues concerned the production of wealth rather than its distribution. America had been building for three hundred years a civilization which, more than any other civilization the world ever knew, was the result of capital combined with the labor of men. Yet it was a rural civilization, for the most part agricultural, was that old civilization of our first three hundred years; a pioneer civilization, with rough and ready ways, great distances, remote cities, far-reaching enterprises. Time and space had not been shrunk and cramped as the next three decades were to shrink and cramp the old verities on the American continent. A President in our first century was a figure, a person whose very presence brought awe by reason of his office. And McKinley exemplified the old order as the man aloof. ¬He was the last President to stand apart from the people, pedestaled, shielded from publicity, with the divinity that doth hedge about a king. And no European ruler west of Moscow was so jealous of his democratic dignity as William McKinley. He cherished the ideals of the old order to his last breath. He had lived so long alone in politics that he sloughed off his attitude as an individual and gradually become a public man, like the American rulers before him —soldiers, gentlemen, scholars, and statesmen, but always a race apart.

With McKinley's exit the wheels of change began to whirl rapidly. Scarcely had he mounted the marble pedestal on his monument in the statehouse yard at Columbus, Ohio, before the nation had forgotten the issues that McKinley emphasized. The tariff, pensions, the currency—indeed, all thought of economic measures tending to promote the production of wealth—were discarded for new issues. These new issues were deeply divisive between class and clan. They concerned the regulation of trusts, the control of railroad rates, the branding of foods, the conservation of mines and forests, a postal savings bank. Coördinated with the demand for these economic reforms came political changes which tended to exalt the common man; the primary, the initiative and referendum, the direct election of United States senators, political corruption acts, the secret ballot, and a long line of laws which put power into the hands of the citizen that he might control government in the interest of a fairer distribution of the common wealth of the nation. It was enough in the seventies, eighties, and nineties to brand these issues as socialistic. But they came crowding into practical politics after McKinley's death. They brought new problems, made a new epoch, a new day wherein new methods were accepted and new men rose to power. Against these new issues old leaders known as the Old Guard fought a desperate, losing battle for a decade, and went down before the cohorts of the new era. The new era came from the impact of a new industrial civilization contending with an old rural civilization; the old civilization highly individualistic, the new as complex as the interdependence of men and nations, and as highly socialized. Looking across the state house yard out of his marble eyes, scarcely less lively and animate a figure to-day than he was in his pomp and power, William McKinley must have seen the clamor and violence of our new day as a world gone mad. In his life he was as remote from that world as Lincoln or Jefferson. There he stands in glory, gathered to the Fathers of the Republic; all statesmen of the old individual rural America that has passed forever. There they all stand, those petrified fathers, with McKinley their last child. Placidly, even in proud complacence, he seems to be shepherding them from the ravening wolves of modern industrialism with its harsh realities; he, quite as remote from life in the marble as they were aloof from life in the flesh.

PART III

TWO WARWICKS

"I am understanding. . . . By me kings reign and princes decree justice."

King Demos has his Warwicks, and by them ye shall know his fruits. In the America of the generations passing in this second decade of the twentieth century, two men of large stature, politically, were known not for their power as rulers, but for their power in making rulers and setting kingly tasks. These two men were Mark Hanna and William Jennings Bryan. Each gave color to his times. Hanna made the way easy for McKinley. Bryan was the voice crying before Wilson; Bryan was even herald to Roosevelt; Bryan, who never warmed his own throne.

Truly Yours
M.A. Hanna

Mark Hanna in 1896, from a sketch in *Leslie's Weekly.*

By courtesy of Judge Publishing Co., Inc.

MARK HANNA

CHAPTER XVII

"HE SHAMBLES FORTH IN COSMIC GUISE"

FIRST, let us look at Cleveland, Ohio, as it was in the last years of the old century. If for no other reason, let us look at Cleveland on the theory that man and the other creatures of the earth are the reflections of their environment. Thus we may know something of our hero's earthly habitat.

Cleveland, Ohio, like Falmouth, "is a fine town, with ships in the bay." There, in the middle of the nineteenth century, the smoke of a hundred furnaces stained the sky, and the clang of iron with the tinkle of gongs formed the din of a restless commerce. It was a town of workers when Mark Hanna began to know it. It was a town of workers when he dominated it. When he died and was buried in Cleveland, it was an industrial center. Even a quarter of a century after his death men still talk business at the clubs, and talk shop in the movies which have replaced the saloons; they take their business to bed with them o' nights after joy-riding, and still work in their dreams and dream at their work.

In 1900, when Hanna was the commercial overlord of Cleveland, beautiful homes on broad avenues led away from the lowlands where forges glowed. Solid public buildings were scattered along the streets where the tall, well-designed business houses rose, and pretty parks, solemn statues, and appropriate monuments in the wide squares adorned the town with a decent respectability. The homes, the public buildings, the commercial strongholds, the parks and their adornments, were accounted up to date in those golden days. Cleveland held half a million population. The houses and the people were all commercially profitable.

Down toward the mouth of one of the city caverns, before it spills its human stream into the industrial cauldron, swirling below the hills, stood a square, redstone building. On the sixth floor of this building was a suite of rooms, and on the door entering this suite was the legend:

M. A. HANNA & CO.
Coal, Iron Ore,
and
Pig Iron

The inner room of this suite was large. On the walls of the room, finished in mahogany, were a number of photographs of Hanna's home under the elm trees, surrounded by grass and flowers; also photographs of the members of the Republican National Committee of 1896, and a photograph of the interior of a power house, where four huge engines—all trim and solid and mechanically eloquent of power—stood waiting the touch of the master to release their energy. The photographs looked down on a directors' heavy mahogany table with massive round legs. On the table was a litter of blue-prints—engines and architects' designs—embryo boats, power houses, smokestacks, and many strange cross-sections, ground views, and perspectives of industrial edifices. Solid chairs of nondescript design were set near the edge of a crimson rug. In a corner beside the broad, deep window stood a massive desk. At the desk, leaning heavily on a clutter of letters and documents, was a stocky, long-bodied man, with his small feet hooked desperately to the supports of a pivoting chair. As he whirled about nervously, his quizzical, humorous smile animated the place and humanized it. This was Marcus Alonzo Hanna. Wherever he was, Hanna's personality exuded from everything. In his office the photographs of the great engines became vitally a part of him. The blue-prints seemed to crystallize themselves into him. The politicians' faces, the chairs, the table with the shapeless legs, all in an instant became living, component parts of this man's existence. The room, the building, the town on the inland sea—they also were parts of him and products of him, and he was a part and product of them.

Mark Hanna in the last decade of the old century was an American type. In 1895 he was engrossed in business. He felt that a crisis faced the country. He made the crisis himself. America was going through a siege of Populism. It was the early Populism of Altgeld, Weaver, Tillman, and Jerry Simpson, known as the Sockless. It was a crude Populism, striking blindly at the forces of the organized plutocracy—chiefly with a demand for an inflated currency, but incidentally with demands for Government control of railroads, trusts, and banks in the popular interest. Also, the Populists of the day had a political program: The Australian ballot, the primary, the direct election of United States senators, the initiative and referendum—a menacing battery of political guns.

So Mark Hanna set out to fight Populism, dramatized the fight around a hero, and made the crisis himself. He sloughed off his business. He became a political leader, and—as patriots go—a patriot. By sheer mechanical force, using money, the one lever of which God gave him mastery—a decent and handy device in his day—Hanna set millions of flags to waving. He manufactured and distributed, securely wrapped in packages of assorted sizes ready for immediate consumption, more lofty ideals of "civic integrity" of his own brand than the country had consumed before in a score of years. A weaker man than Hanna, with more emotion in his make-up, might have felt more deeply and perhaps more intelligently; but only a man like Hanna could have acted in the time of stress so effectively. With the hot, practical energy of a trip-hammer, Hanna converted dollars into patriotism, and saved the nation from a calamity which he feared. While he was at his work, men reviled him, bullied him, abused him—just as they did to the end of his career. He was Kipling's American personified. He knew men hated him.

> Which knowledge vexes him a space;
> But while reproof around him rings,
> He turns a keen, untroubled face
> Home to the instant need of things.

The story of his business life is like the biographies of thousands of other successful Americans. It is the dramatization of energy, the romance of industrial achievement. In another century, perhaps, such romances will seem as remote from the life then living as are stories of our Western border in the early nineteenth century,

bloody with Indian wars.   Opportunity in industry may
not always stand knocking at the gate for American
youths.   But at any rate, the story of Hanna's rise is a
brave tale, and one well worth the telling.

Hanna was born in 1837, in New Lisbon, Ohio.   Of
his ancestry it is sufficient to say that he died a member
of the Scotch-Irish Society of Philadelphia, in full com-
munion and good standing.   His grandfather was bound
out to a Quaker, and for a century before Mark Hanna's
death the Hannas were Quakers.   In 1852 Hanna's
father moved to Cleveland and brought along his seven
children.   The older Hanna started a grocery store, trading—more or less in a wholesale way—on the lakes, particularly in the Lake Superior country.   Young Mark
plodded through the public schools and got enough education to admit him to the Western Reserve University.
But in 1857, after a year in college, he returned to Cleveland to learn the grocery business, which was growing
and had become exclusively a wholesale concern, with
customers all over the lake region.   A year or so later
the elder Hanna was stricken, and the management of the
store fell in 1862 on the boy, Mark—a heavy load for a
young man, barely past his majority.   The responsibility
put grit into· him and gave him the luck-stone of his
life—the habit of industry.   It schooled him, as no university would have done to a man of Hanna's type, in
the uses of self-reliance and courage.   The wholesale
grocery business made a man of him at the time of life
when other older youths are addicted to the picnic habit.
When he closed up the store successfully five years later,
he knew all about the grocery business, and his energy

was proverbial in the town of Cleveland. He was thirty
years old when he married. He had always a romantic
streak in him and married a girl whose father first for-
bade Hanna the house, then tolerated him, and generally took a high and mighty attitude toward him. The
young Hannas lived alone, went broke, and finally moved
back into the house with the old folks and went into
business with the esteemed father-in-law. His father-in-
law was Daniel P. Rhodes. The firm, Rhodes & Co.,
dealt in coal, iron ore, and pig iron. The Civil War
had just closed, and with the close of the war old
America—the America of the farm and the rural village
—began to fade slightly and to change greatly. A new
industrial America began to appear. Young Hanna
threw himself into industry with passionate enthusiasm.
He learned the iron trade from the bottom, omitting no
circumstance. He was insatiably curious. He had an
artist's thirst to know the how of things. He learned
about coal mines and bought coal lands, learned about ore
and bought iron mines, learned about boats and bought
boats. Then he took his iron and his coal, and built the
first steel boats that ever plowed the Great Lakes. He
established foundries, forges, and smelters. Men worked
for him from western Pennsylvania to the base of the
Rockies. He knew his men and he knew the work they
did. He knew the value of a day's work, and he got it—
he also paid for it. Where there were labor troubles, the
contest was short and decisive. Hanna met the men himself. Either things were right or they were wrong.
If he thought things were wrong, he fixed them on the
spot. If he believed things were right, the work went on.
He was master. His workers were dependent on his will.

Serfdom was disappearing with the decline of agriculture; but a new problem was appearing—the labor problem, ancient as the differences in men.

In the early seventies the miners in Rhodes & Co.'s mines formed a union. Hanna studied the union as he had studied mines and ores and ships. He mastered its details, got the hang of it, and got up another union—a union of employers. Then, when the men at a mine had troubles, they conferred not with the mine operator, but with the mine operators' union. The two unions got along without friction, until the walking delegate found himself deposed, after which came trouble and Hanna's union dissolved. But the mining operators' union, while it lasted, gave to organized labor the first public recognition which it had received at that time. It was Hanna's invention. It worked—for a time. After the dissolution of the mine operators' union strikes multiplied. A number of arrests followed some shaft burning. Hanna went down to western Ohio to prosecute the men under arrest. They were defended by a young lawyer named McKinley—William McKinley—and he did his work so well that most of the miners went scot-free, and those convicted got short terms. Hanna took a liking to the young lawyer whose tactics had won the legal battle that Hanna had lost. A friendship began which was famous in contemporary history. Hanna had won his point in the strike. Perhaps he was in a mellow, expansive mood, which may have prepared him to admire the attorney for the strikers. Hanna was that way—a Celt and proud of his magnanimity.

The regularity with which Hanna won in his labor contests gave him business prestige. He declared in his heyday of industrial power, in the eighties and nineties, that he never let the men deal more fairly with him than he dealt with them. He used to brag that his office door swung inward as easily on its hinges for the dollar-a-day man as for the superintendent. In Cleveland, men said that there was an automatic spring on it for the chronic grumbler, for the shirker; and for the walking delegate. The door used to swing out upon these men with force and emphasis.

Hanna was a satrap in industry; wise, kind, even generous—but always paternal. He was a hard worker. He asked none of his employees to work as hard as he worked. His industrial intelligence made work easy and increased the capacity to do work. Genius is something of that sort. System was Hanna's secret. After he had reduced mining to a system, he added shipping, then he reduced that to a system and took on shipbuilding. Reducing that to its lowest terms, where the machinery works smoothly, Hanna built a street railway—made his coal and iron into cars, and his steel into rails. When he came to man that railway—the Cleveland City Street Railway—he had reduced the labor problem to such an exact science that while he owned the cars no strike was called on the line, although the cars of other lines in Cleveland were tied up frequently. About this time he took a fancy to the theatrical business. He bought the town opera house and began studying the gentle art of making friends with the stars of the theatrical world— went into the Mæcenas business wholesale! He learned the business of friendship as thoroughly as he learned the iron and coal and steel and ship and street railway business. He omitted no detail; he went the whole length—

put on a play by Mr. William Dean Howells, the wise and gracious pioneer of realism in American letters in the latter nineteenth century. Hanna invited the author out to see the job done properly. It was one of his fine small vanities to display to the end of his days the friendship of actors like Joseph Jefferson, Henry Irving, Francis Wilson, Stuart Robson, William H. Crane—and the best of the playwrights. His patronage of the gayest of the arts set off the ironmaster well. Hanna really loved the artists. His affection was never feigned. He was deeply loyal. The actors and playwrights could trust the appreciative eyes that laughed so easily. He knew all the actors' stories and could find the paths that led to their hearts. Hanna enjoyed hugely, with the gorgeous, expansive, conscious but self-deprecatory vanity of his race, sitting in his box at a play in his theater when some star was shining on the stage. There Hanna beamed like a moon, bowing and smiling at the gentry and nobility about him in the pit— the cadi of the village and proud of it—deeply appreciative of the caper he was cutting. That habit of tickling himself with a straw in his high moments never left him.

In the early eighties—apparently by way of diversion, or because Satan finds some evil work for idle hands to do —when the coal and iron mines, pig iron, steel, shipping, railway, and theatrical businesses became nerve-wracking monotony, Hanna started a bank. He took the presidency of it, and devoured the minutiæ of the new business ravenously. As he watched the wheels go around, looking at the levers and cogs and making the bank part of his life, Hanna began to notice baffling movements in the banking works. Some years the flywheel would not revolve. At other times it whirled too rapidly.

He went through the machinery with hammer and screws, but he found that the trouble lay outside the bank. He traced it to iron ore, through that to coal, and still it eluded him. The trouble lay outside the things he knew. It was in the lodestone of politics.

CHAPTER XVIII

"THE CELT IS IN HIS HEART AND HAND"

So Hanna went seriously into politics. In 1880 he had organized the Cleveland Business Men's Marching Club—a silk-hat platoon! The idea was a new one, and it took all over the country. That was the year when the tariff began to assume proportions as a national issue. Being a dealer in coal and iron and steel ships, Hanna made a discovery. Heretofore business had been business, and politics politics; the hypothesis that business and politics were allied was a theory in the nebular state, floating around in classrooms and debating societies. Hanna congealed the theory into cold, hard fact. The business man in politics was Hanna's American invention. During the seventies he trudged under a political torch. But in 1880 he put a plug hat under the old leaky can of the flambeau, and the oil that leaked from the can lubricated his mind. For he ground up one startling fact of politics rapidly: that money makes the mare go. He had begun at the ward caucus, even in the late sixties, and for ten years was a factor in his ward and in his county and in his state; but he carried politics as a side line; a matter of no more importance than his religion. Having acquired a bank, he bought a Cleveland daily newspaper and annexed politics as a branch of his business.

Hanna was always Hanna. In politics he used the technique which had made him successful in iron, in banks, in railroads, as a patron of the arts. He was direct,

forceful, self-reliant, unbound by conventions. He acted
upon hunches quickly, sometimes with terrific energy.
Observe his first maneuver in national politics. James A.
Garfield was nominated by the Republicans. General U.
S. Grant had been defeated after a long deadlock in the
national convention. His friends were sulking. Grant's
leader was Roscoe Conkling, his lieutenant, John A.
Logan—both temperamental; both vain, and Conkling
hungry for vengeance. They came to Ohio perhaps on an
alibi-ing excursion, merely to show that they were supporting Garfield and the Republican ticket. They did not
go to Mentor, where Garfield lived, but put on a great
parade at Warren, Ohio; a grand, hollow, harmony
parade. Grant came. Conkling came. Simon Cameron,
of Pennsylvania, came. General John A. Logan came
from Illinois. They came in a special train. Hanna had
charge of transportation. Without consulting any one,
Hanna arranged that the train should return East from
Warren by way of Mentor. Hanna, a neophyte among
the great, was not invited to the luncheon given by Senator Perkins, of Ohio, at his home in Warren, for the
Olympian gods of the party. Hat in hand, however,
Hanna called, was shown into the dining room where the
luncheon was in progress. Hanna knew his crowd.
Grant was generous, Conkling imperious, Cameron cunning, Logan proud. Hanna picked Grant and said, without batting an eye, looking the general squarely in the
face:

"General, it has been arranged that we return to Cleveland by way of Mentor, and if you propose to stop and
see General Garfield we shall have to start quickly."

The party about the luncheon table gasped. They had

come to Ohio to save their faces, not to surrender to Garfield. The question was up to Grant, the titular leader. Conkling, the real leader, clouded up, proud as Jupiter. Grant, seeing the danger and sizing up young Hanna, replied almost on the instant in his quiet, firm, soft voice:

"We'll go to Mentor."

So the train stopped at General Garfield's town and Conkling, the imperious, Cameron, the cunning, Logan, the proud, passed in review before the new leader of the party and Garfield won the election. Hanna always told that story with chuckling glee, working his long loose Irish upper lip convulsively to strangle the grin of joy with which he recalled the episode.

In his middle forties politics became as important in Hanna's life as shipbuilding, or street railways. Hanna had a dozen sides. But in 1880 he learned definitely that politics, properly controlled, prospered every business that he touched. So he set out to make a brand of politics as profitable as his mines, his ships, his railways, and his banks. In 1884 Hanna had learned the business of politics well enough to go into the national market with his own product. In the convention that nominated James G. Blaine, Hanna appeared as John Sherman's political manager.

To understand Hanna it may be well to identify John Sherman. Sherman, a brother of the general of that name, entered Congress in '55. In '61 he was a senator whose chief activity during the war—as Chairman of the Finance Committee in the Senate, was to guide the financial operations of the nation. He advocated the issue of legal tender currency—fiat money—during the war

and secured the passage of a bill to establish the National
Banking System.　It was charged that he paid the soldiers in paper, and a few years after the war he was
responsible for the Refunding Act which his enemies
charged, insured the payment to the bondholders in gold.
This latter financial operation was known as "the crime of
'73," and Sherman was cartooned by the Grangers,
Greenbackers, and restless cults of the day as the arch-
plutocrat of his time.　In '77, Sherman became Secretary
of the Treasury under Hayes, and two years later kept
the Government's promise to resume specie payments,
thus putting the country definitely upon a gold basis.
Sherman was the Gold-bug of the devil myth in that day.
In '81, he returned to the Senate, where he remained until
1897, when we shall see him again in this story.　But it
was in '84 that Mark Hanna picked the arch-plutocrat of
his day as Hanna's candidate for President.

He was to Sherman then what in 1896 he was to
McKinley.　When Sherman lost, Hanna went on the
Advisory Council of the National Committee.　He learned
how the machinery of national politics runs; what its fly-
wheels do; what its pulleys move; where to oil it; and
where the power is generated.　In the pre-Convention
campaign of '84, in which Blaine defeated Sherman for
the presidential nomination, Hanna began working with
Major William McKinley, a congressman from the
Mahoning Valley industrial district, who was a member
of the Ways and Means Committee of the National
House of Representatives.　In the Convention which
rejected Sherman and nominated Blaine, Major McKinley
was the Chairman of the Committee on Resolutions and,
probably more than any one else, guided the draft of the

platform. Hanna, the business man, had enough influence in the convention to attend to that little detail. He was beginning to be an insider in the game. Hanna helped to handle the campaign fund in '84, helped to collect it, helped to disburse it. And four years later, in '88, Hanna became one of the auxiliary committee of the Republican National Committee, whose specific duty it was to solicit campaign funds. He walked up and down the industrial world of America, among the tariff beneficiaries rather than among the bankers, and collected his funds with no nonsense in his attitude. More money was raised in that campaign than in any previous campaign. So much that after the election Hanna returned to the donors their share of the surplus. Hanna knew where it came from and what it was expected to buy. He was a delegate in the national convention; there he had supported rather casually the presidential ambitions of Major McKinley, whose candidacy suddenly developed surprising strength. General Benjamin Harrison was nominated for the Presidency, but McKinley came out of the Convention a power of the first magnitude. And with him emerged Mark Hanna, twice defeated as king-maker, but none the less a powerful figure in American politics.

Hanna's insatiable curiosity, that had made him master of other trades, made him adept in what is known as practical politics. Without knowing where his greed for facts was leading him, Hanna became an amateur political scientist. He knew none of the rules of the game as the books laid them down; the theories of scholars were unfathomed in his reckonings. But, as the Yankees say, he "sensed a scheme" of the relations of things in the worlds of business and politics, and unconsciously this scheme took possession of him. His scheme was simplicity incarnate: High tariffs keep foreign goods made by cheap labor out of American markets. Politics controls Congress, and Congress makes high tariffs. Money influences politics. Those who benefit by high tariffs should contribute the money which influences elections and controls politics!

Now, a man whose business leads him to the daily contemplation of men working in their undershirts is not going to sit down and dream up an economic system for a world full of men in Nile-green neckties and lavender trousers. The spectacle of human perspiration was never so entirely shocking to a man of Hanna's habits and antecedents that any plan of his would eliminate it from human existence. So Hanna's idea was not particularly Utopian. He was not tinkering at the abolition of poverty, for instance. His was simply a device to provide for more work, more sweat, more business, more dividends. And that wasn't the least of Hanna's discoveries. Quite incidentally, and more or less casually, Hanna saw that in the administration of President Cleveland, the currency crankshaft of the National Works was crooked and shaky, and needed straightening; that it was wobbly because it was crooked and was crooked because it was wobbly. It did not occur to Hanna to bother with the crankshaft. He was busy generating power.

In the seventies, eighties, and nineties, Hanna's friendship for William McKinley had been growing. This friendship grew as most friendships grow: by reason of propinquity, which came from common political interests. Friendship was a master passion with Hanna. He was deeply emotional, being Scotch-Irish. He grappled his friendship for William McKinley to him as he grappled his business ambition—with all his heart and mind. But it was not a platonic attachment. Each needed the other. Hanna was impulsive; McKinley was a man of measured emotion. But neither was a fool. This friendship became as much a part of Hanna as the mines and the ships and the steel things that he loved. McKinley satisfied something in Hanna. The men were complimentary opposites. The Canton lawyer was industrious. He was decent. He was reliable. He was ambitious but self-contained; a bit too unemotional, too far-seeing for a really satisfying friendship. But Hanna's friendship displayed McKinley's more pleasing virtues in the market of public esteem, and held them there at their par value. In 1896 Hanna's energy incorporated McKinley, and every business house in the United States, from Wall Street to the carpenter's shop on the alley, subscribed for McKinley stock. Hanna promoted the presidential candidacy of McKinley before the Republican National Convention at St. Louis. He put into the campaign, which ended in the National Republican Convention at St. Louis, every trained political faculty that had made him a successful captain of business! The outcome was interesting.

American politicians—generally a slipshod lot—who depend much on brass bands, claquing, flag waving, oratory, and beating of tom-toms in politics to swarm their bees, were astounded to see a campaigner use the exact, businesslike methods of the general manager of a railroad. Every other Republican presidential candidate in 1896 sent out letters by the bushel. Hanna sent McKinley's letters out by the peck. But he picked his corre-

spondents with the care with which he picked the officers
for his lake ships.   It was Hanna's purpose to give the
preferred stock in the McKinley syndicate only to men of
commercial honor, business standing, and political capacity.   The whisperer, the Janus-face, the blowhard, and
the promiser—and how that lot throve in those good old
days!—were permitted to speculate if they chose, but
only upon the general-prosperity issue of the series.

The Republican National Convention at St. Louis in
1896 was the meeting of a large board of directors in
a business concern.   Emotionalism, despite the factitious
claque and clamor, was as remote from the constitution of
that body as a skyrocket from a table of statistics.
Hanna had planned the syndicate.   He had promoted it.
He had made it go.   He didn't know exactly who would
make the motions, nor who would write up the minutes,
nor what phrasing would be used in the prospectus.   But
he knew the men in the majority, and he knew that they
were there to vote for McKinley.   He knew that they
were men who ordinarily accomplish their ends.   It was
an old story to Hanna—the picking and handling of men.
There were at that hour, in June, 1896, eight thousand
men on his pay roll at Cleveland—on the docks, and in
the mines, and at furnaces, and at desks, and on street
cars.   There were one-tenth as many delegates at St.
Louis; and besides, the St. Louis convention was a co-
operative corporation.   So Hanna didn't worry.   Yet
certain things puzzled him.

CHAPTER XIX

"MINE ANCIENT HUMOR SAVES HIM WHOLE"

DESPITE the fact that reporters and editors of what might have been called, with professional courtesy, the loathed but esteemed contemporaries, said unpleasant things about McKinley and the Hanna promotion scheme, in double-leaded types and short paragraphs; and even though the reporters and editors claimed that the convention was sewed up in a sack; and more, that it was branded, gagged, and delivered; and, still further, that it was the personal property, chattel, and common appurtenance of Mark Hanna and of his heirs and assigns forever—still, affairs did take a turn that would have astounded Hanna if he had claimed property right in the delegates. Hanna had gone into the battle for McKinley's nomination with a seven-devil lust for tariffs. The currency question was one of those things dreamed of in Hanna's philosophy, along with the Civil Service and the Alaskan boundary and Cuban independence. Hanna had never opposed the gold standard; but, while he was struggling for the nomination of McKinley, Hanna seems to have believed that by taking thought of the currency question he could not add one cubit to McKinley's stature. Moreover, McKinley had a bad record on the currency question—from a gold-standard viewpoint. So Hanna sat in his office in Cleveland and listened to the saurian snort of his barge whistles, and fixed his faith in ad valorems and tariffs and other accouterments of his campaign.

As the spring of 1896 opened, the earnestness of the New England Republicans for a gold-standard declaration amazed Hanna. He went to the St. Louis convention with that amazement unabated. He was not angry. But to him it was as though all the men on the Cleveland City Railway had decided to paint their left ears green, something which they had a perfect right to do, but which did not add to the speed of the cars nor the service of the line. He did not fear the growth of the gold-standard sentiment—so far as McKinley's candidacy was concerned. But it did not occur to Hanna, when he went to St. Louis to complete the task before him, that the adoption of the gold-standard declaration in the Republican platform would relegate the tariff question to a place in the campaign beside pensions and the interstate commerce. And so because the men he trusted—and needed, chiefly the New England contingent—favored a declaration for gold, Hanna accepted it. His friends were his friends. They wanted to declare for gold. Hanna loved them. He did nothing by halves; he thereafter accepted the gold-standard plank. Its ways were his ways, its people were his people, and its enemies provoked his wrath.

But even before the Republican National Convention assembled at St. Louis in June, the Western Republican delegates began to issue dire threats setting forth what they would do if the Eastern Republicans insisted upon a Republican declaration for the gold standard. The Republican party had gone without a party bolt since 1872, when the Horace Greeley defection—a flash in the pan—seemed to threaten Grant's second election. This

TRYING IT ON.
HANNA AND PLATT. — Vell, vell, vell, vat a magnificent fit!

TRYING IT ON.
Hanna and Platt: "Vell, vell, vell, vat a magnificent fit!"

threat of the Westerners to bolt gave dramatic zest to the whole convention. Hanna realized that it did not seriously affect McKinley's nomination, whatever it might do to the election. Surely he did not foresee that the fiat-money champions would capture the Democratic convention the following month, nor dream what a turmoil the silver Republicans and the fiat-money Populists would make in the land from July to November. Drama was in the air. Hanna was a business man who overlooked the component parts of his new trade of politics—emotion moving human machinery into a dramatic progression. Hanna was one of the few men in the Republican convention of 1896 who did not realize the dynamics of tragedy that charged the atmosphere there. Senator Teller, of Colorado, one of the founders of the Republican party, was leading the whole region west of the Mississippi out of the party to which he had given a lifetime of devotion.

When the Republican platform had been reported by the Committee on Resolutions, and the clause endorsing the gold standard had been read, Senator Teller, advocating the free and unlimited coinage of silver at the ratio of sixteen to one, made a speech favoring the adoption of a minority report of the Resolutions Committee, which report eliminated the gold-standard declaration. While Teller spoke, a pudgy man, broad-shouldered and of robust girth, sat fidgeting in his narrow chair among the Ohio delegates, but one row removed from the aisle. He was Mark Hanna.*

* I was a reporter in the convention. I wanted to see how Hanna would take the bolt of the free silver men which the reporters knew was coming. I went to the floor of the convention and slipped into a seat left vacant by a North Carolina negro delegate, directly in front of the Ohio delegation, one chair to the front and one chair to the left of Hanna. The above account of the bolt is from my report written that hour.

The loose muscles about Hanna's mouth twitched irritably as Teller's silver swan-song rose and fell. Occasionally Hanna lifted a broad hand to a large, bumpy cranium, as if to scratch. Instead, he rubbed the rich, healthy, terra-cotta hide on his full, firm neck. His bright brown eyes took the orator's mental and moral measure with merciless precision. But with the rise of passion in Teller's oratory Hanna's expression changed from a mobile smile to a vicious iron glare. When Teller sat down sobbing, Hanna grunted his relief; but he was nervous. He kept rubbing his jaw. His long upper lip twitched from side to side. The muscles under his eyes quivered. Others spoke in favor of the Teller resolution —perhaps an Idaho man, maybe a Montanan, from a chair behind the Ohio delegation. Then a dapper young chap, with a boutonnière on his perfectly fitting frock coat, came chasséing down the aisle, and received Chairman Thurston's recognition. "Who's that?" asked Hanna of Congressman Grosvenor of Ohio.

"Cannon."

"Who's Cannon?"

Mind you, it was Mark Hanna who was asking these questions—Hanna, who was popularly supposed to be omniscient and omnipotent at St. Louis that day. Yet here was a United States senator whom Hanna did not know; Hanna, who really held the convention in the hollow of his hand.

"How did he break in?" growled Hanna.

"Senator—Utah," replied Congressman Grosvenor of Ohio.

The Westernor opened his mouth to read his address.

"Well, for heaven's sake, goin' to read it! Lookee

there—" And Hanna's broad, fat head waved toward the orator. "Perty, ain't he?" Hanna's eyes slitted. He sneered: "Looks like a cigar drummer!"

The orator soon abandoned his manuscript. Hanna showed a wise serpentine tongue between his thin lips and snapped:

"So that's Cannon!"

And after appraising the dapper young man, Hanna jeered to Governor Bushnell beside him: "Why, it's a regular stump speech. Listen there!"

The man on the rostrum continued. He made an acrid reference to the gold standard. A small-boned, fat leg flopped across its mate, and Hanna changed his weight from one hunker to the other.

"They ought to admit a lot more of those little sand patches and coyote ranges out West as States. We need 'em!" said Hanna by way of sarcastic persiflage to Grosvenor.

Cannon's remarks were growing more and more luminous. As the orator proceeded, Hanna's brown eyes, which had been twinkling merrily at his own humor, began to glow in heat lightning. His twitching mouth clicked two or three times as if to cut off the tail of a truant smile, then spilled its rage in grunting imprecations. The rhetoric of the Utah man was telling. He referred to the Republican party as the party of oppression, and began to threaten to leave the party. Then Hanna's harsh voice blurted out across the multitude:

"Go, go!" He stopped, then renewed his courage and lowered his voice. "It's an insult. It oughtn't to go in the proceedings of the convention," grumbled Hanna.

Grosvenor swore a couple of bars. Bushnell carried

the bass. Finally Cannon, shaking a flamboyant head of hair, put the threat to bolt in a rococo period of rhetoric, declaring that the Republican party had seceded from the truth. Hanna, uncoupling his short, fat legs from behind his chair, stretched out in nervous wrath. A steel sneer wired its way across his face as he groaned in a flat, harsh snarl:

"Oh, my God!"

There was a tragic half second's silence. Ten thousand eyes turned toward Hanna. Evidently he could feel their glances hailing on his back, for his flinty auburn head bobbed down like a cork. He was still the business man in 1896, and this blab was unbusinesslike. It was political. Hanna, the ironmaster, ducked. The orator on the rostrum had used the phrase: "The parting of the ways," famous through the whole campaign to follow. It was Hanna's voice that cried out: "Good-by," an instant later. The whole convention was firing "go's" at the rostrum. Then Hanna, the politician, rose proudly from the small of his back, and got on the firing line. After that the Utah man was in the hands of a mob. Hanna devoted himself to the pleasurable excitements of the chase. He stormed and roared with the mob; he guyed and he cheered with the mob. He was of it, led by it, enjoying it, whooping it up. Then, when it was all over, when an hour or so later the gold-standard platform had been adopted, Hanna climbed into his chair, clasped his hands composedly behind him, threw back his head, let out his voice, and sang "America" with the throng. Where he did not remember the words, his dah-dah-de-dah-de-dums rang out with patriotic felicity, and his smile of seraphic satisfaction was a good sight for sore eyes. For Mark Hanna was giving an excellent repre-sentation of a joyous American citizen, with his wagon hitched to a bucking but conquered star, jogging peace-fully down the Milky Way of victory.

By this token may the reader know that Hanna was intensely human. There was nothing god-like, nothing demoniac, nothing cherubic, nothing serpentine about him. The dollar mark, which the cartoonists put on his clothes a few weeks later, belied Mark Hanna, the man. They only represented Hanna the politician, possibly the states-man. For he was frankly a plutocrat in his creed. He was a plain man, who stood in the last ditch with his friends and fought his enemies to the death. As a man, he enjoyed a good joke, a good fellow, or a good dinner; and liked all three served, if possible, at the same table. Often in his political life he won brilliantly, sometimes lost conspicuously; made a fool of himself occasionally, laughed at it good-naturedly, and did it over again. He wore on his bones the clay of the inexplicable old Adam— rich in weakness and strength, graces and foibles. Withal, he had the philosophy which sustained the shepherd of Arden. But his strength was more than his weakness, for he had the virility of common sense. He was never happy crocheting tidies and adopting ringing resolutions. He was a man of deeds rather than of explanations— yet sentimental as a girl.

Hanna had a cash-register conscience; he was never a man of attenuated ideals. Between his purpose and its execution the path lay in a straight line. If gentlemen in spectacles crept into his life, stretching across his path strings of ethical obstacles and planting in his way the potsherds of certain moral scruples, Hanna pushed for-

ward, kicking away the strings and crushing the pottery
under his feet.   Later, if he had time, he devoted a few
lurid minutes to the spectacled gentry before he closed the
incident with a bang and went about his business.   In
politics Hanna was a partisan.   He was perfectly willing
to admit that certain theories of government were beautiful, perhaps even logical; but he insisted on his American
privilege of voting for the majority report.   With him
the mugwump was entitled to the same consideration
that was due to the guerilla in time of war.

Yet through all the pomp and circumstance which
trailed behind him in his day of glory, Hanna kept his
head.   His sense of humor saved him whole.   After the
election in 1896 that made McKinley President, Hanna
was a political star of the first magnitude, a power poten-
tially greater than the President.   His friends and
admirers arranged a Feast of Belshazzar for him; also
many parades.   Coming home to Cleveland after one of
these orgies, Hanna—like a Roman emperor—riding
before the procession in his triumph—saw an old and
modest friend on the sidewalk.   Knowing the doubts and
fears in his friend's heart, Hanna winked, twitched the
nervous muscles of his big Irish mouth, and said in sotto
voice above the blare of the bands as he waved at the
procession and pointed to himself grotesquely:

"Me, me!   Heap big Injun, me!" and chuckled until
his fat torso undulated in merriment.   He could always
laugh at the vanity of man—even when he was the man!

CHAPTER XX

"OR MATCH WITH DESTINY FOR BEERS!"

In his political career, after 1896, Hanna became the acknowledged high priest of a triumphant plutocracy. During the reign of McKinley and later, when that plutocracy was challenged under Roosevelt, Hanna had three clashes with strong men. Two bouts he won. Before the third he fell. These bouts were with Thomas B. Reed, the first czar of the House of Representatives, whom Hanna deposed as Speaker. The second was with Sherman, who resigned as United States senator and went to McKinley's Cabinet to make a senatorial place for Hanna. And the third contest was with Theodore Roosevelt, whose accidental ascension to the Presidency brought Hanna to death grips with the young leader. He was a sick old man when Roosevelt challenged his leadership, and time was Roosevelt's strongest weapon. When Hanna mastered Reed and Sherman he was in the pink of his political power.

Reed was from Maine, a huge six-foot, gelatinous walrus of a man, who brought into a dull and sordid day in our politics a keen mind, a twinkling eye, an iron will, a sense of humor so gorgeous that he scorned his own power certainly, but before that despised the weakness of his adversaries. He had a scholar's erudition. Wise saws and modern instances were always at Reed's

217

command. He was the idol of the House, but he also was tainted with a certain New England mugwumpian independence. He stood four-square—stronger than McKinley ever stood—for the gold standard; but to Reed the tariff was not sacrosanct. He had his moments of doubt about the spoils system and loathed its acolytes. Party regularity was a conventional garment with Reed, but not a high priest's robe. And as he held the strings that moved the House of Representatives, Reed's dictum about legislation had to be considered by Hanna and McKinley. Hanna felt that it was the McKinley administration, and questioned the right of Reed to rule the House. Hanna had followers. The mattter would have come to a clash. Hanna went straight to Reed. The two, behind closed doors, in the presence of a mutual friend, had their differences out. It was Reed's cynical humorous sense of the futility of a dirty game that made him turn from politics, quit the House of Representatives, and go into law in New York. But he took with him a merry loathing of Hanna and his kind.

The struggle against Sherman was a short horse soon curried. Sherman was old. He had nothing but the prestige of his long record behind him. Senility stood around the corner threatening him. When Sherman was a candidate, almost a successful candidate, for the Republican presidential nomination in the seventies and eighties, Hanna had been Sherman's devoted friend; his campaign manager, in fact. Sherman had been the target for the enemies of sound money, and withstood all the beasts at Ephesus for the cause which Hanna had won so gloriously in the campaign of 1896. But Sherman was a weak reliance in the Senate for McKinley. So Hanna put Sher-

man out with a comic little ceremony, promoting him into
the Cabinet, for which he was sadly unfitted, vouchsafing
him only a few well-chosen resolutions of respect. Behind
Sherman was no machine; behind Hanna was the phalanx
of the business man in politics which at the moment was
controlling the Ohio Republican organization.

With these conquests behind him in the closing years
of the old century, Hanna, vigorous, pugnacious, triumphant in his early sixties, unbroken by time, faced the
world of politics happily. He was the militant plutocrat,
howling the joy of his plutocracy unashamed. When the
Spanish-American War threatened in 1898, Hanna tried
to avert it. He felt that the war might endanger the
stability of business. He had no use for the few Wall
Street gamblers who would risk the nation's prosperity
for a chance to bet on disaster. But the war lust in the
hearts of the people, taking the case of the inhuman
reconcentration camps of the island as an excuse to go
on a crusade, rose stronger than the will of the ironmaster, and McKinley was forced reluctantly into the
war. After it was over, Hanna had no qualms about the
loot of battle. Hanna stood for taking the Philippines;
and, under his leadership—in spite of McKinley's pious
contention that it was our "plain duty" to be chivalric in
tariff matters in Porto Rico—Porto Rico was retained
as an American colony.

Hanna walked about the Senate Chamber in those days
with a brisk little trot, whispering to this senator, smiling at that one, putting his arms affectionately upon the
shoulders of another, throwing the fine, warm glow of his
big brown eyes into the countenance of a fourth; a leader,
beloved and respected, but too busy and too effective to

make love and respect an asset, a considerable asset, in his business.

When he went into the United States Senate he kept books on everyone in Congress. He knew the powers at home who sent the congressmen there. He knew every senator's railroad master—if he had one, and generally he had! Hanna knew the string in his district that would pull every Republican House leader. And he worked at the job of politics as he had worked in business. His business tops were spinning and he wound up politics with a skillful hand.

He was incarnate partisanship—a high priest in his temple. Hanna would endorse a political proposition not authorized by his party caucus and his party platform about as readily as a general would take orders from a newspaper. In his party, Hanna had disputes, differences, and contentions; but he knew when he was whipped, and respected a similar knowledge in his adversary. When a fight was over, it was over with Hanna. He bore no malice, carried no knife from the conflict to use another day, and had a scorching contempt for the contentious and—to Hanna—impossible persons who insisted that a question is never settled until it is settled right. From Hanna's point of view the ways of the reformer and of "the serpent on the rock" were beyond understanding.

Hanna's solicitude for the people was as tender as that of the late William H. Vanderbilt, who said: "The people be damned!" Hanna believed in every man for himself and the devil take the hindermost. Little social altruism tinged the simplicity of his creed. To him the failures in life were failures. He did not mince matters, nor go into heredity nor environment in locating the blame for their condition. Yet, working with material problems in a material way for material ends, he was fair according to the lights of his generation. When he went into politics he went with the dollar mark of a money-devil cartooned on his clothes. He was broiled in public scorn as a conscienceless boss; was called a crusher of labor, an industrial octopus, a commercial Moloch. He took his punishment like a gentleman. He truckled to no other ideal than that which made his record. He could have been a demagogue and pretended to subscribe to ideals which he did not hold. But no enemy of Hanna ever added to the gayety of nations by calling Mark Hanna a demagogue. He was a blunt man, too proud of his opinion to simulate others, too pleased with his record to go back on it. If a large, jagged, brown damn was needed in a diplomatic situation, Hanna furnished it. If a laugh was needed, Hanna was never afraid to use it. If an open fight was required, Hanna made it. He was a man of simple instincts and single purposes. His relations with certain of his senatorial colleagues were arranged in their biological development millions of years ago.

Senator Thomas C. Platt, of New York, was one of Hanna's antipathies. Platt was a tip-toer in politics. The fortunes of the Spanish-American War made Theodore Roosevelt Governor of New York. He kept the outward covenants of faith with Senator Platt, who controlled the New York State Republican machine; but Roosevelt violated instinctively the inner spirit of allegiance to Platt. In 1899, as Governor of New York, Roosevelt allowed Platt to save his face by sponsoring the Roosevelt appointments and the Roosevelt policies after Roosevelt had chosen them. Roosevelt's gorgeous taste for rather innocent intrigue matched Platt's insatiable lust for Machiavellian intercourse; but in the struggle between them, Roosevelt was master. Senator Quay, of Pennsylvania, and Platt—blood brothers in indirection—came to some kind of an understanding, in the Republican National Convention at Philadelphia in 1900, by which Quay agreed to help Platt get rid of Governor Roosevelt by making him the Republican candidate for Vice-President, in spite of Hanna's protest and in the face of Roosevelt's determination to continue for another term as Governor of New York. It was a part of the slimy conspiracy that the two old sheep-killing dogs, hunting together, took a circuitous route to their object. In their own way they found in the West noisy delegates who were amenable to the kind of influence that Quay and Platt used so effectively. The noisy Westerners clamored through the Republican convention, fooled Roosevelt, who was easily susceptible to any Western demonstration, and, what with the New England delegates, who never cared deeply for Hanna—and the New York and Pennsylvania delegations, the Westerners were able to take the convention out of Hanna's control and nominate Roosevelt. Whereupon Hanna was full of wrath. It was vocal. He regarded Roosevelt as a wild ass of the desert.

Hanna would have made a most dignified campaign in 1900. It was McKinley's second campaign. The McKinley campaign of 1896 was not a pleasant memory. Ugly and probably unjust accusations were made against Hanna's conduct of the '96 campaign, and he would have his canvass in 1900 eminently respectable; a silk-hat campaign, appealing to the lofty ideals of America in justifying the retention of Porto Rico, and the Philippines, and the American sovereignty over Cuba. But Roosevelt burst into that campaign, his first national appearance, with all the flare of a skyrocket, with the incessant clatter of a riveter; and with a new, gorgeous vocabulary of erudite vituperation, Roosevelt challenged an acclaim which eclipsed Hanna's presidential candidate for the hour and elbowed Hanna off the stage as the savior of the nation. Hanna loved McKinley sincerely, deeply, as a strong brother loves a weaker one. Perhaps subconsciously Hanna was jealous of Roosevelt, the pirouetting young dervish of a Teddy who took the spotlight in the drama of the hour.

If Hanna had realized that Roosevelt was the voice of a new spirit, that he was not mere commotion but the incarnation of a movement which would overturn much that Hanna had lived for, Hanna would have been implacable in his hate. As it was, he was only irritated and confused. But this is Hanna's story.

Hanna's conscience, which was affronted by the devices of Quay and Platt, was the conventional conscience of commerce. Wrong was wrong and right was right, in Hanna's clicking cash register. Everything came out of it either black or white; he was color-blind to the mauves and grays and electric blues of political conduct. If a man lied, he lied; if he stole he was a thief; if he cheated, the man was a liar and a thief; and that was the end of him with Mark Hanna. Quay and Platt, who for their own ends suborned political chicane, and Roosevelt, who was big enough to tolerate it for a cause, Hanna could neither understand nor well endure. Hanna liked a man with good red blood and a strenuous spirit and common sense; as for the other sort, they were all one to him— the sort that "might be made after supper of a cheese-paring," and he would have none of the breed.

CHAPTER XXI

HANNA was really always an outsider in politics, though he wore the high priest's robe, though he functioned among the temple Pharisees, he was of another dispensation—the dispensation of business. He ruled in politics for five years, but he was never of the dynasty of politics, as Quay and Platt were, or as Tweed was, or as —many years later—Senator Boise Penrose was. Hanna was an extra-constitutional power for five years, but not a national boss. No man with a twinkle in his eyes and a smile always teetering on the threshold of his countenance could view with composure the deadly hunger for "a little brief authority" which often moved men to sell their souls for it. This power-hunger is the mainspring that makes the boss a joss. In politics, he who laughs at the visceral convolutions of the joss is lost. Hanna had to laugh at these things, and when he could not laugh, he swore—which brought relief to his soul!

Yet in national politics Hanna was unlike Pontius Pilate, but like Herod. Hanna was a force, not an intrigue.

The election of McKinley in 1896 and his reëlection in 1900 exalted Hanna's power in America to a degree which few men have enjoyed outside of the presidential office. Inside the White House McKinley dominated Hanna, but outside the White House Hanna had a reputation as a king-maker. He liked it. In the Senate he really was vicegerent of McKinley, as also in Wall Street. In the Republican national organization he was a first-class power in his own right. He had half a dozen desks where he did half a dozen things, different things, splendidly. Fawning men disgusted him, but they must have given him a lively sense of his power. His power was for the most part outside his personal relation with the President; but somewhat Hanna held his power because his power outside the White House was not challenged inside the White House. Then, at the height of his triumph, suddenly came the madman's bullet that killed McKinley. And when McKinley died, Roosevelt, twenty years younger than Hanna, came to the White House; Roosevelt, whom Hanna had publicly declared was not McKinley's choice for the Vice-Presidency; Roosevelt, whom Hanna had tolerated with polite derision during the presidential campaign a year before. The men had many different ideals, but they had several common traits. Candor, courage, industry, loyalty were their common virtues. Hanna lost more than an ally when McKinley died; even more than a friend. He lost the aim and ambition of his life. McKinley's death was not a political event to Hanna. It was a personal calamity. Hanna received the blow with McKinley. The two went down together.

So Hanna's third contest was his last. The end of Hanna's career was tragedy, but he walked on the stage set for tragedy like a soldier and a gentleman. He had conquered old men when he deposed Reed and put Sherman on the shelf. But Roosevelt was young. Moreover, Roosevelt had most of Hanna's good qualities plus an energy that more than matched Hanna's even when Hanna was young. In addition to their common qualities

Roosevelt had what Hanna lacked—moral intelligence,
and a sense of the economic situation in America and in
the world. Roosevelt's sense of economic conditions
brought him to a living realization of the injustices of the
prevailing political and economic systems. Roosevelt knew
what the House of Hanna stood for; knew even better
than Hanna. All over the land, following the Civil War,
there assembled vast aggregations of wealth—capital
slowly combining to control the major industries of the
land. These industries manufactured and sold the com-
modities necessary to American life: oil, lumber, coal,
iron, steel, transportation, communication, cotton, wool,
copper, cement. These large aggregates of capitalized
wealth were militant in their attitude of aggrandizement
toward the government which would regulate them.
Hanna's political efforts in their behalf were only incidentally corrupt; corrupt where he felt corruption a necessary weapon; for Hanna was the best of the plutocrats.
Others, not so deeply and decently connected with politics,
would have been more corrupt, more demoralizing to
public life and public morals than Hanna. The menace
of the day was plutocratic control of government through
political corruption. At the moment Hanna stood as
the champion of an order which
to Roosevelt seemed to menace
his ideal of America. So Roosevelt snapped his eyes and clicked
his teeth and set out first of all
to overthrow Hanna and his
hierarchy.

After Roosevelt was elected
Vice-President it was odd to

see Roosevelt and Hanna bowing and scraping to each other; Roosevelt deferring to Hanna where he could, opposing him frankly, almost brutally, where he must and apologizing afterwards like a gentleman, maintaining the outward forms of gallantry. Probably each held deeply the inner form of admiration and respect for one another.

His first four years in the Senate broke Hanna's body. By 1901 he seemed to be ten years older than he was in 1896. The ruddy terra-cotta skin that glowed with health in 1896 had faded to an ashen pink. The mobile smile that was a conversation without words was hardening a little—but only a little. The lower parts of his legs were slightly uncertain, and his feet almost shuffled. The large, firm hand gripped his heavy cane with something like nervousness. The thin hair hung listlessly to the head; but the jaws were wired with steel, even then; and always. The brown eyes, Hanna's harbor lights, twinkled with the fervor of a schoolboy's.

After McKinley's funeral, when Roosevelt was inaugurated, Hanna did a characteristic thing. He went to Washington, greeted the young President, and sat down before him like a father. Roosevelt has told the story of that meeting many times. He declared that Hanna spoke at once, out of his sorrow, and told the new President frankly just how far Hanna could go with Roosevelt. He kept his word to the letter. He supported the Roosevelt policies where he could, cordially, generously. He had not promised to support Roosevelt for President. He may have hoped, probably was definitely ambitious, to be nominated for President himself in 1904. A group was organized inside the Republican Committee to gather up Southern delegates for Hanna, and to pick up dele-

gates in certain Eastern states dominated by New York
and the commercial interests of lower Broadway. But
through it all, Hanna played fair with the young President. It must be remembered that Roosevelt differed
profoundly with Hanna about the conduct of the administration, about the relation of business to government.
Roosevelt was the first Republican leader of a new cult—
the liberalism of the young century. Hanna was the best
of the old. Hanna believed that government existed to
protect, encourage, and fortify business. Roosevelt believed that government existed as an agency of human
welfare to promote justice between the citizens, and that
commerce was but one of many necessary functions of civilization, not so important as education, not so dear as
liberty. Roosevelt from the first, although formally following the McKinley policies, proclaimed his own doctrines, preached his own creed—and Hanna knew what it
meant. Nevertheless, Hanna admired courage and forthright dealing. He never broke with Roosevelt. There
grew up, in the two years and a half of their association
in Washington, one of those shy, fine friendships between
men of different generations.

In spite of this friendship the fight between the old
order and its challenger was a fight to the death. Roosevelt had been a year and a half in the White House when
the fight climaxed. He was carrying out the McKinley
policies, but denouncing the fundamental principles which
would have made those policies instruments of what he
called "aggrandized capital." His popularity was widening and deepening. Populism had submerged and was
reappearing in Republican insurgency. The West, which
by reason of discriminatory freight rates in the Missis-

sippi basin, had been the seat of unrest since 1870, rallied
to the Roosevelt standard almost instantly. Populism
shaved its whiskers, washed its shirt, put on a derby and
moved up into the middle of the class—the upper middle
class—and followed Roosevelt circumspectly, but with an
enthusiasm which revealed the Populist blood. Before
the National Republican Convention of 1904 it was
presumed that Hanna and Roosevelt would fight a battle
royal. The first skirmish came before the Ohio Republican State Convention early in 1903. Hanna went out to
Cleveland to stop the Roosevelt forces in the convention.
A resolution was proposed which would have endorsed
the Roosevelt administration. And two days before the
convention it was known that the resolution was ready.
The nation's political eyes were focused on Ohio.
Hanna's machine wheeled into position. An endorsement
of Roosevelt meant the death-knell of Hanna's political
hopes. Hanna's factional enemies—the Foraker crowd,
which afterwards became the Ohio gang—helped Roosevelt. But Hanna was not defeated in a factional fight.
All the world wondered what Roosevelt would do when
the Hanna batteries were deployed upon his works. He
sent a telegram to Ohio, and gave out the telegram when
he sent it, asking Ohio Republicans to endorse his administration by passing the resolution. Roosevelt's friends
controlled the convention. When Hanna realized this by
a count of noses he withdrew his opposition. The
young bull had horned the old bull out of the herd.

It was like Roosevelt to write Hanna a letter regretting
that Roosevelt had ruthlessly gone into Hanna's state
and humiliated him. It was like Hanna to know why
Roosevelt had done it and to accept the fortunes of war.

A few weeks later, in his home in Washington, Hanna lay on his deathbed. President Roosevelt called during the morning of February 5 to inquire for Hanna's health. When Hanna knew it, though he could not see the President, he scrawled a note to the young man which reveals deeply the chivalric qualities that always ruled in Hanna's heart. He wrote:

> My dear Mr. President:
> You touched a tender spot, old man, when you called personally to inquire after me this A.M. I may be worse before I can be better, but all the same such drops of kindness are good for a fellow.
> Sincerely yours,
> MARK HANNA.

The next day President Roosevelt sent a note to Hanna, a note from his own heart, equally fine. It read:

> Dear Senator:
> Indeed it is your letter from your sick bed which is touching, not my visit. May you soon be with us again, old fellow, as strong in body and as vigorous in your leadership as ever.
> Faithfully yours,
> THEODORE ROOSEVELT.

Hanna never rallied to the point where he could read the letter. He died February 15, of typhoid fever. Not long before his death Mrs. Hanna, the wife of his youth, was sitting with him. He reached for her hand, and after a long time said:

"Old lady, you and I are on the home stretch. It was a gallant race."

When Roosevelt walked behind Hanna's bier, he went in real sorrow for a brave and kindly man. It was the new generation burying the old. With Hanna power passed finally from the hands of those who had come through the Civil War, whose lives reached back to another age and era in American life. Roosevelt was to represent that interregnum of two decades in which civilization, shifting its conscience, adjusting its morality, recreating its ideals of righteousness, was to pass in the United States definitely from a simple rural civilization to a complex industrial order. Hanna's life was the last pier of the old bridge upon which men crossed out of the old order and approached the new.

BRYAN

CHAPTER XXII

THE BOY ORATOR OF THE PLATTE

WILLIAM JENNINGS BRYAN was a dramatic and powerful figure in American politics from 1896, when he became the Democratic presidential candidate, until 1925, when he died. His place in history will be comparable to that of Blaine or Clay; each led America for a generation. Both Clay and Blaine, striving for the Presidency, dramatized important causes. Bryan, in seeking the high office, often had the smoke of revolution in his garments; a revolution which he led for a time but never entirely understood. It is a long span of years from the nomination of Samuel J. Tilden, which Bryan saw as a lad in his teens, to the administration of Calvin Coolidge, yet Bryan linked the two epochs. When he entered Congress McKinley was just setting out to run for President; Roosevelt was an unknown young silk-stocking in the Civil Service Commission. Taft, scarcely more than Big Bill, the football gladiator of Yale. Harding was a country printer. Wilson was an unknown schoolmaster teaching political science to the boys in Princeton. McKinley, Roosevelt, Taft, Wilson, Harding—all rose to power and left their names in history, while Bryan did chores around the Hall of Fame, hoping for a niche there. His only important place in the national government was as Secretary of State, where he was accounted a failure by those who keep books with material counters. Yet he knew the office well. He had known, officially, every Secretary of State from Bayard to Kellogg—a succession of forty years.

Leaders like Clay and Blaine and Bryan, who come and go during the generations, are of a higher grade generally and are worth more to their country than the common run of Presidents. In sixty years America has had but two Presidents who could get votes for causes as well as for themselves outside the White House— Cleveland and Roosevelt; one might add Wilson, if he had lived. To lead a movement requires a man of real capacity, some element of greatness in him. Bryan had the plus qualities which gave him distinction, yet he was, like all great men, at bottom a common man but not a common leader. With all his force, and it was tremendous at certain crises of his career, he was static; the same man when he left the stage in 1925, as when he entered it in 1896. The habits of his youth were not changed by environment, by the assimilation of knowledge, by the gift of higher, finer wisdom through all his days.

We may best know that by looking at him in youth; for there he foreshadowed clearly, with sharp lines, the man that was to be. Let us take him as he was in his twenties, in the late seventies; a tall youth in a small freshwater college in Illinois. His father was district judge, a man of importance in his community, who ran for Congress and was defeated. The Bryans lived on the outskirts of a little town. There was Irish in them. Back in the eyes of William Jennings Bryan the twinkling orbs of some ancestor of the old sod often peeked out timidly. Bryan's figure was all Irish. His loose hanging arms were Irish. His sturdy, well-pegged legs were Irish. And there was an Irish grandsire—who probably used to smoke a clay pipe—who liked to come back and rest his bones, that have been under the "ould sod" these hundreds of years, by sitting on the small of his grandson's back to view the world from across his grandson's elevated knees. Doubtless, if the scion could have brought himself to "take a little something to take"—even catnip tea—at such times, the Irish ancestor would have come out of the past to give the young man a philosophy that could smile with the world at man's weaknesses and shortcomings. But—alas!—Bryan was handicapped to the end of his days by an overweening sense of his sobriety, one of his minor virtues. He was one of those men who neither smoked, drank, chewed, nor swore—and his pride of abstinence plagued him like a secret sin! So the "ould one" from the green isle kept his place and listened while his offspring sighed at the misery, wickedness, and woe of this melancholy world. And it was really too bad to suppress the "ould one." He might have made Bryan President.

The youth in the Illinois college, from the day of his matriculation until he was graduated with the class of 1880, was an orator—a college debater and an orator. In Bryan's book, "The First Battle," published in 1897, his wife wrote a short biography of him. She tells how he did odd jobs on his father's farm, how he hunted rabbits, how he joined the church and decided—as many boys decide at some stage of their lives—to become a preacher, but compromised on the bar; how he went to

school, and how he "developed an interest in the work of
literary and debating societies." This debating society
business was young Bryan's ruling passion; his wife puts
it happily thus:

A prize always fired Will's ambition. During his first year
in the Preparatory Department of Illinois College he declaimed
Patrick Henry's masterpiece and ranked well down the list.
Nothing daunted, the next year found him declaiming "The
Palmetto and the Pine." The next year, a freshman in college,
he tried for a prize in Latin prose and won half the second prize.
Later in the year he declaimed "Bernardo del Carpio," and gained
the second prize. In his sophomore year he entered another contest with an essay on "Labor"; this time the first prize rewarded
his work. An oration on "Individual Powers" gave him a place
in the intercollegiate contest, held at Galesburg, where he ranked
second.

For his second prize, which consisted of ten dollars'
worth of books, he selected an Oxford Bible with a con-
cordance, and a volume of Shakespeare. He would have
made that his choice on the day of his death.

Of all the members of his college faculty, Bryan in
his memoirs written at the close of his career and published after his death gives us a picture of only one man
—"a large man with a strong face and a piercing eye"—
his teacher of dramatics and elocution, who "preferred the
oratorical style," and who complimented young Bryan by
saying that he "declaimed oratorical pieces so well" that
the instructor could not be of much assistance to him. Still
he trained Bryan "in modulation of voice and gesticula-
tion," and Bryan writes naïvely that his use of the professor's advice "has been unconscious rather than inten-
tional." In his junior year he seems to have attended
a state oratorical contest at Jacksonville, Illinois. Here

Bryan raised his Ebenezer, for he writes: "From that day this vision was before me, and my work as a declaimer, as an essayist, and in the delivering of orations" was patterned to this end. In his Memoirs he sets down only two kinds of memories of his college career: those relating to the lady who was to become Mrs. Bryan, and those relating to his college oratory and debating. If he learned anything about the material universe, about the pilgrimage of men on the planet, about the gorgeous procession of the stars, about the laws of trade, this learning did not stick in his memory. But recollections of contest in debating, in essay writing, in orations, came to him in his sixties when he set him down to write the story of his life. One episode may be transplanted here, for he says, "My good wife often refers to it"; "good wife" being exactly the phrase that Bryan would have held in his heart through the passing sophisticated decades to the end—"my good wife!" The incident to which his good wife often refers is this: Practicing for an oratorical contest he went out into the woods surrounding an adjacent insane asylum, where he was heard by some college picnickers ranting and chanting his mellifluous oratorical lines. They, being frightened, took him for one of the inmates, and only the dear lady who was later to be "my good wife" recognized the voice that was to breathe over America for a generation. In college he was interested in Edmund Burke; he heard Wendell Phillips deliver his lecture on "The Lost Arts," and another peripatetic spieler and spellbinder, Doctor Conwell, in what Bryan calls "his remarkable lecture on 'Acres of Diamonds.'" The Apostle Paul impressed Bryan more as an orator than as a philosopher; and Bryan quotes the beginning of an oration which he used at the state oratorical contest,

a speech on "Justice," which begins: "Plutarch tells us
that man entertained three sentiments concerning the
gods—they feared them for their power, respected them
for their intelligence, and loved them for their justice."
In his Memoirs he refers to the local papers' account of
his speech and to the fact that, though he had only second
prize, "his college backers insisted, as college boys are
wont to do, that he ought to have had first prize." He
won fifty dollars—and bought an engagement ring for
Mary Baird; a modest garnet set in gold, which was, he
said, "sufficient to satisfy our simple tastes," and adorned
Mrs. Bryan until she lost it in the campaign of 1896. He
was a contestant for one more prize in his senior year and
again came off second. The man who defeated him went
to a protracted meeting and was re-born, and Bryan says:
"I have never known a man more completely consecrated
to the service of God and to a life patterned after the
example of Christ." Here is the eternal Bryan—magnanimous, sanctimonious, full of the ineptitudes of the
single-minded and simple-hearted. A photograph of the
Bryan of those days is available. He is standing in an
intercollegiate debating team. One of the members of
the team is Miss Jane Addams; Bryan stands beside her,
the tallest man in a group of nine. He is dressed in a
long, black Prince Albert coat. He wears a high collar
and a black bow necktie of the kind that he clung to all
his days. He wears some sort of white badge to desig-
nate him from the others, and in the bulging front,
between the first and second buttons of his tight-fitting
coat, he has stuck a hand—a statesman's gesture. His
face is lean and tortured by the fires of youth; his serious
eyes burn under heavy brows, and he has a fine poll of

dark hair. He is so clearly the college orator that he
might have sat for the typical portrait of the type that
prevailed in American colleges well into the final decade
of the last century, before the football gladiator pushed
the orator from under the academic halo. Bryan was a
senior in his twenty-first year. He entered life in the
little Illinois town and, of course, made a dead set for
politics. Here the "ould one" from the green isle had his
way. Without an admission ticket young Bryan had seen
the Democratic convention of 1876, where Tilden was
nominated in St. Louis. A policeman boosted the boy
through the window. In 1884, Bryan, the young lawyer,
saw the convention that nominated Cleveland. He
earned his way to Chicago by delivering a Fourth of July
address. If the issues of those days interested Bryan,
if he understood what was in the heart of America in
those first two decades after the Civil War, it did not
interest him sufficiently to occupy a place in his Memoirs.
Yet those were stirring times. Republican corruption was
rampant. It was somewhat the outgrowth of reconstruction in the South, and somewhat the result of building a
vast empire in the West, where the soldiers of the Civil
War went out to homestead their farms with no capital
but their bare hands—and had to borrow billions. In
three decades they built, with borrowed capital, a civilization spick and span, new and bright, equipped with
every modern device to fit the need, to minister to the
comfort, to furnish the luxuries, of a complex civilization.
It was a society erected without a frontier, charmed
full grown from the sod by the magic of capital. And
in those passing decades of the seventies and eighties,
when young Bryan was a student and a starving lawyer,

he seemed to have been entirely unconscious of the meaning of his environment. The various political protests
from the borrower to the lender were rising, clamoring,
and receding in that period—the Greenbackers, the
Grangers, the Knights of Labor.

Bryan saw the convention that nominated Grover
Cleveland. Bryan was then twenty-four. If he sensed the
deep significance of Cleveland's political strength, Cleveland's stolid, indomitable protests against misgovernment
and Republican corruption, Bryan did not set down in his
Memoirs the import of that strength. We know only
from his biography that he was making occasional
speeches, and that in 1887 he went to Lincoln, Nebraska,
where he plunged into politics, helped to elect J. Sterling
Morton, a staunch, old-fashioned, rock-ribbed Tilden
Democrat, as a delegate to the Democratic National Convention of 1888; and so, being honored with a convention ticket in the regular manner, Bryan saw Cleveland
nominated the second time.

In Lincoln, Nebraska, Bryan was too greatly interested
in politics to succeed with the law. He was a poor prac-
titioner; he neglected to prepare his cases, and gained no
reputation at the bar. But he did rise and shine as a
political leader, chiefly because he could talk. He can-
vassed his congressional district in 1888 for J. Sterling
Morton as the congressional nominee, but the tide of
protest against the injustices of prosperity was not running strong enough in 1888 to land a Democrat in a
Republican district. Two years later, in 1890, the crest
of the wave of prosperity was going out; the protest of
the borrower was rising and Bryan himself was elected
to Congress as a Democrat. He served two terms, dur-

ing one of which he was on the Ways and Means Committee, a powerful place in the House. Bryan came home to find moth and rust corrupting his law books, so he closed them and turned to his true love—the people.

Bryan did not realize that he was beginning a career as a revolutionist. Yet during the twenty years following his entrance into politics America and, to an extent, the whole world, passed into and through a peaceful revolution, a time of vast change. Bryan joined the revolution as innocently as a boy follows a mob in the street. He did not know its significance, perhaps he never comprehended the import of his action. Definitely, but rather deeply, in the heart of humanity the conviction was forming that the fruits of industry, agriculture, and commerce were not being equitably distributed. In every age where great changes come, this sense of injustice, vague and often at first voiceless, must lie heavily upon the conscience of the world. In the seventies and eighties political unrest among the farmers and laborers was manifested in Greenbackism and the Grange. The plug-hat brigade felt no twinges in its heart; it took privilege as its right. But popular discontent was hinging upon various issues, some of which were mad and some of which were wise. Slowly many voters came to realize that the laborer was not merely worthy of his hire but that he deserved a "raise"; that the rewards of industry were passing too heavily toward the employers' side of the ledger. So came the unrest of the revolution in the mid-nineties. In President Harrison's time were strikes and lockouts; in Cleveland's time, riots and the approach of anarchy. Also, the embattled farmer appeared in the South and West as the bewhiskered

Populist, with his revolutionary slogans taken from the Declaration of Independence, through which he revealed a mad desire for fiat money. This was the first phase of the revolution, and it was at this phase when Bryan joined it. In Congress Bryan had adopted rather definitely, but probably somewhat fortuitously, the cause of the protesting debtors. The Democratic party was more or less their advocate, as prosperity had been the Republican issue; and the Democrats, being the party of protest and criticism, naturally took the position which made them first criticize the inequities of prosperity and then advocate the cause of its victims. So, in 1894, Bryan, the debater, the orator, the man with an answer but never a reason, ran for the United States Senate in Nebraska, and failed even with a Populist endorsement. It was a Republican year, in the midst of Cleveland's second term, when the people were protesting against the Democratic protesters. When Bryan failed of election he packed his grip and went forth preaching the silver gospel. The silver gospel in those days was a thinly-veiled demand for fiat money. The Silverites insisted that silver should be purchased at the bullion price of about forty-eight cents and coined as a dollar, leaving about fifty-two cents pure fiat in the act of coinage. The silver mines of the West were idle. Prices of farm products were pitifully low, and the advocates of silver endeavored to trace the relation between the price of silver and the price of wheat. Bryan lectured for pay when he could get it; for nothing when he could do no better, but he was incessantly on the go. He may have been a subsidized lecturer of the Bi-metallic League, but he paid his own expenses, even if he had a salary; certainly he made no money out of his advocacy of free silver, but he did acquire fame.   If he seemed to spring into national prominence as if by a miracle in 1896, one must remember that, during the two years before, Bryan had gone into nearly every Southern state and into every state in the Mississippi Valley.   He spoke but one message—the free and unlimited coinage of silver at the ratio of sixteen to one.   He was an attractive figure in those days as he traveled from town to town, from county to county, gathering about him the advocates of fiat money; the disgruntled Democrats whom Cleveland's gold-standard policies had offended, the Populists who were voicing the inarticulate cry for justice that comes from those who are ground beneath the wheels of economic depression; and, last of all, the free-silver Republicans. Bryan's face was so young, so immature in those days that he hid it with a beard, a carefully trimmed Vandyke.   But his eyes—large, luminous, Irish orbs—glowed with youth despite the hirsute evidences of maturity.   His brow was wide, and fair, and high; his mouth loose, sensitive.   He had a slightly cleft chin.   His tall, agile body, topped with sloping Irish shoulders, was made supple by that platform exercise which the orator, daily going forth to wrangle, develops.   Every muscle was trained to express a thought. His voice was finely modulated.   All that his college elocution had taught him which had stuck in his subconsciousness came out in those oratorical days from '94 to '96; for he was fired with his cause.   His sincerity may not be questioned; but it was the sincerity of vast inexperience, the integrity of a closed mind.   As he went to and fro on his silver quest when Populism, outside of the Democratic party, was booming in full tide, pattering a set of speeches which he had learned by heart, he was a pleasant contrast to his fellow workers in that political vineyard. They, for the most part, had come up from the bottom. Their voices faltered; their gestures were rough and angular. The passion in their hearts often choked them. Or they were the oily demagogues seeking what votes they might devour; men who knew better, and showed it in the smug, unmistakable unction of their presence—"gallus-looking slinks."

Physical toil had not twisted Bryan's graceful frame; no complaining at fate had put the rasp of despair into his musical voice. In the throng of men who had fought their way to approximate success by hard, disfiguring knocks, he seemed as one apart from practical life— indeed, as one exalted. He could not know it, but this distinction of innocence gave him his courage. No industrial concern had ever bothered him to act as its director, or as its superintendent, or as its foreman, or even as a laborer. No financial institution had asked him to be its treasurer or its promoter or a member of its advisory board. No social experiment had been put into his hands for development. His knowledge of the actual strength and weakness, quirks and foibles of human nature was a blank page. Upon it he might write a theory of human conduct and argue therefrom with deep, unsimulated feeling. No fluttering wings of doubt, risen from the midnight lamp, doubt that would have brushed by a scholar's eyes and made him stammer and hesitate in his climaxes, disturbed Bryan. His magnificent earnestness was hypnotic, first of all self-hypnotic, because he lost no force of eloquence in convincing himself. The weight of all his rhetoric, of his splendid magnetic presence, of his resonant voice, fell upon the wicked who opposed his holy cause.

CHAPTER XXIII

DANTON

THUS Bryan came to the Democratic National Convention of 1896 from Nebraska. He had been a reporter on the Omaha *World-Herald* in the St. Louis convention a few weeks before, when McKinley had been nominated. He had seen the bolt of the Western silver Republicans; had heard Senator Teller's tragic, sobbing speech as he retired from lifelong membership in the party which he had helped to found. From that scene came Bryan to Chicago, charged with emotion. Those were emotional times. His revolution was in fine fettle. The Democratic National Convention held a majority of angry men who stood not so much to build as to destroy. The demand for justice was in its passionate and destructive stage. The movement attracted few impartial philosophers, but many fanatic dupes and scalawags affected by self-interest, as all new movements attract the unstable. It had its Marats, even its fierce, impassive Robespierres; Bryan, whose words were deeds, became its Danton. He was floor leader, and all over the convention were men whom he had met on his silver crusade. He made friends easily; for he had that grace of manner, that gentleness of personality, which bound friends in sheaves along his path. He was in his mid-thirties and had something of the winsomeness that Dickens gave to

245

Steerforth. As floor leader it was his duty to defend the report of the Committee on Resolutions. That report was practically a Populist platform. President Cleveland in the White House had wrecked his party, had lost control of the organization, turned it over to Populism and political chaos; but there was no leadership in the Democratic forces of Populism during the early days of the convention. No governor or congressman had been preëminent in the silver movement. It was a struggle for principle among the Western Democrats, not a clamor for A Man. Silver leaders conspiring to overthrow the Federal appointees' wing of the Democrats— Cleveland's friends—were not sure enough of victory to give much time to the distribution of the spoils. Richard Bland, a Missouri congressman, was a sort of titular leader of the Silverites; a professional person, dry, colorless, unemotional, convinced by statistics, without mob-appeal; a man in his mid-sixties. Governor Altgeld of Illinois, whom Cleveland had insulted when he sent troops to quell the Chicago riot which Altgeld tolerated, had the mob-appeal, but the silver supporters feared that Altgeld was a step too far to the left. Governor Ben Tillman of South Carolina, an agrarian, a sort of pitchfork Marat, was too wild; he had the hill-billy's lack of poise. That was the list of the silver leaders in the Democratic convention of 1896. They had founded an organization; they had roared out a platform. The sense of that platform was that man is a creature of the socialist state rather than that the state is a creation of man's. It was a new and shocking doctrine for a Democratic convention. So the air was charged with the electricity of controversy. The orator who could arouse

someone, challenge someone, defy someone, plead for
something—that orator would first voice the sentiment
of the majority. That orator was Bryan—Bryan, the
debater, the college hero; who sought not to find truth
but to find answers, posers, climaxes; to make points, to
confound his adversaries, to win applause. He stepped
naturally into supremacy at that talkfest because he had
been training for his famous speech, and for nothing else,
from the hour when he spouted Patrick Henry's address
twenty years before. The practiced elocutionist had even
recited his very convention address to his friends over
and over, just as he bayed his college oration in the woods
near the insane asylum. After Altgeld's harshly resonant
voice had been split to tatters with emotion, after Til-
man's raucous baritone had splintered itself in screams
as he stood madly waving impotent arms to the crowd
interested in his gestures but not his words, the formal
debate arose over a resolution offered by the minority report to the Platform Committee of the convention. The
minority report was drafted by Senator Hill of New
York, William F. Vilas, of Cleveland's Cabinet, Senators
Gray and Poe, a group of congressmen, and ex-Governor
Russell of Massachusetts. The minority report denounced
the silver plank in the platform, declaring "that it would
pass at once upon silver basis in bare contracts, disturb
business, diminish the purchasing power of the wages of
labor, and inflict irreparable evils upon our nation's commerce and industry." The minority report also endorsed
the "honesty, economy, courage, and fidelity of the present National Democratic administration," but did not
dare to mention Cleveland's name. Bryan closed the
debate. It was a tense and dramatic moment. He was

young, god-like in figure. He had himself in hand. In his opening paragraph he cried:

"I come to speak to you in defense of a cause as holy as the cause of liberty—the cause of humanity."

He decried the resolutions that would either defend Cleveland or commend him. With conviction he declared:

"The individual is but an atom. He is born, he acts, he dies; but principles are eternal, and this has been a contest over a principle."

It is hard to realize, a generation after this speech, how such purely declamatory oratory fired the hearts of that convention and, tingling over the telegraph wires of the land, enthralled the nation; yet, up to that moment, probably, no single speech in American history, by any man in any case—not even by Webster, by Clay, or by Calhoun in the Senate, in their noblest moments tuned into the will of Americans so much moving emotion as that Bryan speech in the Democratic National Convention of 1896. It marked the beginning of a revolution. Somewhat, perhaps even largely, Bryan's voice was important. It was soothing but penetrating. It fell upon the delegates as manna in the wilderness. His carefully polished sentences, his studied climaxes, they heard in the hush which his handsome presence inspired; straight, clean-limbed, fiery-eyed, as he shook his mop of dark hair and waved his graceful actor's arms above the multitude. Hundreds of them knew him, loved him; all of them saw and heard in Bryan that day a new leader. He filled them with the frenzy that has created every reckless mob of history. So Bryan's supremacy in the Chicago Democratic National Convention was as inevitable as Danton's in the Mountain. The speech

which gave him his leadership contained not more than
two thousand words. Bryan had stilled the raging
turmoil of the convention. Amid an hypnotic calm
of suppressed emotion, he closed with this rhetorical
challenge:

Having behind us the producing masses of this nation and the
world, supported by the commercial interests, the laboring
interests, and the toilers everywhere, we will answer their demand
for a gold standard by saying to them: "You shall not press down
upon the brow of labor this crown of thorns, you shall not crucify
mankind upon a cross of gold."

From the hypnotic silence which had held it, the
convention awoke to a hysteria of cheering. Finally the
standards of the state delegations began to rise and move
in the howling mass on the floor of the convention, and one
state standard after another, surrounded by each
delegation, formed a moving procession around the hall
to the Nebraska delegation, where each standard flag
stopped and, was lowered before the Nebraska flag. And
all over the country, as the cheering continued for an
hour, the continent thrilled to that speech, and for a day
the nation was in a state of mental and moral catalepsy.

But, after all, it was Bryan's voice that won. Probably
the peculiarity of his talking-box got him further than any
other organ of his body, certainly further than his brain.
Bryan's voice was a high baritone; soft, but never quite
husky, silvern rather than golden, penetrating but never
sharp. In his emotional moments he put a slow inten-
sity into his delivery; an actor's trick of dramatizing himself through his voice. In an hour of tumult Bryan was
calm, restrained, even complacent. His oration was a
college sophomore's assemblage of platitudinous asser-

tions, but his delivery won where thought and composition would have left him stranded. Nevertheless, he performed a miracle that hot July day in Chicago, no matter how he did it. The time, the subject, and the occasion met, and Bryan as a national leader was born.

If the election had been held that summer day, Bryan would have been chosen President. Indeed, all that his opponents did in the three months following his speech was to arouse the American people from their trance. It took much shaking to break the spell, much marching of the patient up and down the land under torches and to martial music to revive the practical, flinty consciousness of Uncle Sam and restore his natural faculties. It is not fair, therefore, to say that the man who put the moral and mental faculties of the nation to sleep in 1896 was not a strong man. He certainly was not particularly wise, for wisdom and oratorical strength are not inseparably allied.

But Bryan's strength was in his deadly seriousness. From the caverns of his inexperience came no cackle of mirth at his own presumption, such as invariably comes to a man of ripe philosophy. Bryan saw in his creed the truth, the whole truth, and nothing but the truth. With him an expeditious compromise was a dishonorable surrender. The easy circumstances of his early life, his environment in the political Elysium, his felicitous career following the beckonings of a mastering ambition—these things conspired to persuade him that he was a statesman of destiny. Men who fight their way up from the bottom of fortune's hill are apt to take personal credit for their victories and believe little in the influence of the State. But Bryan's easy rise so confused him that it was natural

for him to hold that the State can make or break men.
His career made it proper for him to teach that the State,
by proclamation and enactment, could coax the coy millen-
nium out of the roseate dawn and put salt on her tail.
For him to hold another view would argue in him a vanity
that was foreign to him. So he felt that government was
the only instrument of human welfare; politics the only
weapon for reform.

After his defeat in 1896, Bryan, by the sheer force of
a charming personality and a stable character, was able to
hold the leadership in the Democratic party, a leadership
which gave him almost without question the nomination
for the Presidency in 1900. He went about the country
proclaiming his Silver gospel. He offered no new arguments; he attracted to him many Liberal leaders from
all parties and cults and in all sections of the land, but
apparently his leadership did not turn the Liberalism of
his day into a search for truth, but rather a search for
answers, figures for debate, turns and quirks to confound
the Conservatives. He did not broaden in those years.
He was what he was twenty years before.

He had established a home in Lincoln, Nebraska,
which represented Bryan in the flush of his maturity.
The living-room was the library. Around the library
walls were pictures of statesmen—Washington, Jefferson,
Jackson, and Lincoln, prominently displayed; Benton,
Webster, Calhoun, and others, in steel engravings, tucked
away in odd places. A stuffed eagle poised for flight
teetered in front of Bryan's chair. Just behind the chair
was a picture which more than any other illumined
Bryan's point of view. The picture represented Henry
Clay towering almost ten feet high in foreground, badly

out of perspective, pleading with the lilliputian senators
—all in stocks and tail coats, like Clay, and all dignified
and serious, wrapped in improving meditation. Of
course, no human beings ever disported themselves in such
unwrinkled pomp. But Bryan all his life seemed to draw
from this picture his fine Fourth Reader views of the
relations of life.

The books in the library also made an excellent photograph of their owner's mental equipment. Of fiction
there was little. "Caxton Editions" of a number of the
classic novelists were found in sets. Standard histories
and great orations, common in schools of the eighties,
filled much space. Lord's "Beacon Lights of History,"
"lives" of statesmen old and new, collections of poetical
"gems," published by houses that sell through agents, had
shelf room beyond their deserts. On the side of sociology
and economics the books were the sort that may be called
propagandist. They were written by partisans of a
theory rather than by well-known social scientists seeking
the truth. Most of these books might have been issued
by the "committee" or by the "league" or by the "association"; and with a few exceptions they bore the same
relation to sane research in the lines they traversed that
"Mother, Home, and Heaven" and "The Royal Path of
Life" bore to the contemporary essays of Matthew
Arnold and the inquiries of Huxley, Darwin, and Spencer.
Current literature of the first order—new books and
magazines—and those refinements, artistic and literary,
which two decades of invention and industrial organization had brought to American homes in the nineties, were
conspicuously absent from the Bryan library. "Trilby,"
then seven years old, was the latest piece of fiction there.

"Of Course No Human Beings Ever Disported Themselves in Such Unwrinkled Pomp."

Excepting a few economic tracts, the shelves might have been filled by a Virginia country judge before the Civil War.

And this was but natural, for Bryan was always distinctly of the old school personally, despite the novelty of his liberal views. The broad, studded, antebellum shirt-bosom that he affected in his thirties and forties showed this as clearly as did his childlike democratic faith in the omniscience of the people. With him *vox populi* was *vox Dei;* and this, too, in the face of the fact that in modern politics men who affect too much solicitude for the people are called demagogues. The people—that solidarity of citizens of mutual interests, common aspirations, and similar circumstances that once formed the masses of the early Republic—seems in the last fifty years to have resolved itself into a number of individuals associated by self-interest into groups, cliques, coteries, classes, companies, corporations, and municipalities. These units asked chiefly of government, before Bryan came and after he went, only an honest policeman and an incorruptible umpire to see that the fight was fair. Therefore when Bryan first appeared nationally in 1896, a large number of Mr. Bryan's fellow-citizens—a majority, in fact—sniffed at his strenuous clamor for "the people" as the recitations of a demagogue. And, like the priest and the Levite, these fellow-citizens passed by on the other side.

Now the truth of the matter is that Mr. Bryan was not a demagogue then—and never was a demagogue. He was absolutely honest, which a demagogue is not. He was more than three-fourths brave, which a demagogue is not. He was passionately sincere, which a demagogue is not. When Bryan came to Nebraska, in 1887, his town, his congressional district, and his state were overwhelmingly Republican. A demagogue would have joined the majority party. Bryan took up the cause of tariff reform, and fought a losing fight. When he became convinced that free silver was right, he preached it in his congressional district with his party organization and the odds of battle against him. He ran for the United States Senate in '94, with his party's state convention endorsement. If he had trimmed a little on free silver, the Cleveland gold Democrats might have turned the scales in his favor. But he didn't trim; he lost.

In 1898 Bryan enlisted in the volunteer army of the United States in the war against Spain. He was made a colonel. He never appeared in Cuba or in the Philippines, but sat coloneling about in his tent while typhoid raged through the camps, more of a campus philosopher than a soldier, deeply anxious but equally futile about the comfort of his men; utterly incapable of realizing the danger of dirt, the waste of discontent, or the meaning in human terms of the terrible, grimy thing called war. When the army was disbanded Bryan found the Democratic senators in Washington opposing the ratification of the peace treaty with Spain. Bryan did not hesitate to differ with them. He favored the ratification of the treaty because he loved peace, and took a Republican position without timidity, without excuses. In 1900 Bryan found that the silver sentiment was dying in the West. The gold mines of Alaska and of Africa had inflated the currency to a point where the per-capita of gold money was almost as high as the per-capita of fiat money, which Bryan had advocated. Bryan would not have lost an electoral vote by abandoning silver; he would have gained thousands of votes in the East by such a course. He did not study the situation for excuses to change his position. What study he gave to it was for answers to refute the gold-bugs. He believed that the free coinage of silver was right. He would never change; he never changed because he never thought. Facts never budged him. Wild horses could never drag him from a stand.

Then came the day of political change in America. Industrial revolution was beginning to present a new national political phase after 1896. Slowly, as the old century closed and the new one opened, passion disappeared from the cause of distributive justice and with it the menace of anarchy which Cleveland throttled. But in the economic relations of men change was not impeded. The mills of the gods of justice kept grinding. The revolution submerged but moved on. Bryan was the voice of the revolution when revolution was an emotion. But when the revolution was a vision of justice, a constructive hope, Bryan—beleaguered by the phantoms and prejudices of his ignorance—was only bewildered by the movement he had fathered. He could not leave his past to join the revolution. So it went on without him.

Roosevelt's star was rising in that day, and Bryan's leadership, even in his own party, was declining. The independent liberal group left Bryan for a number of reasons: First, because Roosevelt was obviously more erudite, more generally intelligent than Bryan; second, because Roosevelt, when he became President, had the prestige of his office behind his liberalism. Third, because Roosevelt was more energetic, more pugnacious, more clamorous than Bryan. When Roosevelt was nominated for Vice-President by the Republicans, with McKinley for President, in 1900, Hanna, Republican National Committee Chairman, in a moment of inadvertence thinking to get rid of Roosevelt in the campaign, "sicked" him on Bryan. It was a gorgeous shindy. Young Teddy was as noisy as Bryan was vacuous. It was hammer and tongs, hullabaloo, rough and tumble, bite, gouge, and swat—a slapstick battle of the gods! Bryan was routed by the rowdy clamor of Roosevelt's shrewd dramatics. Years later, recalling that day to a friend, Roosevelt sputtered:

"Well, I drowned him out in 1900. I talked two words to his one. Maybe he was an oratorical cocktail, but I was his chaser."

Probably Roosevelt did not regard Bryan as a windbag, but Roosevelt always had a lively sense of Bryan's intellectual incapacity, his abysmal unintelligence about things in books. But fundamentally it was because there was more wind in Roosevelt's trumpet than in Bryan's that the independent liberals left the

Democratic party and began voting with the Republicans. Roosevelt's energy overcame Bryan.

Bryan went to Europe, saw the little national railroads of the small European countries which had one problem, and came home feeling that there was a parallel between the small railroad systems of Europe and the vast transcontinental railway systems of the United States with their problems. He had come home after his first contact with the world outside of America. The prestige of his leadership of a major party raised the presumption that he would bring back to America some new issue, some vital thing for his constituents. Democrats were exultant in that hope, Republicans uneasy; those who did not know Bryan, frightened. He spoke in Madison Square Garden to ten thousand expectant Americans. They were looking for another miracle like that which came in the convention of 1896. Bryan began a plea for the government ownership of railroads. It was an academic plea, but—alas!—he missed all the good reasons for his stand and took the cheap ones. He had not been talking twenty minutes before the steady tramp of departing footsteps and the rattle of seats as the crowd left him clicked like musketry and all but drowned his voice. His argument revealed a shallow mind. After that he endorsed Croker as leader in New York, and fell in the esteem of thinking men in America, as surely and as finally as he rose to power at the Chicago convention of 1896. He retained his partisan leadership, something of his personal prestige. He still had his voice. He still held his power of emotionalizing causes by moving the multitudes, but something had gone that he held before that hour.

CHAPTER XXIV

THE LONG, HARD TRAIL

BRYAN was a member of the Presbyterian Church, but until the close of his career he did not seem to add to his other faults the vice of sanctimony. His home life was that of the average well-bred American—simple, affectionate, stimulating. He always took his wife into partnership in all his interests. She was his only confidante and his final advisor. In the town of Lincoln, which never agreed with him politically and rarely voted for him, Bryan bore the reputation of a straightforward, honorable man, whose word was good and whose debts were paid when they fell due. But he stood somewhat aloof from the town politically. In the intrigues of local politics Bryan was not a dominant force. He never reigned there—even among Democrats. He talked himself into his honors in local politics, instead of winning them in the caucus. Most lawyers in Western politics begin at the bottom—run for county attorney or the legislature, are graduated into the judicial nomination, and ascend to Congress at the close of their political lives. Bryan, having framed his life after the models in the old school, began at the top. Politically he was always a Henry Clay in a tail coat, talking to the pigmies.

Bryan had led his party to two consecutive defeats, and in 1904 the Democratic pendulum swung back to conservatism. So Bryan appeared in the National Democratic Convention that year a minority leader. The convention nominated Alton B. Parker, an old-fashioned, high-collared, tail-coated, gold-standard Democrat. The leaders left out of the Democratic platform any declaration on the currency question which was really not an issue. The gold standard had for six years been embodied in the law of the land. But Bryan, in that St. Louis convention of 1904, thought that his cause and his face needed saving—or perhaps he did not think at all; just felt! Judge Parker, who had been nominated by the Democratic National Convention, a Conservative standard bearer, sent a telegram to the convention insisting that a gold-standard plank should be included in the platform. This was to be the sign that the Democrats were done with Bryan and his isms forever! Bryan rose from a sick bed in the night session and for five long hours, far past midnight, led a heroic debate against what he called amending the Democratic platform by way of the Western Union Telegraph Company. Bryan won his victory, but weakened his party. Roosevelt would have defeated Judge Parker, probably, without the Bryan defection, but the defeat of Parker was rather overwhelming. Obviously the Conservative wing of the Democratic party could not win, so the party turned to Bryan again, and in 1908 nominated him for President for the third time at the National Democratic Convention assembled in Denver. William H. Taft, supported by Roosevelt and his liberal followers, defeated Bryan easily. For four years, during the Taft administration, while Roosevelt was advocating the liberal cause in his party, Bryan went up and down the land converting the Democratic party also into a liberal organization.

Bryan's leadership in the National Democratic party

in those days was real. He was a power. He was futile against Roosevelt, but, curiously enough, working in the Democratic party of the South and West, Bryan kept his party abreast of the Rooseveltian movement in the Republican party, so that from 1904 to 1912 the United States was essentially liberal in its political and economic views. Without the prestige of the presidential office, Bryan, almost single-handed, kept his party from becoming merely a critical Conservative party, which it well might have been when Roosevelt was leading Republican Liberalism. In every Democratic state, though not by his political machinations, Bryan created by his influence Bryanesque Governors, and in Congress followers of Bryan, who were Roosevelt's allies against the Conservative East. Bryan did this with two weapons—one, his weekly newspaper, *The Commoner,* which was a broken reed for the most part, but still a wand which he might wave when he wished to call the spirits; the other, the lecture platform. He lectured incessantly and for pay. He appealed to a different group from that which Roosevelt addressed. It was a cut or two under the Roosevelt group, both socially and in the economic scale. Roosevelt appealed to the upper middle class. He was not always certain of having Labor with him. The farmers frequently rallied to Roosevelt, but it was the prosperous farmers—the country gentlemen, more or less; Bryan aroused the tenantry. Labor was always for him. The poor understood his language and believed in him. He could not have talked over their heads if he had tried to do so. So men of the Roosevelt type came to regard men of the Bryan mold as dangerous, not because of what Bryan's followers held to be true, so much as the why-fors of their logic; not so much because of the limit of their intelligence as because of their attitude toward truth. For when Bryan faced an uncomfortable fact his habit was not to search the fact for its truth, but to answer the fact.

His career in those days and always was a parallelism of success and failure. That he succeeded tremendously with his life no one can question who realizes how much the Liberalism of his time owed to him. The tragedy of whatever failure may be read into his career by historians arises from the conflict between his capacity for dramatic emotion and the restrictions of a stunted mind. While his mental acuteness as a debater was a shield that often warded certain truths from his heart, yet he had one simple oratorical trick, and only one: he begged the question. For instance, in 1899 a reporter asked Bryan if the practice of electing senators who happened to be party Democrats in Montana, by the corrupt use of money, was not deplorable. His reply was:

"Don't you think that the spectacle of Senator Hanna voting to unseat Clark for buying an election is incongruous?"

Now the alleged incongruity of Senator Hanna's position in the Clark investigation had nothing to do with the case against the corrupt use of money in elections. But that answer before a crowd would turn the debate into another channel. In his famous Chicago speech Bryan said:

If they tell us that the gold standard is a good thing, we shall point to their platform and tell them that their platform pledges the party to get rid of the gold standard and substitute bi-metalism. If the gold standard is a good thing, why try to get rid of it?

With a mob that passed for argument against the gold
standard. But the fact was, the merits or demerits of the
gold standard were not touched upon at all. In no place
in that gorgeous speech of 1896 was there a single logical
argument offered against the gold standard. Yet the
speech was a perfect piece of rhetoric of its kind, and it
convinced thousands of the iniquity of the gold standard.
Conviction came through bald, unsupported assertion,
repeated a score of times in different figures of speech
and uttered with a manifest sincerity of belief that was
the orator's armament against contradiction. This
method of political discussion was, of course, not original
with Bryan. It is common to all debaters, to all politicians and to many statesmen. But they cannot all maintain the unflinching sincerity that Bryan wore, for if they
are men of much intelligence they see their own sham,
and having seen it, cannot entirely conceal it. But Bryan,
like the lady in the poem, "never could know and never
could understand."

And, finally, it was not the kind of argument that Bryan
used that gave him strength, nor the principles he advocated that drew men to him. At the root of the magnetism which pulled men toward Bryan was the growth
in the popular mind of a faith in Liberalism, and a hope to
see the State lay hold of the industrial system and
untangle its many snarls. During the nineteenth century, with all its mechanical progress, the economic world
literally jumped a cog in the process of its evolution.
Many people believed, in the nineties and the first
decade and a half of the twentieth century, that society
was not properly adjusted, that the machinery of industry was not in gear, and that too many people were being

ground to bits by it. There was a widespread belief that repairs were needed, and because Bryan got out with his oratorical hammer and knocked upon the industrial system and the existing order, unthinking people hailed him as the master mechanic. But Bryan was never a builder, not even a handy tinker. Oratory is rarely constructive. Oratory is an illusion, a legerdemain, and the modern world seems to be learning to dissociate oratory from statesmanship. At any rate it realized in Bryan's lifetime that there was really no more reason for electing an orator to office than for electing a fiddler. Oratory and fiddling alike arouse the emotions. Bryan was a voice—yet a voice in the wilderness.

In 1912, when it was obvious that the majority of the Republican party outside of the Republican organization was Liberal, Bryan, who had reported the Chicago Republican National Convention which split over the nomination of Taft, attended the National Democratic Convention in Baltimore. He was an unofficial floor leader as well as a reporter that year when he came to Baltimore. He was instructed for Champ Clark; indeed, he was more or less tied to Clark by old obligations. Finally, as the session of the Democratic convention dragged along, Clark became through the maneuvers of the convention a representative of the Conservative faction.

Sixteen years had elapsed since Bryan, as the boy orator of the Platte, gallantly strode into the national political arena at the Chicago Democratic Convention of 1896—a handsome, dashing, graceful figure. In those sixteen years he had been speaking incessantly and writ-

ing almost all the time in championship of the Liberal
cause. He had no other interests or attachments. He
was a Liberal political orator, agitator, statesman, as
the word goes, eating, walking, sleeping. His private
life seemed to slough away with the years. He became
more and more a public figure, the embodiment of a
cause. He fed heavily, and except upon the platform
exercised little. He had no hobbies, no mildly mad
diversions, no interesting side lines, into which he could
go for merriment or relaxation. His spiritual life was
cramped by a sort of pharisaical probity; he long since
had choked to death the old Irish ancestor who might
have made Bryan stand aside and watch himself behav-
ing like a basswood figure. A double chin had gradually
swathed his neck in the sixteen years of his public life.
His jowls had become fat; his torso almost pursy; his
muscles leashed to adipose. He talked to innumerable
Chautauqua audiences and his Chautauqua make-up had
become familiar——bagging, uncreased trousers, two-but-
toned alpaca-coat, white shirt, a lawyer's black necktie
still persisting from his college days, a wide-brimmed
Panama hat. He was addicted also to palm-leaf fans.
So when he appeared in the Baltimore convention of
1912, the Liberal leader, some curiously——even tragically
——quixotic aura surrounded the prematurely old hulking figure, sitting like a squatting Buddha, fanning himself; or perhaps more like an Indian chief, in his shiny
alpaca, with the Bryan smile rather fatuously spread
upon the moon-face that was extending higher and higher
up the broad brow toward the back of his noble head.

The sixteen years since Bryan had overthrown the
Conservatives in the Democratic convention of 1896

had wrought a change in the Liberal movement much more striking than the physical change Time had wrought upon Bryan. The "destructive passion for justice" which had dominated the movement two decades before, when Bryan and his revolutionaries turned upside down the control of the Democratic party, bringing the bewhiskered and rampant Populists into the seats of the mighty—that phase of the Liberal movement was gone. Liberalism in 1912 was occupied more with a passion for justice than for destruction. The movement had passed from shirt sleeves and galluses into the high-hat stage. Roosevelt, the son of a rich New Yorker, himself a man of means and consequence, a Harvardian who softened his R's and wore heavy eye-glasses, had given the passion for justice—social and industrial justice were the common words—a vast respectability. The movement was no longer the cry of the oppressed, but the demand of the aspiring. It was no longer indignant; it was constructive. Liberalism in that day represented not so much the attack of the have-nots upon the haves as the vision of a just and righteous relation between men; a plan to readjust obvious inequities by governmental agencies. This plan was promoted somewhat by those who enjoyed the benefits of privilege, largely by those who had no keen self-interest in the matter, and only to a small degree by those who felt the prong of the harrow in their backs.

At the Democratic National Convention of 1912, in Baltimore, Liberalism was at its high tide. Reform twenty years before had been a bull in a china shop. But in 1912 the bull of reform with a ring in his nose was as well manicured as to hoofs and horns as the golden calf itself. In those days Bryan was slipping slouchingly into the decadence of premature old age, while Liberalism was waxing fat and strong. Liberalism inclined to smile benignly but with a certain patronizing tolerance at its old leader. The quixotic angle of his aura was reflected in most of his parliamentary attitudes in that convention. He had written to the various candidates for the Presidency protesting against the choice of the National Democratic Committee for temporary chairman. Judge Alton B. Parker had been galvanized for that place. Wilson, of all the important candidates, was the only one to agree with Bryan. Wilson had good advice from liberal leaders like Colonel E. M. House, the Texas crowd, Josephus Daniels and the Carolinians, Ollie James and the Kentuckians; so Wilson agreed with Bryan before the convention met that Parker should not serve as temporary chairman. Bryan made a sortie against Parker and failed. Then Parker, who won somewhat by courtesy, lost the convention entirely with his opening speech. The delegates faded away from him. The galleries walked noisily out on him. He tried to resume his speech at a night session and was interrupted by the noise of clattering chairs and an ill-mannered public straggling in and out of the hall, waiting for him to finish. Bryan, who never carried a grudge, punished an enemy, nor betrayed a cause, might well have gloated at this sad failure of Judge Parker to rise to his opportunity. But Bryan was facing his own futile hour. He introduced a resolution aimed at August Belmont, of New York, and Thomas F. Ryan, of Virginia. Bryan demanded that these delegates be unseated—chiefly because they were rich and because he felt they were sympathetic with the plutocracy. After some bitter debates in which Bryan rather overdid his oratory, the convention laughed its way out of a dilemma by adopting the resolution under the leadership of the delegations which harbored the two rich men who had been attacked. It was a ridiculous victory. Yet Bryan was a power in the convention. When it was evident that Clark had a majority of the delegates, and that a majority of Clark's majority was composed of the reactionary element of the party, Bryan deserted Clark and led the rush to Wilson. Probably Wilson owed his nomination more to Bryan than to any other man. Not that Bryan's floor leadership was good, but that Bryan, standing as a protagonist of Liberalism, a sort of holy figure with sixteen years of liberal leadership behind him—drew as a magnet from all over the convention, Liberals of every clan, to the Wilson standard.

In the presidential campaign that followed Bryan played a minor part. Wilson took the center of the stage. Bryan was shunted into the country districts. Wilson, ten years before, had expressed a rather low opinion of Bryan, and it was never really changed. The two men were profoundly different. Wilson worshiped his mind; Bryan was moved almost entirely by his emotions; Bryan would sacrifice anything but a cause for a friend; Wilson often sacrificed a friend for nothing! Yet Wilson realized Bryan's power; Wilson's intelligence granted Bryan his leadership of much that was necessary in the Democratic party and in the Liberal wing of the party. Wilson's reason told him that he had no talent to hold that wing; so, against the advice of Mrs. Wilson, the Democratic President made Bryan Secretary of State

in 1913. This was Bryan's first appointive office and his
last. Then came his one day of official glory. It was a
diverting spectacle; much like that of a Southern gentleman in swallow-tails and a choker, but one generation
removed from his periwig, suddenly shot half a century ahead and jammed into the oak-bottom chair of a
corporation president. Our gentleman of the old school
did try honestly to do his duty; but he had such difficult
things to learn, and such an incapacity for learning them,
that he cut many a fantastic caper, and in the end made
as bad a mess of it as a thoroughgoing rascal would have
made. His career in Washington was upon the whole
most unhappy. Liberalism in America had inevitably
become tinged with a certain independence, a certain toplofty attitude toward partisanship. Bryan for the sixteen
years before he came to Washington had been a partisan
of partisans. He, like Blaine, had thousands of partisan
friends who had followed him blindly. He thought in
Liberal terms, but always as a Democrat. Indeed, Bryan
alienated the young independent Liberals who were rallying about Wilson. Bryan alienated these young Liberals
by a narrow partisanship which he justified on the grounds
of his personal obligations to what he called "deserving
Democrats." He acted no worse than other Cabinet
members did, but more was expected of Bryan. And his
partisanship weakened him with the Wilsonians. Also,
Bryan, being a Jacksonian, had small notion of the dignity of his place as Secretary of State. He kept running
in and out of Washington to lecture before Chautauquas
for money; he appeared with snake-charmers, tumblers,
bell ringers, elocutionists, singers, freaks, magicians, and
notoriety seekers—greatly to the horror of the young men

in the State Department who liked to call themselves "clarks." In pre-prohibition days he served grape juice at the state dinners which he gave, and flopped about in his baggy trousers and alpaca coat; a heavy-footed, paunchy, untailored sort of man, in the place where punctilious form contributes much to a secretary's influence. No one could question his honesty, nor his sincerity, nor the fine vision in his heart. But he knew so little! Sixteen years in politics had taught him nothing. All that the American colleges had been giving to American life, all the sophistication that a complicated civilization was veneering upon America, left Bryan untouched. He still read books published by Leagues, by Associations, by propagandists of his own ideals. He had no conception of the newer currents of thought that were stirring in the upper reaches of American intellectual life. He was, in the midst of a highly complex society, the college orator from the fresh-water college of the eighties, who had learned nothing and forgotten nothing of his youthful tricks and manners—a rural bourbon in a gay capital.

He set about with high purpose to negotiate peace treaties with the world which would have made war between America and her neighbors on this continent—and somewhat in Europe—rather difficult. He negotiated many such treaties, and was possessed of a genuine pacifist ardor at the beginning of the Great War which that holocaust did not dampen. He went about with bland and smiling innocence, distributing tracts directed toward the vast conflagration which was burning up an old and wicked world.

He became more and more detached from reality.

The cosmos which he knew as a youth and in which he could function as a man, even if falteringly, was changing. The actual world was nothing like the thing that Bryan fashioned in his heart as the counterpart of life. So in the midst of war, the dazed old man in the baggy trousers, the alpaca coat and the campaign hat, with his treaties and his tracts and the college orator's smart retort, slowly faded like a ghost on a screen from the terrible verities of the times.

CHAPTER XXV

THE SUBSTANCE OF THINGS HOPED FOR

As the war came nearer and nearer to America, Bryan seemed to feel no sense of danger, even when diplomacy all about him was a sour mess of lying and intrigue. He tried simplicity and candor amounting to naïveté, was laughed out of countenance, and gradually edged from his desk into obscurity.

In June, 1915, he resigned his portfolio as Secretary of State more under a cloud of derision than of obloquy. His mood mocked and offended the world about him as Daniel's must have offended the Babylonian king. Bryan's day was done. When the war came to America he was useless and almost dumb. He was faced with facts which did not fit into his cosmos and he went about the land broken-hearted and forlorn, lecturing about "The Prince of Peace" and the Bible heroes. He could not fight back as LaFollette fought—or would not. Yet he seemed to hate the war even more bitterly than LaFollette. And when it was over he took up the cause of prohibition, and appeared in the National Democratic Convention of 1920 in a debate with Bourke Cochran upon a resolution which Bryan introduced, declaring for the enforcement of the prohibitory law which Wilson had vetoed. It was evident that his party had left him and he was a rather sad, lonely figure, surrounded by a new generation of

Democratic politicians to whom 1896 was but a tale that is told.

He trudged up and down the Chautauqua trail until 1924, when he appeared again in the National Democratic Convention, this time not as a delegate but as a reporter for a syndicate of newspapers. He was a reporter as well as a delegate in 1912 and in 1920. But because he was an honored figure in the Democratic party, who had three times led it in the presidential race, at every Democratic convention, he was accorded the privileges of the floor. He appeared there several times in 1924, once opposing a resolution denouncing the Ku Klux Klan, where he made a rather poor fist of it and was hissed and hooted and booed by the gallery and most uncivilly received by the delegates. He turned and walked away, a weary old man, and sat in his shirt sleeves at a reporter's desk with his head pillowed in a handkerchief resting upon one hand, while another hand slowly moved the palm-leaf fan that cooled a tired brow.

For half a dozen years before, Bryan had been the leader of fundamentalism in the sessions of the Presbyterian General Assembly, and had made much headway there. So when the State of Tennessee passed a law prohibiting the teaching of the theory of evolution in the schools of the state, Bryan appeared as a counsel for the state in the trial of a young school-teacher at Dayton, Tennessee, charged with teaching the subversive doctrine. There Bryan met for the first time in his life erudite, skillful, criminal lawyers who showed no respect for his years or his prestige. They set about deliberately to heckle and terrify him, to break his morale, to confuse, shame, and abase him. In their hands he was a pitiful figure. He

WILLIAM JENNINGS BRYAN.

knew it. He had read little and understood nothing technically about the doctrine of evolution, about modern ideas of social progress, about the higher critics who had been studying the Bible text for a hundred years. The whole literature of the subject with which he should have been familiar when he volunteered to appear in the case was a vast, unexplored waste to him. His opponents were merciless. Bryan, crushed, humiliated, saddened, but never for a moment in doubt about his faith, heard for the first time in his career something more terrible than boos and hisses—the cruel, cackling laughter of a shallow, heartless crowd. Also, he must have felt the disapproval of those forces in American life which even he surely understood were the intelligent forces. He could not fight them as he fought the gold-bugs in 1896 and as he defied the imperialists in 1900. He was at last without resilience. For the first time in his career his naïveté was punctured; he was dazed and confused.

This attitude, somewhat physical, somewhat spiritual, rode him after the trial. He wrote a long speech or statement of his cause to be delivered in court. It was not in his best form. It lacked the bounce and assurance of any Bryan whom his friends or the country knew. He ate a large Sunday midday dinner—chicken, stuffing, mashed potatoes, green peas, and pie—such as Americans love to consume. Then he lay down for an afternoon nap, and died. Perhaps faded is a better word than died. For Bryan in his later years, indeed for a decade and more, even in his hour of pomp and power in the State Department, was only a tradition. His day of glory was in the nineties. There he was Danton. If a kindly ax clicking upon the guillotine block could have taken

Bryan in his thirties, what a figure he would have been! But life was cruel to him because fate needed him for menial work in the Augean Stables of politics. So this Danton lived on and on. He saw his enemies triumph. Roosevelt clanked upon the stage like Napoleon and conquered the world with Danton's soldiers. Taft came like Louis the Eighteenth; Wilson, like a Talleyrand, with his "hundred days." And so to Charles the Tenth. Then, in a day of reaction, amid the pasteboard pomp of a rampant plutocracy, this dashing young Danton of the nineties, grown old and fat and seedy, trudged heavily out of life into the blessed immortality of a fame that once had crowned his youth.

It is hard to establish Bryan and his place in his times; it is so easy to exaggerate either in praise or defamation. He was a forceful figure in a day when a man with less moral sense and more intelligence might have been vastly dangerous. He was greedy, of course, but for his causes, not for himself. Once at Crestline, Ohio, in the campaign of '96, tradition declares that Bryan came along on a B. & O. train and a committee asked him to get out and make a speech. He refused to talk until one hundred dollars in cash was contributed to the cause. He kept no penny of it, but carried the odium of holding up his hearers for cash. He would wrangle with a committee while an audience waited, on his lecture tour, until he had turned into cash the checks which were offered to him for delivering a lecture on "The Prince of Peace." This was blindness, bred in ignorance of social forms and the canons of good taste.

Bryan showed his greatest personal strength in the fact that he was utterly without a political machine.

Other men in American politics stand or fall for reasons outside of their personality. Mr. David Bennett Hill, a contemporary Democratic leader from New York, for instance, was a geographical location. McKinley was a kind of syndicate. Roosevelt impersonated an ideal of civic righteousness. Mr. Richard Croker represented an impudent appetite. Senator Matthew S. Quay, of Pennsylvania, was a system of wireless telegraphy. But Bryan always was Bryan, and Bryan was his prophet. More power for good or evil rested for twenty-five years under Bryan's black slouch hat than under any other single contemporaneous headpiece in America. And Bryan was machineless, not because he abhorred the machine, but because he ignored it. He did not know what to do with captains and lieutenants. When his party began to turn from him, Bryan could not call, "What ho, warder, let the portcullis fall," in a score of states and check the stampede. He had only his clarion voice. Oratory could not stop the panic; the multitude left him as it came to him. After which he went on lecturing till that gave out, and running for the Senate till that gave out. Finally he became an emeritus statesman. He had saved some money. He could always draw a crowd, with a fairly good stipend at the gate. And at the last he espoused queer causes. He pleaded them in a plausible way, using with pleasant facility short Anglo-Saxon words that often move juries, but are not so telling in briefs.

As he walked further into the sophisticated world his gaucherie made him seem selfish where he was only cautious, sordid where he intended to be careful. He just did not know about life. And so, despite the fact that he was always battling for something, or attacking something or crusading in one holy land or another, he really touched life less and less as the years went by. He spoke more and more as an oracle, and put barriers against intimacies; barriers to everyone except to Mrs. Bryan. She who had been his boyhood sweetheart remained his lifelong friend. But others felt in dealing with him as they would toward an actor or a play-boy. He spoke too often with his associates like a man in a trance, or masked, who proclaimed his wisdom in high-flown words containing many semi-vowels. His enemies felt that he posed like a prophet, but vanity never directed his ways; rather a passionate earnestness controlled. If ever American politics developed a meek, generous Christian gentleman, it was William Jennings Bryan. He will have no trouble matching virtues with the saints, even though the philosophers lift an eyebrow when he appears in their paradise.

Bryan's contribution to his time was important. As men go, in American politics, he was a great man. He prepared the way for others. Yet he reaped also where others before him had sown. He respectabilized the doctrines of the Greenbackers and the Grangers, the Farmers' Alliance and the Populists, by carrying those doctrines into the National Democratic platform and giving them light and leading, as the National Democratic candidate. Bryan made it possible for Roosevelt to restate and reconstruct the Bryan dogma in realizable ideals, many of which Roosevelt left on the doorstep of the Wilson administration. Wilson took them and made them his, and so those issues passed out of politics into life.

Bryan was first and last an agitator. He had few

talents, none of which he ever wrapped in a napkin. He was the good and faithful servant who, if he had no important intellectual qualities, had moral sense, moral courage, and tremendous emotional energy. He was the heart and the voice, rather than the brains, of the earlier Liberal movement. When he stopped to examine, to reconstruct, to build, he was courageously futile, even to the point of absurdity. But when he pointed truth home, even if it wasn't his own truth, even if it was that half truth which the Populists could understand, Bryan was a power; a power for righteousness. His life, on the whole, was on the side of the angels. At least, Bryan always wished to work with the forces of righteousness, and when he erred it was an error of intelligence and not of courage. He seems to have had no relations with women, no women friends, no romantic contacts of any kind except with Mrs. Bryan. If he ever, from early youth to his dying day, felt a desire to tread the primrose path, he sublimated it completely and the desire never appeared in a hard or bitter attitude toward life. He was an optimist and never a dreamer. For he energized his faith; made his private opinion public opinion where he could, but he could not institutionalize public opinion as Roosevelt and Wilson could.

Certainly Bryan's mental processes were slow, lumbering, and inaccurate. Yet he had a curious instinct which might be called an instinct of political diagnosis. He knew when things were wrong. He did not know how they were wrong, and he never offered an adequate remedy for the wrongs he saw. Yet he was right fundamentally, as often as any statesman of his time. He was right when he proclaimed that the country needed more money

in the mid-nineties. He was wrong in demanding that it
should be fiat money. He was right in his instinct that
the transportation problem needed serious consideration.
He was wrong in standing for government ownership in
1900. From the viewpoint of a partisan Democrat, he
was right in opposing imperialism in 1899, but he was
wrong from the same viewpoint in advising Democrats
to ratify the peace treaty with Spain, which gave us
Porto Rico and the Philippines. In the Democratic convention at Baltimore, in 1912, Bryan was right instinctively from the start to the finish, and yet on any particular motion or at any parliamentary stage of the proceedings his case could hardly be justified upon the
intelligence and the information of the hour. As Secretary of State, his chief and only official act of importance was his endeavor to secure peace treaties between
America and the world, yet the treaties themselves did
not avail much. They will hardly hold water. But his
attitude toward peace did tremendously strengthen the
hand of Wilson after Bryan had left the Cabinet, when
Wilson held a vision of world alliances and universal
peace.

Probably Bryan will not loom a large figure in another
generation. He coined no phrase which will outlast his
time. He originated no policy which is linked with his
name even in this generation. Yet he was one of the
saints in the apostolic succession who have moved
America and so have influenced the world. Without
Bryan, Roosevelt would have been handicapped. Even
Roosevelt's energies alone could not have carried the
Progressive cause to the climax of 1912. Certainly,
without the climax of 1912, Wilson could not have come
into power. And without Wilson there would have been

no League of Nations. Probably in history the Liberal
movement of the nineties and the first two decades of
this century in America will have one major contribution
to Western civilization: that will be the idea first institutionalized in 1919, at Paris, of a World Association
in the interests of international welfare, justice, and
peace. The economic and political expansion which came
as a result of an enlightened conscience in America, came
as the natural expansion of the economic life of the world
under the stimulus of steam and electricity. A rough
approximation of justice has followed this natural expansion, which brought in a late phase of the new world
revolution that started in the midst of the nineteenth
century; the marvelous distribution of goods necessary
under mass production, quick sales, high wages, and low
costs. Justice has followed this last turn of the wheel—
justice of a kind. The next variation of industrial life
must be in world organization. And in its rudimentary
forms the Wilson idea marked a notable change, a forward movement in the evolution of mankind. It was to
that end, unconsciously, that Bryan, the pioneer revolutionist of the nineties, lent his strength. All the clamor
and the turmoil of 1896, the recrimination and hullabaloo
of the twentieth century's first decade, seem to-day as
remote from the idea of world association as they do from
human slavery. Yet Bryan was the sower who went forth
to sow the seed of this new Liberalism. These seeds, falling in the earth, through the miraculous alchemy of the
forces of life appeared as a strange new impulse in the
world, an impulse that was only vaguely in Bryan's
dream. So life unfolds and manifests itself in many ways,
"Lest one good custom should corrupt the world."

PART IV

THE GREAT REBELLION

"All we have of freedom, all we use and know,
This our fathers bought for us, long and long ago!"

Those were surely Cromwellian times—from 1901 to 1917. What a lot of liberty we bought "with lance and torch and tumult" in those days from Roosevelt to Wilson! In those days the America of *laissez faire*, the Jeffersonian America, passed. The morality of the people restated itself in the laws and institutions needed by a complex civilization. If ever our land had a noble epoch, America enjoyed it in those days of The Great Rebellion.

THEODORE ROOSEVELT*

CHAPTER XXVI

"A HAPPY GENTLEMAN IN BLOOD AND LINEAMENTS"

THEODORE ROOSEVELT was a giant; an overgrown personality. He was one of those sports that, appearing once or twice in a century or in an age, work tremendous havoc or harmony, and disappear apparently without spiritual progeny. Greatness, generally speaking, is an unusual quantity of a usual quality grafted upon a common man. The thing which the gods gave Roosevelt in excess was energy. He was Gargantuan in his capacity for work. It was one of those utterly unthinkable coincidences, coincidences so rare, so unbelievable that they almost force one to believe in the minute Divine direction of human affairs,

*The reader should be warned that Theodore Roosevelt was my friend and probably I cannot be fair in estimating his weaknesses. This article was edited and somewhat rewritten more than nine years after his death. Yet he seems as vital now as he ever was in my life. Still his own justification of incidents in his life—as, say, his cruise in Panama, or his quarrel with Wilson—seem to me reasonable and on the whole inevitable, being what he was, and on the whole tolerable. So what I tried to make an honest estimate is scarcely better than a eulogy.

that a man of Roosevelt's enormous energy should come
to the Presidency of exactly that country which at exactly
that time was going through a transitional period—critical, dangerous, and but for him terrible—between an old
rural, individual order and a new highly socialized
industrial order. Of course the transition did not come
abruptly. The transition period began in the eighteen-
fifties, before the Civil War. It has not closed as these
lines are written in 1928, but the peak of crisis was passed
somewhere between 1905 and 1916, a time during which
Theodore Roosevelt was either in the White House or
was a political leader of the first magnitude. In that
period he went through his late forties into his early sixties, the ripest time of his life. He stood in 1912, when he
was in the midst of his most important activity, a stocky
man of five feet ten or eleven, long-legged, short-bodied,
never pursy, though at times too heavy. He kept himself
well trained physically; and electric energy seemed to exude
from his body and emphasize his personality. His walk
was a shoulder-shaking, assertive, heel-clicking, straight-
away gait, rather consciously rapid as one who is habitu-
ally about his master's business. He shook hands vigorously with a powerful downward pull like a pumper, with
a firm but never rough handclasp. His shoulders sloped
a little off the square line, and his head often, perhaps
generally, was thrust forward from the neck, a firm short
pedestal for his face; indeed, his neck was a sort of muscular part of his face, which jammed his head forward
without ever requiring a stoop of the shoulders. His
countenance was dominated by a big, pugnacious nose, a
mustache dropped to cover a sensitive mouth in which a
heavy underlip sometimes protruded, indicating passion.

Occasionally he used the loose lip as a shutter, purposely to uncover a double row of glittering teeth that were his pride. He knew that his display of teeth was effective as a gesture of humor or of rage. His slightly cleft chin could shoot out from a broad jaw, and when he was excited he worked his jaw muscles with an animal ferocity. They swelled and undulated in his moments of excitement, furnishing a physical outlet for his inner stress. Even in his thirties, when youth was still strong upon him, he had a wide, high brow, and to the end kept his hair intact. Probably his hair did not retreat a fraction of an inch in all his life. It was always stiff hair, inclined to curl, fairly close cropped, always trimmed, and gave his countenance an aspect of virility so real that, looking at Roosevelt's hair, one could understand how Delilah thought she would sap Samson's strength by shearing him. Roosevelt's eyes always peered through glasses, generally nose glasses when he was indoors or in civilized environment, and the glasses often gave a glint to his face which was absent when he took them off; for his grayish blue eyes were the least ferocious features in his face. Out of his countenance two men were wont to gaze at the world: One was a primitive—impetuous, imperious, splashing in a reservoir of vigor; the other was sophisticated, not ever quite furtive, but often feline. There, sometimes, glanced obliquely from his face the shadow of some inner femininity deeply suppressed, some exquisitely well-bred but devious female ancestress who sometimes flicked catwise out of his subconsciousness into the light and back again, as he clicked his glittering ivory teeth while purpose was surging from impulse into measured words. He rarely spoke hastily, but never acted

tardily.   Yet in his moments of inner debate one could
see that old catlike great-grandmother hiding behind the
shadow of his smile, or beneath the umbrage of a glare.
She was always a minority report, but never entirely
absent.   Mostly Roosevelt was canine, and spiritually
kicked dirt behind him and barked; perhaps in certain
hours he gave tongue loudest to convince himself—bark-
ing at the treed cat of his own ancestry.   But he surely
was big, overwhelming, towering, monumental, a very
Goliath of a personality inflated out of a common man by
surplus energy.   Every faculty, every purpose, every
impulse, every physical and spiritual inch of him was over-
engined.   Yet his qualities were coördinated.   He made,
with all his Cyclopean features, a well-balanced man and
mind.   If he was a freak, God and the times needed one.

THE AMERICAN LION.

A French artist's impression of Roosevelt.   The African journey furnished
the occasion for this spirited cartoon by Frueh.

CHAPTER XXVII

CHILDE ROLAND AND HIS DARK TOWER

So much for the picture of a gorgeous fighting, laughing, loving, hating, robust man. Now for the background, for the battlefield upon which he wrought. Let us put his time of bitterest and most useful strife between 1902 and 1914, a dozen crowded years. Before he appeared on the national scene as a major figure, America was in the midst of a struggle between two civilizations, an agricultural civilization and an industrial civilization; the one strongly individualistic, philosophically Puritan, economically self-sufficient, spiritually earnest, and aspiring; the other necessarily deeply socialized, highly dependent upon every wind of whim for existence, anchored somewhat in luck and naturally gayly fatalistic, lacking the Puritan vices and hating their virtues. In the three decades following the Civil War, a rural civilization for the first time in the world had to call in capital. Probably the homestead law, more than any other one factor, was responsible for the new condition that faced America following the Civil War. This law, as it emerged finally in the sixties, gave to every federal soldier a homestead of one hundred and sixty acres. The Union veterans of the Civil War, young men in their late twenties and thirties, with their young wives, flocked into the West by the hundreds of thousands and took up the rich, raw land of the Western Mississippi Valley. They had energy, courage, vision, and the decent puritanical ideals of the English-speaking races; took joy in their physical work, but had only their own hands for their capital. They had to borrow, and they mortgaged their land as soon as they had title to it; mortgaged it that they might improve it, stock it with cattle and hogs and horses, fence it, clear it, build homes and cultivate orchards upon it. The whole new West was built on borrowed money. And when this outside capital came to the farmers in the Western Mississippi Valley it took away some of the farmer's independence; socialized him to a certain extent and in spots made him a socialist when pay-day came. The Grangers, the Greenbackers, the Farmers' Alliance, the Populists, the Bryanites, a slowly widening and gradually diluted brand of American socialism, attracted the farmers of the Middle West in the seventies, eighties, and nineties as mortgages fell due. Mostly the ten- and twenty-year mortgages, which were executed following the Civil War, when the soldiers went West to establish their homesteads, fell due in the nineties. Then the Populists joined the Democrats in the South and West. Under an expanded currency in the late nineties debts were settled, mortgages renewed, stability appeared. But the problem of a changing agriculture struggling with an expanding industrial civilization was by no means settled. Populism, led by Bryan and greatly advertised by adoption into the National Democratic Party, was standing for measures which would curb industrialism, take power from the hands of industrial captains in tariff-protected New England, and curtail the power of the railroads in the newly settled mid-continent.

The Populists demanded a secret ballot, the direct

primary, the initiative and referendum, to give the individual voter strength and dignity at the ballot box. They demanded also government control of the railroads, government regulation of the trusts. The Populists stood for postal savings banks and expansion of the currency. All these socialistic measures put into the hands of unsocialized voters of rural communities much authority and power. The fight for these Populist measures had well begun, but was only a decade old, when Roosevelt came to the White House. The Republican party was committed definitely against these measures. Roosevelt, as a candidate for Governor of New York, had not espoused them. Yet as a governor he had stood for what he regarded as a square deal and had dramatized somewhat the more equitable of the Populist demands for regulation of capital affected by public use, in several sharp conflicts which he won and, winning, shot terror into the hearts of the party leaders. As Vice-President he had combated Bryan on the stump; out-talked him. Also he had been writing essays for magazines that were deeply heretical. Yet Wall Street Conservatives suspected him, not because he was irregular in his creed, but because he was free.

Now all this agitation on behalf of broader political liberties and wider participation in the economic gains of the country presumes some considerable subtraction of political privileges and economic rewards from a lively minority. Such a minority assumes the presence of some sort of organized effort on the part of those holding the desirable privileges and benefits. That organization was rapidly becoming a static plutocracy. Politically it was Hamiltonian and eminently respectable. It had the charters of both party organizations behind it. Politics and business were merged in a gorgeous fabric, woven so that business supported politics by doles and politics supported business by setting up special privileges for business. The merger of business and politics was called, at the time, "the system," and the local expression of the system in a town or a city or a state was called "the machine." The head of the machine, whether he was a Democrat in Democratic communities or a Republican in Republican communities, was the boss. The boss always was local—a ward boss, a town boss, a city boss, a state boss. Only Mark Hanna might have been called a national boss; and he was so much more a business man than a politician and he had such a sense of humor that he failed as a national boss, and at best or worst was the "business man in politics," and was less effective probably in politics than in business. His talents were of business; his instincts of politics. A national boss never arose out of the system. Bosses and machines under the system locally rose, fattened, rotted, and fell. But the system went long undisturbed. In the Republican party, which was after all the firmer stronghold of the plutocracy, bosses and their machines tended to flourish in state-wide units and upon state-wide business organizations. The Democratic machine flourished typically in the great cities. A wide difference existed between the two kinds of machines. The Republican machine was put together by a ruling boss, who gathered district and county bosses around him and passed to them the largess which he received, either officially as State Republican Chairman or unofficially as caliph of the region, from large business concerns seeking protection from the barbarian hordes of unrest and the predatory vandals of corruption clamoring in every countryside, village, and farm. Contributions came to the State Republican boss from the railroads, from the insurance companies, from the packing houses in the West and the manufacturers in the East and other large industrial concerns which desired to control, as they saw fit, hours of labor, working conditions, competition; also to be free from drastic regulations. The boss received the contribution from business and generally retaining for himself a decent percentage of the tribute, passed the remainder down to the district and region bosses—who, in turn, saved something for themselves and passed it to those who controlled the towns, wards, townships, and precincts; who also took personal retainers before distributing to the smaller fry. It was the business of the smaller fry and the little bosses to control caucuses and conventions. These minor boss-controlled caucuses and conventions had to name as Republican candidates for various offices touching the legislative, judicial, and administrative departments of the county and state government, men who were "safe and sane." By "safe and sane" one means officials who would not disturb the entente cordiale between business and politics. To disturb that pleasant relation was a form of treason, mild or damnable in proportion as it trifled with details or struck at the heart of the organization.

The Democratic machine, in the North at least, was largely a city machine. City bosses generally, throughout the North, were Democratic bosses. They were allied with vice; levied tribute from saloon-keepers who desired to violate the laws which regulated the saloons, also from gamblers, often from dive-keepers, and always from

lawyers who defended the bolder criminals, and from the
operators of public utilities—the electric light companies,
the gas companies, the street car companies, and occasionally came tributes from banks financing these companies. The Democratic boss was not as respectable as
the Republican boss. No state university gave the Democratic city boss honorary degrees as colleges heaped
degrees upon the plug-hatted, graven image who controlled the Republican state organization. The Democratic boss rode in no private car, hobnobbed with no
railroad president, belonged to few country clubs, and
when his daughter married he came with his hat in his
hand to the respectable morning paper with her photograph, hoping that it might be printed in the society
column of the Sunday paper. The daughter of the Republican boss, home from her Eastern women's college, was
married like a princess. Private cars, even special trains,
hurried across the land to join her cortège, and she often
tripped gracefully from the society department of the
newspaper to the first page upon her wedding procession
with a royal swish of her train. Her divorce later came
politely hidden under a one-line head over on the want
ad page. Business organizations like railroads, insurance companies, and large financial houses, which backed
concerns engaged in interstate commerce, owned the local
state bosses; and these local state bosses, assembling at
national conventions of the party, took orders from Wall
Street or, being proud, sometimes gave orders to Wall
Street in small matters, like the nomination of a Vice-
President or a pension plank in the platform. But the
system was set and institutionalized. It was as respectable as the Constitution, and the Constitution was held up

before the eyes of innocent children as the inspiration and defense of the system. Money controlled caucuses; caucuses controlled conventions; conventions nominated candidates; candidates became officials; officials were controlled by politics; politics was owned by business.

The system was human; being human, it had human faults and human virtues, and, being human, its human faults were overbalanced by its human virtues. Good men did frequently, even generally, come into office, high and low. Man in any organized institution is attracted by the leadership of the best, the bravest, the noblest, the kindest, the wisest. So out of this system, yet always resting upon it and more or less conscious of it, the statesmen of the day arose. If they were Republicans these statesmen had a deep and sometimes lively appreciation of property rights when those rights conflicted with human rights. The protective tariff was sacrosanct with Republican statesmen. They were strong nationalists, naturally believers in bureaucracy, regularity and centralized government based upon the obedience of the many to the few. If the statesmen were Democrats, the tariff was not a sacred cow in their cosmos. Their notions of the rights of property in conflict with the rights of man were sometimes dubious. For they were Jeffersonians, yet unconscious believers in aristocracy. They were stiff-necked, high-collared, unpurchasable, and often highly vocal in their advocacy of a decentralized government, home rule, states' rights, freedom of the individual. From the South came the brigadiers of the Confederacy; proud, aloof gentlemen, addicted to fine-cut tobacco and fervid rhetoric, as remote from reality as marble gods in the Parthenon, but honest, courageous, and generally futile.

It was the system of government which gave America these static statesmen, against whom the Grangers, the Greenbackers, the Farmers' Alliance, the Populists, Bryan and his followers, came clamoring and raging through the seventies, eighties, and nineties. In '96 the mob terrorized the citadel of privilege. In 1900 the mob was disintegrated. The citadel seemed safe, a mighty fortress of business defended by politics. This stronghold loomed before Vice-President Theodore Roosevelt. Then suddenly he was called down the mountain one dark night, when McKinley died, to take the oath of office as President of the United States. When he appeared in Buffalo he wore his black slouch hat and a business suit with trousers all bagged and wrinkled from a tedious journey; a day's beard on his face, youth in his eyes, high visions glowing in his countenance, and justice crying in his heart. He stood in the Milburn parlor as he took the oath of office among the frock-coated, high-hatted dignitaries of the day; a sort of political stepchild, to be taken into the fortress of a privileged plutocracy and tolerated there for a brief season and maybe smothered in its gloomy dungeon. "And so Childe Roland to the dark tower came."

CHAPTER XXVIII

JUST BEFORE THE BATTLE

In the early part of this century a story circulated about the elder Morgan, John Pierpont II, which possibly may not be true; at least it is unverified, but, like many apocryphal stories, it is important as showing how the myth-making mind of man works its ideals into its folk tales. The story tells how the news of McKinley's assassination came to Wall Street. A reporter from an evening paper, bearing a telegram signed by the Associated Press, dashed into the Morgan office. They brought the banker out of his private room and the reporter presented his telegram. The great financier took the paper, read it, and spat out a few incredulous damns. He whirled about once, like a man who is shot but feels no pain. An instant later the shock of the news got into his leather-covered consciousness; his face flared red, and he staggered back to his desk, where he sat ashen-gray, his head nodding and his jaw a-tremble. Personally he did not know McKinley well. The two men were merely acquaintances. But the quaking hands controlled not merely millions but a billion dollars that were being hoisted into permanent organization by a thousand pulleys hanging to the crane of prosperity. McKinley was the man in the engine room who steadied the crane, and if it wobbled that load fell. The terror of this man at the thought of McKinley's death typified the fear of all

295

organized capital. The keepers of the citadel were surely in terror when the strange knight appeared inside the moat.

Yet, if Theodore Roosevelt had died before September, 1901, his name in the tables of Vice-Presidents of the United States would probably mean no more a hundred years hence than the names of Daniel D. Tompkins, Richard M. Johnson, George M. Dallas, and other obscure Vice-Presidents. In dictionaries of American literature, two inches of brevier type would record that he had written ten or a dozen books, and give a list of the positions he had filled. An infinitesimally small number of Americans of the next century, historians, and advanced students of the period of American development from 1870 to 1899, would have a look at Roosevelt's "Winning of the West," "American Ideals," "With the Rough Riders in Cuba," and in so much as the style of these writings reveals the man, scholars would know him as a frank-spoken, sturdy fellow, a hater of shams, and a friend of every one who gets things done and over with. No doubt American biography in the next century will tell of stories of similar characters—fine enough, of course, but almost unknown and of limited influence. Roosevelt rose somewhat upon the ordinary rounds of political promotion; from a state legislator to a city office, Police Commissioner of New York City; from that to Federal office, Civil Service Commissioner; and later to a higher Federal office, Assistant Secretary of the Navy, and from that to Governor of New York. So he was trained in politics. But that does not explain his rise. Whence his strength? How did he win? To answer these questions, it is first necessary to find the keynote of

YOU'VE GOT TO CUT LOOSE, MR. PRESIDENT, IF YOU EVER EXPECT TO REACH
THE TOP.

From a drawing by E. W. Kemble in *Harper's Weekly*.

Roosevelt's character. That was his ambition. And his ambition—the one great, ever-active purpose that, lying nearest to his heart, was the mainspring of his life—was to set an example before Americans, and especially youth. Always he saw himself in every public performance mirrored in the heart of youth. This reflection kept him always young. He was forever imagining himself as a man of the highest ideals, derived from good birth and liberal advantages, demonstrating to the youth of his country what such a man can do in politics in all honesty, without soiling his hands, for the betterment of American life and the progress of the world. In his early career he failed to realize his ambition. The country for the most part misread his motives. Men roughly regarded him as a pugnacious, impetuous, honest, but eccentric young man, or at best, perhaps, a harum-scarum, "bronco-busting" lover of notoriety, a poseur who liked a fight for its own sake and had no regard for the amenities of political relationship. Few of his partisans and fewer of his opponents saw, until he was well into his career, that they had a rare species of politician on their hands, one whose training had been moral rather than political. The American creed is that most politicians of all parties are bad, the worst ones generally being in the other party, and the good ones all dead or out of office. Americans believe that to get an office and enjoy it forever is the chief end of a politician's existence. Roosevelt had held office more than half his life, between his majority and the day he came to the White House. These offices entailed more labor and brought Roosevelt more enemies than glory or material reward. Only as Governor of New York and as Vice-President was his official salary as much as he could make writing for magazines and publishing books. But he never felt the need of money.

He went from Harvard to the New York legislature with a distinct purpose. He was reëlected because of his capacity to accomplish things. Purpose pushed him from one office to another, purpose and a rather noble Narcissan ambition to shine in the hearts of men of his caste and class as a knight errant of democracy. He was Civil Service Commissioner under Benjamin Harrison in his early thirties and Police Commissioner of the City of New York at thirty-six, and at thirty-nine, in 1917, he was Assistant Secretary of the Navy. The place required much hard work, offered no glory. Roosevelt resigned from that office to be a soldier in the Spanish-American War. His training as a soldier in Cuba increased—what a brief Western experience had already given him—his understanding of men, the love of direct, individual action, and the comforting knowledge of his own personal bravery. In those days he told his friends that until he was in his first battle he did not know surely whether he was going to bolt or not. It was a toss-up between the cat and the dog in him!

He won the office of Governor of New York in a whirlwind of enthusiasm that followed the Cuban War. As the Republican candidate for Governor of New York he owed no political gratitude to Senator Platt, the state Republican boss, yet in an interview with the reporters, Roosevelt said, in so many words, that in making his appointments he "would consult Senator Platt." The politicians concluded at once that Roosevelt had stultified himself. Platt was the head of the Republican organization in New York; a Republican governor who refused to

consult him as the head of his party would disrupt the
party to no good end.   Roosevelt's critics failed to see
that a man brave enough to say squarely to Platt's
enemies that he would consult Platt, would make that
consultation honorable.   Platt found this out.   At these
consultations Platt suggested the names of several unfit
men for high offices.   Roosevelt refused to appoint them.
Platt vainly pleaded, blustered, threatened.   Roosevelt,
courteously, yet finally and with emphasis, told Platt to
name honest men or none.   Platt named honest men.
They were appointed.   So Roosevelt "consulted Mr.
Platt."   There were other consultations.   Platt desired
the governor's signature to what Roosevelt believed were
bad laws.   Platt could not get it.   Roosevelt favored a
bill taxing the franchises of corporations.   Platt opposed
the bill.   Platt schemed and intrigued.   Roosevelt openly
brought to bear the direct pressure of his gubernatorial
influence.   The Franchise Tax Bill won.   Passing that
bill, Roosevelt was learning to be President.   The consultations with Mr. Platt grew less and less frequent,
though they were always frank, always free and fair.
Roosevelt sought them.   Platt grew tired of them.   The
wily Platt, checkmated in New York, sought aid from
afar.   He intrigued with Quay of Pennsylvania and some
Westerners, and made Roosevelt Vice-President against
his wish and will, not to praise Roosevelt but to bury
him!   Roosevelt, in so far as he directed his political
fortunes toward the White House, came there not
because he aimed high but because he always aimed to hit
a mark worth hitting—and generally he rang the bell.
Common sense is so common that few of us really value
it, and when a man like Roosevelt comes along and will
have nothing else for his mental food and moral drink but

the ordinary wisdom of the race, men are appalled and call him many strange names—superman among others. Roosevelt was no superman—except physically in his capacity for hard work. Indeed he was much like the rest of us, and always knew it. The spiritual quality which raised and glorified him was his honesty. Honesty is not rare, but Roosevelt was so intensely what he was that his honesty glowed—a burning flame.

The average man, sitting by the average grate fire in the average club living-room in the United States in 1901, would have proclaimed the same opinion about civic morality and public honor that Roosevelt proclaimed. If Roosevelt had dropped in, there would have been amiable discussion, but few differences between the clubmen in spinning theories. But when the average man left his club for the caucus or convention, the legislature or Congress, he would accept things as they were and thank God he was not as other men. Roosevelt balked. He fought for things as they should be and can be. He spent his life trying to do much that the common man had dreamed should be done.

Moreover, Roosevelt started out to do many things that were left undone. And so, while Roosevelt had worked for a time as legislator, leaving that work unfinished; for a time as ranchman; as civil service commissioner; as governor, leaving work to be done by others; even as President with rough ends showing; as agitator for liberalism, in the midst of his task he quit his career with certain definite achievements. His life as a whole was efficient; chiefly as a definite, consistent inspiration to like-minded Americans. In that much his ambition was fully realized.

CHAPTER XXIX

THE CAPTURED CITADEL

THESE remarks about Theodore Roosevelt, the man
and the statesman, are necessary to explain why the
tickers that record the Wall Street market recorded
danger when McKinley died. Yet the market had to live
with Roosevelt. The politicians had to live with Roosevelt. And in a year life had settled down to a fairly
comfortable status. Roosevelt had developed a technique in handling politicians at Washington. During the
first two months the President and the statesmen devoted
their time to getting used to one another. The statesmen had one way of doing things, Roosevelt another.
There was friction, plenty of it. Each side gave in a
little. The trouble began when the President insisted on
being a party to minor appointments. He refused to let
senators and congressmen assume the responsibility for
bad appointments. The President made them withdraw
the names of undesirable men and substituted the names
of better men for all offices, post offices, minor Federal
jobs in the state. Congressmen and senators began to
rebel at the humiliation; indeed formed a cabal, referred
to Roosevelt as "His Accidency"—a title left over from
Grover Cleveland's first term—which soothed their feelings and amused Roosevelt. In January, following the
September when Roosevelt first took the oath as President, Congress reassembled after the holiday recess with

the Republican majority mad all the way through. Senators and congressmen had pledged their word to give certain offices to certain undesirable candidates, possibly for certain rather questionable work at polls and in the caucuses. If these candidates were turned down, naturally they would think one of two things: that their sponsors were playing double, or that their sponsors had lost caste at the White House, either of which alternatives the Republicans in Congress viewed with consternation. Probably the President took counsel, possibly he himself saw the danger of a break in the Republican party. He tacked. He permitted a number of particularly vicious candidacies to hang up—that is to say, he did not appoint them nor reject them. The statesmen sponsoring the vicious candidates, being thoroughly scared, generally presented other candidates for the office, on the whole acceptable. These were quickly and cheerfully named. As the winter drifted into spring, statesmen —seeing that the President was firm—quietly withdrew their offensive candidates for Federal appointments, got them placed comfortably either in state offices or in business jobs, and before hay time nearly all the friction was over. At the end of the year, politicians knew better than to endorse a man with a bad record for a place under the government at Washington.* The moral atmosphere of the nation was purified with ozone and a violent display of thunder and lightning was averted. Statesmen of the more pharisaical caste probably felt that

* Of course this statement is only broadly true. Theodore Roosevelt was not a god. He made many mistakes. He compromised when he had to compromise. But if he was looking the other way when a bad man passed the gate he turned his head not in cowardice or connivance, but in inadvertence. His intention was good; his performance much better than fair, though of course, far from angelic.

Roosevelt was disrupting the Republican party, because certain candidates in their states whom they had indorsed had not been appointed by the President. Yet it was a curious fact that while four or five prominent candidates for the Republican presidential nomination were about to enter the race in 1901, after Roosevelt had been in office a year and a half he stood practically without opposition. The thing which saved Roosevelt, probably, was his laugh. Time and again he punctured the cant and sophistry of an argumentative statesman with a twinkling grin and a gurgle:

"Oh, come now, Senator!"

He made friends with Senator Hanna. The two men were too much alike and had too much twitch in the corners of their mouths and too much curvature of the vest to quarrel seriously. After a man fills up a forty-two inch waistband a number of things lose their relative importance and honorable peace seems desirable. So it was with Hanna and Roosevelt.

Peace was the more easily obtained between Roosevelt and Hanna because of the scrupulous exactness with which Roosevelt had kept his pledge to follow McKinley's lead and keep McKinley's word in matters of national policy. McKinley was Hanna's idol. And so exactly had Roosevelt held to his promise at the beginning of his year's work that he had done practically nothing in the way of forming new policies. He had been clearing up the work that McKinley left unfinished. The Panama Canal, left over from the McKinley administration, was actually begun and practically finished under Roosevelt; so was the establishment of civil government in the Philippines. Reciprocity, particularly Cuban reciprocity, originated with McKinley, and Roosevelt followed McKinley's intention to the letter in this matter. In the politics of the day was no more pathetic spectacle than that of McKinley pleading through the lips of Hanna with the rebellious senators to stand by Roosevelt and Cuban reciprocity. When certain senators refused to listen, feeling that defeat would rebuke Roosevelt, they were treading on Hanna's softest corn, and gave Roosevelt Hanna for an ally. But men on the wrong side may always be trusted to do the wrong thing.

Early in his presidential career Roosevelt had tremendously disturbed the reactionary wing of conservatism by his patronage fights with the Senate, by his demand for Cuban reciprocity over the opposition of the sugar interests, by the appointment of Oliver Wendell Holmes, Jr., to the Supreme Court. Holmes was regarded in Massachusetts as rather an unsafe and unsettling Liberal, a book lawyer and a Puritan Brahmin. Finally, Roosevelt disturbed the right wing of Conservatism by instituting a suit under the Sherman Anti-Trust Law against the Northern Pacific and the Great Northern railroads, charging them with establishing a merger in restraint of competitive trade. During his first year he made no important declaration of Liberalism, but it was obvious to the more intelligent Liberals of the country that Roosevelt was rather definitely committed to their cause, and also that he was using the thin edge of the wedge to drive his principles home.

Even at the end of his second year in the White House Roosevelt had not declared formal war upon the defenders of the citadel of special privilege. That citadel stood upon the firm foundation of Republican tradition.

But Roosevelt was mining it. There sprang up out of the grass a group of young Liberals, men at whom he had been unconsciously aiming all his life, who were coming into politics, and particularly into Republican party politics, not for the spoils, not to strengthen the machine, but for the fun of the game and the glory of God. They were mostly young men of means and some leisure, young business and professional men. For some strange reason, though Roosevelt all his life was the friend of Labor, the Labor movement never followed in his train. When he was a Bull Moose candidate ten years later, Labor remained aloof from him. But this young Liberal group, probably sons of mugwumps of the eighties—and Roosevelt was friendly with the mugwumps in the eighties—formed the nucleus of a faction inside the Republican party. It was evident in the second year of his administration that this faction might form. It was the first faction that had formed since the Silverites bolted in 1896.

For an impulsive man, Roosevelt was conspicuously cautious in those first years of his presidency. Yet certainly he was noisier than McKinley. He filled the White House with all sorts and conditions of men; Western bullwhackers, city prize fighters, explorers, rich men, poor men, an occasional black man, editors, writers; and around his festal board gathered three times a day, from early morn until night, men whose faces never had been seen in the White House before. Party managers, to whom the White House table was an altar before which they bowed, were disturbed at the motley crew which Roosevelt called in. That assembly also was a sign of the times, a sign that Roosevelt had turned his back upon the citadel of privilege and all that it shielded and was looking into a new day to begin another struggle.

He was a book protectionist; not a political protectionist. He fried fat gingerly, holding his nose; whereas the party under the leadership of Hanna for twenty years inhaled the fumes of protective fat frying, as high priests love the blood of the altar. Roosevelt preached the simple life and became a book agent for a Swiss pastor's sermons on simplicity, advertising "The Simple Life" in a speech in which he attacked the trusts. And when he preached simplicity, it was a part of his cult to live his creed. In the White House his life as a father, as a husband, as a citizen, as a politician, was most interesting, but almost primitive in its simplicity. Few forms were observed. He cut red tape. He talked state secrets in a loud voice to statesmen in the presidential workroom, so that reporters could hear. He went on long walks through the parks in the environs of Washington, taking fat military officers with him, who panted along a step or two behind him. He tolerated no sacred cows. The generals of the army and the admirals of the navy, as generals and admirals, did not overcome him. Yet as an individual any man in the army or the navy or the State or Interior Department might command Roosevelt's esteem, even affection. But the officer's gold braid and rooster feather clearly got no homage from the President. He wore for the most part the black slouch hat of the type he had bought when he was Police Commissioner, fashionable in the early nineties. It became him. He liked the style. He stuck to it. And except upon extremely formal occasions, as when reviewing a fleet or when at a state function, Roosevelt wore his slouch hat

and his business suit. The white-vested, black string-tied,
gray-trousered McKinley in his Prince Albert coat had
set a fashion for politicians. Roosevelt ruthlessly abolished the fashion. And, curiously enough, in abolishing
the fashion of ceremonial garb—as in a score of other
unconventional and revolutionary innovations—Roosevelt
was dropping powder in the mine to blow up the citadel
of privilege. So much of the cult of politics depends upon
interior ceremonies, empty forms, tin cornice, and false
fronts. His rejection of the pasteboard shams of life,
social life, business life, political life in and around the
White House, as much as his Anti-Trust suit against the
Northern railways, and more than the appointment of
Holmes to the Supreme Court, influenced the thought of
the times, took away the magic of the cult of high priests,
and turned America's heart from a solemn plutocracy to a
rather noisy and aspiring democracy.

The death of Hanna, in 1903, removed the last possible
aspirant for the Republican presidential nomination,
excepting Roosevelt, in the election of 1904. It was evident even before Hanna died that Roosevelt had overcome him. The President had the patronage of the White
House, and in the Southern states showed his determination to use it. He had a growing acclaim in the Middle
West. Academic, highly protected New England had
small use for Roosevelt in those days; but that mattered
little. He had settled a menacing coal strike. He had
strengthened the Trust laws. Before Hanna died Roosevelt had even contested Hanna's rule in Ohio—and won.
He had cleaned out the thieves in the Postal Department.
He had put new energy into the diplomatic wheels that
were to build the Panama Canal; wheels that were slow-

ing down under McKinley. Roosevelt had wrestled publicly and successfully with the machine element in every
state in the Union, where the machine had tried to
impose upon him for Federal appointment candidates
whom Roosevelt regarded as unworthy men. And these
tussles with the machine had always been advertised.
His few defeats and inevitable compromises were forgotten. The spotlight of publicity followed Roosevelt all
his life with curious devotion—by no means without
Roosevelt's encouragement. Certainly McKinley had
stood for clean men in high places. Many of McKinley's
appointees had been men of the highest type. It is only
fair to say that McKinley, on the whole, found better
men for high places than Roosevelt chose. It was in
choosing high-grade men for the minor appointments and
fighting for these men that Roosevelt made his mark.

McKinley had a fine intuition for character in men.
But if he fought the organization, he suppressed the news
of the combat. He remained regular, a part of the established order. Roosevelt, in his battles with the Republican
organization for men in minor places, called out the brass
band, rang for the fire department, put on a military
parade, and the nation saw the show. But in three years
he had won.

He was unopposed for the Republican presidential
nomination in 1904, because he was right in the sense
that he was following the deep and probably righteous
tendency of his times. He had strength to review both
sides of many proposals, and physical weakness did not
tempt him ever to take the easy way. It was his habit
to seek and follow the lines of greatest resistance; which
habit made him seem deeply courageous where he was

only mentally and morally acute.   In these three years
he had revealed to Congress and to the nation a man
of abnormal energy.   He often arose at six o'clock,
took half an hour of violent exercise, breakfasted at
seven, and was in his office at seven-thirty, grinding
away upon the day's work which a less energetic
man might have postponed until mid-forenoon.   At luncheon his table was crowded with visitors and he talked
incessantly, yet never lingered over the table; ate heartily
but not too heartily; enjoyed with a zest good food, and
knew about it; drank one glass of sherry and no more;
came back from lunch bursting into his office, where he
saw senators, Cabinet members, bureau assistants, and
chiefs, congressmen and citizens in a long procession, and
with the valves of his dynamic force pumped them
through the White House in a steady stream.   He decided
minor questions quickly and with seemingly almost brutal
casualness, even nonchalance, but really drawing from
deep wells of past experience in each decision.   Of a late
afternoon he went for a short drive, or went walking, riding, swimming, and sometimes all three, spending an hour
before dinner in vigorous exercise.   At dinner, often he
met a multitude.   If he was a bit weary he directed the
conversation, primed this man to tell a story, that woman
to talk, but kept the dinner table from breaking into stag-
nant pools.   It was one big powwow—that presidential
dinner table in the Roosevelt day.   Generally he did the
talking, ate well but not gluttonously, and by nine o'clock
had dismissed the casual guests and probably picked out
two or three.   These he took to his library and with them
wrangled over the day's passing problem.   He was a
swift, greedy reader, reading by pages rather than by

sentences, yet always absorbing the gist of any matter.
He read widely—current literature, Greek classics,
biology, the physical sciences, besides following many
curious, winding by-paths of literature that led into odd
places. He discovered once that Senator Quay made a
hobby of Icelandic sagas. Roosevelt crammed up on the
subject, invited Quay to dinner, and the two jabbered
away for hours, never mentioning the big fundamental
differences that had arisen between them. Having
charmed Quay and acquired his respect, Roosevelt found
it easier than before to conquer Quay in the political
matter between them. He must have slept soundly and
with deep refreshment, for often after an eighteen-hour
day he was up and about at six. But with all his splendid
vigor, time was not frittered away. It was directed with
a rather indomitable purpose to the day's work—the
thing in hand—the goal of the hour that he was seeking.
He did not win because he was all-wise, Jove-like and
morally thrice armed. His victories came to a great
extent because of the boundless might of his physical
body, wherein his brain was as well trained as his legs
or arms, and as tightly in leash as the corn sheller of a
stomach which ground his food into blood and energy.
This knight was no pale dreamer who came to the dark
tower of American politics, dominated it, and set it free.
He ruled not because he was brave and wise and kind,
though he was all three, but because his courage, his
wisdom, and his heart were hitched to a dynamo, which
gave him a sort of imperial authority.*

* Again the reader should be warned that this book is written by a
convinced Liberal who verily believes that "reason and the will of
God" are with the men who struggle to establish among their fellow-
men more and more equitable relations.

There was no fight in prospect in the spring of 1904, and so the Republican National Convention, opening in Chicago on June 21, was the first Republican National Convention held in forty years wherein every one could get a seat. Empty seats might be had for the asking the first day, and when the convention opened, hundreds of delegates' seats were vacant on the floor of the Coliseum. The fighting interest was lacking in the spectacle. Roosevelt was in control at the Republican machine. He had put rings in the noses of the holy cattle of the little temples and had assembled the herd, docile if not happy, in the great arena to nominate him. But they came without enthusiasm. The cheering was mechanical. When Roosevelt's name was first mentioned in a polite period by Mr. Elihu Root, temporary chairman of the convention, the pandemonium of applause lasted exactly one minute. The name of Hanna got exactly one minute in the same speech, and a minute was doled out to McKinley. Evidently the claque was doing its cheering by the day and not by the piece; for it refused to put an extra second of lung work on any name to give the performance finish and the verisimilitude of joy. The only burst of pure felicity came from the convention to greet Joe Cannon, who stood in Washington, even in Roosevelt's first term, as the type of old-fashioned "honest politician," whom the President's enemies openly worshiped as their political god. After three days of dreary platitudes from suppressed and subdued orators and favorite sons of the various states, Ex-Governor Black, of New York, who disliked Roosevelt instinctively and also for cause, and who had attacked the President covertly at a public dinner two months

"ALL IN FAVOR OF THE NOMINATION WILL SAY AYE!"
Chicago, June 21, 1904.

before, was called upon as the titular leader of the party
from Roosevelt's home state to place Roosevelt's name
before the convention as a presidential candidate. Black
nominated Roosevelt in an electric fountain of rhetorical
icicles. The speech may have thrilled the country; for
them Roosvelt was a people's President, but the enthusiasm in the Coliseum Hall was only a stage picture. One
almost wondered who was the costumer. The galleries
cheered heartily, for Chicago admired the President.
The politicians on the floor of the convention had to do
something, so for twenty long, weary minutes they turned
loose and cheered like mummers suddenly turned in upon
a wedding feast. When they felt that the amenities of
the occasion had been satisfied, when they felt that it
would not make "talk" for them to quit, the mummers
eased into silence. Senator Mat Quay, at St. Louis eight
years before, got a larger demonstration when he ran
against McKinley than Roosevelt got at the Chicago
convention that nominated him unanimously.

But the people were for Roosevelt, and the politicians
obeyed the popular mandate. Roosevelt secured his
nomination working openly upon the Republican organization in the country. He threw pretense aside. He
assembled the platform. He chose the officers of the
convention and he put his secretary, Mr. Cortelyou, in
as Chairman of the Republican National Committee to
conduct the campaign. He assumed full responsibility
and asked the people to be his witness that it was his job.
He probably picked Charles Fairbanks, of Indiana, as
the Republican candidate for Vice-President. Of course
over-nice people objected to the Roosevelt manner. They
preferred the punctilios of hypocrisy which certain other

Presidents had felt constrained to use under the rules of the political game. Such bald * candor as Roosevelt's had not been seen in the White House since Jackson's time. Roosevelt succeeded because in all his demands of the party he asked for no improper thing. There was his strength. He had moral sense as well as moral courage. His moral sense kept him from tripping. The politicians of the old order and the high caste in his first presidential years felt that Roosevelt's audacity was a sign of weakness, forgetting that audacity for the right is golden, and that mere impudence, for the sake of winning, is brass.

* His enemies called it brazen.

CHAPTER XXX

INSIDE THE DARK TOWER

In three years, Roosevelt had overcome and bound the defenders of the citadel of privilege and had occupied the dark tower himself in his own name. He did not wantonly destroy privilege with a sweep of his hand. He could not have done so. But he had implanted in the popular heart a faith in a new kind of democracy. The lesson to the Republican National Convention of 1904 was rather briefly this: That in the United States political institutions were safe. The party system, when turned over to spoilsmen, makes government merely an agency of priests of prosperity; but the same system is always at hand to serve the decent government when the people, properly led, know how to use government for the ends of justice. And more than this, the convention made it plain that though the party system had bred corrupt men and held them in power because the rank and file of the party sanctioned questionable leadership, when a brave, honest man like Roosevelt rose, strong enough and wise enough to use the party machinery for good ends, then the party system worked as easily and effectively for good ends as for bad ends. So at the close of his first term, his accidental term, Roosevelt functioned with his highest value as an example. It was not what he did, not even what he said, but how he said his say and did his work that counted.

It was worth infinitely more to America to have the picture of Roosevelt, triumphing over the Republican machine, stand at the head of the nation where the eyes of young men might see him, than it was to have prosperity and protection maintained, or to have the trusts brought to time, or the currency established upon a sound basis. Roosevelt was valuable to his country in that day, not because he stood for prosperity, and he did stand for prosperity after a fashion, but because he was a flaming prophet of justice, a Jeremiah enthroned!

From the day he entered American politics, standing on a chair in the Republican National Convention in 1884, snapping his teeth and shaking his fist at the Blaine crowd, until he walked down the steps of the White House in 1917, after calling on President Wilson and offering his services in the army, a period covering a generation, Roosevelt was first of all—and probably at the end of all—a prophet of justice. When he was sworn in for his first elective term in March, 1905, he sloughed off obligation to the McKinley administration and began making an administration in his own right. Then came the fight for the Roosevelt policies.

Theodore Roosevelt began the contest for the so-called Roosevelt policies when he delivered his inaugural address in March, 1905. The address was a challenge. He was no longer McKinley's successor. He was a militant Liberal, ready to take the Liberal leadership of the world, to join the movement which was interested not in policies looking toward the accumulation of wealth, but rather policies which were looking to government as an agency of human welfare, which should enact laws and form a new tendency in the world—a tendency moving toward the equitable distribution of wealth. This policy regarded prosperity as an incident of life, emphasizing justice in human relations before prosperity. This policy appealed to the farmer, to the merchant, to the small manufacturer outside of the trust, to labor in its upper levels, to skilled labor, the railroad brotherhoods, and to the country banker and the professional man.

The Roosevelt policies found their most cordial welcome in the middle West; their bitterest enemies in New

HIS FAVORITE AUTHOR.

From an original drawing by Mr. Everett E. Lowry. This is said to have been Mr. Roosevelt's favorite cartoon.

York and New England. The South cheered for Roosevelt, but did not follow him politically. When Roosevelt
announced his policy the holders and supporters of what
he termed "aggrandized wealth," "militant capital,"
turned upon him with righteous indignation. He had,
indeed, departed from the ways of the fathers. He
was trying to point his country to a new highway, to a
new destination. He was following Bryan rather than
McKinley. And throughout the land a furor arose. After
all, those who lived in the citadel of privilege were by no
means confined to Wall Street, Beacon Street, and the
homes of the investment bankers. Roosevelt's stand was
revolutionary, and every Conservative mind was shocked
at his pronouncement.

One must remember, in considering this Roosevelt pronouncement, that the wave of Populist protest had submerged even if its force had not subsided. Prosperity
had come to the land and blessed it. Only a man of
indomitable power could have turned America in that
hour from the business of accumulating wealth to a consideration of the equitable distribution of wealth. And
how he went at it! He took the Congress that was elected
with him and tried to hammer it into a usable instrument. The congressional leadership was frankly against
the Roosevelt policies. Cannon, Speaker of the House,
and Nelson Aldrich, official leader of the Senate, were
openly, bitterly, cynically against Roosevelt and his program. Which fact did not ruffle him. When he found a
senator or a member of the House of Representatives
difficult to handle, when, in the discussion of a problem,
senators raised factitious questions and would have
befuddled the issue, Roosevelt, under his black slouch

hat, clicking his white teeth, partly in rage, partly in joy, and partly from nervous exultation at the thought of combat, went out over the land into the districts of men who opposed him, preaching his doctrines, lending the prestige of the presidential office to the lever of his logic. And so America moved upward. His method in dealing with congressmen was direct, generally courteous, and always forthright. He loved intrigue of a harmless sort, but used it for amusement rather than gain. His Machiavellian strain was grafted upon his sense of humor. But his sheer brute strength and awkwardness won battles for him rather than his finesse and cunning. For four years he fought the good fight in the White House; precious years, fighting years, crammed full of eighteen battle hours a day. But always his contests were led by a man who could laugh. Roosevelt never giggled; he chuckled, and was not above a guffaw, and loved a roaring belly-laugh. Yet one must not forget that he was a Harvardian, a person of erudition who knew about music, painting, sculpture, history, poetry—the softer, finer things of life; one who had been reared observing the amenities, the son of a philanthropist, born indeed with the silver spoon in his mouth. And if he railed and preached in Gargantuan laughter, it was not the raucous clamor of a vacant mind. And so day after day, month after month, for four busy years, Roosevelt in the dark tower fought to let in the "light and leading" of Liberalism.

Now the Roosevelt policies were not confined to the list which Roosevelt made. These were largely legislative. But his attitude as an administrator also was sufficiently marked to make a policy. The legislative program

and the administrative attitude were in truth an attack
upon the citadel of privilege, nothing less and scarcely
more. It was, after all, as an agitator that Roosevelt
found his greatest usefulness; as an agitator against the
unsocial attitude of a wicked and perverse generation,
the rulers of the land, indeed the rulers of the world;
for the Liberal movement of America was going neck and
neck with the Liberal movement in Europe. Morley,
Asquith, Lloyd George in England, the Socialists in
Germany, Clemenceau in France, Nitti in Italy, were
men of a common purpose. And Roosevelt in America,
while he won victory after victory in Congress and established justice in a score of bureaus and in every department, his victories and his administrative establishments
were preachments of a world-wide creed of Liberalism,
first object lessons in justice. He was the Moses who
was teaching us the new Ten Commandments. Speaker
Joseph Cannon sneered at him as one who had discovered
the Ten Commandments. But the dullness of Cannon
and his kind, in not perceiving that there must be a new
Ten Commandments for every new order, made overthrow of the Cannon-Aldrich leadership in Congress
inevitable.

The actual list of achievements of Roosevelt in his
second term, viewed as a legislative or administrative program, is not imposing; viewed as a crusade for justice it
is a revolution. He made men see that the crafty imitation of honorable conduct which the political and financial
rulers of the land were often simulating was treason to
the social order. He would have swept away the loaded
dice of contemporary commerce and instituted at least the
vision of a square deal. He applied to the problems of

the day a keen, sometimes offensive sanity, a sturdy impatience at unjust traditions, an aggression which startled and finally overcame the well-fed prosperous alliance between politics and business by arousing the popular conscience.

The Roosevelt policies provided for the conservation of the natural wealth of the land; the honest branding of food and drugs; the establishment and construction of the Panama Canal; the establishment of a Department of Commerce and a Department of Labor; the promotion of peace through world organization backed up with a rather militant preparedness ("speak softly and carry a big stick" epitomized his idea of foreign relations); the restoration of competition in industry; the regulation of the railroads; a more scientific attitude toward the tariff.

This list is not the catalogue of the achievements of a revolutionist; but, backed by continual preachment for righteousness hurled defiantly at the nation as the jeremiad of a prophet, this program aroused emotion, got into the common will of the common people and produced a new spiritual attitude, revolutionary, dynamic. Roosevelt found America in 1901 spiritually mud. He left it marble.

Perhaps his most important work as an agitator came after he left the White House. He had brought about the nomination and election of President Taft. The two men had been friends for nearly twenty years. Taft amiably refraining from dissent where he disagreed with Roosevelt, but effectively taking orders as a member of the Roosevelt Cabinet, convinced Roosevelt, who was easy to persuade of the virtue of his friends, that Taft was a Liberal. He was a wool-dyed Conservative. And Roosevelt's astonishment became anger when Roosevelt found that he had given his political endorsement to one whose creed so conspicuously differed from his own. Roosevelt went to Africa on a zoölogical exploring expedition to give Taft a free hand. Taft revealed his free hand. Roosevelt came home in 1910 to find that Taft was overturning the temples of justice which Roosevelt had erected. Roosevelt's wrath was volcanic. He raged across the land denouncing the reaction of the times. Early in 1912 he became a candidate of the Liberal Republicans against Taft, carried a considerable majority of the presidential primaries in Republican states and claimed, probably justly, a majority of the Republican convention. Certainly he had an overwhelming majority in the convention of delegates from those states which make the Republican majority. The South in the hands of the Taft administration combined with New York, overwhelmed Roosevelt in the convention; and he started on the war path, formed the Progressive party, went out as a roaring Bull Moose agitating for righteousness and, losing, won. Woodrow Wilson was elected President. Roosevelt's moral triumph was a pyrrhic victory, but no less a victory. He rearoused the American people to a sense of their rights and duties.

For four years the administration of Woodrow Wilson was busy enacting the Progressive party program of 1912 and putting into administrative effect the pronouncements of the Progressive candidate. Wilson reaped where Roosevelt sowed.

It was predestined and foreordained that Roosevelt should hate Wilson, and that Wilson should distrust and

THE PRODIGAL FATHER'S RETURN.

Bill Taft. "SAY, IF THAT'S POPPA'S NOTION OF 'LITERARY CALM,' I WISH HE'D NEVER COME HOME."

Mr. Roosevelt, replying on September 13 to a request to comment on the Democratic victory in Maine, is reported to have declined, his reason being, "I have just returned from a hygienic tour to steep myself in literary calm."

Sir Bernard Partridge's impression of Roosevelt's return from Africa. Reproduced by permission of the proprietors of London *Punch*.

despise Roosevelt. The two men were of different breeds. Where Roosevelt was robust, Wilson was frail. Where Wilson was secretive, Roosevelt blurted things out. Wilson took small counsel and gave no credit. Roosevelt was forever feeling out public sentiment. He was a sort of popular initiative and referendum in his own right, and delighted to bestow the knighthood of credit upon his subordinates.

"This is Gifford's plan," said he, of conservation. "That is Knox's idea," said he, of the fight against the timber thieves. He gave Bristow full credit for cleaning out the Post Office Department. But Roosevelt took all the blame for the intrigue in Panama. Wilson was jealous of those he trusted when their worth and greatness was advertised. He dismissed friend after friend from his court in suspicion. And Wilson lacked magnanimity; when he was done with a man he was done. Roosevelt fought and gouged and bit, and arose bloody but unbowed and extended his hand to his antagonist. In his magnanimity he swallowed his pride, unbuckled and laid aside his hatred of Wilson, went to the White House to offer his services in the Great War when Wilson brought America into the conflict. But at the White House Roosevelt was met with the fishy eye, the clammy hand, the dead voice, the distrustful mien of one who felt too deeply to forgive. In Roosevelt's most magnanimous moment he had from Wilson only the courteous palaver of one whom rancor, poison, and hatred had numbed. Roosevelt, instinctive in his judgment of men, knew the Wilson kind and walked out of the White House hopeless and heartbroken, but not without his proper pride and decent wrath—which he poured upon the President even

in wartime with unabated fervor, till death checked his
hand. When the war was over, Roosevelt, by virtue of
his opposition to Wilson and by virtue of his leadership
of the Republican party for eight years, was the logical
candidate for President. He was preparing his platform.
It was to be a Liberal platform. He said to his friends:
"Let us forget the war."

He did not realize that the war had opened a new
world. He who had brought righteousness to an old
order passed with the day of his triumph. For twenty
years Theodore Roosevelt had dominated the political
thinking of America and had been one of the world's
great Liberal leaders. The day of Liberalism was drawing to a close. The conscience of the world had accepted
the new creed. In a new day other forces were coming
than those which Roosevelt knew, forces which would
dominate his country. A new industrial order was rising.
It came under Harding, whose administration saw the
dawn of the new order; and shame came with it. Yet
when that order was more definitely established, the
Roosevelt creed—justice, righteousness and a sane peace
finally were shot through the new order; and Roosevelt's preachments, Roosevelt's ideals, Roosevelts militant
joy in justice some way beneath it all still lived in the
hearts of his countrymen.

Without the interregnum of Liberalism which came
from 1901 to 1920, an unbridled, corrupt, and arrogant
plutocracy might have firmly established a Babylon on
this continent. Roosevelt for two decades hobbled the
Hamiltonian plutocracy, gave the people new ideals,
established righteous ways, and when in the new day corruption and greed threatened his country, the Roosevelt

traditions in the heart of the American people finally
revolted and drove the money changers from the temple;
and that without national leadership, with no great voice
calling across the land. The seed he sowed had fallen on
good ground.

Now to say that Theodore Roosevelt was merely the
sower who went forth to sow seems so little to say; so
inadequate a figure to describe the tremendous personality that arose from his store of spiritual energy. The
man was gigantic. In his generation he was unique.
Men who lived with him died without seeing his kind
again. He vitalized everything he touched. For thirty
years he maintained a friendship with Henry Cabot
Lodge; a friendship that knew no faction or politics.
For in factional politics they were not agreed. Lodge
was not a great personality, but he had keen perspicacity.
"Thin soil highly cultivated" was Tom Reed's character-
ization of Lodge. Yet Lodge, a New England Brahmin,
emotionless, ageless, circumscribed and circumspect,
cried out in the Senate—where he stood among the Scribes
and Pharisees of his kind—when Roosevelt passed:

"Greatheart has gone!"

Greatheart he was—passionate, brave, generous, kind
and wise; a great heart that revived to righteousness a
nation that was fattening in greed, languishing in iniquity.
Greatheart he was, untouched by the years until he died;
always young, ardent, with the merry heart which maketh
a glad countenance; always haloed with that divine madness which makes for a gorgeous but charmed audacity.
He stalked through the world, a Greatheart indeed, who
made his little day a great epoch!

TAFT

CHAPTER XXXI

WILLIAM HOWARD TAFT, our twenty-seventh President, was born politically out of his time. As a President
he was both a throwback and a forecast, a terrible muddle;
a throwback to the eighties of the last century, a forecast
of the twenties in this century. An amiable, placid, easy-
going, physically unemotional and mentally roly-poly
man, he must have lived in torture during the four
years of his incumbency in the White House. For never
before in the memory of living man had the White House

been the scene of such pulling and hauling, intriguing, contention, bickering and strife as it was in the years from 1909 to 1913. It was occupied during those restless years by this kindly, well-meaning, soft-voiced, rather simple-hearted, lumbering, fat gentleman of six feet two. He stalked into the historic corridors of the White House a "career man" in American politics, as McKinley was—indeed, as most Presidents are. But in all his long career of office-holding, beginning with 1881 and lasting through his life until he ran for President, he was elected to office only once, and that as Judge of the Superior Court of Ohio, where he had no contact with politics in his campaign and served but a few months. He was, at one time and another, Assistant Prosecutor, Collector of Internal Revenue, Judge of the Ohio Superior Court, United States Solicitor-General, Judge of the Sixth Federal Circuit Court of Appeals, Dean and Professor of a School of Law, Chairman of the Philippine Islands Commission, Secretary of War in Roosevelt's Cabinet, representing the United States in many important negotiations, Civil Governor of Cuba, Professor at Yale, Chairman of the Central Committee of the American Red Cross, President of the United States, and finally Chief Justice of the United States Supreme Court; always in public service, generally in public office, and only once, before he came to the White House, did he face an election—and that once he was shielded behind the phalanx of judicial dignity. He was as insensible of public opinion and of currents of public thought as an Oriental satrap. It was well said by him by O. K. Davis, a reporter who knew him for a dozen years at the height of his political activities, that Taft's bump of political saga-

Mr. Taft as a Student at Yale.

city was a dent. To look back now at the time that was, when Taft was President, and to see him floundering, for the most part patiently, always pitifully, through problems which were almost exclusively concerned with public opinion or public clamor, it seems inconceivable that even the most ironic of the fates should have led such a man to such a destiny. Figuratively, he used to come out upon the front stoop of the White House and quarrel petulantly with the American people every day. He was a big blond man who had been molded between two six-foot parentheses, bulging gorgeously in the middle, his trousers wrinkled, his vest creased, his coat bumpy, his collar flaring at an angle of forty-five degrees above a decent dark tie. Above that collar a generous short neck supported a large florid face, criss-crossed about the eyes with good-natured wrinkles, with slightly sloping jowls, and all topped by a thinning crop of chestnut hair. Blue eyes, kindly, expressive, intelligent, always a-twinkle even when they opened wide in rare moments of passion, lighted a beaming countenance. His mouth smiled easily under a blond mustache. In college he was an athlete, a football man, the college "Big Bill" in the late seventies at Yale. He walked with a vigorous gait when he chose to, lay down when he could, loved good food, good fellows, and a good night's sleep. His hands were large and soft, and his handshake lacked the pump-handle enthusiasm which many politicians consciously put into their greetings. Not that he was indifferent; he had no experience in electioneering. He was a clubman and a gentleman in his private life, and he maintained a vastly larger area of his consciousness in private life than in public. To him, in all good conscience, a public office was a private

job, to be run according to the dictates of his own judgment, his own experiences and his own intelligence, which
was never low except upon matters touching public relations and public opinion. He spoke little in public, but
with a pleasing, soft, high voice that carried well so far as
it went, which was not far. Being a lawyer, he trusted
to the spur of the moment to inspire him when he spoke;
this partly because he was indifferent to what he said,
not remotely realizing the import of the spoken words of
a President to a multitude; and again, partly because he
would prefer to talk to his friends, take his ease, and
do some other task rather than prepare a speech. He
had no sense of the importance of a speech as a speech,
nor of any other public contact as a part of a statesman's
job. He conceived a statesman's job as an opportunity
to do his work honestly, intelligently, courageously; and
he sublet as much of it as possible. Hence, at the pinnacle
of his temporal power in the White House, Senator Dol-
liver, of Iowa, described President Taft as a large, amiable
island, surrounded entirely by persons who knew exactly
what they wanted. Probably the phrase amused no one
of our ninety millions of people at that time so keenly
as it amused the President. It was impossible even for
his bitterest enemies to cast him for a villain in their
hours of curdling hate, because of the easy gurgle of his
laugh and the sweet insouciance of his answer which
turned away wrath. He was a man who could giggle out
of an earthquake, even though he was himself the least
salvageable part of the débris in the cataclysm. And the
American people who chastised him, observing him
chuckle as he rubbed the red place where their rage had
blistered him, loved him for his merry countenance.

Which is all very well if the people would only profit by their mistakes. The nomination and election of William H. Taft to the Presidency in 1908, when the Liberal tidal wave was sweeping across the land, was one of the most spectacular mistakes ever made by a democracy. Of course, Roosevelt sponsored that; Roosevelt, who in his day was probably the largest private consumer of human gold bricks in the country; Roosevelt, who knew issues, loved men, understood the populace. But whether Roosevelt tolerated men who loved him, or loved men whom he came to tolerate, or was just fooled in their qualities, no one knows. This also should be remembered: For seven years Roosevelt had faced all the dragons, hobgoblins, man-eating tigers that organized capital, seeking special privileges under government, could command. Roosevelt's fight had been spectacular and successful, a daily first-page pageant of triumphant righteousness. He may have thought, as his seven years were closing, that he had killed the dragons and conquered the materialism of high finance. Perhaps unconsciously, deeply subconsciously indeed, Roosevelt felt that he had fought so well and so effectively that it would be safe to leave Taft on guard. But the moment Roosevelt withdrew, the whole menagerie of a greedy and unconquered empire of pagan materialism was turned into the ring, and Taft had no desire for martyrdom, no technique but flight.

When it was too late, Roosevelt remembered, and vociferously declared in palliation of his error that "Taft was a good lieutenant but a poor captain." Roosevelt recounted then how Taft, as Secretary of War, used to come to him with problems—presenting them evenly balanced for Roosevelt's decision. Decisions cost Roose-

velt little of his store of energy. Taft, despite his
powerful physique, lacked energy, shirked decision,
put away unpleasant circumstance when he could.
He had served Roosevelt and McKinley well. As Federal judge, his opinions were carefully considered and
always were based upon sound legal principles. In the
Federal judiciary during the nineties, he was not in the
midst of clamor and strife. In the serenity of his judicial
chamber, he made up his mind generally to a conservative view of a legal question. In 1906-'07, when
the Liberal element of the Republican party began looking for a candidate, they centered naturally upon Governor Charles Evans Hughes, of New York. Roosevelt
distrusted Hughes. The distrust was natural. Hughes
did not come along with the Roosevelt faction, though
Hughes was a Liberal then in his own right. Roosevelt
picked Taft. Roosevelt trusted Taft. Roosevelt's
Liberal associates did not. Taft had engaging qualities,
even blandishments. The Liberals were in control. He
captivated them rather against the judgment of many.
Taft's attitude toward the Liberals in 1907 and '08,
before the Republican convention, was probably consciously, certainly conspicuously charming. Liberal newspapers printed the story of Taft's "folksey" ways. Liberal writers, of whom the subscriber hereto was one, filled
magazine articles with impressions that Taft was a candid, big-hearted, bluff, affectionate man of the people,
who hooked up his wife's dress in the back and ignored
diplomatic conventions when he stood in the presence of
kings. Some one must have known better, but Taft's
cordiality, his charm, the affectionate glow in his countenance, the easy manner in which he met the powerful, and

the anxious way in which he looked after the lowly were social graces that hid a deeply ingrained suspicion of democracy. Taft's manner was the denial of democracy by an aristocrat, born to the manner spiritually, mentally, and for that matter physically. He had lived a sheltered life. Yale schooled him. His family supported him, promoted him, placed him. He had never fought his way. He had never tried a case before a jury, fought it on appeal through the highest courts and back, lost and won, and won and lost, in all the days of his youth. His pugnacious qualities were atrophied. He had no defense against rudeness, because he had never encountered and overcome the "slings and arrows of outrageous fortune." He was sunny, genial, jolly, because he had never had occasion to be anything else. His family by which one does not mean those of his household, but his brothers and those near to them, those who shielded him behind the family phalanx—felt that Taft's amiable ways had made him a popular idol. The country did recognize his charm, but that was all. Roosevelt, dominating the Liberals and controlling the Southern delegates as any President may if he will, made the nomination of Hughes impossible, and Taft became the presidential candidate of the Republican party in a direct apostolic succession from Roosevelt.

After he had secured the Republican presidential nomination in 1908, Taft's attitude began to change. Speaker Joseph Cannon, of the House of Representatives, began rather open attacks upon the Liberal program and incidentally, not too covertly, upon Roosevelt. After protest from the Liberal leaders, Taft, or some of his friends, managed to quiet the Speaker. Taft himself was innocent of politics. Senator Foraker, of Ohio, who hated Roosevelt with good reason in a bad cause, made no bones in the campaign of his anti-Rooseveltian prejudices. Taft was slated by some Ohio friends to speak from the same platform with Foraker. And not until the reporters called Taft's attention to the probability that he would have to listen quietly to abuse of Roosevelt or rise and defend him, did Taft realize the trap into which he was being led. He canceled the speaking date with Foraker. He made few speeches. To those around him who urged him to define himself clearly in a series of speeches, he sighed as he lay on the couch and smiled benignly:

"That would be a long, hard work."

Roosevelt asked but two things of Taft: First, that he name James R. Garfield Secretary of the Interior; and second, that he make William Loeb, Roosevelt's private secretary, who in reality had been an assistant president in many minor matters, Secretary of War. Roosevelt believed that he had Taft's assurance that these appointments would be made. Roosevelt received no word directly or indirectly from Taft that these appointments would not be made until he read in the newspapers that Ballinger of Oregon had been named Secretary of the Interior, and Jacob M. Dickinson of Tennessee, Secretary of War. In politics that particular kind of indolence is generally regarded as beyond the pale. Roosevelt naturally smarted under the snub. Taft might easily have made the appointments he made, but to make them without acknowledging his obligations to Roosevelt was unhappy; unless, of course, you assumed that Taft said in his heart:

"The Long, Long Trail."

From an etching by J. N. Darling.

"Well, who is Roosevelt, anyway, that I should consider his feelings?"

In 1908 Roosevelt took the lead in the campaign in which Taft was elected President. It was Roosevelt's fight against Bryan and for Taft, not Taft's. Naturally, during the campaign, the Liberals gathered about Roosevelt, and naturally, after Taft was elected he was hedged about with friends and relatives and leaders who cautioned him against the Roosevelt influence. So Roosevelt's friends soon found themselves displaced in the Taft administration. The crowd of poets, pugs, playwrights, professors, inventors, visionaries of one sort or another, that had romped for seven years through the White House, coming at Roosevelt's beck and call from the ends of the earth, found the doors barred to them. Regular, respectable, high-hatted statesmen and solemn, anxious-faced business men occupied places at the White House table often, that in other days had been warmed by a gay company which did not meter its mirth. The new President accepted the Cannon and Aldrich leadership in Congress, deeply Conservative, even reactionary. Roosevelt had used it. But there was a nice difference between the using and accepting of the reactionary leadership. The tariff was revised, with downward rates and upward administrative regulations which would greatly increase the benefits received by protected industry. The legislative joker of the administrative clause was exposed before the bill became a law. The President did nothing to remove it. It is possible that he did not realize it. It is probable that it did not seem important to him. Soon popular wrath rose and beat upon the White House. The President's friends thought it wise to take the Taft

smile and what might be called the hereditary appurte-
nances thereunto appertaining "which shook when he
laughed like a bowl full of jelly" out on a swing around
the circle. His friends felt that he could laugh off the
cyclone. Clearly the President had no notion of the
rage that was rising around him. He prepared no
advance speeches, for he had no sense of publicity. He
went into the congressional district of James Tawney
of Minnesota, who had turned Conservative though representing a Liberal district. There public feeling was
forming against the pending tariff bill. Without thought
further than to inquire at the water tank the name of the
town a few hundred yards ahead, the President arose and
made the famous Winona speech. He accepted then and
there the wool schedule—administrative joker and all—a
particularly obvious fraud, and gave the full countenance
of his administration to what the country generally
believed was an iniquitous measure. After that the President returned home satisfied and happy. When an old
and valued newspaper friend, Oscar K. Davis, who had
written an authorized campaign life of Taft, appeared
at the White House after contributing to the New York
Times, a most conservative paper, some account of the
resentment burning in the heart of the Minnesota people,
Taft refused to see Reporter Davis. The presidential
secretary explained:

"We don't like your stuff!"

Thus do tyrants behead the bearers of bad news. It
was easy after that to keep protesting Liberals from the
circle that surrounded the President. He seems to have
heard nothing of the truth about the popular revolt, or
if he heard rumors, the deep distrust of democracy which

instinctively controlled those about him made him feel
that popular clamor would die in a day or a week, or a
month, or a year, and that it could be ignored as passing
fustian. No sense of the reality touched him.

The reality was this: The angry whitecaps of the waves
of bitterness that broke about the President were not
evidences of a passing storm. He was trying to dam
a sweeping current of Liberalism which had been an
undertow in the days of the Greenbackers and the Populists, which rose rudely in the days of Bryan, which was
running strong through all the channels of world politics
but had not spent its force. Taft was destined to go
down beneath it.

In the midst of that tidal flood, from 1909 to 1913,
Taft battled futilely, desperately, stupidly; an unhappy,
ill-fated figure. Taft's plight was Roosevelt's fault as
much as Taft's, perhaps more than Taft's. Roosevelt
might have seen what Taft could not see, that Taft was
untrained for combat; that his mind was not pugnacious,
nor were his habits strenuous. He was a man of peace
who was merely petulant in battle. He stewed and fretted
with the people through four years, unable to speak to
them, unable to understand them, dazed and at times
impatient, but never exhibiting either felicity with his task
or understanding of it. In 1910 Roosevelt, returning
from a lion hunt in Africa, saw the situation clearly. He
broke with Taft politically and said bitter things about
him.

"Taft means well, but he means well feebly," was one
of the gentlest of the Rooseveltian shafts. There seems
to have been a vain exchange of notes between them, some
attempt to retain the old affectionate relations before

the public break which was inevitable came. Taft was
surrounded by Roosevelt's enemies. He trusted Roosevelt's enemies. They were fighting for Taft a contest
which it irked him even to hear about. He could not
abandon his army, his fortress, his cause, even for Roosevelt. And Roosevelt, whose friends kept him stimulated
with a lively sense of the President's ingratitude, finally
decided to oppose Taft for the presidential nomination.

Taft's friends controlling the national patronage easily
secured the delegates of the Southern states, which never
vote for Republican Presidents. And, what with fraud
in Indiana, the machine in New York, chicane in Ari-
zona, Taft's supporters controlled barely enough delegates in the Republican National Convention to secure
the majority for Taft, a narrow majority. The faith
of Taft's Conservative friends in the triumph of force
over reason was admirably dramatized by the procedure
of the convention which they controlled. The National
Republican Committee was in the hands of Taft's friends.
It made up the roll of the convention, and most arbi-
trarily seated contested delegations that were favorable
to Taft, giving those contested delegates a right to vote
for the officers of the permanent organization of the
convention who should finally pass upon the ultimate
right of those delegates to sit in the convention. Without the votes of the contested delegates, Taft would have
been in a minority. Roosevelt's friends demanded that
contesting delegates on both sides stand aside until the
convention was permanently organized, and that all contested delegations then go to the Committee on Credentials with their claims to a seat in the convention. But
because they had force and authority in the National

Committee, Taft's friends—ruthlessly abrogating parliamentary procedure—produced a majority out of a minority and forced his nomination. They were blind to currents of public opinion, deaf to the din of protest, trusting curiously to their distrust of democracy in a time when democracy was awake, armed, and militant. A more egregious blunder never was made in American politics. It was the kind of blunder that men have made throughout history who have great power in their hands. They believe that this is a world of force. They do not allow the imponderables—for instance: public sentiment, the lust for vengeance, the aspiration for justice—to enter their reckoning. It seemed to the Republican National Committee sitting around the table of the Credentials Committee in Chicago, in June, 1912, that their majority of the committee would enable them to enforce their will upon the convention. They counted on party loyalty to enforce their will on the nation and reëlect Taft, whom their action around that board renominated. Their judgment failed. In the failure Taft went down; and, with a divided party, Wilson came into the Presidency.

Wilson was a new man in national politics, a stranger in world diplomacy who was confronted, sixteen months after his inauguration, with the greatest decision that ever challenged an American President: the decision to take sides or stand as neutral while the World War was brewing. Either Roosevelt or Taft knew the ropes of the international game. Roosevelt knew well the men at Potsdam, at Vienna, at Moscow, at Paris, at London, who were considering the issues of war. Probably either Taft or Roosevelt, certainly Roosevelt, would have thrown America's weight into the balance for peace in July, 1914. Wilson naturally hesitated. But Wilson came to the White House because the members of the Credentials Committee at Chicago, representing Conservative forces in America, were ruthless in their eagerness to win. They were of one piece with those other Conservative minds sitting around the green baize tables of diplomacy in the capitals of Europe. So came the World War, out of the world's lack of faith in men, out of a long chain of denials of the power of things of the spirit. When these practical men have their way, even God cannot help the world.

Of course, Taft's friends in Chicago sensed nothing of this. No one else dreamed what the pent-up waters behind the dam of their arrogance would do. The Conservatives nominated Taft, defied Republican sentiment, split the party, and gave Wilson to the world.

Roosevelt, in that crisis of 1912, was surely a visionary. There seems to be conclusive evidence that in the Republican convention Roosevelt could have defeated Taft, either by taking the nomination himself at the end of a deadlock which certain Michigan delegates for Taft offered to create, or by securing the nomination of Senator Cummins, of Iowa, or Governor Herbert Hadley, of Missouri. But Roosevelt refused to compromise unless the roll of the convention was first purged and the contested delegates on both sides removed, so that the convention could be organized without the votes of delegates whose seats were in doubt. Roosevelt, writing to a railroad king, in 1908, said:

"You and I are practical men."

Four years later, in the crisis of the Republican convention in Chicago, refusing dubious compromise to his own gain, Roosevelt followed the counsel of perfection and proved himself an idealist. Many of his friends who were close to him felt that he came back from Africa a changed man, deepened by the solitude with a sense of the insignificance of material rewards. Possibly this is so. Certainly no man ever "stood at Armageddon and battled for the Lord," with a nobler vision or a higher ideal than Roosevelt's, in those big days of that grave contest of 1912.

Taft saw only a wild man of the woods, raging through a wilderness of monkeys, as Roosevelt plunged and lumbered his way to tragedy. Taft in the White House saw nothing of the significance of the contest in the Chicago convention. To him it was politics, the clamor of the mob led by a vain and ruthless demagogue against the calmly considered plans of those who represented the wealth, the power, and the respectability of a happy world.

Historical perspective was denied to Taft. He could not see that he stood in the midst of an ancient feud; the contention between those social forces on the one hand which demanded a stable conventional attitude toward life, and those forces on the other hand which cried out for justice before stability, and preferred to set up new standards rather than be oppressed by old conventions. Taft did not realize, in 1912, that human institutions are formed to preserve justice and yet, if left alone, always tend to strangle justice. And he did not see that the fight to socialize capital, to set its metes and bounds, to make this new social force that has come into life with the discovery of steam a force for righteousness and not an arm of oppression, was the task of our age. He felt that to hamper capital would overthrow capitalism; while those pitted against him believed that capitalism only might be saved and the world held from chaos by preserving capitalism tempered by justice.

During the campaign of 1912 it was evident that the storm aroused by the President was not abating. In the election Taft carried two states, Utah and Vermont. And for eight years his party dwelt in a far country and lived upon husks.

In the wave of disillusion which followed the world peace of Versailles, amid the hate and clamor that assailed President Wilson for fumbling a great cause, the Republican party came back under the banner of Warren G. Harding, of Ohio, and with the return of the party came quite another crew from those who had gone down with President Taft in 1912. He had associated himself with the highly respectable, rather deeply disinterested representatives of a proud plutocracy. Harding brought with him, as his personal adherents, too many political errand boys, the commissary sergeants, the stable men of that plutocracy, who moved into Washington like the procession of the Forty Thieves.

When a vacancy occurred in the Supreme Court by the death of the Chief Justice, President Harding called Gus Karger, a reporter for a Cincinnati paper owned by William Howard Taft's brother, and said:

"Gus, I am going to appoint Big Bill, Chief Justice."

Karger rushed to a copy desk, scrawled the message of the President on a piece of cheap print paper, signed it "Gus," and sent it to Canada where the future Chief Justice was at work upon a lawsuit. He opened the envelope, saw a penciled note, and thus learned that at last he was to "walk in the green pastures and lie down beside the still waters." And so a Chief Justice was named for the Supreme Court of the United States. There Chief Justice Taft had found a task for his talents. There the clamor of the mob and the movements of the democracy are all the same to him and his court.

How lightly the clamor and bitterness of the few years in the White House touched this man! Ten years is a long time for an ex-President to live. The average life of a man who leaves the White House is under five years —so do his harrying duties break a President's body. The imperturbable Grant lived but a dozen years beyond his presidential term. Roosevelt survived a scant nine years. But the serene and cherubic Taft has outlived every ex-President of the Republic in terms of years. Perhaps his longevity is due to his happy philosophy; perhaps his length of days follows the sheltered life of a jurist. He is the leader of the most powerful court on this planet.

There, in the atmosphere of pure justice, modified by such human qualifications as are required to apply sound judicial procedure to the day's work, he sits, one of the high gods of the world, a smiling Buddha, placid, wise, gentle, sweet, and as noble as a man may be in this poor worm-eaten earth.

WOODROW WILSON

CHAPTER XXXII

OUR FIRST FOLK MYTH

AMERICA, being a young country, has contributed to the world few folk tales. One of the few is the story of the Aztec youth who was chosen for human sacrifice. As the tale runs, the fairest youth of the Aztec realm was chosen to be worshiped as a god. For a year after he was taken to the temple, every wish was gratified. Every sense of his physical body was satisfied. Every yearning in his heart was answered. No wish was denied him. He lived surrounded by love, nurtured by adulation, lifted to the pinnacle of fame and joy—for he was to become a god—powerful beyond the ambition of men, happy as humanity could make one of its kind. And then, at the end of a year, leading a great procession of his adoring people into a mountain, he ascended an altar and laid him down to have his heart ripped out by the high priests while he still lived and breathed. Perhaps in another age—in the Golden Age men dream of—they will tell the story of Woodrow Wilson in terms like these when he shall live as the mythical god of the first world peace.

Thomas Woodrow Wilson, the twenty-eighth President of the United States, was the first Southern gentleman to walk into the White House after James K. Polk left it. Zachary Taylor was Southern, but he was the

345

symbol of more or less Jacksonian boots and whiskers
in the White House. Andrew Johnson was Southern,
but of the poor whites of Tennessee, an illiterate until
after his marriage. Wilson, born in Virginia of a fine
large Irish father and a sweet, quiet, aloof lady whose
father came from the Scotch border—Wilson, in whose
blood ran no American soldier stock except that of his
Irish father, who was a chaplain in the Confederate
Army—Wilson came from the upper middle class in the
South at a time when there was no higher social estate;
when the Southern aristocracy of the first half of the
nineteenth century had been reduced to penury and
shame by the Civil War and by the reconstruction days
in which humiliation followed, even more poignant
than defeat. Woodrow Wilson, whose parents were born
in Ohio, in some way was marked indelibly by the South.
It was, of course, only the environment of the South that
marked him. Yet during his youth as a preacher's son
—the son of the Reverend Joseph Wilson, an orator and
a leader of the Presbyterian Church in his day—young
Wilson was a migratory boy. He moved with the
preacher's family from town to town—from Virginia to
Augusta, Georgia; to Wilmington, North Carolina; from
North Carolina to Columbia, South Carolina. And
because he was not set in the matrix of one town's tradition the legends of his boyhood are slight. Yet the
remembrance men have of him in each town is the same—
that of a spindle-shanked, awkward, rangy, milk-eyed,
freckled boy, with auburn hair and a long solemn face;
a boy who carried the handicap of spectacles when he
was eight years old and until he was mature. At Augusta,
at Wilmington, at Columbia, they recalled him—studious,

aloof, mischievous but never naughty, wistfully watching "the young barbarians at play" who romped through woods, swam the creeks, fished in the brooks, and fought in the fields of the South in the days of the sixties and seventies. The royal blood that was in Woodrow Wilson was surely Celtic. His paternal grandfather, a newspaper man, legislator and state senator in eastern Ohio and his paternal grandmother came from the north of Ireland. They were Protestant Irish. His maternal grandfather, a Scotch Presbyterian preacher of renown in Columbus, Ohio, and Chillicothe, and his maternal grandmother came from the north of England on the Scotch border, and were accounted Scotch by their neighbors. Both branches of his family were Calvinists. Wilson himself, to the last—though he lies in an Episcopal cathedral— was an uncompromising denominational Presbyterian by way of creed, and a Calvinist in philosophy. The Joseph Wilsons were a neighborly, expansive, contentious lot. The Woodrows, his mother's people, were reserved, scholarly, meticulous in the performance of their duties, prouder than Punch and conscientious to their own hurt. Wilson's father, a Princeton man, a pulpit orator, a good fellow in every town and an effective money-raiser in every church, smoked his pipe, took his nip, loved society, was a national church leader, helped to organize the Southern Presbyterian Church, and was a figure in his world. Wilson's mother was not a good preacher's wife. She was standoffish. She paid her full and exact obligations to life consistently, but without much joy; was governed by her sense of duty and given to her moods. She made few friends and lost them easily. Out of this blood and environment came Wilson's heredity. As a boy who grew

up in three towns he had no lifelong friend; no friend who
went with him to the end. He was frail and never ganged
with his fellows. It is important to consider the boyhood
of this preacher's son, the first boy born to middle-aged
parents and the adored idol of two elder sisters who
shielded him, coddled him, and of course pampered and
hampered him when he should have run wild, a young
beast of the field, releasing his energy, trying his fists,
his arms, his feet, and his brain in a thousand contests
with his fellows; contests that would teach him to give
and take, fight or fly, stand or run, and pay for his
bad judgment of his fellows with his hide, after the
ancient manner of boys in the vast man factory of their
youth.

In the small Southern college where he went for part
of a year he tried to play baseball, but his glasses bothered
him. His eyes failed. He went home and studied with
his erudite Princeton father, went in his own turn to
Princeton in the middle seventies, and there, in his
adolescence, for the first time he found his gang! But
his qualities of leadership never moved men or boys of
brawn. His leadership was purely intellectual. In college he was business manager of the baseball club, but did
not play. He led the glee club and sang well. His singing was an outlet for his emotional nature, which was
never well coördinated. Leaving Princeton with an A.B.
degree and Johns Hopkins with a Master's, having a year
in a law school, he first taught English in a women's college, but rejected teaching women and went to one of the
small but first-rate New England colleges, Wesleyan at
Middletown, Connecticut, where he made an impression
on the faculty and was a favorite with the students. He

coached the football team and took an interest in athletics
—vicariously—as a promoter. He returned to Princeton as a teacher in 1887, a handsome young man in his
late twenties, with a sensitive, refined face, smooth
shaven, well set up, spick and span in his tailoring and
toilet; a married man who was none the less popular
at teas; but who, tradition says, in Princeton refused
to be the life of the company after or when other men
came to the party; that kind. He taught the social
sciences—history, economics, sociology, political science;
wrote books about history and political science—books
that became textbooks in other colleges; good books of
their kind, academic but prepared with pains and understanding, adducing and defending theories of political
thought that were popular in American colleges in the
eighties and nineties. These political theories he was
compelled to abandon in practical politics; chiefly
because the world had moved and changed its theories
between the eighteen nineties and 1912. New facts had
come into American civilization—indeed, into the new
civilization of Christendom; facts which disturbed the
old theories. And it is no discredit to Wilson that he
changed with the times. At Princeton he became a popular professor. His classrooms were crowded. His
lectures were most illuminating. He delivered himself
in a fine, clear, happy voice in carefully selected language,
with here and there a dash of humor indicated by the
asterisks of twinkling eyes. For those years were the
happiest years of his career. Ellen Axson, his young
wife, also Southern, also Presbyterian, was bearing him
lovely children. The students liked to lounge in his
study. He was the idol of the tutors and instructors. He

gathered about him in the college a Wilson cult. His
class of '79 was proud of him and, returning on high days
and holidays to Princeton, delighted to honor him. The
fine Irish smile which illuminated a rather sober countenance, a smile composed somewhat by flexing thin lips and
gathering gay wrinkles around hazel gray eyes, a muscular smile withal, was on his face frequently in those years
of the eighties and nineties. He was one of the demi-
gods of the American academic world even before he
took the next upward step in his career. His books about
books concerned with history and political science,
written largely for textbooks, were bringing him fame
in American colleges. He became an authority when he
still was a teacher, an authority on the science of government as it is taught, not—alas!—as it is practiced. He
was a contributor to magazines of the better sort; always
in demand as a speaker of the occasion at academic,
dedicatory services, and inaugurations; also, he was a
figure at those pleasant unions of business and college
politics centering about alumni meetings of Princeton and
the other first rate colleges of the East. He wore a silk
hat well, and graced state occasions in the cloistered
academic circles where good breeding and a certain air of
distinction and refinement are required. Among the ten
thousand who ruled America in the nineties, Professor
Wilson was a Distinct Somebody. Then he took an
upward step, became president of Princeton, and was
Somebody Rather Important. For America makes education a religion, and her educational leaders become
ex-officio high priests. In making public sentiment, and
so, ultimately, in ruling America, the president of any one
of the first ten American colleges—if he take his place in

public life without any further official distinction than
his academic rôle—has as much power and authority as a
senator, and if, in addition to that, he has the knack of
leadership, he is as important as a Cabinet officer in the
American system, all without bothering with elections or ·
the leadership of a national cause. Dr. Woodrow Wilson, president of Princeton, in this list of ten educational
high priests, moved in the first five, possibly the first two
or three, as the century closed.

In his inaugural address as president of Princeton he
attacked the tendency in American education to follow
the materialism of the German universities and stood
for the humanities. Thus he challenged an evil, and took
the leadership of a national cause. So Woodrow Wilson
became, after a fashion, a pundit with spiritual powers.

CHAPTER XXXIII

FATE SMILES AT OUR HERO

But by a curious irony of fate Wilson's talents led him into a channel where he functioned badly. The presidency of Princeton was his first executive enterprise. There he encountered opposition. There pride, which he had released so joyously as an intellectual leader, had to be curbed with tact if he hoped to succeed. There he had to meet and master men. There, if he stood up as an academic leader, he had also to function as an administrator. And there he failed; not miserably, for he had intellectual vigor; not cravenly, for he staged his failure about a noble ideal—the ideals of a changing world. To give practical expression to his democratic ideal, he began a fight for the democratization of Princeton. He was in a way becoming a hero. Princeton, in the first decade of the new century, was, as nearly as an institution might be, the embodiment of the old aristocracy. It was Calvinistic in philosophy, set in its ways, proud of its past, unashamed of its wealth, the harbor of a decent, if sometimes arrogant, conservatism. A well-housed college was Princeton, beautifully conceived architecturally. Its outward phase reflected the dignity of its inner aspirations, a rather tough and gnarly stem upon which to graft the tender buds of the new democracy not yet respectabilized by Theodore Roosevelt.

Explicitly, Wilson's point of attack upon the aristocracy of Princeton was through its fraternity dormitories. Wilson desired to buy the luxurious fraternity houses which had sheltered the gilded youths of Princeton for a century, and use these houses as residences for student groups which should live with faculty preceptors to guide their work. Being thus grouped, the aristocracy of the fraternities would be undermined. Also other issues arose. A graduate school was proposed, and Wilson would have merged this school into the university. Those who opposed him desired the graduate school to assemble in its own buildings and with its own faculty, rather a separate faculty, but not, of course, independent of the university. This division would make the leveling-up process of the undergraduates—the Wilson ideal—more and more difficult. He staged his fight well, and in it he had two weapons. First of all a coördinated brain; then a felicitous faith in himself, and some needed spark of joyous resilience which inspired confidence in others. It was more than charm; it was more even than Irish blarney galvanized with wisdom. It was as though his guardian angel at birth had picked for him the spiritual pulchritude of Apollo, Hyperion, Adonis and Narcissus. But—alas!—in a mischievous gesture of irony his angel soured his birth brew with a drop of the blood of a moody Scot. The spiritual comeliness was always there, the nimble wit, the merry heart; but always,—in the wings of Wilson's drama, squatted the Scotch Caliban waiting to wreck the scene.

Wilson, in the first decade of the glowing new century, was moving with the current of his times. Roosevelt, the most considerable Liberal leader of the world, was in the White House preaching economic democracy. In a score of gubernatorial mansions minor Roosevelts were preaching political democracy. The initiative, the referendum, the primary, the recall were coming into American life generally, all to the exaltation of the average man. The gimp of arrogance was being dampened in the top dog of the social contest. So the world saw this Wilson reflecting a gay heart in a merry countenance, battling against the privileges of wealth in Princeton, and hailed him as a new knight and contender for righteousness. But—woe was he!—the bruises that came from the bludgeons of the strong men on the Princeton Board of Trustees and in the Princeton faculty, men whom Wilson had antagonized with his democratic program, these bruises hurt; the Caliban in his heart howled in wounded vanity.

The aristocracy of Princeton was by no means decadent. Grover Cleveland, a director on the Princeton Board, backed by a strong Wall Street coterie of Princeton alumni, faced Wilson in his contest for academic democracy. Wilson—with all his intellectual strength, with all his spiritual felicity—could wave no scepter that would hold back foes when they were men of Cleveland's caste and kind. Moreover, Wilson's life had not prepared him to meet and defeat such enemies. He tried intrigue —and they discovered him. His personal dignity behind the fluttering banners of his gracious Celtic decorum was deeply affronted; seriously wounded. In all his life as a lonely pampered child, unganged in boyhood, a frail student, a youth seeking paths of least resistance, he had no background, no guide of experience to show him how to meet the opposition of brutal, direct, determined men. He preached the righteousness of his cause with smiling serenity, but that did not suffice to heal his inner wounds.

So the battle raged in Princeton. The rich alumni piled up millions in largess for buildings and endowments to establish the graduate school and overthrow the causes which Wilson defended. It was in those battle days that the Wilson of the ebullient, happy professorial period became a man of moods, of good days when he was very, very good, and of bad days when he was horrid. His nerves were strained. He took long rests, and came back from each of his vacations a little less restored than he should have been. In 1910 he was going steadily, inexorably, to a rather splendid failure as president of Princeton. And then, before final failure came, because Woodrow Wilson was a darling of the gods, Opportunity began tapping gently on his door, and when he opened the door he saw politics coming from afar. Politics approached deviously and abashed, but quickly, hat in hand, all but dropping curtsies. The New Jersey Democratic machine, which had been more or less financed from Wall Street, where Wilson's enemies did most congregate, asked Wilson to run for Governor of New Jersey. He accepted their suggestion, being at the end of his academic rope for the moment, also being broken in pride and corroded in vanity. He could not, being what he was, take entire comfort in the righteousness of his academic cause. He could talk bravely about the triumphs of defeat. That was an intellectual conviction. But that defeat was personal with Wilson; defeat always was personal, with him.

Woodrow Wilson was elected Governor of New Jersey in 1910, when the insurgents were getting ready to impale President Taft's head on their pike, and when the waves of political Liberalism were running strong and mounting high. Wilson's cause was politically a restatement of his democratic theory in education.

The measures which he championed in New Jersey had been in the program of Liberal governors of both parties in America for half a decade. They looked to one thing—the exaltation of the common man: by giving him political power through the primary; by protecting him against the cheats and swindles of trade; by curbing the privileges of unregulated corporate capital; by checking corrupt practices in politics and in commerce. These measures, which Wilson championed at Trenton, appealed keenly to the voters. When a governor was entrenched in power, it made him a hero to champion these measures; and if, as Wilson was, he was a man of tact and breeding, given to happy phrase and merry quip and common sense, the hero could go far in the politics of those days. So things came his way. He revived as a pundit; indeed, became a political pundit, with the magnificent trappings and background of his academic career. Again the smile came back—the seductive Irish smile that had won the boys of Princeton in his professorial days. Again the expansive manner returned. His wounded pride was healed by the balm of political success. Wilson, at Trenton, was only sixteen miles from Wilson, at Princeton, in the matter of solid space, but in the matter of temper and felicity he moved in another world. Success pampered him again. He was happy. He even learned to flip an occasional spiteful "damn" at his foes, for which he felt entitled to be called a good fellow, but not so good that anyone ever dared to caress him. Wilson never was embraced by the political hug with which small leaders like to fondle their idols publicly. No man ever got near enough to Wilson physically or emotionally to take him "by the right hand to kiss him" and therewith smite him "in the fifth rib and shed out his bowels to the ground." Wilson, in his gayest hours, in his times of greatest happiness, stood always aloof, distrusting men instinctively. It was this suspicion of men, founded upon ignorance of men, which led Wilson always to question the strong, to fraternize with the meek, and to break ruthlessly and irrevocably, without defense or explanation, any friendship which threatened his own prestige.

In New Jersey, Governor Wilson got his political education. A group of young Irish Liberals, out for a crusade and a lark after the Irish fashion, took Wilson in hand when he broke faith with the bosses who made him governor. These Irish lads spoke to something deeply submerged in Wilson, some Celtic sense of fairy adventure. They taught him the language of the political game. He learned quickly, on the whole profited by his mistakes, and after a manner succeeded; but succeeded only because he was riding the Liberal wave which was mounting a strong tide. Breasting the waves, Wilson surely would have failed.

Of course, there was geography in Wilson's success. As Governor of Nevada, or of Mississippi, doing something like the same job, Wilson would not have been available as a presidential candidate. The accident of geography was in his favor, but something more than geography made him loom large after two years as Governor of New Jersey. The Liberal movement was coming rapidly from flower to fruitage. The momentum of forty years of political agitation was behind Wilson when he began to rise on the horizon as a presidential candidate. It seems strange, when one considers Wilson as he was in 1912, to number him among those in the caravan of crusaders for Liberalism, whose bones have bleached the desert of failure in the past: Ben Butler, a sort of Falstaffian Murat; General James B. Weaver, of Iowa, grim, gray, deadly serious, the Greenback candidate for President in the eighties; Colonel Leonidas L. Polk, Jerry Simpson, Mary Elizabeth Lease, and Altgeld, the rabble-rousers of the early nineties in the Farmers' Alliance and Populism; Bryan, the pied-piper, who led the ragamuffins of Populism into the respectable mountain of democracy and lost them; LaFollette, the implacable dervish of reform; Roosevelt, robust, dynamic, noisy, raucous in his joy, electric in his rage, deeply intuitive and highly emotionalized. Slowly, in the hands of these leaders through the generation, Liberalism had grown from a joke, through a menace, to a mass plea for justice. And here was Wilson, with his Irish heart, his Scotch dignity; well-tailored, silk-hatted, straight, erudite and aloof; the professor in the political bull-ring—none the less a hero, even if not the perfect toreador. How the old Grangers, the Greenbackers, and the Populists must have turned in their graves to see this man pulled out of Princeton by Wall Street, turning his back on Wall Street with some show of perfidy in his righteous desertion, leading their cause, the cause of the common man, the cause of the old agrarians, facing their rulers in an industrial age. What a tableau this long procession of revolutionists must have made, from Ben Butler to Woodrow Wilson. But because he was an outstanding figure in his party, because he had won his New Jersey fight, and because he was unquestionably an intellectual leader in his party, Wilson assumed presidential size.

He accepted the new political dictum of the hour. To it he applied his mind and heart. He gave to Liberalism his best endeavors. From 1913 until the close of the Liberal epoch in America with our entrance to the World War, he became, by reason of his prestige and somewhat by reason of his intellectual capacity and greatly because of his charm and grace of personality, the leader of Liberalism in America.

CHAPTER XXXIV

OUR HERO RISES IN POWER AND GLORY

FAME came suddenly to Woodrow Wilson. In two years he moved from the academic circle where he was in the midst of intrigue and alarm, where he had paid no attention to politics, where he voted irregularly, where he never attended caucuses or primaries, where, indeed, he had only a book knowledge of the ways of our ruling classes, and found himself in the highest office in the gift of the world's most important Democracy. Fate has rarely played so gorgeous a game with a man apparently so unprepared for fate's caprices as she played with Woodrow Wilson when she led him off the campus of Princeton University into the White House.

Here it becomes necessary to consider the major influence in Wilson's life. For when he married Ellen Axson, in the beginning of his academic career in the mid-eighties, he attached a balance wheel to his temperamental nature. She was the type of wife who tried not to spoil her husband. She gave him what was good for him. She was a restraining influence. Being the daughter of a Presbyterian minister, she had a conscience and her emotional nature was well poised. Her advice was temperate and judicial. Her husband's greatness had come upon her so gradually that she was not awed by it. She had known him when he was less favored of fortune, and she knew what the wife of every man's youth knows—the limitations of his qualities and the

360

danger points in his nature. She had seen those danger points threaten when he was a young instructor, when he was a professor, when he was president of Princeton, when he was Governor of New Jersey, and she did not ignore them when he was President of the United States. She knew the boy in him; the gentle, aloof, shy, sensitive, sometimes over-jealous, often over-suspicious boy, who stood apart from gangdom wistfully and found his place in the world only in the days of his adolescence. She shielded and mothered that boy, and so matured and strengthened the man.

She was not impressed by the spectacle of his power, and while she lived she tried to hold him in the ways of the meek. But the pressure of responsibility, the sense of power which comes to a President, must have inflamed his intellectual vanity in spite of himself; even in spite of Ellen Axson.

Yet he held a firm hand at the steering wheel of his life. Liberalism had advanced him; had given him his leadership, even though to be a Liberal leader he had to abandon his academic conservatism. So to the end he was a Liberal leader, and as nearly undefiled as men may be and live a practical life with practical men. The high gods were giving him his heart's desire, showering him with blessings, marking him for their choicest favors.

When Ellen Axson died, Woodrow Wilson was fifty-eight years old. He had been watched and tended for more than thirty years by a maternal wife. He took her body sadly to her former home in Georgia and buried her in a narrow plot—too narrow for his own dust and ashes! After the funeral, and during the first few months of loneliness and grief, new duties came to him, new visions

opened before him, and for the first time in his maturity
he made his decisions with no one at his elbow to check
him. Henry Watterson often said that there were two
Grover Clevelands: one before his marriage, another
afterward. Those who knew Woodrow Wilson best
always felt that there were two Woodrow Wilsons: one
before the death of Ellen Axson, another afterward. No
man who lives for thirty years in the relationship of
marriage is the same man he was before he entered
into that relationship, nor is he the same man after that
relationship ends. It takes two to make one, and when
either integer is changed the equation changes. It was
inevitable that Woodrow Wilson would take another wife.
He was essentially a woman's man, as Grover Cleveland
was a man's man. Yet, no matter what his domestic
qualities are, strong or weak, in domesticity a man takes
the color of his domestic environment, of his wife's
opinions, prejudices, desires, aspirations; in short, the
color of her personality.

The year after Ellen Axson Wilson's death, President
Wilson married Mrs. Galt, of Washington, and at sixty
began a new experience. He was happy in his new relation, and in the new spiritual environment that he found;
probably he looked at the new felicity as he had looked
at his new fame, in wonder and in joy. Here he was with
a youthful wife, the praise of a hundred million of his fellows, and a powerful place in the world.

Wilson's brand of Liberalism had come to differ from
the Rooseveltian Liberalism in its attitude toward peace.
As the war in Europe began to cast its menacing shadow
over America in the midst of Wilson's first presidential
term, the American attitude to that war and to war in

general became an acute political issue. As early as 1914, the war, diverting men's minds from consideration of political and economic issues which had interested them for a dozen years, was one of the forces which demobilized the progressive party and left Roosevelt with a following of progressive captains and colonels, but with no progressive rank and file. The Germans began to fire on American vessels in their submarine warfare. The British violated United States ships searching for contraband. It became evident to the more intelligent of American statesmen that America's attitude toward the European conflict would have to be declared. It was inevitable that we should either join the Allies in the war or maintain what to many Americans seemed a shameful neutrality. When Roosevelt was counseling men to speak softly but carry a big stick, Wilson still continued to plead for this neutrality. He coined the phrase "Too Proud to Fight," and the campaign slogan of his Democratic managers in 1916 was "He Kept Us Out of War"—but that slogan was only a part of Wilson's program of Liberalism. Roosevelt's attitude to the war became the major part of his program of Liberalism. He would have challenged those who were hectoring us. He would have put a fighting face on Uncle Sam. Wilson kept turning the other cheek. He was forced into a feint of preparedness only by the clamor of the Rooseveltians; and Woodrow Wilson, winning the election of 1916 as the Liberal leader, took Liberal leadership definitely from Roosevelt, who was at the moment interested in the Great War. To Roosevelt, the war seemed to threaten civilization. He had no patience with the Wilsonian neutrality.

Roosevelt, in 1917 and 1918, became no casual political opponent of Woodrow Wilson. In the campaign of 1912, it was the strategy of the Progressive party to attack Wilson, the Democratic candidate, and to let Taft, the Republican candidate, alone. Roosevelt, during the primary fight, had said all that was necessary to say about Taft and perhaps a word or two more. Anyway, Taft was clearly the weak candidate; Wilson, with the united Democracy behind him, was clearly the strong candidate. So Roosevelt, day after day, week after week, for three long months in 1912, hammered away at Woodrow Wilson, the presidential candidate of the Democratic party. The Roosevelt barrage was cruel. For the first time in his life Woodrow Wilson received blows publicly from an opponent of his own size. In New Jersey he had fought more or less with little state bosses, while he loomed as a national figure. In Princeton the details of the fight were for the most part under cover. But, in the campaign of 1912, Roosevelt lambasted Wilson right and left and laid to with a vigor of phrase which must have rankled the proud heart of the Southerner. So when Roosevelt espoused preparedness, and gathered General Wood into a military camp and practiced preparedness, Wilson, being human after the fashion that he was, refused to be stampeded by the clamor of the military party. He was convinced of his righteousness somewhat by the kind and character of his opponents, and again, being what he was, despised them bitterly. The knowledge that Wilson despised him was not soothing to Roosevelt. He glorified in antagonism, delighted in combat, even chuckled at another man's wrath; but he rankled under Wilson's contempt, and Wilson, fortified by presidential prestige, was able to triumph in his contempt; which was wormwood for Roosevelt.

As Wilson's first term drew to a close and the nation came further and further into the shadow of the war, the Liberal movement in American politics, which had fructified under Wilson, passed, a casualty of the World War. It was strange that a man of just his temperament —this erudite, complacent, bookish man from the cloisters —should be the instrument used by the Fates to write "Finis" to a national movement which he had championed less than half a decade. But with the eclipse of Roosevelt, Wilson became the instrument which, in so far as Liberalism ever was solidified into institutions and legislation, gave the cause its political direction at the close. It was the Roosevelt progressive platform and the LaFollette measures which engaged the Democratic Congress, under President Wilson, from 1913 to 1917; the laws protecting American seamen, establishing the Federal Trade Commission, the Federal Tariff Commission, stabilizing credit and the currency, shortening the hours of labor and regulating the railroads, were enacted in those years. Wilson, with genuine enthusiasm, led Congress and the people into the adoption of those measures. He was at his best in those years; they were years of triumph, and hence years of his happy moods. By 1917 he was a convinced Liberal, who sensed in the approach of war the downfall of his cause. He knew, being a student of government, how reactionary war is, what entire denial of liberty it must be. But the hour had struck. Forces stronger than he were running across the hearts of men in Christendom and he could not check the debacle.

Probably humanity was not ready for further progress, men being what they were—lusty for blood and war. And the age-long struggle for equitable distribution of property, equalization of social and political opportunity, and for glorification of the common man, came to an end because the common man had gone as far as his light would lead him. Man must suffer in shame and sorrow until, free of conceit, in all humility, he comes into a larger wisdom which lights him further along the way into a more abundant life. Some of these things, most of these things, Wilson knew as he sat in the White House that night before his great decision to lead his country to battle, and looked into the abyss before him. Few statesmen have made war who knew so well as he what it implied. Yet if he had seen the meaning of his action less plainly he would not have visioned his work so well when the war was done. Other statesmen have led their nations to combat. But whatever high-sounding slogans other rulers may have proclaimed, and however they may have protested the righteousness of their cause, actually and in truth, Wilson is the first who ever led a united, disinterested nation into war for no reason other than the hope of permanent world peace. Therein lies some of his greatness.

Now, despite Wilson's contempt for him, Roosevelt, from 1914 to 1919, was, next to Wilson, the greatest figure in America. But beyond America, in Germany, another figure was coming into the circle of Wilson's detestation. Kaiser Wilhelm the Second dramatized for the Allied world, and particularly for Wilson in the White House, the barbarism of war, the savagery of physical combat. The Allies, for one reason or another, were heroized in America. The Central Powers carried the contumely of willing the war. This contumely came, perhaps, because of the savagery with which the Germans waged the war on the sea with submarines. Americans were killed. Wilson protested with a show of more dignity than rage.

Let us remember that this Princeton teacher was standing before kings. There must have been a certain balm to his pride in the fact that he, who less than a decade before was putting boys through their paces, was now lording it over Roosevelt, America's popular idol, and wrestling before Christendom in a great debate with the world's villain; the incarnate devil of the Central Powers, Wilhelm the Second, King of Prussia and Emperor of Germany. Cinderella in her golden coach knew no finer thrill than Woodrow Wilson, who had been snatched from the ashes of a cloistered life, and transported to this high estate; discussing terms of war and peace with kings and potentates; happy with his newly married wife, who—as good wives will—admired his strength and ignored his frailties. Napoleon and Cæsar had really less reason for their arrogance than this lean, solemn-faced figure who, to use a Rooseveltian phrase, "looked like an apothecary's clerk," and had to play Mercurio, and Romeo, and Richard of the Lion Heart all in one.

In early April, 1917, Wilson took America into the war. It was an hour of triumph, this world acclaim for him; that day when he stood before Congress, before the Supreme Court and before the diplomats of the nations— gaudy in their blazing emblems of power—and read the eloquent message to Congress which led America from neutrality to battle. It was a message worthy of the occasion. Wilson spoke well because he thought clearly and dramatized the issues of the hour as they were marshaled in his heart, with convincing language. In an age of physical miracles, we are sometimes blind to spiritual marvels; the marvels that move the human heart and mind. Wilson's speech, taking America into the war, was one of those cataclysms which transform human life and the courses of human destiny. For months before Wilson declared for war, the war party was growing stronger every day in America; but when Wilson joined it, America was well-nigh unanimous in its war spirit and the President suddenly became the most powerful man on earth. One hundred millions of his countrymen joined in his praise and, in praising him, surrendered their liberties to him. This surrender quickly expressed itself in legislation, and in many ways was implicit without legislation. By the very declaration of war, eloquent as it was, Wilson came into a power more absolute than that of Wilhelm the Kaiser, or Nicholas the Czar. It was a terrible thing to happen to a human being, and as well as a human being could, Wilson rose to it.

In his rise, his virtues were expanded, his vices magnified; and certainly his expanding virtues dominated his life. His virtues were of the mind, his vices of the heart.

It was as though the speech before Congress where he was surrounded by all the pomp and panoply of power, had released a current that moved some vast lever which changed the direction of human life on the planet. Thereafter millions, hundreds of millions, all over the earth responded when he pressed buttons; gave their property, their lives, their heart's desire to him to have and hold and use. And he, feeling the impact of this overwhelming force, behaved under his responsibility as well as an ordinary mortal could.

Wilson's words melted even Roosevelt's rancor. Roosevelt was never a grudge-bearer. Magnanimity was one of his conspicuous virtues. The day after Wilson had sounded the war tocsin in his message, Roosevelt rode up the long curving pavement to the White House, where he had not been before for nearly a decade. Hat in hand, he knocked at the President's door. In token of his loyalty to Wilson and the war, he had come to congratulate Wilson, to offer his services to Wilson as liege lord, to let Wilson put his heel on his neck.

Wilson was busy! Roosevelt was turned away.

A few days later he appeared again, as a private citizen with no appointment. Again he knocked and stood hat in hand before the President's private door. It was opened. The two men faced each other; measured each other. Wilson was courteous. Roosevelt was punctilious. Roosevelt offered his services; would have raised a division, trained it and taken it to France. The President listened with smiling politeness, and with smiling civility —nothing more—shook hands with Roosevelt at parting. Each knew in his heart, when the door closed, that that episode was over. Roosevelt walked out of the White House, stopped a moment to gossip with the reporters and hurried down the broad steps. He rode away in his carriage, scorned and rejected—and he knew it. He was scorned and rejected in his most heroic hour. For he would have given his life to serve his country. But Wilson, being what he was, suspected Roosevelt's motives, and in his secret heart must have sucked some solace for his vanity out of the deep implications of the conventional scene. That day the gods were pouring for Wilson a heady wine. His cup ran over. The berserker rage of Roosevelt which followed when his rejection was made public, probably did not dull in Wilson's heart the thrill of triumph that he had power to humble his adversary. His counselors advised him in his course, as they would have advised another course had Wilson been generous. No one near him, except Colonel House, dared cross Wilson with a demand for a noble gesture in that scene. Possibly his habit of omnipotence was turning his head. He sent Elihu Root to Russia at the head of a fact-finding commission, and when Root returned Wilson imperiously refused to see him to get the commission's report because, forsooth, Root had talked to a reporter on his way home. Root waited about Washington a week and finally left, with no word from the President to explain his august retreat. So Wilson ever rationalized his conduct, squaring his prejudices with his righteousness, and drank the sweet poison of revenge while he walked his royal way. Then he turned to Kaiser Wilhelm, King and Emperor. There was a foe worthy even of Wilson.

What a man this American President was in those terrible days from April, 1917, until February, 1919! The world of democracy has never seen his like in power, in glory; but no chance caprice of fate brought him and held him on his throne of triumph. His own qualities, his own mind, his own eloquence, his own intellectual equipment—powers that for thirty years had been growing for that day—came to him, strengthened him, emboldened him, and ennobled him. He was indeed a looming figure—as great men are esteemed in this world; comparable with Napoleon and Alexander, save that his greatest work was not with arms, though there he was

German Press Bureau Photographer: "Costume perfect, Sire—accessories admirable; but, in view of all these 'victories,' dare we suggest that the *expression* might be just a touch more *jubilant?*"

Reproduced by permission of the proprietors of London *Punch.*

competent, but with words; winged, barbed, fiery, devastating words; words that were deeds and more than deeds. They were disembodied energies that rocked the world; words that conquered and scattered an army with banners.

The struggle between President Wilson and the German Kaiser, which began when the Central Powers used submarines with which they attacked American vessels along with the vessels of other neutrals, assumed international importance early in the naval phase of the war. The Kaiser was a world figure, possibly the world devil. He stood, at least in the Allied countries and somewhat in the neutral lands as well, as the embodiment of autocracy in government. He was pictured by the mythmakers as an arrogant, malicious, ruthless creature, who had gathered into himself as their embodiment the forces of evil in the world and was malignantly threatening democracy. The truth is, as they tell it who were near him in those years, that the Emperor came into the war after years of boredom on the throne, when nothing in particular was happening to stimulate his joy except a repetition of drills and parades and empty functions. As the war wore on and as the German military leaders realized that victory was not assured, their doubts obsessed the Kaiser. Behind the scenes he was irritable, mean, fitful, jealous of his prerogatives, which were slipping from him unconsciously. His hair was graying and his face breaking in wrinkles; a vastly different creature from the hell-god created by the Allies. But it was the hell-god that Wilson attacked. The notes from Germany to Wilson were merely signed by the Kaiser. They represented the German will to conquer, not the personal arrogance of the old flutter duck of Potsdam. This Wilson could not know. So, with his Presbyterian hate of devils, with the one weapon God gave him, his pen, Wilson rode out in front of the world and began charging the mask that was the German Emperor. Here Wilson was full panoplied. For he was essentially a crusader. Wilson came from a race of dragon-fighters, and the Kaiser—a fine pasteboard dragon—was a shining target for Wilson's wrath. Wilson managed quite unconsciously to dramatize himself as the world figure who should meet and vanquish the dragon. But the Kaiser was not entirely vanquished with arms. At the head of his army, Wilson was a minor figure in the war. No military group surrounded him. His Secretary of the Navy wore a soft sugar-loaf hat on shipboard. His Secretary of War was a philosophical pacifist, but a practical man at that. His Secretary of State, Mr. Bryan, was a grandmotherly Presbyterian elder with millennial illusions. After America came into the war, Secretary Lansing headed our State Department. He wrote a good Spencerian hand and took orders. The President's confidants were soft-spoken idealists—Colonel House, Bernard Baruch, Jesse Jones, of Texas, Edward M. Hurley of the shipping board—not a sabre-rattler in the lot. He even had small use for Wall Street. In the midst of the war, after much urging, Wilson went to New York to review a great civilian parade for the last Liberty Loan—or perhaps the Red Cross. Wall Street urged him to ride in the parade in a carriage surrounded by Wall Street notables in high hats, flanked by soldiers, guarded by major generals in glittering accoutrement. But Wilson said "No."

"No! I have never been tied up with that Wall Street crowd. They don't know me. I don't like them. No, I'll not be paraded down Fifth Avenue attached like a captive to the Wall Street chariot."

Instead of riding with Wall Street in pomp, Wilson headed the parade on foot, accompanied only by a little group of secret service men from the White House. He walked with his shoulders thrown back, his face aglow; a fine figure of a man in his early sixties under a shining tile. He was dressed in a dark afternoon coat with gray trousers, a dark purple necktie, and a suitable collar for his long neck. He had the easy swinging gait of young Tommy Wilson in Princeton, leading the parade across the campus when his glee club sang.

His battle with the dragon was going well. He had stated the terms of the Allies, the ideals of the Allies, and in a way had remotivated the war. He had made it seem to be a war for democracy; a war to end all war which came from the arrogance of aristocratic autocracy.

Then science put a new weapon in his hand. Woodrow Wilson was the first world leader to use wireless transmission for spreading his propaganda around the world. Because the device was new it seemed miraculous. So his words sang through the wireless spaces, and were heard in far-off lands. Germany heard them. The Kaiser heard them—the fretful, peevish, moody old gentleman in his gray cloak and his uniform splashed with gold braid and tinsel. The Kaiser heard Wilson's words, surrounded by a Cabinet jealous of his army and an army slowly undermining his own power. He heard Wilson's words, but they meant nothing to him. But his people listened to Wilson and were disturbed in their sorrow, puzzled as they hungered, harassed with a doubt of their own cause as they suffered. The German push of the spring of 1918 failed in the summer. American soldiers were before the German trenches, and Wilson's eloquence, striking behind the lines, demoralized the German Government back of the trenches. As he walked so proudly down the Avenue that autumn day Wilson knew, in his heart, that he was the master of the world.

CHAPTER XXXV

THE MAN WHO WOULD BE GOD

THIS knowledge should have ennobled him into god-like conduct. But Wilson's words were fairer than his deeds. General Leonard Wood, who defied the President in 1915 by talking preparedness and by setting up a training camp in the midst of peace, trained the Eighty-Ninth Division and came with it across the land to embark for France. On the eve of embarkation the general was stopped by the President, and sent back to Kansas to train another division. Wood was humiliated before the nation! The President explained afterward that certain army officers in France had asked him not to send General Wood to Europe. The army was wise, knowing Wilson. He got from France the excuse he needed. Roosevelt and Wood had their lesson. But the faith of the American people in their hero was for the moment shaken. Despite his consecration to a holy cause, and in the face of the inspired and rounded periods that carried the bolts of his dialectics, there lived in Wilson still a spoiled child. He had a lofty mind, an inspiring soul, and no particular heart. His capacity to rationalize great causes also enabled him to rationalize mean conduct. Man is that way sometimes.

As Wilson's discourses upon democracy electrified the world, doubts of the righteousness of their cause were heralded into German hearts by hunger and sorrow and shame. Slowly, during the spring of 1918, virtue—that curious power that follows the surrender which men make of their liberty to kings—left William II, Emperor of Germany and King of Prussia. One ally after another deserted the German standard. Inside his shell of power the little dried pea of a man rattled for nine months longer. At him Wilson aimed his shafts of eloquent logic, while one chancellor after another came and went, somewhat at the behest of the army, somewhat under the influence of the Reichstag.*

When the tank attacks of the Allies succeeded in 1918, Wilson's Secret Service Department told him of the crumbling morale behind the Rhine. He knew that Wilhelm's army was at the end of its rope. Wilson, before Wilhelm, knew that the unrest of the people was reflected in the signs of mutiny at the front. The Czar was gone. Bolshevism had come. Austria was in collapse. Autocracy all over Christendom was passing. Democracy, with America as the economic leader of the new order, was coming into power. It was this knowledge which threw Wilson's head back and called out of his inner heart young Tommy Wilson, who marched down Fifth Avenue so proudly that autumn day at the head of the big parade.

Finally, the Socialists captured the German Government. The commanders at the front were demanding an immediate armistice, fearing rout and anarchy. Between the lines of the German papers, whose contents were cabled to the White House every day, Wilson read this story, too. His thunderbolts had made at least the German world safe for democracy. That was in October, 1918. Disaster followed disaster as the days swirled by.

* Credit should be given to Emil Ludwig's WILHELM II, published by G. P. Putnam's Sons, for the description of the fall of the German Emperor.

Not armies, not navies, but the reasonableness of Wilson's eloquent plea for world peace, under democracy, had moved figures behind the iron line on the western front. Then, on November 9, Prince Max called the Emperor on the telephone. Imagine telephoning the All-Highest! Prince Max said he could no longer rely on the German troops, that red flags were flying all over Germany, which Wilson knew better even than Wilhelm; and, ultimately, Prince Max breathed into the Emperor's ear the stabbing truth that Wilhelm's abdication was all that would avert anarchy. Then the final picture.

In the White House it is the hour of triumph, of tense excitement; the hour whose every minute brings in its own trophy of victory. The President's long face is flecked with smiles, with complacent, mechanical smiles. But across the world the Emperor stands shivering before a wood fire, leaning against the mantelpiece, listening to Generals Groner and Pleseen, who are reporting upon the operations of the troops in the interior of Germany. The Emperor lifts his dull eyes and sighs:

"I desire to come home in peace at the head of my army."

Then General Groner stood up and spoke brutally:

"Under its leaders and generals the army will march quietly and steadily home, but not under the command of your Majesty; it is no longer behind you."

A little bluster—and that is over. Hindenburg adds this drop to the poison of Wilhelm's agony: "There are no loyal troops left; would to God, your Majesty, it were otherwise!"

In Washington, smart young officers in shiny puttees are hurrying up the White House steps with news of the collapse of Germany and the steady retreat of the German troops. Newspaper reporters are buzzing like wasps in and out of the President's office. Congressmen, senators, Cabinet members, sleek dollar-a-year men clinking their millions, all are bustling through and out of the President's room, waving such kindly peacock feathers of flattery as he will take, all singing to him their hosannas of praise and glory. The great of the earth, through those electric currents which have abolished space, are huddling about Wilson in those last days of the lonely, shame-stricken old Emperor, warming Wilson's heart with their acclaim.

The Emperor, draining the cup of Hindenburg's poison, gloomily shook hands with his old commander and went out. Suddenly the royal train appeared outside the headquarters. The Emperor had not ordered it, no one could say how it came there. Wilhelm boarded it. He had no alternative. And before midnight the exulting group at the White House, surrounding Wilson, the world conqueror, had learned that the royal train was speeding to the Dutch frontier. In the dawn there, the next morning, an old man in a gray uniform and cloak, with a few soldiers about him, tried to pass the frontier guard. A mere civil officer stopped him. At that frontier, shorn of his glory, Herr Wilhelm Hohenzollern, late Emperor of Germany and King of Prussia, was just a man. The guard let him into a little iron cage, where he sat and waited while the telephone and telegraph bore his prayer to enter Holland to the Queen and her council. An hour he waited—the Emperor. Two hours—three! Another two, and still another long hour, he sat in the little iron cage alone, under the gray cloak that had been the symbol of power for thirty years. At last the message came. The iron gate clicked and creaked on its hinges and an old man—no longer an Emperor—trudged out to his motor car and sped away from the German border.

Woodrow Wilson had winged the gray eagle of the cliff. The world turned to its new hero and ruler with the fine fervor which that fickle courtesan, the mob, turns upon any new lover.

In that hour, when the world bowed before him, when humanity was warm with joy over the end of the war, when governments were forgotten and the popular heart was beating fast, Woodrow Wilson, by lightning-like insistence, possibly might have established his League of Nations by proclamation. For in that hour of the armistice, nationalism submerged. Christendom was almost Christian.

But the golden moment passed. Wilson could not know it passed. Perhaps the cynical ones knew. But out of the exaltation that followed the end of war—in a week, at least in a month—nationalism began to recast the new world on the old, old pattern. In those months after the armistice, Wilson's defects were revealed in cruel detail. He had no great vanity for personal glory, but all his life he had exalted his own mind. Just before the armistice, he wrote a letter asking for a Democratic Congress, thus transferring the war from a national to a party basis. And after the armistice he narrowed the peace into a personal proposal.

President Wilson had been working quietly with Colonel House and a group of European statesmen from 1915 to 1918, developing the idea of a League of Nations. It was characteristic of Wilson that he thought

THE MODERN MOSES.

"LITTLE JOHNNY HEAD-IN-THE-AIR."

A more or less friendly jibe at the President's fourteen points.—*The Passing Show* (London).

and worked in secret. For he feared criticism, never for himself, but always of his ideas until they were well born and established. He said nothing to the American people, nothing to the leaders of the country, of the League of Nations he had planned. He trusted to his intellectual prowess to force his ideas upon America. He was aflame with his vision—like Paul on the Damascus road. But he told no man except his household intimates. Because his heart held the Ark of the Covenant, he rose and took it to Europe. He decided to go to Europe—not, as his enemies thought, to receive the adulation of the multitude; probably he cared less for that than even his friends realized. He went to Europe because he could not trust anyone else with his precious charge, the child of his intellectual loins. One faithful friend advised Wilson not to go to Europe. It was Colonel E. M. House, who had been his loyal messenger since he came to the White House. Colonel House felt that Wilson in America would be in a stronger position to enforce his will upon the Peace Conference than when sitting at the peace table with diplomats. With Wilson in America, his representatives in Paris could hold him up as the unreasonable but uncompromising absentee ruler; he would be master of the situation, and so bring Europe to terms. But with Wilson at the peace table, the European diplomats could trade him out of his eye teeth. Colonel House's plan provided a strong American delegation; not the sort that Wilson took.* Certainly he would not trust the wicked Republicans, as, for instance

---

* The President's colleagues on the Peace Commission were honest, amiable gentlemen: Secretary Lansing, Colonel E. M. House, General Tasker Bliss, and Henry White; excepting Colonel House, entirely without American political influence.

Hughes, Root, and Taft, who had been leaders internationally, for nearly a decade, of an organized world peace movement. Yet their minds were as keen as his. "I have sucked his brains," said Wilson once of Root, meaning that he had got from Root all he was capable of giving; a vain, even puerile statement. But Wilson trusted only errand boys. So, surrounding himself with men of soft approach, and surrounding them with men of academic background and of no political training, of no sense of public opinion, Wilson was wafted to Europe and across the land, through an everlasting throng, from London to Rome and back to Paris, in a cloud of glory. Now he did not seek this glory. It came as a minor incident in his life. The glory followed his mad decision to pit himself, his prestige somewhat, but largely what he regarded as his god-like intellect, against the statesmen of Europe, because in his vast conceit he could not delegate his powers. In the gaudery of his intellection, like Satan, he fell. He would not be warned by the loss of Congress in November, just before the armistice, which followed one display of his precipitance. He would not be warned by an obviously growing hostility to him in the Senate. Nor would he let his friends tell him of the danger which beset his European adventure. For his European glorification bred the jealousies of small men, "men of pigmy minds," if you will, who still had senatorial votes, and also—which was rather more important than the votes—had personal and political following. So, while Wilson preened across Europe, at home the forces of destruction organized against him that wayward wanton, public sentiment. If he had known less of political science, and more of practical politics, he might have avoided tragedy. But he sat down with men as wise and shrewd as he, who had no fine scruples. Clemenceau, Lloyd George, Sonnino, Balfour, Robert Cecil, found Wilson unguarded except by courtiers; and the Europeans, trading their national needs for his international aspirations, outplayed him at his own game. He went to Europe a god. He sat down at the green baize table in the Room of the Clocks at Versailles, a philosophical prig. He arose the incarnation of a tragedy. For old national aims came back and ancient national greeds were restored. The new Europe was revealed as the old Europe. And while Wilson was in Paris, the American jingoes joined the world jingoes, and took charge of things.

It was in these days of tension and excitement that Wilson broke with Colonel House. House, in running Wilson's errands, had learned the ropes of Europe, knew more than Wilson, and was not without glory in the capitals of Europe. When he advised Wilson against his will, Wilson distrusted him, and incontinently cut off and brushed aside a political friendship in which his obligations were deep and unmistakable. He banished House to England, and refused to see him in America— an indefensible gesture. House might have brought the Senate to Wilson's cause. But there, in Europe, Wilson was on his heaven-kissed throne. He who had burned with the ardor of his dreams for a League of Nations, who had crossed the ocean, who had stood before kings, who had thrown kisses at all the world, who had waved gay hands at multitudes and was the equal of potentates; even he—the schoolmaster, Wilson—who in his triumph was the spiritual ruler of Christendom, came back to

America to find his own kingdom rotting beneath him.
When he tried to make his vision reality, touching shoulders and elbows with men, they found that he was clay.
Wilson's emotional defects amounted to moral defects.
And whatever failure came to his career at the end was
moral failure, greedy vanity for the quality and caliber of
his own mind. Too often in his career—at Princeton, at
Trenton, at Washington—he had prided himself on his
ability to separate himself, as a man, from his personal
obligations; to follow what he regarded as a principle,
irrespective of the cost. He was suspicious in his dearest
friendships. He broke personally, time and again, with
men to whom he owed moral obligations, when he
thought these men were not loyal to his intellectual conclusions; which means bluntly that he could not get along
with men who differed with him, however much he might
owe to them in decent human gratitude. This quality,
at the last, isolated him. This quality attracted sycophants; but in his great crisis, it repelled strong men.
In all his courts, from Princeton to Washington, where
Wilson set up his intellect as a graven image, always
there was some Rasputin to grovel before it. Intriguing
sapped his strength and undermined his power. Wilson's
aspiring intellect gave the League of Nations to the
world; Wilson's emotional defects withheld his gift from
America. As a world visionary he walked and talked
with the high gods. As an American politician, trying
to realize his vision, he was possessed of a devil. But
his vision lives. Perhaps some dumb, kindly man will
one day bring the vision home to America and so put
Wilson on his pedestal.

Humanity had come as far toward perfection as

humanity could without a miracle. Wilson, his head in the clouds and his feet so prone to trample on the necks of his enemies, denied the world its miracle. Back in America he found his dream shattered, and in the end, even in the twinkling of an eye, his glory gone. Between December, 1918, and June, 1919, the Hero of the Armistice became, in the hearts of millions of Americans, the betrayer of the American birthright. They felt that in making them part of the United States of the World, he was making them less important as citizens of the United States of America. It was in the midst of this fight that Wilson received his death call—some sort of stroke, partially paralytic, fell upon him, affecting his brain, the organ of his pride. In that crisis he might have lost a leg, an eye, an ear, or an arm, and survived; but when disease touched his brain, Wilson fell. With calumny rampant around him, he tasted the ingratitude of his Republic—the statesman's ancient cup of hemlock. No wonder that, on the high and empty altar where the flame of his fame was quenched and the cold, charred ashes were strewn, he lay helpless while the high priests of the temple cut out his heart.

And so ends our hero tale that some day, when peace shall come to the earth, will be a folk tale. So ends the tragic story of a man who would be God.

PART V

THE RESTORATION

"Here is naught at venture, random or untrue—
Swings the wheel full-circle, brims the cup anew.
Here is naught unproven, here is nothing hid;
Step by step and word for word,—so the old Kings did.
Step by step and word for word; who is ruled may read:
Suffer not the old Kings—for we know the breed!"

Harding in the White House was a protagonist prince of reaction. Not that his brains made the times; he had few and mediocre talents. The gods of the times created him out of the red Ohio mud and put him to dry against the fence outside the Executive Mansion; and when they breathed the breath of opportunity into his nostrils, he walked in—Fate's tragic mannikin. Then came Coolidge, the Restorer of the Faith in a Hamiltonian plutocracy!

HARDING

CHAPTER XXXVI

ENTER THE WALKING GENTLEMAN

WARREN GAMALIEL HARDING came into the White House as President of the United States on the crest of a wave of hate. He was elected in 1920, when he was fifty-five. He had been in politics a third of a century, chiefly Ohio factional politics; where, until six years before his election to the Presidency, he was a third-rater. He was a henchman of the Foraker faction in the Republican party in the eighties and nineties of the last century, and during the first decade of this century. There is a story which cannot be authenticated, but which Herbert Croly, who wrote the "Life of Mark Hanna," and who read all of Hanna's letters—feels may be authentic, that in his rage at some insulting proposal made by Harding, possibly for Foraker, Hanna kicked Harding out of his office. It is one of the things that Hanna would do and one of the things that Harding, in Hanna's day, might easily have deserved. For in Hanna's day, Harding was not even a third-rater in politics, but merely a striker or fixer for the gallant Foraker. Foraker was often involved in scandal. His career closed when letters were found and published which involved him as a supporter of the Standard Oil Company's Ohio politics and policies, and designated him as a dependable senator in the Standard's national political enterprises.

The Ohio gang which Foraker had organized about his person, as a sort of political bodyguard, maintained its lines even though its leader fell. It was a feudal organization, controlled largely by that gratitude which is the "lively anticipation of favors to come." Under the leadership of National Committeeman Harry Daugherty —later Attorney General of the United States for Harding,—the Ohio gang finally backed Harding for senator, even against Foraker. That was in 1914. Harding was in his forties; Foraker in his seventies. Harding horned Foraker out of the herd, yet ever maintained for Foraker an affectionate regard, even in his victory over him. Their relations remained unbroken. Before he came to Washington as a United States senator, Harding had served two terms in the Ohio state senate, one term as liteutenant-governor, and had suffered defeat as a gubernatorial candidate by James M. Cox, a rival fellow-editor at Dayton.

Foraker might well have picked Harding in the eighties as a henchman for three important reasons. First, Harding was biddable. He "took program" easily. Second, he was a handsome young dog, a little better than six feet tall, straight, with well-carved mobile features, a good shock of black hair, dark olive skin, fine, even teeth, and an actor's mouth; and third, Harding had a silvery voice that carried far—a trumpet-like instrument that stilled the multitude. Such a bit of equipment was valuable before the invention of the loud speaker. At any rate, Harding became a spieler in the Foraker show. In Ohio he was never much more.

Harding's father was a country doctor, who operated from a farm; and in his teens young Harding, who had the common school back of him and three years of high school education, taught country schools, moved to the village, read law and took charge of the failing, starved little weekly newspaper; learned the printing trade in his own office that he might save expense, worked steadily, made friends, moved to Marion, bought a newspaper, was diligent in town politics, solicited advertisements, job printing and subscriptions himself, wrote local items, and conducted his own editorial page after the manner of any country editor of his time and place. He played a tuba in the town band, ran with the town gang of young sports, which ranged over the countryside among neighboring towns and villages. With these bucks and blades he was in and out of the saloon by day, playing a little poker in the frowsy, surreptitious gambling room over a store by night; charging noisily and with ostentatious detachment in and out of the isolated shanties of neighboring towns, where the primrose path ended among the sunflowers and jimson weeds. So he grew up as an average young American of the country town, bred in the last quarter of the old century; no better, no worse than the common run of small-town sons of the upper and ruling class. In 1891, in his middle twenties, a most important thing happened to young Harding. He married Florence Kling De Wolfe, a widow, five years his senior, in her early thirties; the mother of two children. Florence Kling was a strong woman; the daughter of the town banker, socially a cut or two above Harding. Hers was the dominant spirit, and physically she was always his equal. They made a husky, lusty, ambitious pair. She seems to have been a maternal type of wife, though by no means without charm. But she caught the gay, devil-may-care, free-and-easy young blood, who was more or less hell-bound in several ways, tamed him, and put him to work with a purpose. She came to the printing office and helped him. When they started a daily she took charge of circulation, helped with the advertising, did a man's hard work. Her parents had objected to Harding on obvious grounds. She set about to conserve what energy she had married and direct it to a decent material end. She had something to work with, namely: Harding's lovable personality, which amounted to winning ways and a talent for public speaking with a magnetic voice. The young man became known, even noted, in his county and in adjoining counties as a silver-tongued orator, who was always available on public occasions. He mouthed high-sounding phrases; caught and recoined popular shibboleths into alliterative slogans. Thus, while his paper was growing slowly in circulation from one thousand to two thousand and then to three thousand, in the nineties, his fame as an orator was extending far beyond the bounds of his newspaper circulation—which was confined to a radius of ten or fifteen miles from the front door of his office. But when Harding went to the state senate, became a floor leader of the Foraker forces and, later, the oratorical mouthpiece of the Ohio gang, Florence Kling's husband was a somebody in central Ohio.

Warren Harding came into his forties a perfect example of his type, the oratorical mid-western politician. Although he became United States Senator in 1915, his first really national appearance was when he presented Taft's name to the Republican National Convention at

Chicago against Roosevelt, in 1912. He was chosen to strafe Roosevelt, and he strafed him heartily. Four years later he went still further in national politics and was elected permanent chairman of the Republican National Convention in 1916. He was a delegate-at-large from Ohio. He had then become the spokesman and respectable outside man of something more extensive, but not more decent, than the Ohio gang. Harding represented, in that convention of 1916, the National Republican organization. It had been disgraced and discredited by the election of 1912, when Taft was defeated, carrying only Vermont and Utah. When Roosevelt polled the majority vote of the Republican party, and Wilson, with a divided opposition, came to the White House, this National Republican machine, which controlled the Republican party, organized the National Convention in 1916. The machine was implacable in its malice toward Theodore Roosevelt. The National Republican Committee in that day was controlled by a rather crooked minority, which was led and exemplified by Harry Daugherty. Daugherty was a lawyer who practiced extensively in legislatures. In the National Republican Committee were other politicians called lobbyists, not so widely influential as Daugherty, but cocks of their own dunghills. Certain interstate commodity industries, like oil, steel, insurance, lumber, coal, food, flour and grain, had interests in state legislatures and in Congress. Half a dozen or so of these Republican National Committeemen, or their kith and kin just outside the organization, knew Harry Daugherty as a leader of their gentle band. Roosevelt for sixteen years had been lambasting them and their trade. He had almost ruined their business in

certain states. He had defeated Taft, the Conservative
candidate, whom they had nominated in spite of the
obvious demands of a majority of the party.

When the Republican convention, at the behest of the
Republican organization, named Harding—the spieler of
the Ohio gang—for permanent Chairman of the Republican National Convention in 1916, it was for two purposes. First, and chiefly, to make impossible the nomination of Roosevelt by the Republican National Convention that year. Second, to glorify and reward the man
who, four years before, in presenting Taft's name to the
Republican convention, had villified Roosevelt most
bitterly. The last Progressive National Convention was
in session in 1916, in Chicago, while the Republicans met.
There was hope of fusion, or, if not fusion, at least a step
toward harmony. The Bull Moose Progressive leaders
were outside the Republican party. The Republican
organization picked with meticulous care the delegates to
the Republican convention with one object in view—
the rebuke of Roosevelt. That convention was cold with
hate for Roosevelt when Warren Harding rose to take
the gavel as chairman. But the cold hate chilled the
enthusiasm of the convention.

It was easy to get seats at that convention. The morning when the permanent chairman made his address
found the galleries only fairly filled and the floor of
the convention scarcely comfortably covered. Reporters
referred to the place as the Mausoleum. Warren Harding, the permanent chairman, stood upon the rostrum
beside the speakers' table, a tall, well-built man, just
turning fifty, vigorous, self-contained almost to the point
of self-repression, but not quite; handling himself, as

to gestures, the tilt of the shoulder and the set of
the head, like an actor. His clarion voice filled the hall
and he was obviously putting on a parade with the calm,
assured, gracious manner of the delegate from some
grand lodge exemplifying the work to the local chapter.
When he smiled, he knew he was smiling. When he
frowned, it was with a consciousness of anger. His
robust frame was encased in well-tailored clothes, creased
and pressed for the high moment. His eyeglasses were
pinned elegantly to his coat. He used them in his gestures—histrionically. His statesman's long-tailed coat, of
the cutaway variety, and his dark trousers were of the
latest New York mode. Fifth Avenue was tailoring Senator Harding in those days. This fact is one of more than
passing importance, for the Hardings were coming along
socially. In the United States Senate they were edging
into a gay young set—second-generation aristocrats—
good livers, good spenders, good fellows. Little use had
this crowd for the austere, highbrow, puritanical galaxy
that gathered around the White House in the first Wilson
term. Observe this handsome, well-set-up man on the
rostrum of the forum where the Republican National
Convention met in 1916—this man who was chosen to
hold the curb upon the convention and defeat Theodore
Roosevelt. Full, fair notice was served, with Harding in
the chair, that the old crowd would have no fusion, was
ready for no armistice with the soldiers of Armageddon.
Harding stood there on the rostrum that fine June morning of 1916, the well-schooled senatorial orator, with his
actor's sharply chiseled face, with his graying hair and
massive black eyebrows, with his matinée idol manner,
tiptoeing eagerly into a national limelight; which—alas!

—he was to catch and keep from that day until he fell in tragedy. He had come a long way up to reach the height which he had attained. As he stands there with one hand poised, about to speak, let us leave him and look at the journey he has come, with Florence Kling, in a quarter of a century.

CHAPTER XXXVII

THE STAGE SETTING AND SOME PROPERTIES

HE is editor of the Marion *Star,* a daily paper with a circulation of something like ten thousand, which is making from fifteen to twenty thousand dollars every year. He was born a Seventh Day Adventist, of which church his father and family were members. The rollicking, roistering young buck of the late eighties has slipped out of the picture into some inner consciousness of the man, but still flips his Rabelaisian quips and comments upon this dignified town booster who has taken the roisterer's name, and who holds his festive memories in their common heart. Warren Harding has become a man of consequence in Marion, a Mason of high degree, an Elk, a Rotarian, chairman of many important committees in the Chamber of Commerce, supporter of civic progress, a platform sitter at all important public gatherings, member of the reception committee when the great and the powerful visit Marion. In short, he is the Prominent Citizen. In his paper he plays Providence to the town, but not out of his own will or desire. He belongs to "the bunch that does things"; that small group of interlocking directories—the banks, the churches, the schools, the factories; seventy-five or a hundred men and women who hold the power of life and death over community projects. Sometimes they break into factions. He represents his faction and his paper voices the fac-

397

tional sentiment, or the larger group sentiment, as the
case may be. He is not a leader. He is one of the
fellows—"the fellows that count." He has no special
convictions. He is as easily handled in Marion as he is
in Ohio politics; not pliable, just obliging, yearning tremendously for the good opinion of his kind, keen for
"service." That is the idea—service in such enterprises
as are commonly esteemed to be for the public good. If
his crowd fights, he fights. If they lie down, he lies down.
If they compromise, he compromises. He "goes along."
That is his boast. But Florence Kling pushes him ahead,
as he "goes along." She is strong. She is known among
Harding's cronies as "the Duchess"! She mothers him.
If now and then the roistering youth comes out of his past
and leads Warren Harding on a little detour from the
straight and narrow way, Florence Kling eases him back
into the main road, and the episode seems to be forgotten.
She gives him his reins as a man. The Saturday night
poker game has been substituted in his life for the dingy,
dowdy gambling room. There, in a lawyer's office, or in
the back room of the bank, or in either of half a dozen
of the large gracious homes that sit well back on velvet
lawns amid high elms, the "bunch" gathers to have its
ease and its fun. They smoke a lot, drink a little, play
until morning with no one much poorer. The banker,
we will say, furnishes the liquor, the lawyer furnishes the
cigars, the doctor the gossip, and Warren, whose life is
touching the big world in a wide political arch, brings in
the new stories—which he tells well, such as they are.

This gallant group meets more or less with the consent, if the dubious approval, and sometimes under the
culinary patronage, of Florence Kling Harding, still

known as "the Duchess." Her name and fame are to follow her into a broader field. For when Harding goes to
glory, flanked by the Ohio gang, the more intimate members of that body of distinguished bandits will still refer
to her, half in fear and half in affection, as "the Duchess."
It is a mild bacchanalian orgy, that Saturday night poker
game in Marion, from which men recover in time to go to
church by eleven o'clock the next morning. No one is
much the worse for the bout, and it goes on through the
pleasant years more or less regularly, in spite of death
and high taxes, which sometimes reach out grim hands to
withdraw one of the revelers or to push some outsider in.
Harding's thumb is in many a jam pot in the town of
Marion in these days. He has a little stock in this, and
a share in that enterprise, and possibly a rake-off from
another—all legitimate enough, as the morality of the
time and place go. He has never written a line that has
been quoted beyond the confines of his state, and has
rarely taken a position which has attracted more than
local notice. His paper is as impersonal as the town
crier, from which the country newspaper was descended.

The Marion *Star* made money in those days, but not
on account of its leadership; rather because its editor
belonged to the nobility and gentry of the place and was
supposed to speak with authority in the town. He had
risen in politics, not as an oracle but as the figurehead of
power, the power being the Republican machine, later to
be known as the Ohio gang. He was the head, the apex
of the flying wedge, chiefly because of his sweet though
vast assurance and his clarion voice. He was the god
from the machine, good-natured and kind-hearted, profoundly loyal to his friends with the loyalty of genuine

gratitude and affection, a good hater because he was a good friend. In his town and in his state he had won his way, not by force, but by the charms and graces of good-fellowship. In June, 1916, he was charging upon the Republican leaders of the United States Senate with the same glucose-dipped spear that had stood him in such good stead in Marion and in Ohio.

In the United States Senate, Harding was also the voice of the organization. He was not consulted about policies. He "took program" on the floor, while others made programs in committees and in cloakrooms. He had the air of a Roman Senator, and in the midst of his oratorical flights would drop in an occasional apostrophe, "Oh, Senators," or "My Senators," or "Senators," by way of adding a certain ponderous unction to his phrases. So he was accounted an orator of parts. What he said was trivial. But he said it with a manner and spoke it with a flare—with a gracious, crystalline voice that had in its timbre a certain soft, disarming insouciance. Even in the Senate he was still the dignitary from the grand lodge, home to exemplify the work to the local chapter.

In the Senate he was following the leadership of the Republican organization. Because Wilson had twice defeated them, and because, from the start, Wilson had championed the Liberal cause and was making a Liberal President, so far as it was possible with a divided party, the Conservative leaders in the Senate, and the Liberal Republicans likewise, felt it their duty to honor Wilson with their bitter opposition—which, because they were little, had to be personal. Wilson was the object of abomination, as Cleveland had been two decades before.

But Wilson, also being narrow, hated back. He loathed
the leaders of the Republican caucus. A merry row arose.
Harding, in those martial days between 1916 and 1920,
was appointed at odd times by the Senate Republican
cabal to stand up, all tailored and barbered and bouton-
nièred, in his place in the Senate and berate the President for the delectation of the Republican galleries. He
made no important record as a senator. He voted against
the confirmation of Louis D. Brandeis as Associate Justice in the Supreme Court, supported the war against
Germany, and the draft and espionage bills. He
championed the death penalty for spies. But it may be
said in passing that his kind heart got the better of him
when he was President, and he granted amnesty to political prisoners, even Debs. He opposed the Federal control of food and fuel, as did many of the Republicans,
fearing that it would aid the Democratic machine. He
favored the prohibition amendment and voted for the
Volstead Act—voted, indeed, to pass it over President
Wilson's veto. He stood for the anti-strike clause of the
Cummins Bill, and voted to return the railway lines to
their owners after the end of the war.

When the fight on the League of Nations arose, there
Harding's clarion voice, as impersonal and mechanically
controlable as a phonograph, played a star part. Harding himself was one of those who voted all around the
lot to hamper President Wilson's plan to adopt the
covenant of the League of Nations. Then he voted
against the hampered plan. He voted for the Lodge
reservations and voted against the ratification of the
treaty, as submitted by the President. He supported
the Knox Resolution, declaring, independently of the

Allies, that the war with Germany was ended. In short, he was one of the Irreconcilables.

Harding had no personal grudge against Wilson, nor had he any deep conviction about the Wilson foreign policy. It was the plan of the Republican organization to wrangle with Wilson, and the Senate leaders clicked Harding on mechanically as chief wrangler. He spoke bitterly, even if mechanically, but—alas!—mechanically he could not simulate conviction. So his words wounded, but did not change, the President's friends. Harding in his six years in the Senate talked much but said just nothing. He left in his senatorial record, as he left in his editorial career, no phrase that characterizes a situation, no illuminating comment or convincing argument upon any subject. He was, at the height of his statesmanship, a mere bass drum, beating the time of the hour, carrying no tune, making no music, promoting no deep harmony; just a strident, rhythmic noise. In the Senate he repeated his Ohio program. He played some poker, drank some liquor, was a conspicuous ladies' man, ran with the gay crowd, took orders, talked when talk was needed, voted when votes were required. His arm was ever on the shoulder of some colleague; his feet were ever running errands, not merely for the great and powerful but for the poor and needy senators, who scarcely knew their way about the Capitol. He was smart, as the word goes, had the ear of the powerful, and banked his loyalty with Boise Penrose, the boss of the Senate.

In the meantime he took what care he could of the Ohio gang. They had no convictions. They were spoils-hungry, and he had little to offer them. For in Ohio, the Democrats were in control of the state house. In

Washington, the Democrats controlled the Federal government. But a little war pickings here and there kept the Ohio gang alive and sustained its hope for a brighter day. Of course, the gang leaders were tremendous patriots, Red-hunters, spy-chasers, witch-burners by way of diversion, but they knew that their redeemer lived in Warren Harding. Harry Daugherty, head of the Ohio machine and high in the councils of the Republican organization, saw every day how far Harding was going, realized how well he was entrenched in the Senate. In 1919, Theodore Roosevelt died. It seemed likely, at that time, that he would have had, by acclamation, the Republican nomination in 1920. His death threw the contest into the hands of a party without great leadership. In that day, facing the campaign of 1920, the Republican party was composed nationally of half a dozen groups. There was the Senate cabal, greatly excited about foreign relations, somewhat because the cabal hated Wilson. There was the Republican organization, which controlled the Southern delegates and in a certain measure controlled those states where no strong Republican senator held sway. There was the remnant of the Progressive leadership, which had mostly scattered after Roosevelt's refusal to run in 1916. Opposing that particular group was the Wall Street crowd, secretly, but mildly, opposed by the protective tariff contingent from New England. Chiefly and most powerfully represented among the financial interests was oil; oil and the new oil kings; not Rockefeller and the old crowd, but a strange new breed in national politics.

CHAPTER XXXVIII

IN WHICH THE PLOT THICKENS

THIS was the stew in the Republican pot in 1920; a hell's brew if there ever was one. Naturally, there was a reputable element. On guard at every National Republican Convention is the plug-hat phalanx, which believes piously in prosperity and patriotism and a decent eight per cent on its investment. That element was in evidence in 1920, but the controlling minority was held by the Senate group. And it was somewhat, if not largely, dominated by a rather personal interest in large campaign contributions, which were presumed to be available if the new oil group was satisfied. Jake Hamon, national committeeman from Oklahoma, a particularly odoriferous gentleman who was killed by his mistress a few months later, was much in evidence around the place. The Sinclair interests and the Doheny interests were conspicuous. Oil had a room in an office building and presumed to summon potential presidential and vice-presidential candidates to that room, where men good-naturedly discussed our foreign relations with Mexico in the oral examination which was given to those whom oil was about to bless with its support. There can be no doubt in the mind of any one who reads the testimony in the numerous oil suits brought later by the government that oil controlled the Republican convention of 1920. It worked through the Senate cabal, led by the irreconcilables—who were so busy hating Wilson that they became easy victims of the greed of oil. A story has been printed, and fairly well verified, that General Leonard Wood, a candidate before the convention, banged his fist on the table and told the oil kings to go to hell, and so lost the nomination. Lowden would have done as much; but Harding—no. Harry Daugherty, leading a coterie of his kind in the National Committee, had his heart set on Harding. No fool was he, this Daugherty. In February, before the convention met in June, he gave out this cynical interview:

I don't expect Harding to be nominated on the first, second, or third ballot, but I think we can well afford to take chances that about eleven minutes after two o'clock on Friday morning at the convention, when fifteen or twenty men, somewhat weary, are sitting around a table, some one of them will say: "Who will we nominate?"

At that decisive time the friends of Senator Harding can suggest him and can afford to abide by the result. I don't know but what I might suggest him myself.

Daugherty dominated the group which controlled the Southern delegates. That group was necessary to the Senate cabal, and friendly with the oil interests instinctively. Daugherty knew what he was talking about. The nomination would have to be made when the Senate leaders and the Southern delegates joined forces, and they could not join forces until the oil interests were satisfied. Only one candidate before that convention held the key to the solution. That candidate was Warren Harding, an amiable senator, the frontispiece of the Ohio gang, who had many opinions and few convictions —certainly none about oil. That he knew exactly what would be asked of him from the oil interests is doubtful, but also immaterial. Harding was no Machiavellian trickster. His part in any program was to talk, to stage the part of the walking gentleman in the show. He appeared at the convention, in its preliminary stages, a "looker-on in Venice." When the combat between the giants, Wood and Lowden, was staged, he seems to have lost his nerve, for his candidacy was at that time negligible.

Friday afternoon, after the adjournment which marked the second day of deadlock, Harding slouched around the corridors of the political hotels, a most unromantic figure. His clothes were wrinkled, his soft hat was crushed awry. He had a thirty-six hours' beard on his dark skin, which gave him a forbidding look. His eyes were tired, as though he had been playing too much poker with whisky obbligato. His hands were sunk in his trousers pockets as he wandered about on rather aimless errands, and he had anything but the look of a man who, twenty-four hours later, would be acclaimed "Thane of Cawdor . . . that shalt be King hereafter." His was a weary, disillusioned countenance, not heartbroken at all, but just cynically dubious of the goodness of man and the purpose of God. His face was not mean. When his countenance was illumined the light came from the generous heart of a man who, according to his lights, was trying to be reasonably decent. Warren Harding was never the villain in the piece. Always he was the gentleman who comes on with his hat, his stick, his gloves, his smile, to do the dumb, impossible thing. So, even disheveled and forlorn at the opening of the big second act in that Chicago convention, he was the good kind gentleman confronting what he believed was the steam roller which was about to flatten his hopes. And his face seemed to say "Not that I care, but the cigars are on Harry," meaning Daugherty. He disappeared from Chicago that night, probably led away by Harry, so that he would not have to appear as hero in the next act without a new make-up.

In the convention balloting, Harding had thirty-nine votes from Ohio on the first ballot and twenty-five scattering votes. On the eighth, after Wood and Lowden had wounded each other to the death, Harding had less than one hundred and forty votes. It was on the ninth ballot that the signal came. Senate leaders sent the word thrilling down the line for their delegations to leave Wood and Lowden and go to Harding. Daugherty's prophecy was verified. Friday night the senators, the hucksters in Southern delegates, and the oil crowd got together. When the delegations came to the Coliseum, Saturday morning, it was known that the die was cast and Harding would win. On the ninth ballot he had three hundred and seventy-four votes and on the tenth he secured six hundred and ninety-two votes.

He was nominated in spite of the Progressives and of the high-hat phalanx. The senators who named him knew him, but believed they could control him as they had controlled him in the Senate. The oil interests knew him, and they knew Daugherty, and if they asked questions the answer was superfluous. Daugherty also won over the National Committeemen who controlled the South. There it was—the remnant of the anti-Roosevelt faction; greedy oil, and the oily greed of the elder statesmen, whose chief distinction had been their hatred of Wilson. Hate and greed flavored the pot in which Harding's nomination had been cooked up.

Warren G. Harding, the Republican nominee for the
Presidency, in the beginning of the campaign of 1920
seems to have been deeply impressed at odd times with
the dignity and solemnity of his position—but only for
short intervals. He kept his whisky out of sight, tried
to backtrack from the primrose path, and sent for the
respectable leaders of his party—Nicholas Murray Butler, Will Hays, Borah, Johnson, Lodge, Hoover, Root.
Root, coming forth from the consultation, answered the
clamoring reporters at the gate:

"Gentlemen, I have known intimately five Presidents,
and each of them was eager for counsel—before the
election."

So Harding aspired and yearned for righteousness
amiably, but never as the hart panteth for the water
brooks. Always the good fellows, the boosters, the gay,
half-drunk, hard-boiled, moral eunuchs of party regularity, hungry for fat pickings, were near him. He tried to
serve two masters. He appeared through it all an affable,
weakly, facetiously pompous figure, partly Dickens' "Mr.
Casby" and partly his good-natured Cheeryble brother—
a portly, befuddled gentleman who tried to be as decent
as possible in a difficult time.

He made a front porch campaign in 1920, much like
McKinley's in 1896. He refurbished, so far as he could,
the McKinley make-up, the McKinley gestures, the
McKinley attitude toward the cosmos. He even reproduced McKinley's gentle faculty of getting on both sides
of a question which he did not understand and in which he
was but slightly interested. He denounced the League of
Nations bitterly; yet, in response to a public suggestion
from Republicans like Hoover, Hughes, Root, and Taft,

declared his convictions that "an Association of Nations" was necessary. But the campaign was made upon two fundamental issues—the hate of Woodrow Wilson, which was fanned by a cheap supernationalism, and the return to "normalcy"; the word "normalcy" being practically the only contribution which Harding has left for posterity. Harding, on his front porch, in a dark blue coat and vest and white trousers, and a saw-toothed straw hat or a Panama, as the occasion demanded, received the multitude—whose spokesmen were always coached before they came. Marion, Ohio, which, upon the whole, liked its Warren, bedecked itself in gaudy bunting and flickering flags the day that Harding's campaign opened. Every store front was a giant bloom of red, white, and blue; every store front but one. And when the reporters asked about it, they heard one of those stories about a primrose detour from Main Street which Florence Kling, the Duchess, had chosen to ignore. But otherwise, certainly Marion paid tribute to its leading citizen. He was their embodiment. He was Main Street in perfect flower. During the campaign, the Ohio gang remained decently submerged. The gang never was eager for publicity. However, Republican leaders, Senate leaders, and others, who knew what might reasonably be expected of Harry Daugherty, and knew how completely Harding owed to Daugherty his gratitude for the nomination, did not hesitate to warn Harding against him, did not even hesitate later to threaten Harding if Daugherty was named Attorney General. But in the campaign where hatred of Wilson and his international program was the noisy paramount issue, Daugherty and his kind could work almost without disguise, certainly without masks. For the people were so angry at what they feared might be going on in Geneva, that they did not see what was clearly happening in America. It is that way when pick-pockets cry "Fire!" to rob the crowd.

Harding was shunted into the White House as a passionate protest of the people against a number of unrelated things, for which the Democratic party was only partly responsible. For all that had happened during the eight years of Democratic incumbency—for getting into the war too early; for getting in too late; for getting in at all; for conscription; for leniency to conscientious objectors, and for punishing them at all; for the debts of the war; for the waste of the war; for the peace, as being too hard on Germany, and too tender of her feelings; for the League of Nations, in that it was too loosely defined and too restricted by language; for prohibition, and for the lawlessness that followed; for high taxes and low morals, and, chiefly, for the complaint called Wilson (a word that had become a byword and a hissing through some cruel irony of the sardonic Fates)—all these things the Democratic party answered for at the election which made Warren Harding President—and answered chiefly in hate.

But also Harding and the Republicans won somewhat, because the people demanded a leaderless nation. For the first time in twenty years, we were tired of men with burning convictions, curative or palliative panaceas or reforms; ideas that might develop into causes. We were sated with all kinds of spiritual fidgets. The land was more or less afflicted with moral shell-shock. So amid moaning and groaning, sighing and bitterness at the need to do it, but with a prescience deep and deter-

mined, America—tired beyond words, hating Wilson,
fearing LaFollette, disillusioned at the war and rejecting a futile peace—turned to Harding as the man of the
hour, of the zero hour of our courage and faith. So Mr.
Harding, carefully repressed, perfectly garbed in body,
soul, and spirit, perfectly composed, the sinister symbol
of hate and fear, entered the stage alone, the "walking
gentleman" of the piece.

CHAPTER XXXIX

THE BIG SECOND ACT

WHEN Harding came to the White House, surely something happened to him. No man can stand unmoved and unchanged in the terrifying presence of the responsibility which we have put upon our Presidents; that same being somewhat in the constitution, somewhat in the demand for extra constitutional leadership in the Presidency, and somewhat in the times. We have loaded the world upon us as we have loaded ourselves upon the world, whether we will or not. And any man capable of reaching the Presidency, even under the most deplorable circumstances, is perhaps astounded, and perhaps even aghast, at the way world problems beat in upon his desk. A man of the oratorical cast of mind, who makes a point and pauses for the claque; a man who is instinctively kindly and has lived a neighborly life in Rotary and in the Chamber of Commerce, in the intimate association with his fellows which a country editor must have; a man who by reason of his temperament and his job feels keenly the hurt of his fellow's wounds, standing before the broad, flat-topped mahogany desk in the White House, must feel like Moses before the burning bush. Harding stood appalled. If his friends saw in him strange moods; and they did, and spoke of what they saw—if his old poker pals in the Senate were first annoyed and then confounded by certain signs of change in the man, what

they saw and felt was only the reaction of a kindly heart
to a crushing sense of responsibility. But, for all that,
Daugherty came to the Cabinet, and so came Fall, who
carried his own warning in his mien and manner. But
also came Hughes and Hoover, strong men, idealists of
the practical sort, to whom the President turned, sometimes pitifully, for information and guidance. He knew
them, being a good politician, and could trust them.
And he felt that Daugherty, who had been his dear and
intimate friend, would not betray him; which feeling
merely indicates that his conversion before the great
light of duty was rather superficial. Or, perhaps, something within him had rotted away; maybe while he was on
those primrose detours from Main Street, maybe through
contamination with the Ohio gang. Or, again, maybe it
never was there—that substance of soul which could
grapple a great faith and so regenerate a man. So there
he stood dumfounded. When he turned for diversion, as
was his life's habit, to his poker, and to its spicy human
and spirituous condiments, the spell was shaken. But there
were the elements of great tragedy, as, time and again,
Harding—before his desk in the quiet office of the White
House—talked with whatever gods there be who wrestle
with rulers and those in places of great power.

Evidently, soon after the inauguration of Harding
those who dominate the forces of our politics, which play
Providence with affairs on higher planes, took a serious
look at Harding as a President. They saw that he
would have to be helped along. Men like Root, Hughes,
Nicholas Murray Butler, Wadsworth and Lodge realized the startling truth about Harding. They knew
something of the American Presidency as it was devel-

oped by Roosevelt, as it was more or less forced upon
Taft, and as it was brought to perfection under Wilson;
and these Republican leaders realized that, under Harding, the Presidency—as it had been conducted for twenty
years before Harding came into power—would have to be
either abolished or suspended. These leaders put the
country, or thought they did, into the hands of a syndicate. Harding used a phrase which explained the situation when he said that, as President, he would call about
him "the best minds of his party." "The Best Minds,
Inc.," took over the country after the election and set
it back to McKinley as nearly as possible. Of course
executives differ, but, broadly speaking, there are two
kinds: the stamp-lickers and all the others. The first kind
of executive goes into exhaustive details in the business of
his subordinates, and the others trust their subordinates
and consider results only from their departments.

Roosevelt had an addict's passion for stamp glue;
though not every Cabinet officer's glue at one time.
But while Roosevelt was President, no Cabinet officer
was immune from a stamp-licking visit from the President—a time when the Chief Executive might take a keen
and competent interest in the work of a department, or
in the business of a bureau, or in what was going on in a
division. Chief clerks or division superintendents were
constantly called, over the heads of their superiors, into
consultation with the White House in the Roosevelt days.

That was too much for Taft. He couldn't keep the
pace. He tried to rely on Cabinet members for help and
information in governing a sovereign people. But the
department heads and bureau chiefs and second assistant
private secretaries or third assistant clerks, having got

the White House habit under Roosevelt, couldn't take it or let it alone under Taft. So they, whom he mistrusted, wrecked his administration, with the cheerful, dumb, and never-failing help of those whom he did trust.

Wilson ruled from Olympus. No stamp glue ever stained his pure lips. Where Roosevelt stood throughout his administration (like the man in the almanac, surrounded by the signs of the zodiac), showing his digestive paraphernalia to the wide world and proud of the short and ugly word for it, Wilson posed, disdainful and heroic, apart from man in the midst of alarms—Ajax defying the lightning!

President Harding was more like the figure described in the old Fourth Reader, which reads: "And Eugene Aram walk'd between, with gyves upon his wrists!"—a most modest and almost downcast figure; not at all the bridegroom coming out of his chamber and rejoicing as a strong man, but rather the innocent man enduring tolerantly an unjust sentence, ready to stand anything rather than make a fuss about it. But much of his complacence was a seeming. He really did not stand everything. But he made little fuss about it, which was the trait of his undoing.

Two concrete examples will demonstrate Harding's executive method. At the Paris Peace Conference, President Wilson had with him, as Peace Commissioners, four estimable gentlemen whom he plainly regarded as waxworks. He gave the lecture, and it was their business to stand around and look pleasant. The Lansing book and the Bullitt letters reveal but a fraction of what Colonel House or General Bliss or Mr. Henry White might have exposed of the sweated life of the second

fiddlers. Mr. Harding called his armament limitation
conference, attended the first meeting, made the speech
of welcome, and did not show his face again while the
conference was deep in its problems. One cannot con-
ceive of Theodore Roosevelt following either example.
He was forever telling giant stories; gabbing to White
House callers about the marvelous qualities of his friends
and associates. There were giant rumors around Wilson.
But no one ever verified them—least of all, President
Wilson!

Then suddenly the giant stalls were sadly empty in the
White House. Mr. Harding was never quite up to giants
—not even to the giant crooks who played about the
White House in his day.

In making "The Best Minds, Inc." the holding company of his administration, President Harding was following the leading of his better nature. Here he was
Dr. Jekyll undefiled. The men who dominated "The
Best Minds, Inc." were chiefly senators, representatives,
and Cabinet members, and chairmen of congressional
committees.

Now, the directors of "The Best Minds, Inc." may be
threaded easily upon a string. Politics runs through each
name but one, as the conspicuous reason for its distinction.
That one is Hoover. He was an accident of the war.
The others would have been in a Harding council twenty
years ago; they will be in Harding councils fifty years
from now. "The Best Minds, Inc.," were politicians who
came up out of the soil of most practical Republican
politics to serve a President who thought in political
terms; to whom policies, measures, bills, and all the
achievements of an administration were considered first

in terms of elections, primaries, majorities, popular feeling, and public sentiment. This party syndicate knew what public sentiment was; even if the syndicate ignored public sentiment at times and for sufficient cause.

It is the politician's job to get votes counted on the tally sheet of the election returns—and little more. Now, the trouble with reformers is that they sniff at that game. That game is a good game in a Republic—not the highest game; but sometimes it makes good men. It makes resourceful men, courageous as well as cunning men, shrewd men, tactful men, often kindly men, and it selects generally loyal men. The incidental thieves, cowards, and double-dealers—let us say for example "the Ohio gang"—who appear in politics are not made by politics. They are scamps who are attracted to politics by the chances for plunder. And, in the higher reaches of politics, the scalawags are generally discarded.

Sometimes, at the top in politics, the deadening sense of power callouses the qualities which give men leadership; the practice of omnipotence would make a tyrant of an angel. But in politics men get their power by qualities of loyalty, of tractability, and of good-fellowship. The Best Minds, Inc. and "the Ohio gang" were political minds; and as this is a political government, sometimes miscalled a government of parties, a government by political minds will, in theory, get results. But —alas!—for poor Harding, the bad results will be remembered and the good interred with his bones. His failure was due to his aim. He and his associates thought too much in terms of party advantage, and of the common good only as an incident thereof.

The game of "The Best Minds, Inc.," therefore, was

obviously not to save the world, but to smear the blood of the Democrats over the front page of the newspapers, the first Wednesday morning after the first Tuesday after the first Monday in every other November. Such was the distressing fact. Yet it has its bright side. The seers and altruists and practical students of affairs were not weeping with Harding in vain. Indeed, the louder they wept and the longer they wailed, the better.

They—the philosophers, the economists, the keepers of various arks of the covenant—had, and always have, direct access to the people. The children of light had but to go to the people with their theories, their visions, their plans for a better world, and if the people were ready—which they were not in Harding's day—the people would receive the visions. But as for the men themselves who held these high plans for humanity, their day in Washington was done. The scribbler went back to his attic, the dreamer to his study, the ascetic to his cloister. Roosevelt had invited them to the White House. Wilson encouraged them to go to Congress. Taft politely told them to go to the devil, but Harding didn't even do that! The agitator in Harding's administration had no place to lay his head. He had to go to the people —where he was not wanted—or cease to function. So he rested.

CHAPTER XL .

EXIT THE WALKING GENTLEMAN

PRESIDENT HARDING, the head of "The Best Minds, Inc.," was a politician trying to become a statesman. The transformation back and forward is no new miracle. It happens typically that the statesman who jumps full panoplied into public affairs ends as a politician—and a rather measly one at that. And the politician who becomes a statesman is rather the commoner and more inspiring figure in our national life. Lincoln was a politician who became a statesman. Harding, in the Foraker gang in Ohio, was going to a fairly good school for statesmen. Being a politician, he must have known how small a part his own wisdom or force or courage played in the events which made him President. This knowledge would explain a certain gracious and contrite heart which President Harding, on his better side, was forever showing to the world. And it was not always a pose, this self-effacement, this impression that he gave that he could summon the indomitable strength of the humble. But he could not grapple with the men who made him—with the Daughertys and the Falls.

Also, we must not forget that the bars were down and that the hungry herd of capitalism came raging into the green pastures when Harding began to rule. We had turned an important corner during the World War; the American farmer found himself crowded into second place. America was making more things than she was growing. And in this ascendancy of industry a new element had entered. It was oil. Railways gave industry its impetus in the sixties, seventies, and eighties. They revolutionized business and politics. In the nineties of the old and the first decade of the new century, the farmers conquered the railroads; put railroading in its place, turned it out of politics. But oil, as power, the fuel and lubricant of the gasoline engine; oil, a different creature from the oil of mere illumination and incidental industrial grease—this new oil, as an industrial force, was a new devil god. The new devil should have been taught new morals; should have been put through his paces as a fellow in democracy; indeed, put in livery, made to serve and not to rule. Harding set the new devil at the first table and gave it the keys to the house. Oil, leading the trusts, the railroads, the investment bankers, and the tariff barons in a new assault on the government, came out of the metes and bounds of political decency which had been set for our industrial servants in other decades —militant, rampant, triumphant. It was field day for Plutocracy when Harding came to the White House. His slogan, "A Return to Normalcy," meant, being translated, the return to respectability of those capitalistic forces of greed and cunning in American life which Roosevelt had routed and Wilson civilized. Only in this were they new forces—they stank of oil.

Probably oil put Fall in the Cabinet, as Harding's gratitude put Daugherty in the Cabinet. With Daugherty came a group of scoundrels, some of whom have gone to jail, others to death by their own hands, while others have disappeared into the obscurity from which they were ele-

SECRETARY FALL

vated to do their dirty work. Harding had known most of these men in Ohio. But in the White House these crooks and grafters rang bells under his coat and burned incense before him. With them he drank, played poker, relaxed. And while the aspiring man in Harding's heart slept, he was shorn by the Delilah of his own moral indolence. He was not typical of his kind. Of all the men paraded before the Republican convention of 1920, as candidates, Harding was the only one with the peculiar weakness which overcame him. Except for that one weakness the American theory of democracy would have worked, even in Harding. Our democratic theory seems to be based upon the proposition that if you put one red shot and two hundred black ones in a double-barreled shotgun and fire both barrels at a National Convention of Elks, the man hit by the red shot will make a good President. Occasionally, even generally, it works. But in Harding's case it failed. The man hit with the red shot had a weak heart and a thick head.

In Harding's day no great issues divided the people. Party lines were sharp enough, but without significance. One party was held together in the South by fear of negro domination, in the cities by fear of Puritan rule. The other party was held together by the property-minded agricultural voters of the West, who desired to make the Eastern industrial captains disgorge. And in the same party were the Eastern financial leaders who at the time seemed determined to make the farmers disgorge by a policy of deflation—and did it. The President had no political ideals, except to make an honest administrator of the laws on the book. Whatever aspiration there was in that day—and there was precious little—came from the people. They were disillusioned and suspicious; victims of two devils that always beset the disheartened, fear and credulity. The simple Pharisees were obviously upon fairly clubby terms with the money changers. That was the background upon which Harding worked.

Now for the tools and weapons of his equipment. Spiritually and morally he was dull, so he was full of fears—fears sired by his ignorance.

Harding, standing before a Rotarian audience, or a Masonic conclave, or a Christian Endeavor convention, seemed to have almost human intelligence. He used strange, etymologically silly words like "common sensical," "normalcy," "citizenry," and the like, which passed for erudition. But, beyond his narrow political orbit, the man was unbelievably uninformed. His scholastic education had been slight. He had read some fiction, but evidently his mind could not grapple with serious books. Once, in 1921, when a deeply puzzling tax problem was before him, a problem upon which his financial advisors differed —Mellon and Smoot, for instance—and upon which Wall Street was divided, and the Republican economists by no means unanimously agreed, Harding—at the end of a hard day's listening to figures that he could not comprehend—walked, head down, all weary and a-slump, into the office of one of his secretaries. The presidential hands were in his trousers pockets. He took a turn or two upon the carpet before the long flat table, and cried out:

"John, I can't make a damn thing out of this tax problem. I listen to one side and they seem right, and then —God!—I talk to the other side and they seem just as right, and here I am where I started. I know somewhere there is a book that will give me the truth, but hell, I couldn't read the book. I know somewhere there is an economist who knows the truth, but I don't know where to find him and haven't the sense to know him and trust him when I did find him. God, what a job!"

He had the courage to do, the desire to do, but not the wisdom to do the right thing in cases like this, where his friends were not involved. But where his friends were involved, he had perhaps the wisdom to act, but lacked the courage to act; lacked at first, perhaps, even the inclination in his kindly heart with his warped loyalties.

CHAPTER XLI

THE TRAGEDY

At the end of Harding's second year in the White House, Washington was beginning to know the truth about the Harding administration, though the country still remained in ignorance of the corruption that was breeding. The Ohio· gang was collecting money in blackmail wherever it could. Jess Smith, a simple-minded country merchant from Washington Court House, Ohio, who knew a little national politics and had no political morals, appeared in Washington as a sort of Smike for Fagin's gang. Money extorted from violators of the prohibitory law or donated by them—distillers, brewers, large operators in illicit liquor—came to Smith's hands and was passed on. His name became a scandal among those who knew the situation. Harding seems to have heard of Smith's activities. Probably Harding protested. Smith, in the midst of his activities, under a threat, probably from the White House, of prosecution, killed himself—or was murdered by those whom his confessions might have involved. A major scandal was created by Smith's death. Stories of looting in the Alien Property Custodian's office were afloat. Forbes, the President's friend, was suspected of stealing and wasting millions appropriated for sick or crippled veterans. The Fall scandal was gathering and about to break in the spring of 1923. Out

of the backbiting and intrigue which Harding encouraged
by his amiable disposition, the realization surely came to
him that his friends of the Ohio gang had led him into
a sad morass. But even then he had moments when he
spoke beautifully, almost eloquently, and probably aspired
seriously to deserve the trust which the people had
bestowed upon him.

In those nobler moments Harding must have been
assailed by the devils of his past. What leering imps
came to sneer at his high resolve as he stood, "oiled and
curled like an Assyrian bull," bellowing platitudes, somewhat to bolster his own convictions, and to hold fast his
high dreams of righteousness? Always there must have
been, in the dark periphery of his consciousness, cackling,
ribald voices: Daugherty's voice, Fall's voice, drunken
voices, raucous in debauch; the high-tensioned giggle of
women pursued; the voices of men whispering in the
greedy lechery of political intrigue; cynical voices crack-
ling like the flames of the pit in scurrilous derision at the
booming presidential rhetoric, Harding's highfaluting
yearnings. This was his hell; the hell which he could
only escape by sinking further into it, and forgetting his
lofty emprise. So fools rattled their heels in the White
House and on the decks of the *Mayflower* while Harding
relaxed.

His two years in the Presidency whitened his hair,
blanched his face a bit, and chiseled lines at right angles
with his mouth. He stood by his desk in the White
House, a well-made, squarish man in those last months of
his life, rather taller than the common run of men. Upon
a full neck set a large head, and a face with well-marked
features, to wit, a good nose, a generous, sensual mouth,

kindly eyes, a large but pleasant jaw with no nonsense in it, nor much brutality. His straight, tractable, gray hair was always well brushed; his heavy eyebrows neatly trimmed. His figure was well clad, his clothes well considered, pressed and speckless. His necktie and collar were severely inconspicuous. Emotion cropped out nowhere in his public manner. Men about the White House declared that he was lazy; but sloth was not in evidence in his rather over-nicety of sartorial attentions. He betrayed his indolence in his voice, which rarely was querulous—as drawling voices sometimes are. It was a considerate voice, self-deprecatory in many of its modulations, never assertive. His distinguished, dark waxen face, his conventional clothes, his modest dignity, made him the ordinary American, a country man, never urban. He wore a certain obvious assumption of urbanity, the mask of the unsure. Yet Harding was no bound boy at the husking; far from it. No American President ever enjoyed the palace life more than Harding, and no first lady ever took her task more seriously than she who was known among her husband's fellow sybarites as "The Duchess."

While "The Best Minds, Inc." dominated much of the routine in the office of the White House and ran the office as a syndicate, with the President as a firm but gentle director, the parlors, reception rooms, and banquet halls of the White House were under the spell of the "Best Fellows, Ltd." This group was hardly political. If it got into official life, it went because you can't keep the society bud out of Congress. Here one found the second-generation senators, men like Elkins and Hale, and festive statesmen like Frelinghuysen, and rich young men like McLean—a gala butterfly bevy, who knew how to play and how to enjoy capering.

These youngsters and their pretty wives made lovely interior decoration for the White House on otherwise solemn and state occasions. They had no relation to the business of government. The President could have more fun with these gay lads and lasses than with a box of monkeys, and they had about the same political status. They trooped down to the *Mayflower,* the presidential yacht, and they scampered around with the President on pleasure trips, and they gave him always as good an imitation of the happy days at Marion, past and gone, as any imitation can give of the real thing. All that his hungry heart hoped for, in his busy life, of the departed joys of "Main Street," he got in this merry party.

There was no Nietzschean strain in Harding's philosophy, nor much of the Whitman tolerance. He was born a Seventh Day Adventist, and was rather Wesleyan or vaguely Billy Sundayan in his Baptist theology, wherever his theology affected his dealings with people. He was no grudge bearer nor grouch warmer, and certainly he had little use for a hog. The rich man by his mere wealth did not impress Harding. He came from a state and from an era where the politicians had bossed the rich manufacturers since Hanna died.

In New York it was the other way around. Your New York statesman always has a vest button off here and there from crawling before the rich. The New York crowd in Harding's day hadn't a frontal button from its collar to its shoes. And it was not particularly strong at the White House. For the President's instinct was not to kowtow to the rich. He acted generally, and in so far as the Comptroller of the Currency reflected the President—and they were from the same Ohio town, and spoke the same financial language—as if he thought New York was getting too large a share of the country's credit.

He was to the last a small-town man, the Prominent Citizen of Marion, Ohio. He saw life from the office of the *Daily Star*. Certain New York capitalists felt aggrieved at Harding. They judged politicians by their own kind of hand rubbers and hat carriers. They forgot that when a man runs a country newspaper that is making from twenty-five to forty thousand dollars a year, bankers are, to him, just two-legged men whose economic justification is to renew an occasional ninety-day note. This mild-mannered, gentle-spoken, drawling, well-set-up, and well-kept countryman, who owned a business in his own right, was a puzzle to a plutocracy that was used to dealing with messenger boys. They never quite got him. Probably they would have captured him in a year or so. Death was Harding's best friend.

So that is the kind of man that President Harding was: a modest, kindly, complacent sort, who got along well with politicians; distrusted all big business that was bigger than Ohio big business; enjoyed the idle rich so long as they remained idle; believed in party government and sacrificed his opinions for party success; loved to play so much that he often sneaked an early-morning game of golf, bemoaning the while over lower-middle-class hooting at the game; was sincere, and not industrious —a prosperous, courteous country news merchant, with no annoying convictions, no scholarly inhibitions upon his political folly, and few moral predilections that interfered with party teamwork.

It is easy to see that Harding could never have been a great leader, for leaders must represent causes, which rarely change. Harding was interested only in elections. The hero business, with its martyrdoms and dramatized defeats, its fine phrases and rousing slogans, bored him to the verge of tears.

He loved to chew tobacco, and often when the President was going about the land he made confidants of strangers by letting them see him take a surreptitious chew which he hid from the public. It was his idea of good-fellowship. He called men by their first names easily, with the harlot's ingratiating familiarity which politicians imitate so well. And—alas!—he always took the light relation, which he and they assumed, for friendship and for real affection. Thus he presumed upon a loyalty which he did not inspire. Some way he established about his court a free-and-easy comradery of thieves, yet without the traditional honor of their cult. For they robbed him of his name and fame while they broke his bread.

In March, 1922, Harding stood well with the people. He had made some bad appointments and some good ones. His Cabinet seemed to be working well. He was edging toward the endorsement of the World Court under the guidance of Hughes and Hoover. The crooks and grafters that were working like moles beneath the surface of his administration were only occasionally visible. Fall, Doheny and Sinclair, with Daugherty's knowledge and more or less with the approval of the Secretary of the Navy, Mr. Denby, were working out the plans which were to disgrace the Harding administration and cause upheaval in the nation. If Hoover and Hughes knew

about the plans of Fall, Doheny, Sinclair, Denby, and
Daugherty, they did not make their protest felt. Probably they knew little of what was in the wind. But one
way or another, generally in a rather bad way, a way
which the courts have denounced as fraudulent and corrupt, the plans went forward to separate America from
her naval oil reserves. And so the second anniversary
of Harding's inauguration passed. But in the spring of
1923, in New Mexico, men were whispering about the
sudden prosperity of Secretary Fall. His record in New
Mexico was such that many honest men conceived that
his prosperity was irregular if not corrupt. New Mexican
papers began to speak out. The scandal was boiling in
the pot, but had not slopped over into wide publicity. In
the Veterans' Bureau, things were happening which made
ugly talk. Harding became worried. Rumor said, probably apocryphally, that he had signed the order for the
transfer of the oil reserves when he was drunk. He was
ill in January, 1923, and at the end of his illness he told
the reporters that he had sworn off, that he did not think
it was seemly for the President of a prohibition country
to drink. At this time, also, according to current newspaper reports, he cursed his friend Forbes, head of the
Veterans' Bureau, out of his office, and laid violent hands
upon him; Forbes later went to prison. Honest district
attorneys were beginning to indict Harding's friends in
Ohio for the violation of the trust laws; for doing in
crockery, or glass, or clay products, what Harding himself did in Marion to get the county printing. He was
worried and baffled. He lost sleep. He seems to have
realized at this time that Harry Daugherty held loyalty
to his own crooked friends which was as strong as Hard-

ing's loyalty to Daugherty, and that the rascals were dominating certain sections of his administration, particularly the prohibition enforcement section. And all the time the weather was fair, the water was smooth, but Harding began to feel the pull of currents beneath the shimmering waves. In June the President started West on his journey to Alaska, somewhat to get away from the scandals, and the strife at Washington. He is quoted as saying to a dear friend, with whom in another day he may have strayed into fresh green pastures along the primrose detour:

"This White House is a prison. I can't get away from the men who dog my footsteps. I am in jail."

When he left Washington in the early summer of 1923, he had prepared speeches which would endorse the American adherence to the World Court, with certain mild reservations suggested by Secretary Hughes and possibly by Mr. Elihu Root; reservations which probably had the endorsement of Chief Justice Taft. He delivered his first World Court Speech, and the outcry of the Irreconcilables filled the air; and at the next stop the President hedged a little. The man yearned for the approval of his kind; the decent Harding was in the ascendant. The Irreconcilables were his friends—and his friends were his friends. But he also had other friends, of a rather different sort. Those friends had to be protected. The things he had done, he had done for them, and he must justify his deeds.

At Kansas City a strange thing happened. The wife of Secretary Fall came to the President for an hour's interview at the Hotel Muehlebach. She ran the cordon of reporters, none of whom knew that she was with the

President. What she said, what her message was, that could not be written nor sent by a less trusted messenger, no one knew. She left the President after the interview, again escaping the reporters, and disappeared from the scene. They were agitating against Fall in New Mexico, talking of investigations and probes. Senator Capper, who was the President's guest at dinner, declares that the President and Mrs. Fall were closeted in the Hotel Muehlebach for an hour. What she told him no one knew, but he went to his speech in Kansas City that evening, perturbed and anxious. His voice rang out across the great hall that night where fifteen thousand had gathered to hear him, but there was in it a note of fretfulness and care. The next day, while riding through Kansas, he said to a friendly new acquaintance:

"In this job I am not worried about my enemies. I can take care of them. It is my friends who are giving me trouble."

He went on to the end of his journey to Alaska. As he put time and space between himself and Kansas City, he grew more complacent, almost cheerful. But just before he left Alaska President Harding received from Washington a long message in code. This message clearly upset him. For a day or so he was near collapse. He recovered somewhat, but remained distraught and worried. He kept asking Secretary Hoover and the more trusted reporters who surrounded him what a President should do whose friends had betrayed him. Should he shield his friends, or should he turn to the country, tell the people the truth, begging their mercy, contend that his experience would fortify him against further mistakes. His conversation, for two or three days, coming

home on the boat, was filled with vague questionings about
this hypothetical President. Harding was indeed in
quicksand. Members of his Cabinet were involved in
scandal. The Republican National Central Committee
was kiting checks to hide its connection with a corrupt oil
deal. The Custodian of Alien Property was under suspicion of malfeasance. How much did Harding know
of all this wickedness? He knew something. He knew
that Forbes was not the only friend who had betrayed
him. Did he realize what Daugherty had done? What
Jess Smith's suicide meant, if it was suicide and not murder? How much did Harding know about Fall's in-
famy? What ghosts of fear must have flopped their
wings across his heart?

He was fifty-seven years old. He had paid small heed
to his physical body. It had been strong. It could stand
punishment—work by day and sometimes rollicking, poi-
sonous nights. But still it stood, and if it sent out warn-
ings, Harding did not heed them. In Alaska he played
with the reporters and the local statesmen gayly enough,
but one wonders if he could suppress the consciousness of
the hidden things, shameful things, which must appear.
Returning from Alaska he became ill on the boat—it was
said, from eating crab meat. But the list of supplies in
the steward's pantry contained no crab meat. Harding
reached San Francisco, and there lay down, gave up the
fight, and died.

Then slowly all the scandal which had been hidden
came out; and with the truth, which was bad enough, came
lies and innuendoes. Before scandal had reached him
men started to raise a memorial to him. A myth was
born that he was a beloved President, a sweet and kindly

man, like Lincoln. But—alas!—the myth was abortive. His friends, cronies, allies, and the Ohio gang were haled into court. Death saved some, the prison took others, shame touched all. And Harding passed into contemporary history with a name so clouded that none would do it honor. Probably no other American President had to run the gauntlet of cruel malice and public odium as Harding ran it during the first four years that followed his death. Some day America will realize the tragic drama in which he moved, will realize how wickedly unfair the Republic was to pick up that man—weak, unprepared, with no executive talent, and with an unused mind—and pinnacle him in the most powerful place on earth. He was as a child in heart and head, set down to fight the dragon, and in the end his terror conquered him.

COOLIDGE

CHAPTER XLII

WHAT DEMOS WISHED ON US

CALVIN COOLIDGE was an odd fish in the White House. Curiously, so was every other President since Washington's day. We have not developed the American presidential type. Looking back over forty years, during which the memory of men now living may be reasonably expected to have retained some recollections of their Presidents, one cannot recall any President, from Cleveland to Coolidge, who was not an odd fish in the White House; who did not have to be explained, almost interpreted to the people. The dynasty of politics which makes the Presidency the climax of a career does not develop in the dynasty a Hapsburg nose nor a Wettin chin, nor a mythical imperious will like that of the Hohenzollerns. During forty years we have had but two Presidents in the White House who were not what might be called career men. They were Cleveland and Wilson, neither of whom functioned in politics more than three years before he was President, and neither, before he came to Washington for his inauguration, had ever seen Congress in session nor entered the White

435

House.   Harrison had been senator, a candidate for
governor, a member of an important Federal commission and a political figure in his state twenty years
before he came to the Presidency.   McKinley had been
in office, or seeking it, from the day of his majority
until the day he died.   Roosevelt had twenty years of
officeholding before he was elected President, and knew
his way about Washington in the dark.   He had run for
office and had known victory and defeat.   Taft had a long
appointive career and only the slightest contact with the
people on the hustings before he was called upon to rule
us; and after leaving the White House, he sidled into
the sheltered life of the Supreme Court as a duck takes
to water.   Harding was a political striker, a henchman,
a part of the Republican machine, grateful for little
offices like state senator or lieutenant governor.   He
fell into the United States Senate as an organization
man, took orders, and was the papier-maché front in the
Senate of a venal and discredited national party machine,
which, allying itself with the new malodorous oil interests,
sent him to the White House.   Each of these democratic
sovereigns who climaxed his career in the Presidency was
as different from any of the others as though he
had come from his own planet in some distant universe.
Yet each was a fairly usual product of American
politics.

So was Coolidge when he came to Washington.   The
moving stairway of Massachusetts state politics had carried him from councilman to legislator, to mayor of his
town, to state senator, to lieutenant governor, to governor, without any display of his genius and without
revealing in him any conspicuous talent for public affairs,

except perhaps a certain dogged faithfulness in working at the trade of politics. When the escalator broadened and landed him at the Vice-Presidency with a shock, his teeth must have clicked as he came to a standstill and looked about him. He had never ridden on a Pullman car until after the vice-presidential nomination. He had never been in Washington before. He had never crossed the Alleghanies, and had scarcely crossed the Hudson. He was peculiarly Yankee, a blue-bellied, Vermont Yankee to the core. He had exhibited absolutely no initiative. He had spoken no memorable phrase. He had appealed to the country but once, and that was as governor, when he delayed day after day until the week had nearly dragged by in the tremendous crisis caused by a police strike in Boston, and then modestly, yet bravely, called out the troops as the strike was subsiding. After the strike he submerged until he appeared in the Vice-President's chair, and later, following President Harding's death, came to the White House. Yet he, like every other President which this generation has seen, was divinely fitted for his job. Each of these queer Dicks whom we have called to the White House from odd corners in our national life has been in the day of his power and glory exactly the kind of man whom democracy, if it had known its conscious mind, which it probably did not, would or should have chosen to represent the spirit of the hour in which he came. Any other President, functioning in the place of either of his predecessors or successors, would have made a mess of it. For each was the embodiment of a definite, even if a passing, faith in the heart of the American people when he came into power. Each President used his power as a defender of

the passing popular faith; Coolidge as much as any, perhaps even more than most.

To understand Coolidge, we must understand the
unique background out of which this prodigy came. He
was—and is—Vermont, blood and bone, horse sense in
granite, a flinty body, a flinty mind, a flinty soul, affected
in expansion by neither heat nor cold; imperturbable,
taciturn, shy, immoderately modest, stingy but never
greedy, abashed only in kindness, voluble only about
economy. But above every other trait his stark honesty
was the keynote of his success. His honesty exalted him
and held him in popular respect, even made him a popular
idol.

Willis Gleed, a Vermont-born Kansan who returned
to his native village, once lifted up his Kansas voice to
declare:

"Vermont should be set aside as a national game preserve and allowed to function as it is for a thousand years,
that the American people may always be able to see
exactly how their primeval ancestors once lived."

Vermont has bred its own kind for nearly two hundred years. The Coolidges came up from the Connecticut Valley in the eighteenth century, well before the
American Revolution. Where they came, they stayed;
living in a bowl of the high hills, as remote as Indians,
with whom they were bred in the half century before; as
prosperous as Crœsus, compared with the Canadians to
the west, and for a hundred and fifty years repeating
their type almost unchanged. These Vermonters speak
cryptically at times, chiefly to be brief, not to be baffling.
More than a hundred years ago, Ethan Allen, coming
down into the Mohawk Valley to protest against certain

injustices arising from land grants, flung at the high powers down there, as he turned homeward, rejecting their offers: "The gods of the hills are not the gods of the plains," and would say no further word to elucidate, or elaborate, or explain.

They understood him at home. He saw no reason to carry an interpreter abroad. The spirit of Ethan Allen spoke through the mouth of Coolidge when he took twelve words, using his verb in pure Vermontese, to lay aside his active candidacy for the Presidency. Vermont has changed in a hundred years—but has changed only to narrow, not to intensify, the scope of her power.

In the early nineteenth century, Vermont was a more important part of the United States than Vermont is to-day. Moreover, most of Vermont's valleys and hills sustained more people then than now. Vermont, a hundred years ago, was teeming with the industry of that time. Little wooden factories were there; felt factories, hat factories, foundries, potteries, textile mills, making the meager tools of an industrious countryside. Things did not move far in the early nineteenth century. Wagons were made in the neighborhood where they were used; plows not far from the fields that they turned; hats and clothing among the people who used them; pottery, chopping bowls, clothespins and potato mashers took no long journeys to find their ultimate owners. And industry in Vermont remained more or less at the cottage stage. It remains to-day somewhat at that stage. There is little itinerant seasonal labor in Vermont. The mills are small. Farmers and their children go from the fields to the factories, and from the factories back to the fields, as the market and the seasons call them. Necessarily, this

primitive industry which characterizes Vermont has stood
still or has shrunken as industry has changed and
expanded with the growing commerce of a new world.
Vermont is static. In the last century Vermont has furnished the industry, initiative, and wisdom for commerce
in every American state. Vermonters have led every
line of human activity in America—but outside of Vermont! For Vermont has been bled white of her courageously imaginative blood. She has retained the solid,
industrious, conservative blood; that has inbred. The
state seems to be inoculated against all the bugs of social,
political, and commercial madness that have bitten the
modern world. And to a certain extent, Vermont to-day
stands for an area in western New England and northern
New York which is affected with the stagnation of
another time. In this placid area, Calvin Coolidge has
lived his life. In Vermont, he came down from the hills
to a country town, a strange boy, to go to the academy
which prepared him for Amherst, where he went, a
strange boy, unnoticed save for his frugalities even in a
Spartan atmosphere. He attended to his collegiate duties
carefully, and solemnly appeared at all extra-curricular
functions with exact regularity, but without joy. Out of
this drab college life young Calvin Coolidge, in his junior
year, bloomed as a bit of a wit by reason of his saturnine
quips at a class-day celebration. In his hill home at
Plymouth, death came into the family in his childhood
and took his mother and sister and left him lonely. His
father lived—as his grandfather, and great-grandfather,
and great-great-grandfather had lived—upon the stony
soil of the hillside, above the hay meadow and the little
fields isolated among the hills. Travelers, wandering

through the woods of the neighborhood, may see curious
pox marks here and there upon the landscape where once,

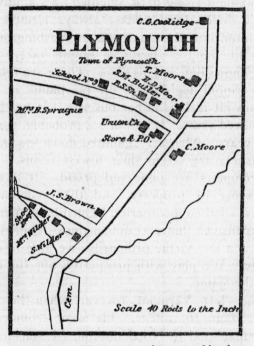

Plymouth Village, 1870, from an old atlas.
The President's home is the house marked
"S. M. Butler." The Colonel's blacksmith
shop marked "B S. Sh." here put next to the
Coolidge house, has been torn down since
1870, and the present one built, across the
road. The road to the left, near the cemetery,
leads down the "Notch" to the "Union." This
map and the drawing on page 435 are reproduced by permission of Mr. John Cotton Dana.

a century ago or more, were homes, occasional villages
that have disappeared from the earth, leaving those who
stayed in the lonely hills even lonelier than before and

bleaker, with fewer human contacts. So out of those silent, granite-ribbed hills, Calvin Coolidge struggled steadily along a rising path, shielded by a kindly destiny, to half a dozen local offices, always elective; out of Northampton into Boston, down to Washington, and so to the White House, always an enigma except at home. Vermont knows him and his kind. There are few fat men in the Vermont legislature, no fat plums in Vermont politics, no fat melons in her business. It has been thus for a hundred years. It will be so, probably, for another hundred years. Men are "gaunted down" in those hills, and measures are set in their lowest terms. It is not that Vermonters are poor and proud. It is that they have a sense of property, and that economy is the high priest of their prosperity. Outside of Vermont, in these expansive, more rambunctious United States, economy is a low virtue ordinarily; we love to dare and to gamble. We play with prosperity, not for the gains but for the game.

Coolidge left Vermont forever when he went to Amherst to go to college. He went from college in his early manhood to Northampton, Massachusetts, but an hour's journey from Amherst, and lived in western Massachusetts until he came to Washington. In Northampton, Massachusetts, while he was forever running for office, he did not mix with the politicians. He was attorney for a brewery and yet appeared at the Congregational Church every Sunday, took his annual drink publicly but solemnly, and when he ran for mayor, completely ignored the saloon issue, which his opponents tried to force upon him. He carried with him into life the qualities of his Vermont environment; good qualities,

wholesome, necessary to the times, but difficult to understand for those who all their lives have been in the turmoil of modern American life, whirled by its currents
from progress to reaction and back again many times in
the last half century. Coolidge, from out of the calm
backwash that is his geographical and spiritual habitat,
looks upon the strange currents of influence about him
with curious interest and veiled astonishment, but little
understanding; much as the inlander who, seeing for the
first time the rolling, restless, booming surf, remarked:

"Must have been raining up the creek. She's certainly
on a bender."

Coolidge, as Vice-President, came to Washington, a
lean, blond man with a sharp Yankee nose and chin, a
typically high Yankee brow, eyes that generally peeked
from squinting lids which, when unshuttered, revealed a
most intelligent, understanding, almost fervid expression
that changed his entire countenance. He had no small
talk, and quacked his casual sentences in staccato, after
the down-East, Yankee fashion. He walked with a certain circumspection, almost cat-wise, on his toes, quickly,
with no shoulder movement to indicate brusqueness, masculinity, or vanity. He played no poker, drank no liquor,
made few friends. And Mrs. Coolidge, who had come
with him from the duplex apartment in Northampton,
Massachusetts, for which they had been paying twenty-
seven dollars a month all their married life, and who
moved with him into one of Washington's rather grand
but noisy hotels, had to work hard, those first seventeen
Washington months of the Vice-Presidency, keeping him
awake after bedtime in Northampton at nine-thirty. She,
being full of joy and appreciating the gorgeous good for-

tune that had fallen to the Coolidges, desired to drink her lucky cup with gusto. He handled his cup gingerly; he sipped it, and kept on his features that curiously characteristic disdain which gives one the impression that he has just encountered a bad smell. Washington tittered in his wake with silly stories of the Vice-President's greenness, his social indifference and zestless acidity. Washington catalogued him as a crab; which was unfair. He was a mountaineer, a Vermonter, self-contained, more bashful perhaps than modest, but of the silent habit of solitary men.

So lived this incarnation of prudence until 1923. Then came a change in the adventurous spirit of America. After the World War the burden of debt piled up by that martial gamble made America pause, throw away her gambler's cloak, and develop a new public virtue. The times cried aloud for a cheese-parer. And out of the earth came this Mayor of Northampton, up the escalator of politics—State Senator, Governor, Vice-President— like one of the genii of Arabian magic, suddenly appearing in the White House. He was certainly most sensible; but queer. This lank, cheerless servant, who materialized when Democracy rubbed the wishing ring, was our leader for those uneventful years in which we economized with almost unbelievable rigor. He incarnated the yearnings of our heart. We prospered under our economy, and our economies came not merely in the public business but in other walks of life.

Commerce was reorganized in the Coolidge decade, under Coolidge's Secretary of Commerce, Mr. Hoover. A thousand efficiencies cut the waste out of business. New ideals even appeared in industry. Your big business man of 1928 was keen not so much for a speculative profit, which he knew was dangerous, but for a small profit with a big turnover. Competition was controlled, even to its necessary restrictions, not so much by government as by Commerce itself. Piracy in business, even in big business, no longer was sure of general applause. The dangers of piracy were likely to overmatch its rewards; which was a changed status for piracy in American business. As government relaxed its hold upon commerce, commerce itself began to do more, through changed methods of established honesty and efficiency, than government could have dreamed of. The political socialism which seemed to be approaching in 1916 was overshadowed by a commercial socialism which came rather definitely in the middle twenties. Under trade agreements every basic industry was organized. Many industries were under a czarlike control of one man or a small board. A thousand waste holes were plugged. Scores of petty grafts began to be taboo. Sprawling business with its unchecked greeds was severely channeled, and as an incident of the channeling it was decently moralized.

Now, of course, Coolidge did not do all this. The Department of Commerce, under Coolidge, directed by Herbert Hoover, gave the movement toward the new commerce vital assistance and some necessary leadership. But as Roosevelt bred his kind, and Cleveland his in a score of state houses, and a hundred city halls, so the Coolidge idea, exalting prudent parsimony and prosperity, and above everything emphasizing honesty, bred across the land leadership of the Coolidge type in every station of American life.

Behold, the mystery! but who can explain it? How

did this genii come when Democracy rubbed the wishing
ring, this Coolidgian servant who could be in a thousand
places at one time, in every aspect of human endeavor?
He had no qualities of leadership, this Coolidge, in Washington, or in the states or in the cities. He was always
an undramatic, unimaginative man who never took time
by the forelock, who hesitated and let the occasion shrivel
and pass before acting. It is not that he was cowardly.
It is not that he was overpatient. He was just careful;
deadly. He had no desire to prance or strut, but would
prefer to get the day's work done as dully and as easily
as possible, and forever put off until to-morrow the
unpleasant thing which just does not have to be done
to-day. So time helped him. Time frequently solves
questions if you will let him. And the Coolidges, big and
little over the land, always let him. There is a saying in
Vermont that no Coolidge ever went West. In so far as
the West is a state of mind, the challenge to yesterday in
behalf of to-morrow, this saying is gorgeously true. No
Coolidge ever went West. He remains Eastern, even
Oriental.

Therefore, Calvin Coolidge went into the White
House in the Oriental magnificence of his honesty, of his
silence, of his caution, of his conservatism, of his faith in
the statu quo; the statu quo being business prosperity.
That faith is the key to his administration. When he
said in December, 1923, that "the business of America
is business," he trumpeted the slogan which would define
his policies of searching economy at home and the protection of American investments abroad. Upon these two
underlying policies he worked through the years of his
presidential service. Upon the economy issue he based

his veto of the bonus bill, and economy was an underlying principle in his veto of the McNary-Haugen Bill.
Because he would protect business from the onslaughts
of political investigators, he packed the Trade Commission and the Tariff Commission with men friendly to the
tricks and the manners of big business. He did this
frankly, proudly, consistently, and the country applauded
him, though he spoke no word to proclaim or explain his
philosophy. It was obvious. He sent the marines into
Latin America to conserve American investments. There
was no nonsense about the idealism which would conserve
friendships south of the Rio Grande ahead of investments there. His diplomacy was in the main a dollar
diplomacy. His hatred of war seemed to take less
umbrage at war's cruelty than at its waste! And although
he winced at the term imperialism he left in the minds of
our Latin friends the same disagreeable convictions about
our altruism which Egyptians, East Indians, and "the
yellow, the brown, and the black" hold in the uttermost
parts of the earth toward the British empire.

CHAPTER XLIII

THE WIZARD OF A NEW ORDER

THE sheer honesty of Coolidge worked like a wizard's spell upon the débris of decency which was the Harding administration. If ever two men were deeply opposite they were Harding and Coolidge. The jump from Lincoln to Johnson, from McKinley to Roosevelt, was not more definite nor over a deeper spiritual chasm than that which the nation made from Harding to Coolidge. All the palaver that garlanded Harding's life Coolidge stripped away. All the courtier thieves, Rasputins, drunkards, harem favorites guarding the intrigues of plunder, all the owlish soothsayers of the high temple of politics—the whole mess of trash in the White House—Coolidge banished forthwith. He put on the wizard's robe himself, to wit: A sack coat and soft hat, well pressed and tailored clothes, a dark four-in-hand tie, an innocuously perfect make-up. In this businesslike garb he wielded the wand of a cold, implacable honesty over the Washington scene, and almost in the twinkling of an eye —in less than six months—he had accomplished a miracle of change. Fall, Denby, and Daugherty resigned. Coolidge seemed to be holding their coat tails as he pushed them out, yet their hats were in his hand at the door. He made no outcry against the crookedness which departed with Fall and Daugherty. He gave no encouragement to the crusading souls in Congress who were dashing out to fight the oil dragons. So far as anyone knew—and, probably, even in his heart—Coolidge had small use for the noisy claque that barked at the departing heels of the guerrilla cavalcade and the infamous Ohio gang; the bloodhounds who were smelling out the tracks of scandal never came from the White House kennels.

In the first half year of his administration, Coolidge made it clear that he was heartily with the tendency toward our Hamiltonian plutocracy and that he had no proletarian leanings. Also, he made it plain that he believed in the honesty of the Hamiltonians; and lo! by the miracle of his own faith he injected an honesty into the works and ways of his allies—which Harding, by his placid, amiable connivance at crime, had tragically weakened. The Liberal movement which came to rest in 1917 had no resurrection under Coolidge. Yet under Coolidge industry began to reform itself. The eight-hour day was established in the steel industry, and became almost universal in other major industries of the land. A new motive thrilled through industry, arising out of mass production, quick turnover, small profits, high wages, low rates of interest. And the great piles of worldly goods, luxuries as well as comforts, which were rolling out of the factory doors every hour were being distributed throughout the land with an equity and a justice which far exceeded the dreams of the Liberals in the heyday of their triumphs. This was not Coolidge's work. It began, indeed, in Harding's day. But Harding did not understand it, did not encourage it, did not sanctify it by faith in it, as Coolidge sanctified with his faith the new industrialism, the new capitalism. More than that, in his desire for stability President Coolidge presented to Con-

gress the first drastic workable treaty outlawing war
between America and a major power. His handling
of the Nicaraguan situation was perhaps wiser and certainly more effective than the policy of the Liberal
Wilson. Nicaragua became a problem, by reason of our
imperialism, long before Coolidge came to the White
House. He used force to get both parties to the controversy to consent to an election, and then maintained a
war against those who rebelled against the agreement.
There was bloodshed, but apparently he was trying at
least to work out a policy of American imperialism which
did not include conquest, even if it required invasion and
the incidence of slaughter. In working out this program,
probably Coolidge had no great part. It was the State,
War, and Navy Departments functioning under the
impulse of a tradition a generation old. But at least it
was honest and forthright, even if it shocked the Liberalism of the hour.

No Persian potentate was ever more practical in his
rejection of the tenets of spiritual progress through altruism and distributive political justice than was this mild-
mannered, silent, self-effacing, conscientious Puritan
potentate, functioning as our ruler with a Jeffersonian
simplicity almost ascetic in its rigor. He gave no tongue in
deep-mouthed baying to his decrees and ukases. Instead,
he quacked dryly. His sentences were well shriveled of
their rhetorical juice when he spoke. Ceremony irked
him, yet he strove to please. The most elaborate of the
ceremonies which presidential duty placed before the
President was to review the Grand Fleet. A President is
presumed to appear in full regalia, wearing a high silk
hat and perfectly tailored clothes, and to stand through

the long hours as one squadron after another passes majestically before him, while he receives the salutes of the admirals. Coolidge appeared in his first review of the Grand Fleet in a business suit and a yachting cap, which he wore as commander of the presidential yacht, *Mayflower!* He stood for a time at the rail, surrounded by all the gold braid and rooster feathers that our navy could assemble, looking silently at the herd of steel dinosaurs of war, as though mentally footing up the taxes which they cost. His eyes, for the most part, were looking down his nose to locate that evil smell which seems forever to affront him. After a time he turned away, and did a most natural human thing. He went abaft the funnel and lay down, either bored or tired or sea-sick, it makes little difference which, while the great engines of war belched forth their expensive smoke and shot their high-priced powder all in vain, so far as Calvin Coolidge was concerned. Whatever the admirals may have felt the nation smiled its sanction.

He decided to go West in the summer of 1927 to see the country and live with Western people. That also was a wise and courtly thing for a President to do. Clearly, he was eager to please. Out West, he put on gaudy chaps and spurs, a shameless checkered wool shirt, and, finally, a terrible cowboy hat; and all shrimped up in this shell of magnificence he minced his way painfully down the front steps of the veranda of the summer White House before the camera men, in a futile, though amiable, endeavor to follow the customs of the country. He could not know that they were the customs of Hollywood rather than Dakota.

The Coolidge mind was a good mind, there in the

White House. He was clear-brained, had capacity for
absorbing facts and reasoning about them. Of course,
every mind is colored by its environment and retains its
prejudices in spite of its logical intentions, but in so
doing Coolidge was merely human. The point is that
he tried. Also, we must remember that in contrast to
Harding Coolidge was a man of books—a college
graduate. In passing, let it be noted that he and Mrs.
Coolidge were the first occupants of the White House to
hold the Bachelor of Arts degree from standard American colleges. Mrs. Hayes and Mrs. Harrison were from
finishing schools or their equivalents. Mrs. Cleveland
was from Wells; Cleveland, from the University of Hard
Knocks. In Amherst, a college in the list of the first ten
American colleges in point of scholarship and standard,
Coolidge was a hard-working student. He knew always
the significance of his words or deeds when he was in
the White House. He knew where to find authorities if
he needed them. He knew how to assemble facts, and
considered them, when assembled, with a tough-fibered
legal brain. If he seemed spiritually a bit moldy and sour,
mentally he was fresh, energetic, and persevering.

Mrs. Coolidge, in the White House, was an unalloyed
joy, the lovely spiritual antithesis of her husband. She
was of the West-Western, a sport from Vermont thrown
forward or backward—Heaven knows which—a hundred
years. Always she was gracious, tactful, ebullient, deeply
kind, wise with the wisdom that comes from an understanding heart. She kept the White House socially
up to its high traditions, and the Coolidges did their full
duty to man and beast with good taste and good cheer
in matters of social punctilio.

Probably the President enjoyed it all. He was human enough under his shell. His shell was partly a Vermontese incrustation, partly the expression of some loneliness which came out of his childhood, where he may have been cruelly cramped and wherein the naturally expansive joys—which come to most of us in exploring a new-found world—may have been so sublimated that they did not rise to the surface of his being. He had a lively sense of responsibility. He could not take lightly his call to duty as he saw it. He was as conscientious as any President who ever sat in the White House; conscientious according to his light and leadings. No political philanderer was Coolidge, making love to friends and enemies alike for the joy of the game, a joy which is heartiest satisfaction to many men in politics, men of warm and expansive natures who love to please their friends, placate their enemies, and hold the high opinion of their kind. Of such were Blaine and Harding. Roosevelt had a nicely tempered taste for royal honey on his hard-earned bread. But if President Coolidge had this taste, that also was suppressed deeply. And, of course, being conscientious, he must have been afflicted with serious questions, castigated in his spirit by "many a conflict, many a doubt." The days of turmoil and trouble which he seemed to pass in such unspoiled placidity, surely stirred him underneath to a weariness of the spirit which he rarely expressed. Those who frequented the White House declared that sometimes at the end of a hard day, when senators had been bedeviling him and problems of the State Department had been pressing him, and all the world pulling and hauling, and the right was gray and the wrong was iridescent in many

issues, and the weariness of the flesh and the confusion of
the spirit were riding him, he would come over to his
wife, stand by her a second, looking down his nose
drearily, then—one can almost see him opening his wide,
handsome eyes to smile as he said:

"Let's go home, Grace."

The gods of the mountains are not the gods of the
plains. He knew for a long time that he had drained the
cup of his fame and power and glory. Looking back, his
friends now know that it was probably a mixture of
mischievous delight and a politician's uncanny desire to
hold the situation until the last possible minute, which
kept him from revealing his attitude toward another
term. He had finished President Harding's term, and
was in the middle of his own first elective term. He might
easily have asked a second nomination from his party.
But he was done; enough was enough. No passing event
affected him. The failure of the Arms Conference at
Geneva did not disturb him. Undoubtedly he had chosen
the fourth anniversary of his presidential service to make
the announcement, but he said nothing to any human being
before he made it. Ten minutes before he dictated the
cryptic words,

> I do not choose to run for President in 1928,
> CALVIN COOLIDGE.

he had not breathed the slightest hint of his intentions.
And until he opened his mouth to his secretary, to dictate
his famous abdication formula, no one knew what was in
his mind. He distributed with his own hands the slips of
paper containing the twelve parsimonious words, to the
reporters, and he enjoyed hugely, but with Indian

PLYMOUTH, VERMONT, IN WINTER.

"THE GODS OF THE MOUNTAINS ARE THE GODS OF THE PLAINS."

stolidity, their bewilderment and amazement. To Senator Capper, of Kansas, who was his house guest, he intimated nothing. Turning from the reporters and going with Senator Capper to his family, he spoke no word even there of what had been done. And when Senator Capper referred to the statement the President had just issued, Mrs. Coolidge asked quickly, curiously: "What statement?"

And Capper told her. Thus deeply are the secrets of Coolidge's heart sublimated in the habits of his life.

The cryptic phrase which puzzled the American people for ten months, from August, 1927, until mid-June, 1928, was translated rather simply by the events at the Republican National Convention of June, 1928. Twice during the ten months the President opened his lips to rebuke friends who were getting delegates for his nomination. But he would not say, "I am not a candidate." Over and over he was importuned to do so. Senator Curtis, of Kansas, a candidate for the Presidency, asked President Coolidge for a frank statement, and in the winter of 1928, Herbert Hoover futilely suggested candor to the President. A short, unequivocal declaration any time before the delegates to the National Convention were selected would have changed the result at the National Convention in June. No one knew this so well as Coolidge. Because he realized the situation, he withheld the candid statement. So long as he was a potential candidate, the controlled delegation of New York, Massachusetts, and Pennsylvania could not be manipulated in favor of anyone whom the President disliked, and his dislike included those who supported the McNary-Haugen Bill, notably Frank D. Lowden and Vice-President Dawes.

His dislike for Dawes was rather deeper than a political dislike. Dawes would have been the choice of the great international bankers who controlled the politics of the three large seaboard states.

In the summer of 1928 the McNary-Haugen Bill became a major issue. It provided for coerced coöperation through the collection of an equalization fee from farmers on each unit of every crop coming under the provisions of the McNary-Haugen measure. This measure, to the President's friends, and particularly to what may be called the Wall Street crowd in various commercial centers, being deeply socialistic, was regarded as highly dangerous. Hoover was the only candidate who openly opposed the McNary-Haugen Bill. He was the only candidate whose nomination would have been an indorsement of the Coolidge administration. The other candidates were running in opposition to the President's record on this major issue. Hence his crafty silence, his refusal to get out of the situation entirely and thus hold away from Lowden or Dawes, and chiefly Dawes, the large Eastern Republican delegations which fundamentally distrusted Hoover—and which, by grace of Coolidge, finally nominated Hoover. Their distrust of Hoover came not from any question about the McNary-Haugen Bill, but came because they believed he was not property-minded; that his Hamiltonianism was tainted with Jeffersonian ideals. A million dollars was not sacrosanct to Hoover. He threw many millions over his shoulder when he closed out his business and became food director in Europe for the Allies in 1914. He was not of the Wall Street kind. But to the President he was the one man whose nomination would perpetuate the Coolidge

policies. Hence by the presidential silence, always holding himself "available" in the background, Coolidge kept
the politicians of the Eastern states away from Dawes,
who· was their heart's desire. Coolidge's friends in the
National Convention of 1928 had to be Hoover's allies.
They organized the convention. They wrote the platform that rejected the McNary-Haugen Bill. Always in
the offing was the shadow of a potential nomination of
Calvin Coolidge until the balloting began. So that his
oracular message of August, 1927, was probably a deliberate, preconceived plot to hold himself in readiness as
a more than possible candidate if his administration and
its achievements were to be even indirectly repudiated by
the Republican convention. He had seen Cleveland,
Roosevelt, Wilson, and Harding repudiated by the
National Conventions of their party, and he was determined to make the National Convention of 1928 his
messenger boy to history, bringing its endorsement of
what he had done.

In that strategic movement one finds all of Coolidge,
his strength and his weakness, his craft and his lack of
candor, his self-sufficiency and a certain ruthlessness to
make his will prevail. But no weakling could do this.
When we see what he did, when we realize the pressure
that was put upon him for ten long months to explain,
to amplify or even to annul his declaration by too
emphatic silence, we realize the strength of this quiet,
taciturn man. No President America has had within the
memory of men living in the first quarter of this century
possessed exactly the qualities of reticence and determination to do what Coolidge did. And the use of the
phrase, "I do not choose," as he used it—cryptic, baffling,

oracular—reveals the man Coolidge, in all his strength and with whatever deficiencies he has, more clearly than any other episode in his career.

Coolidge always knew more definitely what he did not want than what he wanted. His messages were often vague on the positive side, but dazzling in their clarity about his dislikes and aversions. "I do not choose" was a particularly Coolidgian way to put his renunciation of another term. And he will be known historically for his vetoes, which were few but important. He is negation incarnate. As President he bestraddled progress face backward.

He could never play games. His conversation was yea, yea, and nay, nay. The argot of diplomacy, with its vast circumlocutions, its quaint cotillion forms, must have irked him grievously.

Coolidge is a man of anemic emotions. He went through the greatest geyser field in the world, at Yellowstone Park, without pausing before a geyser. If he had curiosity, he repressed it. If the thing awed him, he concealed his awe. He asked few questions, vouchsafed no praise. Talkative men irritated Coolidge. But he rarely raged in irritation; he merely shut up. Sometimes his wrath escaped for a vindictive second; but only for that. But neither did his joy bubble. It merely crackled, like static, beneath the even tenor of his way. Seen close up by those near his person, he may easily have seemed crabbed, taciturn, domineering, stubborn, inflexible. Probably he made a disenchanting portrait to those near his person who "stand and wait." But from afar, the hero's features loomed large. The golden mists of distance gathered and solidified and haloed the picture. To the hundred millions who saw him in respectful perspective, President Coolidge's features stood out clear, convincing. Here stood an honest man. After all, the greatest of human beings are common clay plus a golden vein. Coolidge's plus quality was honesty; honesty backed by a kind of herd courage. Alone he is timid; with his crowd he is immovable, undaunted. And the picture which the millions saw across the gulf which separates a President from his people was the face of an honest man; so they idealized this picture, and saw a man who saved their taxes; a man who was immovable amid clamor; a man who defied the mob; a man who beatified plutocracy by glorifying parsimony; a man who defied untoward events by ignoring them—him they saw as a hero, and blinked his warts and scars. So, in the white light that beats upon a throne, the minor vices of a President sometimes at long range become his major virtues in the public eye.

Calvin Coolidge served his time. He was the man of the hour, the one who alone could have functioned in the White House in the years of his ascendancy. He represented the spirit of the times, the aspirations of his people. Of course there were protesting minorities, many of them; and some of these minorities were deeply affronted and disturbed by his conservatism, by the occultism with which he idealized the gods of materialism. But these disturbed minorities could find no considerable response in the heart of the nation. The puzzle of this conjunction of the man Coolidge and the zero hour of aspiration in the world is one of those mysteries which philosophers must attend to. Certainly Coolidge did not lead the people into his own cautious ways. He had no quality of leadership. Time and again Congress rejected him, even flouted him.

And so far as one could see, the people followed their
congressman, not the President, at the ensuing election.
He could blow no trumpets, could ring no bell, to stir the
popular heart.   But as President he was the symbol of all
that was precious in the popular heart.   How did he get
there?   He came apparently through the accident of
Harding's death.   But why the accident?   How had fate
led Coolidge into the wings of a stage set so perfectly
for him to play his curious hero rôle?   Who was the
prompter that had him ready for his cue when Harding
fell?   What is this great mechanism that moves and
guides events, rough-hews destiny, shapes careers to fit
the times?   Finger the puzzle, fondle it, shake it up, pore
over it as you will, O Philosopher!   In the end, with all
your lore and learning, you can only say, with the idle and
the blind, God knows!

PART VI

THE YOUNG PRINCES OF DEMOCRACY

"He hath veiled the Crown and hid the scepter," warn the Trumpets.
"He hath changed the fashion of the lies that cloak his will.
"Hard die the kings—ah, hard—dooms hard," declare the Trumpets.

Old King Demos begets his kind like a Hereford. Behold two young princes of the new day—Alfred Emanuel Smith and William Hale Thompson—city types. We have had no kings like them, yet soon they and their kind may rule; for we are passing from rural to urban life. When we have sloughed off our rural philosophy—our fundamental Puritanism—we shall crown the young princes. In the meantime the warning is plain: "Put not your trust in princes"!

ALFRED EMANUEL SMITH

CHAPTER XLIV

Now meet and consider Alfred Emanuel Smith, Governor of the State of New York. Observe a stocky man, yet never pudgy, five feet seven, who looks five feet nine or ten sitting down, for he has a long, sturdy body. He is blond, well kept, with clear, fine healthy skin, pink and white in fact, blue eyes, and fair hair that at one time may have been red—or it may have been tow in childhood. He is smooth-shaven, oval-faced, mean-jawed, with a pugnacious set to his head, which wags with fine self-assertion; a self-assertion that is never quite vanity. And as he talks, one begins to realize that he is merely gesticulating with his long neck above sloping shoulders, over a broad chest set upon a sturdy though not distinguished torso, and all built upon a scaffolding of nimble legs. He is articulate in every inch of his body. Now let's dress him, for Alfred Emanuel Smith, Governor of New York, is a dresser—which brands him for a city chap, as do the kind of clothes he wears. Behold a pink hair-striped collar on top of a dark wine-colored bow tie, set above a V of shirt which shows small brownish-crimson figures on a white background with a slight pink thread running through it. Protruding from the top pocket of a dark, well-tailored coat are the scarlet tips of a handkerchief.

Tan shoes, with appropriate silk socks, set off his properly creased gray trousers. He is a tailored man, who gives thought to wherewithal he should be clad; again the habit of a city chap. His blue eyes, looking casually at a man or a scene, remain curtained; bright flickering specks under dark lashes. Only when his emotions begin to rise do his eyelids open. Then his eyes glow with some incandescence which reveals a deeply earnest nature. His laughter is casual and incidental, but purpose glows in those wide scathing eyes. Turn some inner switch in his heart and affection can burn there as well as purpose, for he is a man of passion, with a capacity for feeling almost as strong as his ability to reason. One gets therefore from his spirit, as it is revealed in a well-knit yet nervous body, beautifully controlled, an impression of balance—this kind of balance: a big heart and a clear brain; a balance that makes a man capable of loyalties based upon qualities of both heart and mind. He can be loyal to a friend, but can go to the stake for an idea over the body of his friend—and kept his friend. Nice persons and well-bred come into his office and, seeing him spitting nervously on the carpet as he smokes a big brown cigar, are shocked at his manners. They who place manner above the inner gifts of heart and mind have revolted at a number of our Presidents, indeed at a number of our great Presidents. As, for instance, at Washington's profanity, at Jefferson's often puerile pedantry, at Jackson's brusqueness, at Lincoln's purple stories, at Grant's predilection for whisky, at Cleveland's contempt for public opinion, at Roosevelt's scorn of the feeble, idle rich, at the hoarfrost on Wilson's cloistered manner. All these externals, which have covered stout hearts and exceptional minds, have deeply offended commonplace people who have known our greatest Americans. Alfred Emanuel Smith, beloved of his fellow urbanites as Al Smith, as deeply offends the ultra-mannerly of his generation as any other of our statesmen might offend these nice people. They see on him, these most conventional people, the same horns and hoofs which have frightened men from the beginning of time; horns and hoofs of manners growing out of environmental habits; horns and hoofs which every strong man wears as he comes struggling out of his past into leadership.

Al Smith must rise or fall in our national life, if ever he should enter it, as our first urbanite. Sometimes our cities have brought statesmen into American politics, as for instance, New York City brought Chester A. Arthur and Theodore Roosevelt, each a President by right of another man's death. Our urban life has put a certain veneer upon the few statesmen it has produced—a certain sophistication, a certain debonair contact with men which passes for urbanity; but neither Roosevelt, who was born in the city, nor Arthur, who came from Vermont to the city, was purely urbanite. Roosevelt's mother was from a Southern plantation and Roosevelt's formative youth after he left Harvard was hardened in the Dakotas. His following was never from the great cities. John McCutcheon's cartoon of the farmer with paintbrush whiskers reading approvingly of "Teddy" was a White House icon for seven years. Roosevelt carried the agricultural states of the mid-West with him in his major enterprises. But Al Smith is urbanite with an urbanity unstrained, blood raw with something more than city polish and pink and white skin. Al Smith is city born, city bred, "city broke," city minded, and city hearted. In his public life Smith had exactly the same attitude toward the farmer that Coolidge had toward the city man, an intense desire to know him, a curious feeling that he is real but a baffling sense of futility in trying to get the other man's viewpoint. This division, partly spiritual and partly material, this difference between the city man and the country man, is as old as civilization. The city and the country do make different kinds of men externally. And the externals of men—their manners, their mental and moral attitudes, their various ways of taking joy and meeting sorrow, their different conceptions of social good—do produce different attitudes and contacts which sometimes in politics make men line up inevitably with their traditions and environment, seeing right from varying angles. Thus each kind of man meets and perhaps formulates issues according to his own judgments, and his judgments come out of his environing experiences. As experiences differ, great issues are formed. It was so, for instance, in American history only two hundred years ago, when the question of American political and economic independence was stirring. The Tories, seeing life from their background, differed sincerely with the American patriots. One hundred years ago, when the slavery issue began to form, men and women who grew up surrounded by slave labor saw life one way, clearly, honestly, and those who grew up surrounded by free labor held another viewpoint conscientiously, intelligently—and each had equal courage. We may be facing new issues in our politics based for the first time upon the conflicting interests, the conflicting morals, the conflicting aspirations of a rural civilization as those interests, morals, and aspirations clash in a nation which is rapidly becoming industrialized and urban. Hence Al Smith, with his pink and white skin, his pink and crimson tie and the scarlet border of his handkerchief, his silk socks and his suitable gray trousers, becomes something more than a sporadic figure in our politics. He becomes the symbol of a mighty challenge to our American traditions, a challenge which, if it win in the ensuing struggle, will bring deep changes into our American life.

In early July, 1924, after the National Democratic Convention had wrangled through the longest session ever held by a major party in America and nominated a compromise candidate for the Presidency on the hundred and third ballot, Al Smith appeared after the nomination of John W. Davis had been made. Smith's name had appeared during the long bitter sessions of the convention as a presidential candidate, for days a formidable candidate, always the candidate of a militant minority in the convention. Smith's following came from the Atlantic seaboard and from the states dominated by large cities; Illinois for instance, Ohio somewhat, Indiana more or less. The apparent issue upon which Smith rallied his strength was a distaste for the law prohibiting the sale and manufacture of intoxicating liquors. And certainly the opposition to Smith rallied around the presumption that Smith was a "wet." As a corollary to his wetness came the fact that he was a Roman Catholic, and that fact gained and lost delegates for him in the convention. His strongest opponent, Mr. McAdoo, typified the opposing view of life. Mr. McAdoo unquestionably had the support of the Ku Klux Klan, an organization which at the moment was strong in the South and West, where belief in prohibition prevailed, and where the Klan organized what may be called the lower forces of Puritanism around the Puritan vices. The struggle in the convention, therefore, was between the hard, ascetic moralities of Puritanism and the lighter, happier, mellow philosophy of Catholicism. Supporting the harsher, sterner view of life was the rural civilization in the states south of the Mason and Dixon line, and, generally speaking, west of the Mississippi. There was conflict deep and disseminating between the two ideals in the states east of the Mississippi, north of the Ohio, and west of the Alleghanies. There, in those middle states, the change has not come definitely from the rural to the urban civilization. Ohio and Indiana, in the third decade of the twentieth century, were becoming highly industrialized. The railroad journey through those states resembled strikingly, even if somewhat in miniature, the journey from Philadelphia to Boston, through large industrial centers sprawling over the earth so widely that their remote environs, their country clubs, their fashionable residential districts, their park areas, almost touched one another, with but a small acreage of truck gardens between. In the East, agriculture—as it was known in America forty years ago, had been forced into the hinterland, up into the valleys of the mountains, beyond the broad highways of commerce. In Ohio, Indiana, Illinois, parts of Michigan, and Wisconsin, this rise of an industrial civilization and decline of agriculture as the dominant feature of the landscape was projected but a decade or two in the future.

Now, in that Democratic convention of July, 1924, after the contending factions had struggled over the names of Smith and McAdoo for two weeks, staging

"AL" SMITH.

beneath the surface, but not far beneath it, the struggle
of the rural and urban forces in our national life, the
philosophies of Puritanism and Catholicism, the end was
a meaningless compromise, a truce for breath; and there,
as the convention panted in its impotence, stood Al Smith
that night, delivering a speech to the delegates pledging
his loyalty to the ticket that had been nominated. It was
his first national appearance. The galleries were packed
with his friends from New York, and they clearly were
wild about him. It became evident early in the convention that Al Smith was a form of monomania among New
Yorkers of a political cast of mind. They packed the
halls of the convention that night as they had packed
them every night for two weeks, howling like demons for
their hero, and thus conveying to his opponents the feeling that he was a sort of head devil of the place. When
he appeared the cheers of Smith's friends raged in fanatic
fury. He stood there amid this howling mob, a stocky,
long-bodied figure, with the pugnacious shoulders of a
fighting man. For a moment, in his light suit, with his
hands waving familiarly to his gibbering audience like a
keeper's to quiet a cage of wild beasts—he looked the
exalted bouncer of a boxing pavilion. He spoke in a
loud, raucous voice, wagging his head with rather too
much assurance. His attitude lacked grace and charm,
both physically and spiritually. Obviously it was a
speech of defense and justification, though the actual
written language of the speech did not convey that meaning. He sought to interest a thousand delegates and
two or three thousand of their friends from outside of his state in the provincial affairs of New York.
He reviewed the local issues of his administration at a

time when the convention and the spectators outside of his state and its environs were looking for a broad appeal from a statesman for his cause. The delegates were shocked to hear merely the local manifestation of a cause explained. Smith made a bad fist of his speech. He did not measure up to the occasion. He justified the contention of his enemies that he was merely a local figure. He was just Al Smith of New York functioning in the national limelight.

He did not proclaim himself and his cause because probably he could not realize himself and his cause. Al Smith was even then of national size mentally and spiritually, but he did not comprehend his nation nor think in national terms. He was a borough leader; and no amount of advertising, no amount of propaganda in his behalf could expand him into a national figure until he could find some stage whereon he might dramatize himself as a national hero in a national struggle.

Now let us leave him standing there on the rostrum at Madison Square Garden, under the sputtering blue-lavender lights that evening, shaking his fist, slamming his arms about, bellowing fiercely, wagging his head, sweating like a horse with the vehemence of his conviction, gradually disillusioning his more intelligent friends and sardonically justifying the contentions of his enemies, while we turn to the cause which brought him to that moment of his career; to the cause, indeed, which kept him half a dozen years in the consciousness of many patriotic and intelligent Americans as the potential champion of a new order. Let us examine the changes that have come into American life which give this new kind of statesman the power of a hero.

Expressed in two words, they are blood and iron; but blood and iron affected by another meaning than that which once inhered in the phrase. The blood in this instance is the changing blood of the American nation. The iron is the vast framework of wires and tubes, beams and stringers, girders, and reinforcing, upon which the new urban structure of the material life of America is rising—new blood and new iron. The Pilgrim blood of New England and the Colonial blood of the South for a century and a half had spread a civilization of wood and stone over the American continent. Slowly, for a generation, this old blood had been mixing with new blood, which brought new philosophies and cast the material phrases of an older civilization into a new mold. Thus have ideas and visions, reappearing in material form, changed the outer aspect of the world of substance.

The America of the last quarter of the nineteenth century was essentially an agricultural nation. It fed and clad the world. It furnished wheat and meat and wool and cotton to the workers in mills, looms, forges, and shops all over the earth. Our cities, such as they were beyond the seaboard, were agricultural towns. A city man in the Detroit of 1895, or in Minneapolis, or Cincinnati, or Richmond, or Dallas, or Buffalo, or Omaha, was a skygazer as truly as a farmer. Weather conditions affecting crops affected business in every great American town outside of New York, or Boston, or Philadelphia. A drought or a flood set the pace for commerce in any region as surely as it affected the farmer on the soil. We thought, we aspired, we cast our visions, in terms of agriculture. And because the English blood or Teutonic blood, if you will, naturally takes to agriculture, we were of one blood as we were of one tongue. So as a nation we had one purpose. We were a homogeneous rural people, for all the flash and clatter and brag of the shiny new cities that sparkled upon the plains west of the Alleghanies. The farmer ruled us, either actually by his votes, which made powerful minorities, or by his interests, and traditions and blood, which formed our political thought. Our national leaders thought rurally. Our national policies were such policies as an intelligent, upright, altruistic American farmer might formulate. The world we envisaged was the world which that farmer and his wife would have liked their son and daughter to live in; a decent, well-ordered, carefully regulated, highly moral, entirely just, and eminently respectable world in which each man earned all he got, and in which every man got all he earned by the grace of God —and such amendments to the Constitution as were necessary to establish the grace of God.

All the major movements in American politics on this North American continent have been agrarian movements. Our American Revolution was essentially agrarian. It came from the planters of the South and the New England merchants, backed by the farmers of the North. The anti-slavery crusade, the next great impulse in our politics, was a movement for free farm labor. Following the abolition of slavery came the agrarian agitation of the seventies, eighties, and nineties; the Greenbackers, the Grangers, the Populists. Then came the Bryan, Roosevelt, Wilson epoch, directly descendant from the Greenbackers, the Grangers, and the Populists, carrying the demands of the farmers of the last quarter of the old century into the first quarter of the

new: demands for political power in the hands of the
individual as evidenced by the Australian ballot, the
primary, the initiative and referendum; demands for an
increased and stable currency, for the regulation of railroads, for the control of trusts, for general inspection of
industry by government; the farmer's vision of an ideal
commonwealth. Woman suffrage, prohibition, the income
tax and direct election of senators came into the Constitution through the impulse of this agrarian movement. A
quarter of a century ago, a distinguished New Yorker,
William Travers Jerome, landed a bull's-eye in this movement when he sneered at it as "the moral yearnings of a
rural community."

And now, at the close of the third decade, came the
clash between these moral yearnings of the rural peoples
of America with the urge for another kind of civilization
rising out of the ideals of an urban and industrial population. New issues began to inject themselves into American politics and new kinds of candidates essayed to inter-
pret these issues understandingly. The backwoodsmen of
the last century, of whom Andrew Jackson and Andrew
Johnson were types and Lincoln not far out of the picture,
are menaced by the city type. For a hundred years the
self-made farmer boy has been proud of the rough edges
which he has been too busy to smooth off. American
politics have produced thousands of local leaders with
sixth-grade education—leaders who came out of the backwoods.

Now from the back alley comes Al Smith, the new
type.

There is no reason why the back alley cannot produce
as good moral, spiritual, mental, and physical timber for

politics as the backwoods. The historical equation reads something like this: As Andrew Jackson was to Clay and Webster, so is Al Smith to Coolidge and Lowden. Let us therefore consider the back alley from which Al Smith sprang.

Certainly it was, in the seventies, as clean and whole-some a place as the backwoods from which Andrew Jackson sprang in Revolutionary times. Here was a three-story wooden tenement facing the river front, cobble-stones running down past the old fish market to the tide; square riggers coming in with cargoes and drunken sailors running up over the cobbles eager for the river-front saloon and for the fat prostitute sitting in her window, bare-armed and as alluring as sin in adipose can be. In the third floor of the tenement where Al Smith was born, his father—a dock workman, teamster, day laborer, ready for any job, and a bad man to meet with six drinks in his skin of a Saturday night—maintained his little family, the real head of which was Catherine Mulvihill, an Irish girl whose father and mother were born in America, but who was, nevertheless, of the good old Irish stock, sturdy, faithful, full of visions and dreams, and never afraid of hard work. She was widowed in her twenties and held her brood together by keeping store and doing such honest work as came to her hands; a strong, vigorous character, Roman Catholic in religion and no bigot. For the boy, Alfred Emanuel Smith, went sometimes to the public schools and sometimes to the parochial schools, as the circumstances warranted. And when he had learned to read, write, spell, and figure a little, somewhere between the seventh and eighth grades, he fell out of school and went to work. In his teens, he was a clerk in the fish

market. In his late teens he was in Tammany. And
at twenty-one he was holding office, serving summons for
jurors in the local court of the water-front districts. So
the streets educated him, as the woods and fields educated
Lincoln and as the woods and fields and wars educated
Andrew Jackson. Their backgrounds are typical, even
if different. The psychological effect upon each education—the streets, and the fields, and the woods, and the
war—was exactly the same upon each of these variations
of the pioneer type of mind, the Jackson type, the Lincoln
type, the Smith type. And Smith has exactly the faults
that marked Jackson and Lincoln. Backwoods virtues in
education become back alley excellences. Men of both
types learn about evil early, and if it poisons them it
poisons them and they go down. If it does not poison
them, it gives them faith and clarity, and they rise.
Men educated in the back alley and the backwoods
learn to think vigorously, but without restrictions
and qualifications. They see life in blacks and whites
—not in grays. And so they live with the forces
of life—tragically. Nothing sustains the human spirit
so firmly as the presence of tragedy if the fiber of the
spirit is tough enough to learn its lesson. Al Smith
learned. He moved through Tammany in Croker's time
when it was corrupt, when politics rooted much of its
sinews in vice, in blackmail, and sapped some of its
strength from plutocracy in bribes. The Tammany of
his youth sold special privileges alike to the rich and the
poor, the corporations, the touts, the harlots and the
saloon keepers, with equal frankness and cheerful dishonor. Crokerism waned with the coming of a new century. Croker passed. A new order appeared. All the

politics that Al Smith learned of the old order under
Tom Foley, the local leader, was a capacity for teamwork, a habit of industry, and the precious moral pre-
cept that it does not pay to lie. Much may be said for
the Croker kind of politics. It did make square men
who according to the morals of their day played a fair,
brave game, even when it was dirty. When the morals
changed, the habit of the game did not. And as far
as the game and its morals went, it was as square as
the game that Lincoln learned, or Jackson, in American
politics. All of our Presidents, except Wilson and Grant,
in the past fifty years have gone through that game, and
Wilson and Grant were the losers rather than the gainers
by entering politics late in life. Grant's administration
was in many respects deplorably weak and often obviously corrupt. Wilson's ignorance of politics was his
chief handicap. Because McKinley, Roosevelt, and
Coolidge knew the game, the dirty game, if you will, they
avoided many pitfalls, and were able to walk with the
children of light further than they would have walked
had they not learned much from the angels of darkness.

Al Smith, a young Tammany leader who had worked
his way up through the precinct into the ward and so to
the district, in the moving stairway which takes men forward and upward who are industrious, honest, and intelligent, found himself in his early thirties a member of the
New York Assembly in the lower house of the legislature.
He was there because the escalator took him there, but
there he left the river front. There he moved into
Oliver Street, into a decent house—still in the river-front
district—on a decent street, and maintained a decent
Christian home. He had married Katherine Dunn. Their

children were coming with proper regularity and Al Smith was a man in the district something better than a leader. He was going to school in politics, in Albany politics, under Barnes, Platt, Bill Ward and Lou Payne, Republican leaders, and under the tutelage of men who had their political education from Croker, Bill Devery, Tom Foley, Judge Van Wyck, and later, Mayor Gaynor, who thrust a certain practical idealism into the situation.

But idealism in politics has never greatly affected Al Smith. It was a part of his political education to learn the routine of the public business; how taxes are levied, collected and disbursed; how political appointments are made; what wires hold what men, and what ambitions govern others. His education was not unlike that of a good gambler who comes to know the run of the cards, the hearts of the players, and the rules of the game. He rose in the organization of the Assembly because he was quick to learn its simple, irrevocable rules. He became party leader and Speaker of the lower house of the legislature. Smith's legislative career was curiously typical of the coming new order that he was to represent. He was, of course, from Tammany, and loyalty must ever be a major virtue in an urban organization like Tammany. Smith took orders from Tammany until he was able to give orders. In his first legislative years his record was classed as bad, by the nonpartisan organization which was trying to promote the rather rural program of welfare legislation which occupied the hearts of the political altruists of the hour. Smith voted with the Tammany group against the direct primary, for instance, and certain welfare legislation which reformers were seeking. But Tammany thought Smith's record was good. When he took leadership in the Assembly and when he went to the New York State Constitutional Convention, he was fairly free. It was then that he began to command attention from his political opponents. He was the tough-brained, hard-headed, fact-seeking, ever-ready, hard-working realist that is called "able." Senator Elihu Root took a liking to him. The New York Republican organ, the New York *Tribune,* spoke well of Smith. He grew in power and stature politically.

So he was promoted, riding the moving stairway of party regularity into the sheriff's office. He came back to New York from Albany as sheriff, and took leadership in New York because he had those qualities of heart and mind which make city-bred men leaders of their fellows. He made money easily. He was elected President of the Board of Aldermen. He was honest, hard-working, good-natured, painstaking, and at base, for all his happy Tammany regularity, he was becoming a free man. He had met in the legislature, during his decade and a half of service, the best minds of the State of New York and the great American metropolis. They came there either as leaders in politics or as members of the lobby which at odd times controlled politics. He formed in the legislature many friendships across party lines, being essentially a friendly man, eager for the affection of his fellows. He was the kind who loved a good company, a good cigar, a good story, and a good song after a good drink, and never was ashamed of it. He was a man's man. The primrose path never lured him. He rose, in the councils of his party, upon his social graces; but he rose in popular esteem upon his intellectual qualities. His brain won his adversaries. His heart held his friends. It was a rare combination—the

Al Smith composite. He attended the National Conventions of his party and met, incidentally, leaders from other regions. He did not study politics as a man learns textbooks. He absorbed it as a man absorbs the folklore of his environment. He did not study men like Roosevelt, Ben Odell, Platt, Murphy, Nicholas Murray Butler, Gaynor, George Perkins, young John Rockefeller, William Barnes, Hearst, and Henry Churchill Osborn. He met these men as a part of the daily routine of his job; knew them, not by study but by experience; not by theory, but by more or less intimate contact. And what they taught him was good. He could not have learned it in books. Smith makes no pretense of erudition, but no one who examines his career can deny his wisdom. And let us repeat, for it cannot be too definitely emphasized, that the wisdom of the back alley is just as impregnable as the wisdom of the backwoods. And, possibly, from now on in American politics, as our urban population grows to overbalance the rural population, back alley statesmen may crowd the backwoods statesmen into second place. Smith himself may not rise to a major place in American politics, but he seems to be the forerunner of a new type which shall rise to important and, it may be, triumphant leadership in America. The backwoods are cleared. Crops grow where once the ax echoed in the forest, and cities now cover what were once fields that replaced the woodsman's home. Out of those cities, from the muck of those cities as from the pioneer's rude cabin, are coming leaders of the new democracy, the industrial democracy which in this century will clash and struggle for supremacy with the rural democracy—the America of our past. Al Smith may be only the herald of the new order; or he may be its first champion.

WILLIAM HALE THOMPSON

CHAPTER XLV

THE day was the thirteenth—Wednesday, April 13, 1927; so men said: "He will not come down on the thirteenth and begin on an unlucky day." Others said that anyway he was out late the night before at a cabaret; and still others denied this. He was due to appear at the City Hall at ten-thirty, but no one expected him. He was punctiliously unpunctual. And at eleven all they knew about him at the City Hall was that he was coming. Stragglers began to stop at the La Salle Street door of the great classic pile of smoke-stained stones in Chicago's financial district which houses the city administration, the City Hall. At half-past eleven the crowd at the door had thickened. Policemen were clearing the sidewalks, and in the City Hall, before the elevator, the crowd was milling. On the third floor, from the elevator door to the mayor's office, the crowd— a little more select than the sidewalk crowd and the ground-floor mob—was patiently waiting for The Appearance. At twelve o'clock an aisle formed in the milling crowd from the elevator door to the door in the outer office. The mayor's outer office was a large barren room with white walls. On the walls hung the pictures of the various scalawags and the few gentlemen who in three-

480

quarters of a century have been mayors of Chicago. The room was divided by a heavy railing, enclosing a sort of bull pen. Within the bull pen was gathering a group of minor City Hall politicians. The group parted ceremoniously from time to time to make an aisle through which some paunchy gentlemen in black soft hats occasionally strutted conspicuously past the bull pen rail. They were like pouter pigeons going solemnly to roost in the inner office. Most of the pompous, paunchy roosters paused. There they gathered, circumspectly took off their soft black hats, and looked around to see who else had come. A dozen young women stenographers from the various offices in the building were there. Flowers began to filter through the crowd. A dozen roses, an armful of spring posies, jonquils, narcissus, tulips, and the like, with giant productions of the hothouse, flowed through the crowd and disappeared into a still inner office. That outer office where the fat roosters assembled was a shiny, oak-paneled room whereon hung oil paintings of the more distinguished of Chicago's mayors. The statesmen of the village gathered there were Irish, Pole, Swede, Negro, Jew, and Gentile—the hard-faced, the vacant-minded, the greedy, the uncertain, the hungry, and those who had been filled; each statesman bearing conspicuously his terrible burden of responsibility and proud of his load! On a sofa were half a dozen reporters who, as a matter of principle, kept their hats on with the brims turned down, tired men who jawed gently at the show's delay; men weary of the vain pomp and circumstance of glorious politics—City Hall reporters! Noon passed, and a quarter after twelve came. The reporters lighted many cigarettes and slumped low in their chairs, while the statesmen stood gloomy in their grandeur. The stenographers were flippantly expectant. Twice, at a false alarm, an aisle formed among the solemn liege lords and barons of the realm in the oak-paneled room. And then, because it was late, the aisle became rigid; the milling stopped.

From the street below, through open windows, came the sound of cheering. Down there the multitude, far over the sidewalk, had all but choked traffic. A police squad was working to keep the sidewalk clear. But the cheering gave hope to those in the paneled room three floors above. One could hear it as it followed the figure one could not see, through the lower corridors. A pause, and then came the explosion of lycopodium and the shouting in the outer hall as the photographers clicked their cameras with the flashlight. A cheer rose in the outer office, and down the aisle through the lords of the realm slouched a large man circling lazily a soft, wide-brimmed black hat, waving his free hand, gayly stopping to bow here, to extend a casual hand there, pausing again to give both hands to some lady minion. He was babbling the while in a heavy, beery voice. He hulked briskly across the hall and disappeared into the inner office. The reporters had preceded him; also high satraps and caliphs of the village. There, in the holy of holies, surrounded by the bower of flowers which had heralded his coming, he stood for a moment and, grinning at the retainers, pleased as little Jack Horner with a plum on his thumb, said:

"Well, we are here officially."

And bang! blooey! went the flashlight bomb and William Hale Thompson, of Chicago, made his first reappearance in 1927 as mayor in his private office after a four years' absence. He stood for a second or two blinking after the flashlight picture had been made, grunted some acknowledgment to the Hearst news reporter who had been his lone supporter among all the Chicago newspapers in his campaign, and issued a formal royal statement in chambers. The ukase declared that he was going to give Chicago "a ride to prosperity." Before he had finished, the surge from the street, the corridors, the upper halls and the outer room had jammed into the oak-paneled room and was exuding into the little office. Quickly, as one who knew from long habit how to handle crowds, he stepped from the desk into a small corridor room leading into a side hall. There he squared off, and in a moment had a line passing before him. For an hour the multitude beheld Big Bill Thompson standing with legs apart; six feet tall, in a two-piece suit, with his two-button coat of dark blue serge showing a soft shirt and long, thin dark blue tie, a semi-soft collar. He stood seesawing away at the multitude, while his thick voice purred a slow, beery, diaphonic monotone of greeting over and over: "I thank you. You're so kind, I thank you, I thank you," as he disposed of callers, supporters, office hunters, idlers. Occasionally a face that he knew attracted him—as for instance a colored leader—and he would look at the reporters, or the henchmen grouped in the diagonal corner of the room and say:

"There's a man if there ever was one!" or "Here's a boy for you!"

And then the long, monotonous "I thank you, you're so kind, you're so kind, I thank you, I thank you, you're so kind," proceeded until some new face caught recognition from his eye.

"There comes my boss," he said, as the precinct captain of Big Bill's district walked by.

If the line paused and slackened, he trumpeted into the next room:

"Get a move on 'em! Get a move on 'em! Shoot 'em in!"

His voice had a resonant clarion quality, his oratorical voice throaty, authoritative, penetrating. He stood leaning slightly forward, with a rather longer body than the average man's; above which, from sloping shoulders, rose a bull neck, at the back of which a small bull roll of fat collared his narrow skull and came forward swathing his long, hard jaw. Above his jaw a thick, beefy, protruding underlip made a bad misfit for a loose and mobile mouth, above which was set a pugnacious nose. His jaw and mouth and nose indicated strength without purpose, power without intelligence, force without humor or charm. But his eyes, rising above his lower face, explained why Big Bill Thompson stood there, three times Mayor of Chicago. His eyes also made one understand why this man's political career in the town for a quarter of a century had been a storm center where wrangling, scandal and recrimination have hummed and clamored continually. For out of his eyes looks the eternal boy—beaming forth, not the innocence of youth but its shining inexperience! His eyes give a certain puerility to his face. This bland, blithe, deceptive puerility makes it clear why he attracts and holds for a time with passionate loyalty the millions who follow him.

They are worshiping Pan!

Here is the man who never grew up. Here, behind those flashing, dumb, eager, coaxing eyes, works Big Bill, the Builder, the braggart, the playground blowhard, the . gay leader to whom all political power is a gorgeous toy, who is motived with the ardent loyalty of a wayward child; changing friends with the changing seasons and the passing years, yet always holding those who follow him in the hour's diversion with unswerving fidelity. He is as incapable of treachery as he is of reasoned loyalty. He changes friends, sloughs off old pals, takes on new henchmen, snuffs out old associations, kindles new ardors as innocently as a child or a scarlet woman. He plays each day's game with its own fervor, and forgets yesterday as he ignores to-morrow. He has no remorse, because he has no capacity to judge himself nor the implications of his conduct.

As the returns came in on election night, the year of his third election, after a campaign in which Thompson had raged over Chicago a grotesque figure, bawling "liar," "damn liar," and even "liar" to the third degree, in his big boozy, bellowing bull roar, branding his enemies as cohorts of King George of England, denouncing what he called the "World's Court," the League of Nations, the Federal Prohibition officers, like a silly child making dirty rhetorical snoots at his adversaries, she who knew him best and loved him most, cried in exultation as she looked at the election bulletins:

"They can't beat my big boy!"

And in a day when political issues were chiefly concerned with material things, when the stability of a greedy commerce and the production of business were the chief end of man, in a day when Americans thought as a child and acted as a child and spoke as a child in politics, they could never beat her big boy. He was here to stay as long as the mood that made him lasted. Cheap calleth unto cheap at the noise of his waterspouts!

William Hale Thompson, who liked to be called Big Bill, and referred to himself in his campaign literature as "Big Bill, the Builder," was an interesting but not unusual variant of an ancient type. He was of Cleon's line and carried Cleon's wards. Big Bill and Cleon have interested democracies ever since the first ballot was cast. When they ostracized Aristides, the Just, because they were tired of hearing him called The Just around Athens, some Big Bill of Athens had captured the same crowd that triumphed in the Chicago municipal election of 1927. Indeed, as heroes go, the Big Bills and Cleons of history have swayed more mobs, piled up more majorities, led more armies, quaffed more of the heady wine of fame— even if it was fleeting—than the sons of Aristides. Man turns away from moron leadership in politics only in extreme unction, in times of profound crisis when he longs for the day of deliverance.

It is interesting to consider Big Bill's particular variation in his type. To begin with, he was Boston born; a rich man's son (Cleon's father was a rich tanner). Big Bill came to Chicago in childhood, went to the common schools when they were good schools and in his youth was sent away to a preparatory school in the East like Phillips Exeter or Andover. Schools did not interest him. He must have been a big, fat, wrinkled-wristed baby. For he was a lumbering boy, an athletic youth with some sense of his importance which came from his size, his money, and his prowess—chiefly physical. He came home to Chicago from preparatory school in his late teens, worked around his father's business, went West; where his size, his money, and his sense of social superiority, together with the fact that he did not have to earn a living, set him apart, gave him a certain distinction, encrusted the brass plating on his spiritual façade, and made him walk among the cowboys of the plains country a proud and peculiar figure. Once, after a campaign speech in Chicago, he and his crowd adjourned to a soft-drink saloon where he told his assembled idolators about a race which he once backed out West. He said that he knew it was a crooked race and risked his pile on the outcome. And to be sure that it was crooked in his way he declared that he stood at the goal with a stop watch and a gun to put the fear of God into the heart of the contestant he had helped to buy.

"I am too soft-hearted to play poker with my friends," said Bill to his worshippers. "Once it cost me five thousand dollars to let a friend stay in the game when I knew that I could pull an ace and take the pot."

When his vanity had been well inflated in the West, when he had played the tableaux and charades of the country as the rich young sport from Chicago, and when that game had palled upon him, he returned to his father's house, and worked in the business. He became a yachtsman around the lake, wore yachting clothes, told tall stories about the West, knocked about Chicago a rich young man, big, bronzed, burly, and bull-voiced, a sort of primeval Country Club gladiator before the Country Club came into American life. Business and its regular hours and exacting duties seemed to irk him. He needed no money.

When sporting and yachting wearied him, as his dramatic career on the plains had wearied him, the young man's fancy lightly turned to thoughts of politics. In politics, as in yachting and sporting and dude-wrangling on the ranch, his money helped him and fed his sense of superiority; also it attracted the idle-minded and the greedy. He was elected occasionally and defeated sometimes when he ran for minor offices. But he was always a flashy figure in his ward and leader in the organization, glad to do errands if he could put on the gaudy uniform of authority. In those years of the first decade of the century we see him a gay, gamy, gawky young gentleman whom the forces that controlled the city never worried about. He sat in the council in a notoriously crooked and corrupt régime undisturbed by the scandal, uninterested in the call of reform. If he knew where the money went, and he would have been dumb if he did not know, it did not excite him. Men of his class furnished the money. Men of his ilk passed it around. He had no objection to the use of money nor need for its emoluments. His vote counted one—sometimes a straight one, sometimes one with the questionables, but always one—no more, no less. He went back to his ward and precinct, put on the usual parades that a city politician must promote, got real joy out of the performances, helped his friends in trouble, spent his money, not lavishly, but with a flourish; made it count; played on the football teams of the Athletic Club, cherished the pseudonym of Big Bill, took it into ward politics, gave his conversational voice a chesty, solemn and oracular resonance which in an Irish boss

would have been called a "boozy bass," scampered along.
side—but never quite in—the primrose path; so that
when he breezed into a saloon with his gang or stood
watching a game with his henchmen in the ward, the
gathering cohorts said:

"There's the boy for you! There's your rich young
man who is not afraid to mix with the common people!
There's our kind of folks!"

And they loved him. And what is more and better,
he loved them—with all the affection in his heart which
he did not lavish upon a Narcissan vision of Big Bill,
the boss bountiful, who walked among the lowly with a
royal tread.

What a prancing Pan he was in those halcyon days!

He affected the cowboy hat and sedulously painted
in his cowboy background. Occasionally, in fine condescension, by way of giving the riff-raff of his precinct a
treat, he let them see him as the rich young yachtsman,
the prominent clubman, the sophisticated, brass-plated
man about town. One could not say that he ignored
what is known as the better element. It was just not in his
cosmos. The good government clubs, the civic leaders
who strove for clean politics, those who frequented
more exclusive clubs in the Loop, the Union League, or
the University Club, the haunts of the busy, aspiring, and
more or less virtuous—at least decently pretentious—
citizens of Chicago, were on another planet from Big
Bill Thompson, as they were from those whom he had
gathered about him in his ward and in the town. To
him and to them, the whole adventurous enterprise of
purifying Chicago politics was a sort of Swedenborgian
nightmare, not remotely related to the realities of life as

he lived it—and his followers knew it. They fancied and he vaguely realized that these highbrow uplifters were chasing some queer, iridescent Utopia; but it was as unreal to Big Bill and his kind as the pictures in the Art Institute.

Gradually he broadened—though he never deepened—his sphere of influence. He gathered about him, as friends and followers from a wider and wider area in the city, those citizens who felt as he felt; that life is food, drink and amusement, need, comfort and luxury, flash and show, gayety and substance. This group that crowds the parks, fills the movie palaces, howls at the ball game, blisters on the beaches, works hard, plays hard, dreams little, and aspires not at all beyond the glittering substantial horizon of the day's physical demands and the morrow's material betterment, saw in Big Bill Thompson, the Builder, in his cowboy hat or his yachting cap, their super-cinema hero, a kind of Bill Hart, Valentino and acrobatic Douglas Fairbanks melted into reality. He spoke their language because he understood their hearts.

But Big Bill Thompson was never a demagogue. He knew no better than he did. He talked from the wisdom of his own heart, out of the experiences of his own life, out of the vanity of his own hopes. So one fine day in the middle teens of this century, Big Bill Thompson, with his cowboy hat, came—in the course of the movie scenario that is his biography—into the City Hall as the Mayor of Chicago.

As Mayor of Chicago, Mrs. Thompson's unbeatable "Big Boy" gave his enemies many sad hours. First in sorrow, then in anger, they indicated their belief that

Underwood and Underwood.

WILLIAM HALE THOMPSON.

he was an unscrupulous crook. In most American cities the Thompson type appears in the City Hall and generally controls it. But in few American cities is there so active and so well organized a group of opponents of civic extravagance, carelessness, and irregularity as Chicago enjoyed during the first third of the century. In Chicago, those who work on the side of the angels never sleep. But, it also may be noted in passing, they have plenty to keep them awake. And Big Bill, during his eight years in the mayor's office, from 1915 to 1923, kept the angel choir busy with hymns of hate "through long days of labor and nights devoid of ease." The various good government clubs, composed in Chicago of unselfish men and women of high civic intelligence, being shocked at the mayor's conduct of city affairs, proceeded to paint him a black-and-tan devil, denounced him as a demagogue, railed at him as a corruptionist, and scorned him in the high places, notably the newspapers, the churches, and the public forums. They proclaimed him a grabber, a friend of grafters, with no sense of the decent amenities of politics. His enemies maintained that he had no limit to his extravagance but the bottom of the tax barrel. Now to have been all that his enemies charged, Big Bill would have had to be smarter than they—which is absurd!

In Chicago the mayor appoints the school board, and immediately after Big Bill's election the board proposed a seven per cent cut in teachers' salaries. Sixty-eight school-teachers were discharged without a hearing. A year or so after he first took office, mass meetings of citizens were called to protest against the intolerable conditions in the public schools. Six members of his

Board of Education were unseated by the Supreme Court of Illinois, and a year later Thompson reappointed them. School children were housed in portable schools, and several members of his school board were ordered to jail for contempt of court. The attorney for the Board of Education seems to have threatened the teachers with a salary cut of five hundred thousand dollars if they did not support the administration's plan to sell the school land. So much for the schools.

In the Health Department, the story was something like the story in the school board. In the Welfare Department it was charged that employees had to split their salaries with outsiders. The efficiency staff was dismissed in the Civil Service Commission, and the Civil Service rules were easily broken, bent, or forgotten in the City Hall. The Corporation Counsel seems to have blocked a popular lawsuit against the Gas Company and later, according to the charges of his enemies, he is said to have chloroformed the suit. Early in his administration corruption appeared in the Police Department— which was no new thing in Chicago, nor in any large city. Corruption in American municipal police departments is a common phenomenon. The state's attorney began to quiz the police and to uncover some evidence of graft. The Chief of Police was indicted for corrupt dealing with the underworld. The Grand Jury went after the Police Department for promoting the reign of vice, and the answer of the Chief of Police was to abolish the vice squad. A bloody race war between the blacks and the whites in Chicago raged for all one summer's day, and six hundred people were killed and injured. State's Attorney Hoyne declared that the race riots were caused by Thompson's City Hall politics. Thompson was reëlected!

In his second term Alderman Guerney filed charges of wholesale graft in the Police Department. Governor Lowden declared that Thompson's rule was worse than Tammany's. The Thompson crowd had one fear. It was the judges of the Circuit Court of Cook County. The forces that elected Thompson tried vainly to defeat these judges, but the people waked up and sustained the courts. There the issue was rather too simple to be confused. But Thompson and his group did control the Council Committee and reigned supreme in the City Hall. Colored aldermen from the second ward became Thompson's floor leaders. The state's attorney, Pat Crowe, declared that the Police Department protected vice and gambling. Crowe broke with the mayor. City finances began to go wrong after Thompson had been in office a few years. The people had voted a great sum to make certain city improvements, to create what they called "the City Beautiful." It was charged that real estate experts, appointed by Thompson, received nearly a million and a quarter in fees. Water rates were increased one-third to all consumers. Yet the city went bankrupt, and banks were unwilling to make further loans. The employees got I.O.U.'s instead of cash. Judgments in court against the city for unpaid bills amounted to more than twelve million dollars. The city was obliged in Thompson's second term to issue bonds for eight millions to pay the city's overdue bills. The newspapers began to expose the expert real estate men's fees, which were so obviously extravagant that the Chicago realtors protested. The mayor claimed the right to

spend money without the approval of the City Council.
The president, the vice-president and the business manager of the Board of Education were indicted for corrupt dealings in school funds. Thompson's political boss
was indicted in a million-dollar graft scandal. The head
of the Department of Gas and Electricity also was
indicted. The teachers were able to show a thirteen-
million-dollar increase in school taxes. Yet the mayor
declared no money was available for increase in teachers'
salaries. The resignation of all the members of the
Thompson school board was demanded by clamoring
citizens, who sensed the waste and extravagance in the
administration of school funds. The air was filled with
clamor against what was called the Thompson machine.
Yet, in 1918, as an unsuccessful candidate for United
States Senator, Mayor Thompson carried the city of
Chicago, and in 1921 was reëlected mayor! The charges
against him, the indictments of his appointees, the obvious
carelessness, amounting sometimes to malfeasance, with
which his administration handled the city's funds, did not
shake the confidence of his followers. He answered
charges against him by refusing to allow Viviani and
the French Commission to come to Chicago during the
war and by declaring that Chicago was the sixth German
city in the world. He courted the colored vote in the
black belt. He recognized two colored aldermen, one
of whom was indicted for police corruption, as his floor
leaders. And he gave the colored leaders of the black
belt the kind of government they wanted, the kind of
government that pleased the henchmen of the black
bosses—a wide-open black town.

Now this story of the Thompson administration just

recited is the story as his enemies would tell it. It is important to understand this story in the vernacular of his friends. Thus one can understand why there are Thompsons of various degrees in our American cities and, more or less, in our American politics, and why Thompsons are the first-fruit of democracy. Through all this castigation of his opponents, Thompson appeared to those who supported him a big-hearted, free-handed, fair-minded defender of the common people against the pharisaical, tight-fisted, long-nosed interference of a lot of snobs and snoopers who were trying to deprive the average hard-working, pleasure-loving citizens of certain inalienable rights. Now some of this was before the day of prohibition, some of it after the day of prohibition. Indeed, this attitude far antedates the liquor problem, and has little to do with it despite the fact that, in 1927, when Thompson was reëlected for the third time, prohibition was the particular thorn in the American toe which throbbed. The inalienable rights which these gentle and submerged citizens cherish are restricted by all sorts of sumptuary legislation: health legislation, traffic rules, more or less social legislation, some school laws, police regulation, Sunday closing, censorships, regulatory commissions and the bans on certain amusements. These restrictions on liberty are designed, in the high wisdom of the intelligent minority in colleges, pulpits, newspaper offices and women's clubs, to make life easier, finer and more abundant for the common man. But how the common man resents this benevolent despotism! When the members of the penned and herded mob find a leader who will appeal to their lower passions, who will arouse their smoldering resentments—or show them a big he-man hero with a cowboy hat, a bull-voice crying "liar," "damn liar," and going even further in his blackguard contempt of the uplifter—how the multitude rallies to that leader!

Now the corruption and incompetency of the Thompson administration in Chicago, from 1915 to 1923, were not the result, as its enemies imagined, of a diabolical plot to rob the state, or to protect gamblers, harlots, and thugs in their business. The Thompson administration was not a conscious connivance at the municipal degradation which came as a consequence of Thompson's election. The thing that happened when Big Bill took office was what must happen when any Big Bill assumes charge of an annual tax fund of a billion and a quarter. The "Big Boy" uses the billion and a quarter as a glittering toy, a gingerbread cat! He has no obligations to the intelligent. He feels no restraint of wisdom. He gathers his own kind about him naturally. Occasionally a smart crook slips into the gathering—a man with more brains than conscience. But mostly Thompson, and all the Thompsons in our cities and states—big-hearted and free-handed and dull-witted; big, burly, brainless boys who have run the world since the devil invented the ballot box—throw these billions around, always remembering two things: that their followers want, first, to be let alone; second, to spend the taxes assessed to keep others from being let alone!

We have erected here a government to shield and develop our complex civilization. We have found many places where government, wisely projected, is the only agency which can control the affairs of civilization; affairs that otherwise uncontrolled would limit the rights of the common man. Among other places where government must intervene is in the public health, the public welfare, education, the control of public utilities, the establishment of parks and playgrounds, the control of traffic and fires, the cleaning of the streets. Once all these things were privately managed. Now they must be publicly managed. To manage them publicly, taxes must be levied. Enormous sums of taxes are put into the hands of our Thompsons. Most of the taxes are honestly and intelligently spent, according to routine and under the momentum of long experience; but a few millions drop out in graft and extravagance. But worse than corruption and willful waste are the men whom the "Big Boys" like Bill, the Builder, appoint to administer these laws. These fellows generally are careless, lazy, and stupid. Hence follows much sheerly incompetent waste.

But again, how the average man, who likes to dramatize his political heroes, adores these movie gladiators! How he hates the presence in even minor offices of the careful, the industrious, the intelligent public servant, who gives us good government. Good government smacks of paternalism. It seems to imply a certain social superiority, a kind of high-grade condescension, which is a deep affront to the average man's own attitude toward life. Of course, this average urban voter has his moments of aberration, moments which usually follow some wrangle over spoils. Then, for a day, he turns to good government. His conversion is a short spasm. He does not really turn to good government. He votes his resentment at his own hero of the hour. And when the mob sees what it has drawn, beholds this cold-blooded, conscientious, wise, and meticulously democratic person in power, the disillusioned multitude turns against good government with all the rage of one whose vanity has been wounded and whose purpose has been betrayed. Then Demos destroys good government and enthrones the man after its own heart. And so, as the lady said: "You can't beat my Big Boy," except on a fluke. In American politics and in the politics of the world, more or less, we can only go as far at one jump as the intelligence of our "Big Boys" will take us.

"An army," said Napoleon, "travels on its belly." A democracy progresses on its Big Bills. This statement needs quick and specific qualifications. Your demagogue—even if the Big Bills are demagogues—and his dupes do not control life. Democracy is a number of things; in some degree, education. The educational process is slow, and until the mob and its leaders are educated to the day's needs and in the hour's issue, they impede progress; they never direct it, never stop it, merely slow it down. That is why the mob and the sinister wing of Conservatism are natural allies. The mob goes slow through ignorance; special privilege pulls back through self-interest. And so wisdom, which is leisurely, has come to reason things out in the public mind.

A graph of progress could be made easily enough by thoroughgoing statisticians, showing how the marker moves across the plate, zigzagging one long angle up and three or four peaks down, then a short acute angle up, a short rectangle down and many jagged peaks down as the finger of progress writes its records. Good government is short-lived, sets standards, realizes ideals, gives momentum to orderly processes of politics, and then vanishes. But the forces of disorder never quite force

the line down to its former level: something always is
gained.

In the election of 1927 Thompson polled more than
half a million votes and his opponent something over
four hundred thousand. The forty per cent in any million
votes is often intelligent, frequently dependable, but rarely
victorious. Yet this intelligent minority—modified by
the fools and hampered by them—is in the end the spirit
in our democracy. The demagogue wins, four times out
of five. He steals a little, wastes more, shames us all;
brawls, wrangles, blunders, and bulls his way through the
years of his public service; but public opinion does con-
strain his folly, does more or less direct his energy. In
Chicago, for forty years, Big Bill, under his various
aliases, has occupied the mayor's office more than two-
thirds of the time; and, in spite of the Big Bills, Chicago
has grown. Life has developed. Other institutions, quite
outside of politics, in which the church, the school, and
the arts are nurtured, have functioned and have made a
most habitable city. Despite the fact that protected vice
—gambling, prostitution, the illicit sale of liquor—have
thrived during thirty of the forty years since Chicago
has been more than a big town, and also despite the fact
that crimes of violence have always followed the protection of vice, still, for the most part, the average
approximate of justice is dispensed in Chicago as it is
elsewhere in our civilization. The processes of living
unfold. The dredges still work on the lake front. The
magnificent drives stretch across the city. The visions of
the people are realized as the decades pass—high visions.
And whatever is noble in the hearts of Chicagoans has
found its way into institutions, into stone and steel, into

just and beautiful living. After all, and in the long run, it is not the mob that actually rules Chicago nor any great American city, nor any city referendum. The ballot box is but one form, and in these latter decades a form with diminishing returns of public expression and control. Too often we are discouraged by the verdict which the ballot box spews out. We delude ourselves that some weak, dumb, babbling rowdy, conjured like a witless oaf from the ballot box, is our ruler and not our servant. Certainly the dolt does not mean to serve. He does not know even how he serves. But in so far as he affects real life, through the vacuum of his mind rush the currents that control progress, the spirit that is democracy. And so the booster brags and bullies and goes swashbuckling through the decades down the centuries, flopping his fat hunkers in the seats of the mighty. Being the idol of his kith and kind, he serves well to divert them with the delusion of grandeur while the deeper, swifter, quieter currents that control democracy move and direct our destinies.

There he stands, eternally, a brawny boss, feet apart, his long body lunging forward, sawing away at the hands of the multitude, who have created him in their own image.

"Thank you! Thank you! You're kind! Thank you! Thank you! You're so kind! Thank you! Well, well, so here you are! Glad to see you! Sure, I remember you! Thank you, thank you! You're so kind! Of course I will not forget! You're so kind! Thank you, thank you!"

And then when the lull comes, he leers about with his thick-lipped, loose-mouthed smile, with his eager, shallow, harlot's eyes, and flicks one lewd wink at his audience as he trumpets to his stage manager:

"Shoot 'em in! Turn 'em in! Keep 'em coming! Push 'em along!"

And there he has been standing in tableau as the ages have passed, from the days of Aristides and Cleon even to the latest tick-tock of time, and so, for ages to come, will his figure bulk, dark and sinister, in the path of progress; but only to cheat his followers, to delude his worshipers, whose folly, but for his fumbling, might wreck the world.

INDEX